Unconventional Wisdom

D1566698

Unconventional Wisdom
Alternative Perspectives on the New Economy

Jeff Madrick, editor

A Century Foundation Book

2000 ◆ The Century Foundation Press ◆ New York

The Century Foundation, formerly the Twentieth Century Fund, sponsors and supervises timely analyses of economic policy, foreign affairs, and domestic political issues. Not-for-profit and nonpartisan, it was founded in 1919 and endowed by Edward A. Filene.

LIBRARY OF CONGRESS CATALOGING-IN-PUBLICATION DATA

Unconventional wisdom : alternative perspectives on the new economy / edited by Jeff Madrick.
    p. cm.
Includes bibliographical references and index.
ISBN 0-87078-444-7
    1. United States—Economic policy—1993-. 2. United States—Social policy—1993-. 3. United States—Foreign economic relations. 4. Economic forecasting—United States. 5. Social prediction—United States. 6. Globalization. I. Madrick, Jeffrey G. II. Title.
  HC106.82 .U53 2000
  330.973—dc21
                                                                    00-009975

FOREWORD

One of the things about modern intellectual life that differentiates it from what has gone before is a greater openness to new ideas. In part, this is so because of the diminished role of revealed truth or religion in determining reality. In part, it is a consequence of the adoption of modern ways of looking at the world, such as the "scientific method." Of course, even in the sciences, theories and evidence that contradict the prevailing conventional wisdom often encounter strong resistance or, at least, exceptional pressure to back up the new assertion with especially compelling evidence. Yet, whatever the hurdles that still confront new ideas, this is, overall, a time of great excitement in the sciences. In physics, for example, everything from the age to the composition of the universe is open to lively debate.

In the social sciences, the picture is different. There, perhaps because the application of a strict scientific approach remains limited both by the subject matter and by the shortcoming of available methodology, new ideas face, if anything, a tougher reception. The arguments, pro and con, have more of a legalistic flavor, with reasonable assertions competing as descriptions of reality. These descriptions often are not of current conditions but rather explanations of what "actually" happened in the past or what will eventually happen in the future or what might well have happened but for some small, idiosyncratic variation in circumstances. Sometimes, in this environment where argument and facts are not always closely connected, theories continue to hold sway long after substantial empirical evidence has accumulated that contradicts them. Sometimes, ingenious explanations are offered to account for a bad fit between reality and what theory predicted. And sometimes, coming full circle to the realm of faith-based beliefs, there is a strong element of what can only be called fundamentalism in the insistence that such and such is true—the evidence to the contrary be damned. In the formerly Communist world, there are serious people who still claim that the badly discredited and, one

v

might argue from an empirical point of view, overwhelmingly disproved system of command economics could still have worked—in the long run. And in the West, there are those, more prosaically, still convinced that unemployment levels lower than 6 percent inevitably will cause runaway inflation. These clashes between evidence and belief are the unifying idea behind this volume of essays.

In recent years, The Century Foundation has been exploring the state of economics today, most notably in the late Leonard Silk and Mark Silk's *Making Capitalism Work*, James K. Galbraith's *Created Unequal*, Paul Osterman's *Securing Prosperity*, Robert Kuttner's *Everything for Sale*, and Barry Bluestone and the late Bennett Harrison's *Growing Prosperity*, and we currently are sponsoring, with the Russell Sage Foundation, a substantial investigation into the economics of high-employment. Once we decided to add this volume to that impressive roster of works, we asked Jeff Madrick, editor of *Challenge* magazine and columnist for the *New York Times*, to serve as editor and then asked several bold scholars and thinkers about economics to offer their most imaginative ruminations about the state of the dismal science. We wanted to provoke debate, and the authors have done so. The arguments in the pages that follow also should add new perspectives on some of the central issues in economics and public policy.

We believe that the essays in this volume satisfy one of the main purposes of The Century Foundation: the exploration new ideas, the presentation of fresh evidence, and the advancement of the social sciences. We thank Jeff Madrick and the authors for their strong contributions to this effort.

RICHARD C. LEONE, *President*
The Century Foundation
July 2000

CONTENTS

1

INTRODUCTION

TOWARD AN ECONOMIC DIALOGUE

Jeff Madrick

As this book went to press, America's economy was preeminent in the world once again. Not since the decades immediately following World War II, and never before, had the United States been so widely respected as a model of economic policy and business practice. Success rarely has only one parent, however, and there has been contentious debate over just what America has done right to arrive at this envied place. Some credit the tax reductions under President Reagan for stimulating investment and risk-taking, while others credit the tax increases under President Clinton for helping to balance the federal budget. Some attribute the rapid growth to the success of the long battle of the Federal Reserve against inflation, while others attribute it to the long-awaited reversal of this policy as inflation subsided in 1997 and 1998. To others, rapid noninflationary growth was the inevitable result of a computer revolution. Still others believe the boom was stimulated by the rapidly rising stock market that was driven to dangerously speculative heights.

Whatever the true causes of the new prosperity, a brand of neoclassical theory has become increasingly dominant in the public discourse. In its simple form, the mainstream model stresses markets over government. The main tenet is that reducing the role of government through lower taxes, deregulation, and privatization, not only in America but also around the world, is the best way to stimulate economic growth in richer nations and economic development in poorer ones. America's prosperity provides a foundation for the new view because government generally has a lesser role in America's economy than among its overseas competitors.

1

In truth, however, the mainstream view fails to provide answers to the most penetrating questions of the day. Simply consider how little mainstream economists got right recently. The U.S. economy might have triumphed, but few mainstream economists had expected it to do so. To the contrary, the prevailing consensus had been that the rate of unemployment could not fall below 6 percent or so without higher inflation. As this book is published, however, the unemployment rate stands at 4.1 percent and inflation is not in sight. Similarly, economists generally have not been able to tell us with any confidence why productivity slowed down in the 1970s and 1980s or why it suddenly sped up at the end of the 1990s. They have been unable to settle long-standing arguments about why incomes have become so unequal in America or around the world.

Mainstream economists also invoked the simple neoclassical model to recommend shock therapy in Russia, but Russia descended into financial collapse a half dozen or so years after the reforms were implemented. The neoclassical model also was invoked to promote the removal of capital controls in developing nations in Asia and elsewhere, but such policies led directly to the severe financial crises of 1997 and 1998, many economists reluctantly admitted later. The mainstream economic consensus reinforced attitudes among the decisionmakers at the Federal Reserve that capital controls, such as higher margin requirements, were inappropriate policy responses to speculation in the stock market. The Fed was left with only blunt and painful interest rate increases to stanch demand. We shall ultimately see whether America can avoid a sharp decline in stock prices that might well have been mollified by more direct Fed action.

This is not all. The prevailing economic consensus tells us little about how to reduce America's escalating trade deficit or how long we can sustain the enormous stock of international debt that supports it, even as the International Monetary Fund warns that the U.S. trade imbalance is dangerously high. The consensus cannot explain why ever-lower interest rates in Japan did not reignite its economy. The consensus is the foundation of a bipartisan attitude in Washington that federal budget surpluses should be used to pay down U.S. debt rather than build up public investment because higher levels of savings was the principal path to prosperity. Never mind that the prosperity of the late 1990s arrived despite no improvement in the nation's overall savings rate; federal budget surpluses were offset by falling private savings. We may ultimately pay a price in reduced potential economic growth for the neglect of public investment.

But the ultimate irony is that this powerful consensus does not truly reflect the divergence of views in the academic profession. This assertion may surprise some readers. There is little doubt that the academic community has become increasingly—disturbingly—uniform in thought in recent years, but the practice of economics in Washington, among world financial institutions, and on Wall Street is even more narrowly based. The economic consensus among the influential practitioners simply ignores important ongoing debates among the theoreticians. The media too often overlook these debates as well. In fact, nuance of thought, diversity of opinion, and respect for empirical research are still alive and well in academia. What is needed is a way to make such debates an integral part of the public discourse. The publication of this book of essays is an attempt to redress the balance.

Let me provide a few specific examples. In the 1990s, the so-called Washington consensus, led by the U.S. Treasury, strongly argued for the rapid removal of regulations that might impede the international flow of capital and, as discussed above, the broad, immediate reform of the economy in newly democratic Russia. A casual reader of the pronouncements of the U.S. Treasury, the Federal Reserve, or the International Monetary Fund in recent years might presume that academia fully endorsed the view that government usually and almost always impeded the efficient workings of markets. But the intellectual underpinnings of this argument if anything had been challenged increasingly in academia—and not only by a few seemingly renegade economists. Many of the leaders of this faction considered themselves part of the mainstream, and those who were not were usually as well-versed in economic principles as their adversaries. Central lines of theoretical investigation at the nation's best-known economic faculties increasingly included analyses of the limitations of markets, the economic contributions of political and social institutions, the unequal access to information, the one-sidedness of bargaining power, and the incompleteness of contracts. Their conclusions often included an important place for government in market economies. In practice, these analyses provided support for the use of capital controls as hot global money swelled foreign coffers and a more gradual approach to reform in Russia.

Similarly, a witness to the public policy debates of the past two decades in America might have assumed, given the abhorrence of federal budget deficits, that economists widely believed the only important factor in the growth of a nation was an increase in its savings. To the

contrary, economic research increasingly suggested that public investment in research, education, and infrastructure, to name a few, are
important stimulants to long-term growth. In addition, many economists believed that at times there was insufficient demand for goods
and services, which could in itself retard capital investment.

Critics of the conventional economic wisdom complained that
at the core of this mainstream thought was the assumption that consumers are always "rational." They might be surprised to know that
many economists challenged this long-held view as well. In fact, many
economists increasingly explored alternative hypotheses about the
psychological underpinnings of consumer decisions.

These are just a few of many examples, but they underscore the
reason for this volume of alternative perspectives in economics. A
simplified version of mainstream economics has found its way to the
offices of the nation's top government and business decisionmakers,
and into the press as well. This volume's objective is to broaden the
economic dialogue in America.

This volume presents fourteen essays that deviate in important
ways from the consensus view. The reader need not agree with all of
these essays, but they are all relevant and based on well-accepted economic analysis. Each illuminates an area of economics that too often
is neglected in the public discourse, and bears importantly on public
policy. In many cases, had the conclusions of the authors been followed, we would live in a better world today.

The essays are divided into three broad groups. The first, "Public
Policy," deals directly with issues of government and the markets. In
a lively piece, "Departures from Rational Choice," Robert H. Frank
discusses the limitations of the "rational man" assumption in markets.
Time and again, studies have shown that consumers often act in ways
that contradict their best economic interests. Taking account of this
has interesting consequences for public policy that are often ignored.
In "Capitalism and the Erosion of Care," Paula England and Nancy
Folbre argue that private markets necessarily neglect "caring" labor.
We thus do not have enough competent, well-trained teachers, health-
care workers, and elderly care workers, among others, to nurture the
economy adequately.

Eric Beshers addresses the benefits of federal investment in transportation. In his essay, "High Returns on Public Spending," Beshers
presents evidence that public investment has a serious payoff. In the
often personal and heated debate over the future of Social Security,

Teresa Ghilarducci attempts to separate fact from fiction, as well as serious analysis from vested interests, in her piece, "Myths and Misinformation about America's Public Retirement System." In their essay, "The Social and Economic Determinants of Health," Peter S. Arno and Janis Barry Figueroa present new information about how economic and social status affect our health, a field of research that is only beginning to be explored properly and whose public profile deserves to be raised significantly.

Our second group of essays concerns the true state of America. As this book is published, as noted, the economy could not be performing better. Unemployment rates are at thirty-year lows, inflation is falling rather than rising, and wages are increasing. But this welcome period of optimism is also disguising how far we still have to go. In his essay, "Why Stocks Won't Save the Middle Class," Edward N. Wolff demonstrates that stock ownership, though increasing, is still too narrowly concentrated at the higher income levels to enable us to ignore income inequality in America. Anthony P. Carnevale and Stephen J. Rose investigate the causes of income inequality and find that technological change means something different than is widely recognized. In their essay, "Inequality and the New High-Skilled Service Economy," they find that there is a growing demand for office workers in America that makes new and different demands of the education system. In a comprehensive essay, "Discrimination in the Labor Market," Patrick L. Mason demonstrates persuasively that bias still thrives in the nation's job markets. Those wedded to a pure free-market ideology argue that employers will hire only the best, notes Mason. Evidence shows that despite their pecuniary self-interest, they do otherwise.

How well is America doing, anyway? We present three essays on the subject that place matters in better perspective. Richard H. Steckel looks at social and health indicators of the nation's economic well-being, such as the nation's average height. In his essay, "Alternative Indicators of Health and the Quality of Life," he gathers the data and shows that not all has been well in America. Dean Baker takes a closer look at the economic record of the 1990s. In his piece, "Something New in the 1990s?" he finds that the main policy prescription, which was to raise savings by reducing the federal deficit, did not in fact raise national savings and probably did not produce the economic boom at the end of the decade. As for the key measure of a nation's economic viability, its productivity, economists John Schmitt and Lawrence Mishel review the latest evidence in "The United States and Europe: Who's Really Ahead?" Many nations in Europe, it turns out, have surprisingly high levels of productivity compared to the United States.

The last group of essays concerns globalization and the economic development of nations. As we started preparing this volume in 1998, we were in the midst of a global financial crisis. Market liberalization was the prevailing idea around the world, advocated most aggressively by the U.S. Treasury. But since then, economists increasingly have their doubts. Was shock therapy—the sudden adoption of free markets in Russia—the best way to reform that budding and fragile democracy? In her essay, "Russia, the West, and the Failure of the Free Market," Ngaire Woods argues that rapid reform was exactly the wrong policy to apply. Similarly, capital controls were often thought of as nothing less than villainous in a world disposed to headlong market liberalization. In his essay, "The Case for International Capital Controls," James Crotty demonstrates how useful such controls can be. Finally, what are the major factors of growth and development? In his wide-ranging review of growth theory, "Vision and Fact: A Critical Essay on the Growth Literature," Jan Fagerberg closely assesses what economists know about development and what they are beginning to learn. It's not just savings and free markets that do it.

To repeat, readers of this volume should not expect to agree with everything they read. But each essay is based on well-founded economic principles. What is recognized too little is that the same starting principles can give rise to a variety of policy proposals often not considered in America today. The critical need is to open the debate. Many do not realize how long it has been closed.

Finally, the idea for this book originated with The Century Foundation. The willingness to pursue "unconventional wisdom" in any field requires rare vision. Richard C. Leone and Greg Anrig had this vision, and I thank them for their faith and support. I must also thank the others at The Century Foundation who put so much effort into making this book better. They include Bernard Wasow, Sarah Nelson, Beverly Goldberg, and Jason Renker.

I

PUBLIC POLICY

2

DEPARTURES FROM RATIONAL CHOICE

THE CHALLENGE FOR PUBLIC POLICY

Robert H. Frank

To our considerable benefit, public policy has been increasingly informed over the years by insights from the theory of rational choice. As developed by economists and other social scientists, this theory tells us that people have well-defined, mostly self-interested goals, which they pursue in reasonably efficient ways. The theory has helped us to identify circumstances in which private and public interests are in conflict and has suggested practical policies for resolving these conflicts.

Rational-choice theory taught us, for example, that firms pollute the air and water not because they enjoy doing so but simply because it is costly to filter out toxic by-products of production activities. This simple insight has led environmental administrators to embrace effluent taxes, marketable pollution permits, and other devices for changing producers' incentives. The shift away from traditional command-and-control policies toward ones based on incentives has greatly reduced the cost of achieving cleaner air and water.

The same theory of rational choice, however, also has the power to lead public policy astray. Social scientists now know, for example, that people often depart from the predictions of rational-choice theory in systematic ways. Public policies that fail to anticipate these departures may not only fail to achieve their intended consequences, they may actually make matters worse.

A case in point is the design of public policy for slowing the AIDS epidemic. Influential proponents of the traditional rational-

9

choice approach have argued that potential victims of this disease can be expected to respond in prudent ways to the dissemination of information about how the disease is transmitted. Yet many people appear to ignore this information completely. Failure to move quickly beyond information remedies was responsible for hundreds of thousands of additional infections.

Proponents of the traditional rational-choice approach also urge us to base national savings policies on the assumption that most people have the foresight and self-discipline to save enough to meet their consumption needs in retirement. Yet there is clear evidence that many savings decisions completely ignore these needs. Our failure to adopt stronger pro-savings policies has cost us trillions of dollars in lost economic growth.

One more example: Rational-choice proponents often urge tax cuts as a means of improving our quality of life, on the seemingly plausible view that people know better than bureaucrats how best to spend their own money. Yet individual spending incentives often give rise to spending patterns that fail to take full advantage of existing opportunities. As a society, would we be happier and healthier if we spent less on sport-utility vehicles and more on relieving traffic congestion? Considerable evidence suggests that we would. Yet traditional rational-choice models discourage policymakers from even asking such questions.

My aim in this chapter is to summarize for nonspecialists an emerging literature that describes how behavior departs in systematic ways from the predictions of standard rational-choice theory. I will also describe how the ability to anticipate these departures can assist our efforts to formulate intelligent public policy.

THE TRADITIONAL RATIONAL-CHOICE MODEL

One of the most successful and familiar research programs in the social sciences over the past four decades has been the export of the traditional rational-choice models from economics into sociology, political science, anthropology, biology, and law. To estimate the likely effects of a new policy, these models investigate how *Homo economicus*—the stereotypical rational actor, who is driven by largely selfish motives and endowed with prodigious powers of rational inference—would respond to it.

Research in this tradition has scored important gains. Self-interest *is* an important motive, and people really do try to make the best of existing opportunities. Yet it has long been clear that the classical rational-actor model provides an impoverished account of the way people actually behave in many important practical settings.

Behavioral economics is an umbrella term used to describe a relatively new research movement in the social sciences—one that many view as a challenge to the traditional rational-actor model, but that I prefer to describe as a friendly elaboration of it. But the pattern along which research in behavioral economics has evolved is indeed precisely the opposite, in one sense, of the pattern for the rational-actor school. Whereas its economist proponents have applied the narrow rational-actor model to problems in other behavioral science disciplines, behavioral economics has employed insights from other behavioral sciences to broaden and enrich the traditional rational-actor model.

Behavioral economics began in the late 1970s at the intersection of psychology and economics, stimulated by the pathbreaking work of two Israeli cognitive psychologists, Daniel Kahneman and the late Amos Tversky, and the economist Richard Thaler, then at Cornell University. Its research program has since evolved to embrace, and in turn to influence, research findings and strategies in sociology, law, biology, game theory, political science, anthropology, and other disciplines.

Behavioral economics departs from the traditional rational-actor model in two important ways. The first involves the explicit acknowledgment that because human cognitive abilities are limited, we often evaluate alternatives in ways very different from those assumed in the rational-actor model. The judgmental rules of thumb on which we rely function reasonably well in many settings, yet also give rise to systematic departures from the behaviors predicted by the rational-actor model. I describe such departures as "irrational behavior with regret," on the grounds that when subjects are shown why their behavior departs from the predictions of the rational-actor model in these ways, many feel motivated to behave differently— more precisely, to behave in closer accord with what the rational-actor model predicts.

To illustrate, whereas the traditional rational-actor model predicts that decisionmakers will ignore sunk costs, most people in fact seem to be strongly influenced by them. For example, the fact that the

Concorde consortium had already invested billions of dollars in the development of its supersonic aircraft should not have dissuaded them from abandoning the project once it became clear that fares would not cover even the plane's operating costs. Yet the consortium pressed stubbornly onward, citing its past investments as the reason. There is evidence that learning *why* sunk costs should be irrelevant motivates people to try to ignore them.

The second way in which behavioral economics departs from the traditional rational-actor model is by incorporating a richer account of human motivation. In its most widely applied form, the rational-actor model assumes individuals are motivated only by narrowly selfish concerns. Such persons are predicted to behave in a variety of ways that are inconsistent with commonly observed behaviors. The *Homo economicus* stereotype, for example, will not vote in presidential elections, nor will he tip in restaurants away from home, since these behaviors entail costs yet will not affect any outcomes he cares about. To be sure, many people do not vote, and some people do not leave tips when dining in out-of-town restaurants. Yet millions of others routinely do vote, and most people do leave tips when dining out of town. When it is explained to these people that they could have advanced their narrow interests by not behaving in these ways, few seem motivated to change their behavior. Instances like these I call "irrational behavior without regret."

As I hope the examples I describe here will make clear, both types of departure from rational choice—departures with and without regret—are widespread and important.

SYSTEMATIC COGNITIVE ERRORS: DEPARTURES FROM RATIONAL CHOICE WITH REGRET

Proponents of the traditional rational-actor model do not insist that people never make mistakes. But they often do claim that the mistakes people make are unsystematic. Thus, if some people buy too much of something, others buy too little, so that, on average, decision errors tend to cancel one another. One of the principal claims of behavioral economics is that people depart from the predictions of the traditional rational-actor model in ways that are systematic, not random.

EXAMPLE 1

Imagine that you are about to buy a new clock radio for $20 at the nearby campus store when a friend tells you that the same radio is on sale at a store downtown for only $10. Do you drive downtown or do you buy the radio from the campus store? Next, imagine that you are about to buy a laptop computer for $1,050 from the nearby campus store when a friend tells you that a store downtown has the same computer on sale for only $1,040. Do you drive downtown this time?

Note that in each instance, the benefit of making the purchase downtown is exactly $10. And since the effort necessary to obtain this savings is the same in both cases—namely, having to drive downtown—traditional rational-actor models predict that subjects will decide in exactly the same way in both situations. Yet when these questions are posed to subjects, invariably most respond that they would drive downtown to buy the clock radio, but not to buy the laptop computer.

Since different people assign different values to their time and other implicit costs of driving downtown, there is of course no uniquely correct response to either question. Those for whom the opportunity cost of the extra travel is more than $10 should buy from the campus store, and those for whom it is less than $10 should buy downtown. What the traditional rational-choice model insists, however, is that because the relevant costs and benefits are exactly the same in each instance, people should buy both products in the same location. Yet, in literally hundreds of experiments, subjects say they would not. What seems to account for the observed pattern is that many people estimate the benefit in each case by focusing on the *percentage* reduction in the purchase price they will achieve by driving downtown. Once it is explained clearly why the *absolute* savings is the more sensible magnitude on which to focus, people tend to revise their choices in the direction of consistency. In short, the new knowledge seems to make them regret their earlier choices.

EXAMPLE 2

Imagine that the country is preparing for the outbreak of an unusual disease that is expected to kill six hundred people. Two programs to combat the disease have been proposed. If program A is adopted, exactly two hundred people will be saved. If program B is adopted, there is a one-third probability that six hundred people will be saved, and a two-thirds probability that no one will be saved.

When Kahneman and Tversky confronted experimental subjects with this choice, 72 percent opted for program A, the remaining 28 percent for program B. Note that the two programs have the same expected value, and since there is no other clear, objective basis on which to choose between the two programs, this pattern of choices, by itself, is not problematic. But now suppose the choice people face is characterized in the following way:

Imagine that the country is preparing for the outbreak of an unusual disease that is expected to kill six hundred people. Two programs to combat the disease have been proposed. If program C is adopted, exactly four hundred people will die. If program D is adopted, there is a one-third probability that nobody will die and a two-thirds probability that six hundred will die.

Note that the second description offers a choice between precisely the same two alternatives that subjects confronted in the first description. For example, a measure that guarantees exactly two hundred lives saved (program A) is exactly the same as one that guarantees four hundred lives lost (program C). But under the second wording, only 22 percent of subjects opted for program C, the remaining 78 percent for program D. When the choice is between different options characterized according to the number of lives that will be saved (programs A and B), most subjects choose the low-variance option (A). Yet when the choice is between options characterized according to the number of lives that will be lost, people are drawn overwhelmingly to the riskier option (D).

As Example 2 illustrates, even the most careful judgments are prone to *framing effects,* meaning that the choice of language used to describe the options has a profound impact on the way people choose among them. Framing effects are not confined to subjects in psychology experiments called upon to make choices between hypothetical options. Oncologists who must recommend either surgery or radiation for their patients are influenced, alarmingly, by whether the outcome statistics for each procedure are expressed in terms of the number of people who survive a given period or the number who die during that period.

Example 2 also illustrates the principle of *loss aversion,* one of the most important behavioral regularities identified by behavioral economists. The principle of loss aversion states that losses bring more pain than equivalent gains bring pleasure, making people hypersensitive to the prospect of sustaining a loss. This asymmetry is important. The rational-choice model predicts that people will quickly reach agreement whenever opportunities exist for mutual gain. Yet every negotiation entails possibilities for both gains and losses. Behavioral economists correctly predict that loss aversion will often lead to bargaining intransigence and strong adherence to the status quo, even in the face of opportunities for mutual gain.

New Jersey motorists are offered an inexpensive insurance policy that restricts their right to sue. This plan is the default option, the policy that motorists get unless they specifically request otherwise. They can acquire an unrestricted right to sue by paying a higher price. Motorists in neighboring Pennsylvania have the same two options, only the higher-priced, unrestricted option is the default. In both cases, a decision to switch from the default option entails possibilities for both gains and losses—differences in premiums and differences in the amounts recoverable in the event of accident. Thomas Gilovich, a Cornell psychologist, argues that the fact that large majorities of motorists in both states stick with their respective default options is more plausibly explained by loss aversion than by the alternative hypothesis that Pennsylvania motorists assign far higher value to an unrestricted right to sue. New Jersey motorists were keen to avoid the loss entailed by paying higher premiums, while Pennsylvania motorists seemed determined to avoid losing their right to sue.

EXAMPLE 3

Linda is thirty-one years old, single, outspoken, and very bright. She majored in philosophy. As a student, she was deeply concerned with issues of discrimination and social justice, and also participated in antinuclear demonstrations. Rate, on a 9-point scale, the likelihood that Linda is a bank teller. Then, on the same 9-point scale, rate the likelihood that Linda is a bank teller *and* is active in the feminist movement.

The mean response for subjects given the first rating assignment was 3.3, and the mean response for subjects given the second assignment was 4.5. This response pattern violates the laws of simple logic, since the set of people who are both tellers *and* feminists is necessarily smaller than the set of people who are bank tellers.

Example 3 illustrates the principle that people's judgments of likelihood are often based on little more than an assessment of similarity—a bias to believe that "like goes with like." This bias has been implicated in the widespread initial scientific resistance early in this century to the germ theory of disease (because of the difficulty of associating a big outcome like a serious illness with a small cause like an invisible microbe). It may also lie behind a variety of other invalid beliefs—among them that "you are what you eat"; that handwriting provides accurate signals of personality; and that signs of the zodiac predict character and temperament.

*   *   *

The main conclusion from these examples is that people don't merely miscalculate, they miscalculate in similar and systematic ways. This fact has important implications for public policy. Consider, for example, the implications of loss aversion for the relationship between environmental pollution and economic growth. Among environmental activists, the received wisdom is that economic growth is inimical to the environment. Yet, as the experience of the former Soviet Union showed, even modest levels of industrial activity are capable of causing great environmental damage. Pollution levels depend less on the total amount of economic activity than on whether societies are willing to bear the higher costs of cleaner production technologies. Loss aversion suggests that higher economic growth rates make it easier for societies to absorb these costs. In a society whose income is static, paying cleanup costs necessarily entails having to cut back on other things. But a society whose income is growing rapidly can use some of its extra income to pay for cleaner technologies. It need not abandon material comforts to which it has grown accustomed.

The rational-actor model says that people will be willing to pay for environmental cleanup if the value they place on cleaner air exceeds the value they place on the goods they could buy for the same money. But behavioral economics has shown that the willingness to make this trade also depends strongly on the rate at which incomes are growing.

ENRICHED MODELS OF MOTIVATION

As noted, the traditional rational-actor model assumes that people are essentially selfish. An advantage of this approach is that it helps generate clear predictions about behavior that can be refuted by empirical testing. Traditional rational-choice theorists are often critical of attempts to introduce broader conceptions of human motivation on the grounds that if investigators are free to assume whatever they wish about tastes, then it becomes almost impossible to generate empirically refutable hypotheses. Almost any behavior—no matter how bizarre—can be "explained" after the fact simply by assuming that the individual had a taste for engaging in it.

This criticism is well taken. Yet, as behavioral economists have demonstrated, an enriched conception of human motivation can expand the predictive and explanatory power of traditional rational-actor models in dramatic ways. Let's consider a few examples.

EVALUATING FUTURE COSTS AND BENEFITS

Any realistic theory of human choice must account for how people evaluate costs and benefits that occur in the future. The traditional rational-actor model assumes that people discount future costs and benefits at the market rate of interest in the case of future monetary costs and benefits, and an implicit personal discount rate in the case of nonmonetary costs and benefits. Yet the predictions of this theory differ from observed behavior in systematic ways. Consider, for example, the following two scenarios in which a person can choose between receiving $100 at one point in time or $110 a week later:

A: $100 in fifty-two weeks versus $110 in fifty-three weeks

B: $100 now versus $110 in one week

If people discount future receipts in the manner assumed by rational-choice theory, anyone who prefers $110 in choice A must also prefer $110 in choice B. Yet many of those who choose $110 in A go on to voice a clear preference for $100 in B. Asked to account for this pattern, they typically respond with something like "I want the $100 right away, but if I have to wait a year for it anyway, I might as well wait the extra week and get $110."

From the perspective of the traditional rational-actor model, this pattern doesn't make sense in at least two ways. First, it gives rise to inconsistent choices and behavior. Thus, in the pair of choices posed here, an investigator attempting to determine whether someone is willing to wait an extra week to get an additional $10 would reach one conclusion in scenario A, but the opposite conclusion in scenario B.

The second difficulty is that the observed choice pattern suggests that people often fail to choose the alternative that best promotes their interests. For example, it will be "worth it" to wait an extra week to get the extra $10 as long as the interest rate is less than 10 percent per week. Failure to wait the extra week in a world in which interest rates are more like 5 percent *per year* is simply a bad decision.

As the late Richard Herrnstein (a Harvard psychologist) and his collaborator George Ainslie (a Pennsylvania psychiatrist) have shown, both human and animal nervous systems predispose individuals to choose poorer but imminently available rewards over better but delayed alternatives. These same investigators have shown that observed intertemporal choice patterns can be predicted with great accuracy and consistency on the basis of models in which the psychological attractiveness of a future reward doubles when the delay until receiving it falls by half.

The policy implications of the approaches are profoundly different. Writers in the rational-choice tradition urge policymakers to adopt the rational-actor model when formulating policies for dealing with virtually every important social and economic problem. Richard Posner, a University of Chicago law professor and a federal district court judge, suggests that the rational-actor model provides the best available basis for formulating policies for dealing with the AIDS epidemic. As evidence for this assertion, he observes that homosexuals were more likely to adopt safe-sex practices once they became well informed about how the AIDS virus is transmitted. From this Posner infers that if someone who understands the risks exposes himself to infection, he must be viewed as having made a rational choice, in the same way that we view it as rational to engage in other risky behaviors—such as crossing a street or driving a car.

The behavioral discounting model, by contrast, makes clear that individuals will often choose powerful short-term rewards even when they *know* that these choices run deeply contrary to their interests. It is difficult to conceive of an intelligent policy for dealing with the AIDS epidemic that fails to incorporate this fundamental insight.

The contrast between the rational-actor model and the behavioral model also has implications for policy questions regarding savings. For example, many proponents of the rational-actor model oppose collective efforts to increase savings, even in the face of compelling evidence that the American savings rate is pathologically low. ("People know their own interests," they say, "and if people wanted to save more they would.") Behavioral models of savings, by contrast, encourage us to take seriously the problems confronting people who are overwhelmed by credit-card debt, and the expressions of regret made by people who enter retirement with little or no savings. There are good reasons to believe that these people would be well served by policies that provide greater incentives to save.

The rational-actor model in its most narrow form is similarly ill-suited as the sole foundation for attempts to understand and deal with problems arising from illicit drugs. Many users of illicit drugs wish desperately to free themselves from their influence. Their problem, like the one confronting savers, is that the costs of taking action come right away while the benefits come much later.

Behavioral models of how people weigh the present against the future do not abandon the fundamental insight of the rational-actor model that financial and other incentives affect behavior. They merely stress the need to incorporate the best available theoretical and empirical evidence on the question of *how* incentives affect behavior.

BEYOND NARROW SELF-INTEREST:
IRRATIONAL BEHAVIOR WITHOUT REGRET

SYMPATHY AND COOPERATION IN SOCIAL DILEMMAS

Consider the owner of a business who perceives an opportunity to open a branch in a distant city. She knows that if she can hire an honest manager, the branch will be highly profitable. But she also knows that she cannot monitor the manager, and that if the manager cheats, the branch will be unprofitable. By cheating, the manager can earn three times as much as he could by being honest. Will the owner open the branch in the distant city? The narrow rational-actor model suggests that she will not. She will predict, using that model, that the manager will cheat (since he knows that the owner cannot monitor and punish him). Armed with that prediction, the owner's best option is not to open the branch.

But suppose we relax the assumption that all potential managers are narrowly self-interested. If the owner could somehow identify an honest manager, the venture could then go forward. And in that case, both the owner and the manager would come out ahead relative to the outcome predicted by the rational-actor model.

Can we identify people who can be trusted even though their material incentives favor cheating? Consider the following thought experiment: Imagine you have just gotten home from a crowded concert and discover you have lost $1,000 in cash. The cash had been in your coat pocket in a plain envelope with your name and address written on it. Do you know anyone, not related to you by blood or marriage, you feel certain would return it to you if he or she found it?

In response to this question, most of us report confidently that we know *many* such people. There is also experimental evidence that people can make statistically accurate predictions about who will cheat in social dilemmas—situations in which cheating pays but cannot be detected and punished.

One of the firmest predictions of the traditional rational-actor model is that individuals *will* cheat in social dilemmas. Yet evidence against this prediction is widespread. Many people, for example, return unwanted pesticides to inconveniently located disposal centers, even though they could pour them down their basement drains without detection or penalty.

Cooperation in social dilemmas appears to be motivated not by rational calculations about self-interest but by various moral sentiments—in some cases, sympathy for the interests of specific others, in other cases, a more general sense of duty to the community. Behavioral economists stress that the ability to identify such moral sentiments in potential trading partners creates opportunities to exploit mutual gains from cooperation.

This observation has implications for a variety of issues of concern to social scientists. In the realm of organizational design, for example, it emphasizes the possibility of creating environmental conditions that foster voluntary cooperation on the part of employees. By contrast, the traditional rational-actor model, which emphasizes the impossibility of voluntary cooperation, has focused on attempts to bribe and punish employees. Evidence suggests, however, that mechanisms such as piece rates, surveillance cameras, drug testing, e-mail monitoring, and the like may actually stimulate adversarial attitudes and behavior in the workplace.

There is also evidence that single-minded focus on material incentives will fail to exploit important opportunities for gain in the realm of environmental policy. It is simply not practical, for example, to apprehend and punish people who pour pesticides down their basement drains at midnight. A far more promising approach is to encourage people to refrain from doing so out of a sense of obligation to others in the community.

JUSTICE AND FAIRNESS

Authors in the rational-choice tradition often write with thinly veiled contempt about woolly notions like justice and fairness, describing them as "terms with no content." Behavioral economists, however, have produced a rich experimental literature that defines these concepts in operational terms and facilitates quantitative assessment of the importance that many people assign to them.

One of the most familiar strands in this literature is the so-called "Ultimatum Bargaining Game," a simple game that is played only once by two persons. The first person (who is often called "the allocator") is given a sum of money—say, $100—by the experimenter, and then asked to propose a division of that sum between himself and the second player (who is often called "the receiver"). Thus the allocator might propose $50 for himself and $50 for the receiver; or $60 for himself and $40 for the receiver; or, more generally, $X for himself and $(100–X) for the receiver. (Only integer values of X are allowed.) If the receiver accepts this offer, each gets the proposed amount and the game is over. But if the receiver refuses the proposal, the $100 reverts to the experimenter and both the allocator and receiver get nothing.

The traditional rational-actor model predicts that the allocator will propose $99 for himself and $1 for the receiver, and that the receiver will then accept this offer (on the grounds that getting even $1 is better than getting nothing). Experimental evidence, however, suggests that one-sided offers are in fact extremely uncommon, and that when such offers are made, they are likely to be refused. In one study, for example, a fifty-fifty split was the most frequent offer made by allocators. And when the receivers in this same study were asked to report the smallest amount that they would have been willing to accept, their average response was 26 percent of the total. Further experiments support the interpretation that it is the receivers' perception that a one-sided offer is unfair that leads them to reject it. For instance, one study found that the typical receiver is willing to accept even a very small percentage of the total if that percentage is determined by a random number generator (rather than being an intentional offer by the allocator).

Concerns about fairness have far-reaching implications for issues of interest to many social scientists. A long-standing puzzle in labor economics, for example, is why workers earn persistently higher wages in high-profit industries than in industries with low profit rates. (Traditional economic theory states that even though employers in the former industries can afford to pay more, they have no incentive to pay more than the going rate, since paying even a little more would result in hordes of new applicants from low-profit industries.)

Suppose, however, that workers care not only about the absolute level of their pay, but also about whether their contracts seem fair in the light of their perceptions about employers' abilities to pay. In labor markets populated by such workers, the equilibrium wage will grow with the employer's ability to pay, and hence the observed relationship between wage and profit rates.

Concerns about fairness also appear to explain why union members will go on strike even in the face of overwhelming evidence that doing so will cost them jobs that pay more than they will be able to earn elsewhere. This is what happened, for example, in the fabled Eastern Airlines strike of 1989, which led to the company's bankruptcy filing. In the field of foreign relations, concerns about fairness also appear to explain why nations often take actions that conflict with the predictions of the standard rational-actor model. *Homo economicus* is not expected to set himself on fire to protest his nation's foreign policy, nor would he ever volunteer as a suicide bomber.

Concerns about fairness even appear to explain the reluctance of firms to exploit excess demand by raising prices in the manner predicted by traditional theories. An ongoing challenge to these theories has been to explain why we observe persistent excess demand for Rolling Stones concerts, premium sporting events like Wimbledon finals and the Super Bowl, reservations at popular restaurants on Saturday nights, and air tickets during peak holiday periods. Why don't sellers simply raise their prices? The most parsimonious answer is that sellers are wary of triggering negative consumer perceptions of "unfair" pricing. As one ski area operator put it, "if customers think you've gouged them during Christmas week, they'll go somewhere else in March." The rational-actor model, by contrast, assumes that the skier's willingness to come in March depends only on the price that operators charge in March, not on what they charged in December.

POSITIONAL CONCERNS

Assuming constant price levels, which world would you choose to live in: one in which you earn $100,000 per year and everyone else earns $200,000, or one in which you earn $90,000 and everyone else earns $75,000? In the standard rational-actor model, in which individual utility depends on absolute consumption, the first world is the clearly preferred choice, because its higher income level will support a higher material standard of living. Many people, however, say they would choose the second world. And there is indeed powerful evidence that, once a threshold level of affluence is achieved, human well-being is far better predicted by relative consumption than by absolute consumption.

A long-standing component of the behavioral economics research program explores the many ways in which the positive and normative conclusions of the rational-actor model are altered by the introduction of concerns about relative position. Standard labor-market models, for example, predict that differences in pay among co-workers within firms will mirror differences in the dollar values of what they contribute to their employer's bottom line. But consider the following thought experiment:

Among your co-workers of roughly similar rank, job title, and seniority, try to envision the two most productive individuals and also the three who are least productive. Now suppose that either the top two workers or the bottom three were to suddenly disappear. Which group's disappearance would most reduce the total value of what gets produced in your group?

Most people answer without hesitation that the disappearance of the top two would hurt most. On the basis of this answer,

conventional models predict that the combined salaries of the top
two individuals would be greater than the combined salaries of
the bottom three. Yet in most groups the reverse is in fact the
case. Indeed, for every firm for which the relevant salary and productivity data are available, the distribution of wages is highly
compressed relative to the corresponding distribution of productivity. And this is precisely the pattern predicted by models in
which each worker cares not only about her own salary but also
about how it compares to the salaries earned by her co-workers.
In the presence of such concerns, no one gets to enjoy the privilege
of being a high-ranked worker without implicitly sharing at least
some of her pay with her lesser-ranked co-workers.

   If, as evidence suggests, relative consumption matters more for
some goods than for others, then concerns about relative position
will also affect how people allocate their incomes across different
categories of goods. Compared to the consumption mix that would
maximize overall welfare, people will spend too much on cars, houses,
and many other material goods, and too little on less conspicuous
forms of consumption such as time spent with family and friends.

   The resulting waste is *very* large. Consider the representative
sample of sports cars sold today shown in the right column of Table
2.1. The left column of this table extrapolates how the entries in the
right column will evolve if current spending trends continue to play
out over the coming decade. Given the importance of context for
evaluation, our best conjecture is that each collection of cars will
generate almost precisely the same levels of satisfaction for their
respective owners. Entry for entry, the cars in the left column are
faster and more luxurious than their counterparts in the right column, but by the standards of the year 2010 the established norms
for these qualities will be higher as well.

   The cost of the collection of cars in the left column exceeds that
of the collection in the right column by more than 50 percent. If the
relationship between absolute spending and satisfaction is the same
for other goods as for cars, the conclusion is that we could spend
roughly one-third less on consumption—roughly $2 trillion per year—
and suffer no significant reduction in satisfaction. Savings of that
magnitude could help pay for restoring our crumbling public infrastructure, for cleaner air and water, and a variety of other things that
would confer lasting improvements in human well-being. Since satisfaction from car ownership and other consumption spending depends

TABLE 2.1. SPORTS CAR VALUES

THE UNCONSTRAINED SPORTS-CAR HIERARCHY IN 2010 (PRICE MARKET SHARE)	THE CURRENT SPORTS-CAR HIERARCHY (PRICE MARKET SHARE)
1. Tomorrow's Supercar ($414,000 1%)	1. Ferrari 456 GT ($207,000 1%)
2. Ferrari 456 GT ($207,000 4%)	2. Porsche 911 Turbo ($105,000 4%)
3. Porsche 911 Turbo ($105,000 15%)	3. Porsche 911 Carrera ($72,000 15%)
4. Porsche 911 Carrera ($72,000 20%)	4. Porsche Boxster ($45,000 20%)
5. Porsche Boxster ($45,000 25%)	5. BMW Z3 ($30,000 25%)
6. BMW Z3 ($30,000 35%)	6. Mazda Miata ($23,000 35%)
Average price = $64,320	Average price = $41,620

on context, the incentives confronting individuals are similar to those confronting nations involved in a military arms race. Spending less on cars, or on bombs, would be better, but only if everyone did it. The mere fact that a rearrangement of expenditures would be better is no reason to expect that it will happen.

Incorporation of concerns about relative position also helps shed light on many simmering disputes about the efficacy of the market system. Proponents of the narrow rational-actor model have long insisted that labor and product markets are highly competitive, and that attempts to regulate them in any way are likely to do more harm than good. Opponents of the narrow model invariably counter that large corporations have enormous market power, and that the state must therefore intervene to protect workers from exploitation. On the best available evidence, labor and product markets do, in fact, appear highly competitive. Yet the trend in industrialized countries has been the adoption of ever more comprehensive state regulation of private labor contracts. These regulations increasingly limit the amount of safety risks we can take on the job, the amount of overtime we can work, and the extent to which we can agree to work for lower wages. If these regulations make people worse off, why don't voters oppose them?

The apparent contradiction can be resolved by noting that if workers care about relative position, private labor contracts simply cannot be expected to yield the optimal levels of workplace safety and other amenities. Concerns about relative position create tension between the interests of individuals and the interests of larger groups. Each worker's incentive is to exchange reductions in safety for higher pay, thereby to move higher in the consumption distribution. In the aggregate, however, these moves go largely for naught, since it is impossible for everyone to move higher in relative terms. It follows that collective action to increase safety will be attractive even in highly competitive labor markets.

The incorporation of concerns about relative position into standard rational-actor models also poses a challenge to conventional beliefs about the presumed conflict between equity and economic efficiency. On the conventional view, progressive taxation is thought to compromise efficiency by weakening the incentives of top producers to expend effort and take risks. If concerns about relative position are important, however, then progressive taxes—especially if levied on consumption rather than income—will result not only in a more equitable distribution of living standards but also, by encouraging greater savings, higher levels of economic growth.

OTHER INTERDEPENDENCIES IN PREFERENCES

Interdependencies in preferences and behavior are not confined to concerns about relative income and consumption. The traditional rational-actor model, which denies the existence of such interdependencies, has considerable difficulty accounting for important waves of economic and social behavior. Some examples:

FEMALE LABOR FORCE PARTICIPATION. One of the most striking economic and social changes of the past three decades has been the more than twofold increase in labor force participation of married females. Proponents of the narrow rational-actor model attempt to explain this change by reliance on the usual suspects—in particular, the economic rewards from paid employment relative to those available from not working outside the home. Yet labor force participation of married women has increased for virtually every category—irrespective of movements in the real economic value of labor market opportunities.

There is now good evidence that the recent participation changes cannot be adequately explained without taking into explicit account that the attractiveness to any one woman of working outside the home increases with the fraction of other women in the population who do so—irrespective of the direct economic rewards.

THE SEXUAL REVOLUTION. Traditional accounts of the dramatic increase in the frequency of premarital sex in the years since the mid-1960s emphasize the role of the birth-control pill, which for the first time freed women from the fear of unwanted pregnancy. But alleviation of this fear, by itself, cannot be a satisfactory explanation, since the frequency of premarital sex among women who do not use birth control pills is currently not significantly different from the corresponding frequency for those who do. The dramatic change in observed behavior is unlikely to be explained without taking into explicit account the extent to which the costs and benefits of engaging in premarital sex depend on the frequency with which others in the population also do so. The appearance of the birth-control pill may have helped launch the observed changes, but its direct effect was surely very small.

THE SPORT-UTILITY CRAZE. In 1990, annual sales of sport-utility vehicles in the United States totaled only 750,000 units. By 1997, however, annual sales of these vehicles surpassed 4,000,000 units—more than five times as much. A fall in the real price of gasoline has made ownership of these fuel-inefficient vehicles more attractive than in the past, but this effect is far too small to account for the observed increase in sales. And it is unlikely that any existing social-science models can account for it without taking explicit account that the attractiveness of owning such vehicles is an increasing function of the proportion of others who also own them. Social scientists who continue to deny this influence will someday be lumped together in the public mind with physicians who argued against the germ theory of disease. Behavioral models of consumer choice allow for the fact that ownership of a product may become more attractive with growth in the number of others who own it, up to a point. And they also allow for the fact that proliferation beyond that point may make ownership once again seem less attractive.

*   *   *

Despite the numerous insights that traditional rational-actor models have afforded over the years, the fact remains that these models provide an impoverished account of human behavior in many domains. Models that incorporate simple modifications of traditional assumptions regarding cognition and motivation can often explain observed behaviors that traditional models cannot. This point is important, not just for academics who are curious about human behavior, but also for policymakers. Traditional rational-actor models, which predict how *Homo economicus* would respond to a new policy, often yield a completely misleading picture of how real people will respond to that same policy. The truly rational policymaker is one who looks beyond traditional rational-actor models for guidance about what's likely to work.

3

CAPITALISM AND THE
EROSION OF CARE

Paula England and Nancy Folbre

*When everything is for sale, the person who volunteers time,
who helps a stranger, who agrees to work for a modest wage
out of commitment to the public good, who desists from lit-
tering even when no one is looking, who forgoes an opportunity to free-ride, begins to feel like a sucker.*
—Robert Kuttner, *Everything for Sale*[1]

Robert Kuttner's warning can be rephrased in terms that highlight
its resonance with the interface between capitalism and family values.
When everything is for sale, the woman who devotes herself to her
children, who agrees to work for a nonprofit that cannot afford to
pay market wages, who takes care of sick and elderly relatives that no
one else will tend to, or who passes up an opportunity to get something for nothing, begins to feel like a sucker. A growing feminist literature on caring labor emphasizes a cruel paradox. On one hand,
capitalist development tends to destabilize forms of patriarchal power
that once gave women little choice but to specialize in caring for others. This is to be welcomed. On the other hand, it creates competitive
pressures that tend to penalize women, men, and institutions that
seek to provide genuine care for other people.[2]

In this chapter, we argue that feminist theory offers important
insights into the evolution of care services in the economy as a whole.
Although we apply some of the conventional tools of both neoclassical

We gratefully acknowledge the comments and criticisms of Diane Elson, Jeff Madrick,
and Julie Nelson.

and Marxian economics, we draw more heavily from ecological economics, arguing that personal forms of care for others create "externalities" or unanticipated spillover benefits from individual transactions.
We argue that increased competition in the provision of services tends
to intensify efforts to offload care costs (to make someone else pay), to
reduce care services, and to obscure negative effects on the quality of
care. These processes, similar to those that lead to pollution and deterioration of the natural environment,[3] erode the supply of care.
Ironically, patriarchal control over women has traditionally provided a
partially effective—though extremely unfair—buffer of protection for
some members of U.S. society, especially children. We need to build a
better and more equitable buffer to protect our families and communities from the corrosive effects of the self-interested opportunism that
market forces sometimes reward.

   We begin by explaining the feminist approach to the economics
of caring labor, which emphasizes the tendency to neglect caregiving.
Next comes a description of the caregiving sector of the economy—
how it has changed, and how paid occupations such as nursing,
teaching, child care, and elder care interact with unpaid family work.
We discuss some disturbing side effects of the increased privatization
of caregiving in the economy, such as cost-cutting and reduced quality of services, especially for the least privileged members of our
society. Our conclusion calls not only for more attention to this
problem but also for development and enforcement of a new social
contract for care.

1. The Economics of Caring Labor

Neither a stand-alone competitive market nor a centrally planned
society (nor any simple combination of the two) can guarantee an
adequate quantity or quality of caring labor. The feminist analysis
of caring labor insists that something is missing from both neoclassical
and Marxian economic theory. Care is more than an input into the
development of human capital. It is also an *output,* something we
generally would like to have more of for its own sake. The experiences
of being a parent, a neighbor, a friend, or a lover, for example, offer
direct rewards. For many people, they are ends in themselves.

Worrying about care reminds us that economic growth is simply a means to these ends. As Nobel laureate Amartya Sen points out, our social goal should be to maximize the development of human capabilities—measured by such indicators as life expectancy, literacy, and other skills—rather than trying to maximize collective consumption or even collective happiness.[4] Care is necessary to develop human capabilities, but is also an important capability in and of itself.

Care cannot be planned from the top down, or simply assigned. It flows from social norms and individual preferences. It is also a skill that must be developed and exercised, one that relies heavily on what some psychologists call "emotional intelligence."[5] But we must keep in mind that despite the intrinsic reward, care is also susceptible to economic incentives. In the long run, care that goes unrewarded is likely to diminish over time.

Can we rely on the forces of supply and demand to provide care? Perhaps to some extent. After all, if the demand for caring services goes up, people who provide them should be able to charge more. One obvious problem, however, is that truly caring individuals are less directly motivated by pecuniary concerns, and often reluctant to bargain by threatening to withhold their services. A "rational" economic person, observing the result, might conclude that it is best to avoid situations in which one might begin to care too much.

A more subtle problem emerges from a consideration of the distinctive nature of care services. The price of these services (whether paid as a wage or as a share of family income) is not a good measure of their value, because care creates the positive externalities already mentioned. Many people share in the benefits when children are brought up to be responsible, skilled, and loving adults who treat each other with courtesy and respect. There is a long list of beneficiaries. Employers profit from access to competent, disciplined, and cooperative workers. The elderly benefit from the Social Security taxes paid by the younger generation. Fellow citizens gain from having law-abiding rather than predatory neighbors.

A central economic problem, however, is that these broad gains cannot be fully captured by those who create them. Parents can't demand a fee from employers who hire their adult children and benefit from their productive efforts. Nor can they send a bill to their children's spouses and friends for the value of parental services consumed. Individual transactions cannot compensate them for the value they provide.

When child care workers or elementary school teachers genuinely care for their students, they foster an eagerness to learn and willingness to cooperate that later teachers and employers benefit from. When nurses do a good job, patients' families and employers benefit. Anyone who treats another person in a kind and helpful way creates a small benefit that is likely to be passed along. A growing body of research on social capital shows that an atmosphere of trust and care contributes not only to the development of human capital but also to economic efficiency.[6]

Like other externalities, however, those created by care create an incentive to *free-ride*—that is, to let others pay the costs. Thus, in the absence of collective coordination, or what we might call good "rules of the game," less than optimal amounts of care will be provided because care providers are not fully compensated for their services. Quite the contrary, they often tend to be crowded out by services that can be sold at full value to buyers able to pay for them directly—such as legal or banking services. To explore this dilemma, we need to look more carefully at how care is defined, how it has been affected by the weakening of patriarchal power in this country, and why it is so difficult to provide within unregulated markets.

DEFINING CARE

Care is a word with many complex interrelated meanings, most of which revolve around the basic notion of concern for other people, especially dependents such as children, students, the sick, and the elderly. Many economists might interpret it as a form of altruism, but we argue that it also includes important elements of trust and social obligation.[7] Care may flow from affection, but it often requires work—a very different kind of work from that which economists typically focus on.[8] It is work that requires personal attention, services that are normally provided on a face-to-face or first-name basis, often for people who cannot clearly express their own needs. In our view, the motive underlying this work often affects its quality. Emily Abel and Margaret Nelson put it this way: "Care givers are expected to provide love as well as labor, 'caring for,' while 'caring about.'"[9]

Some writing on care treats it as an activity that is not only intrinsically rewarding, but also morally transcendent.[10] But many feminist economists shun overly sweet descriptions of caring labor, rejecting the implication that it is necessarily more enjoyable or fulfilling than other types of work. Indeed, much attention focuses on the contradictory dimensions of care as an activity that is frustrating as well as rewarding. Workers are forced to engage in such "emotional" labor, required to be polite, encouraging, and cheerful, whether they feel that way or not.[11]

Scholars on the left have traditionally emphasized the importance of unalienated labor, the virtues of producing for direct use rather than for sale in the market. But as the history of slavery, feudalism, and patriarchy shows, work can be exploitative whether it is part of a market economy or not. Did we ever live in a golden age in which personal, family-based relationships fostered egalitarian communities? This is the implication of much communitarian writing, which blames the growth of the modern, impersonal marketplace for many of our social woes.[12] Feminist scholars question this implication for the obvious reason that personal relations have often been patriarchal relations, seemingly designed to assign most of the economic burdens of care to women so as to allow men more freedom to compete or pursue other wants.

The line between caring and "un-caring" labor simply does not coincide with the line between the family and the market. Indeed, feminist scholarship emphasizes the remarkable similarity between women's responsibilities for care in the home and their responsibilities for care in paid jobs such as teaching and nursing. By emphasizing this similarity, the concept of caring labor focuses attention on the gendered character of social norms that shape the division of labor in both the family and the market. Women are expected, even required, to provide more care than men. This expectation is rooted deeply within the history of patriarchal society in the United States and elsewhere.

CAPITALISM AND THE WEAKENING OF
PATRIARCHAL CONTROL OVER WOMEN

Where does care come from? Economists have traditionally avoided this question by confining their attention to the behavior of self-interested adults in the marketplace, and leaving dependents entirely out of the picture. Even neoclassical theory, which is premised on the individual pursuit of self-interest, has treated altruism within the family as a "natural" and therefore relatively uninteresting phenomenon, at least for economic purposes. According to neoclassical economists, women specialize in the provision of care for others either because they have a comparative advantage (they are more "efficient" at it than men) or because they get more pleasure out of it than men do— enough pleasure to compensate them directly for the time, money, and energy required.

But if this particular form of specialization is completely natural and automatic, it is difficult to explain why so many social institutions have historically imposed much greater restrictions on women than on men. As a large body of feminist scholarship shows, women have traditionally had little choice but to specialize in the care of dependents. Explicit restrictions on their access to education and to work outside the home have both reduced their bargaining power and lowered the opportunity cost of time devoted to care. Because they didn't have other opportunities, they weren't giving up as much in order to provide care. Even in relatively egalitarian societies like our own, social norms put greater pressure on women than on men to take care of others, especially family members.[13]

Feminist theory emphasizes the coercive dimensions of social norms of masculinity and femininity.[14] A set of social rules that assigns women greater responsibility than men for the welfare of others can be understood as a system of "discriminatory obligation."[15] It can also be interpreted as a form of "socially imposed altruism" in which women are socialized to act in more caring ways than men, especially toward children.[16] Precisely because these responsibilities were imposed from above, they have been weakened as women's opportunities outside the home have increased, enhancing their bargaining power. Many women are now asking why moms should be expected to give up more than dads.[17]

It is difficult to name a precept more central to the neoclassical vision than its confidence in individual pursuit of self-interest. This confidence has historically been lodged in the presumption, as we have noted, that women would tend to family responsibilities, providing necessary levels of altruism and care. Needless to say, this presumption has been shaken by the destabilization of the patriarchal family and the dramatic movement of wives and mothers into paid employment in the United States. Once it becomes apparent that the family is susceptible to economic reorganization and change, it can no longer be so easily excluded from the larger picture, and it becomes apparent that the larger economy has never been entirely based on the individual pursuit of self-interest. Market economies have always depended on strict rules for the nonmarket provision of care, especially for dependents.

Both personal experience and formal game theory models show that it is generally easier for an individual to avoid responsibilities for the care of others than it is to persuade someone else to assume those responsibilities.[18] Providing care for another is risky, since you cannot be sure it will be reciprocated (hence Kuttner's point about good people being made to feel like suckers). The competitive marketplace is a bit akin to a footrace in which anyone carrying a child or another dependent is at a disadvantage. They do not get their just economic rewards and get left further and further behind. Unless the rules of the race are redefined so that everyone is required to carry a certain share of the burden of obligation, individual competitors have every incentive to offload and outsource their care responsibilities.

INCENTIVES FOR CARE

Many feminist economists will agree that it is better to pay for care services in the market than to extract it coercively from women in the home. That is no reason to ignore the problems built into market provision. As pointed out earlier, care provides externalities that will never be fully rewarded through individual transactions. Furthermore, the nature of care makes it difficult to assure the quality of the services being provided.

One difficulty with creating appropriate incentives for caregiving is that it is difficult to monitor. Economists have long recognized that some forms of work cannot be efficiently based on purely extrinsic rewards for this very reason. Workers who seek to minimize effort per unit of pay can often conceal their level of effort. It is relatively expensive to monitor workers who provide caring labor, because their "product" cannot be weighed or counted. A nanny who seems perfectly loving and nurturing with infants or toddlers when her employers are present may completely ignore them as soon as the parents leave. Some day-care centers now provide videocams accessible from the Web that allow parents to view what is going on from moment to moment. On the other hand, constant scrutiny of someone else's care can take almost as much time as directly providing that care.

Economists studying jobs in the manufacturing sector observe that employers may offer their workers a higher-than-market-clearing wage in part to foster a sense of reciprocity that encourages effort, or simply to increase the cost of losing their job if they are caught shirking.[19] Workers are particularly likely to command such an "efficiency wage" (high enough to elicit greater effort) when employers can easily discern the effects of effort on product quality. But in care work the difficulty of monitoring worker effort is compounded by the fact that outputs are diffuse, difficult to measure, and enjoyed by parties other than those actually paying the costs.

Gathering good information about caregiving is not an easy task. Expert psychologists, much less parents, are uncertain about the effects of caregivers' characteristics on children's development. Social scientists find it extraordinarily difficult to measure the kinds of neighborhood effects that lead to "collective efficacy."[20] So-called third-party problems further complicate matters. We can't necessarily trust children's assessments of whether their teachers are doing a good job or not.

In general, personal and emotional forms of labor have a subtle character that is far more difficult to assess than most other dimensions of work performance. Who is the best teacher? The best parent? It is often very hard to say. The teacher who improves children's test scores the most may not be the one who makes them feel confident and self-motivated. The parent with the hottest temper may, ironically, also be the one who has the strongest emotional connection with the child. Obviously, skill matters. But motivation also matters—we tend to trust caregivers who convey a sense that they genuinely care for their students, patients, or clients.

Workers who provide care must love their work, we tell ourselves (especially if they are cheap, convenient, and polite to those paying the bill). Otherwise, why would they do it for such low pay? As advocates of pay equity have pointed out for years, many nurses are paid less than tree-trimmers, and parking lot attendants earn more than day-care workers. These differences cannot be explained by the characteristics of the people in these jobs. A small but significant pay penalty is discernible for workers in caring occupations, holding education, experience, and other important factors equal.[21] Some people indeed enter caring jobs because they are intrinsically motivated. However, many others enter them simply because no other options are open to them. Furthermore, the conditions of work, which include low pay and little job security, do little to foster genuine commitment. As a result, even our best caregivers often burn out.

Women who specialize in caring for young children, spouses, or elders at home are vulnerable to similar problems. Because pay is strongly affected by job experience, women who leave employment to care for family members suffer wage penalties for years after they reenter the job market.[22] Statistical analysis shows that mothers who work part-time while their children are young also pay a penalty since part-time experience has a lower return than full-time experience.[23] Being employed fewer years also affects mothers' pensions and Social Security benefits. These effects are particularly consequential when caregivers lack the financial assistance of a partner specializing in market work. Children and others dependent on the caregiver suffer as well.

We should expect and demand as much care from men as from women. But no amount of moralistic finger-wagging is going to persuade individuals to make choices that put them at a competitive disadvantage in a race for ever-greater financial benefits. We don't know what level of care can be sustained in an economy that rewards the individual pursuit of self-interest far more generously than the provision of care for others.

2. THE CARE SECTOR

Most service-oriented companies are less immediately affected by the growing international mobility of capital than manufacturing firms are. In the future, we may ship off our children, sick, and elderly to low-wage countries to be cared for—or simply import more low-wage immigrants to care for them here.[24] In the meantime, increased competitive pressure in the production of tangible goods has the indirect effect of intensifying efforts to cut the costs of maintaining and producing our labor force. These efforts impinge directly on the provision of care.

Yet we lack a clear picture of what we could call the "care sector" of the economy. As we know, the nonmarket work of women, a primary source of caring labor, has been explicitly excluded from most economic analysis.[25] The tripartite distinction among agriculture, industry, and services emerged as a classification of types of products without reference to their personal or emotional content.

"Services" have always been distinguished simply by their lack of a material output that could be counted or weighed.

Still, we can patch existing bits of data on time-use and the composition of the labor force together in ways that help explain why caring labor is likely to become an increasingly important economic concern. William Baumol predicted long ago that we would suffer a "cost disease" of the service sector, with increases in relative costs resulting from less adaptability to technological change.[26] His predictions have not been completely borne out. In recent years many services, including banking, retail, and entertainment, have been transformed by waves of innovation. But in an important respect, his prediction was spot on. Productivity growth has been and is likely to continue to be slowest in care services requiring personal and emotional contact.[27] These services have simply been redistributed and in some ways concentrated as other dimensions of work have been transformed.

THE DECLINE OF HOUSEHOLD PRODUCTION

The two most conspicuous trends shaping the historical organization of care in our economy have been fertility decline and women's entrance into paid employment, both under way for more than 150 years. The first of these trends has reduced our overall demand for caring labor by reducing the number of children relative to the working-age population—an effect increasingly countervailed by the growing proportion of the elderly. The second of these trends has reduced the supply of caring labor outside the market by raising its opportunity cost: Women now have access to better-paying jobs than they used to—as a result, the cost of not working for pay has increased. On the other hand, caring occupations such as teaching, nursing, and home health care have increased dramatically as a percentage of the paid labor force in recent years.

The harder one thinks about these trends, the more arbitrary and misleading our conventional picture of economic development begins to seem. We look back on a history of economic growth that we have carefully constructed by "cooking the books." We divided the economy into two parts—the family (considered, like environmental assets, a part of nature) and the market. Household labor was simply not included in the Gross Domestic Product. When women reallocated their work from an arena in which it wasn't measured to the market economy, where it showed up in dollar terms, we registered significant economic growth. But what happened to the underlying quantity and quality of care services? We don't really know.

Economists have just begun reconstructing quantitative estimates that reveal the magnitude of mismeasurement over time. If we assume that women devoted about as much productive effort to combined paid and unpaid work as men did to paid work—an assumption justified by historical research and early census surveys—we can reconstruct estimates of the total labor force of the United States that include housewives with other paid workers providing domestic and personal services. Thus revised, this category accounts for a larger share of the workforce than any other for much of our history. In 1930, for instance, if we combine housewives and mothers without paid employment with other workers providing paid domestic and personal services, we find that they comprised 41 percent of all workers, compared to the 24 percent of all workers providing other types of services and 20 percent in manufacturing, mechanical, and mining jobs.[28] The development of new cooking and cleaning technologies made household work much more efficient—possibly affecting the productivity growth of the economy as a whole more than even railroad and automotive technologies.

The simplest (and also the crudest) way of estimating the value of women's unpaid domestic and personal services is to multiply the number of full-time equivalent workers in these jobs times women's average wages in paid employment in this sector. It is widely conceded that this number represents an underestimate for two reasons. Women traditionally faced discrimination in paid employment that lowered their market wages. Furthermore, if women choose not to work for a wage, it is often because the true value of their home work is higher than the pay being offered, so even a nondiscriminatory wage understates their productivity. Acknowledging this caveat, studies of Australia, Canada, and the United States show that nonmarket activities valued solely on the basis of labor inputs account for a very significant proportion—between 40 percent and 60 percent—of the total value of all output.[29] Total Economic Product (including the value of nonmarket work) grows at a very different rhythm and rate over time than Gross Domestic Product.[30] One summary of these findings suggests that, when declines in the stock of natural resources and environmental health are taken into account along with declines in nonmarket work, we have made no economic progress in the United States since 1970—even though Gross Domestic Product per capita has almost doubled.[31]

Even less appreciated is another measurement problem, rooted in the tendency to ignore the qualitative dimensions of caring labor. Much of what housewives did—and do—involves complex multi-tasking that defies assignment to any one sector of the economy. Serving a salad, for instance, could entail harvesting greens from a kitchen garden while teaching children the names of the plants (agriculture plus education), preparing a dressing while keeping an eye on an infant (manufacturing plus child care), setting the table and welcoming family members to the table (restaurant plus personal services). The modern parent may collect raw materials from the salad bar at the supermarket rather than the garden (hunting and gathering rather than agriculture) but the point remains the same. And within this mix of activities, those with personal and emotional significance—such as choosing something a family member especially likes, or preparing it in a special way—are often far more important than the market value of the meal itself.[32]

Modern time-use surveys often emphasize the distinction between a primary activity and a secondary activity that may be performed simultaneously but is considered of a lower priority, not the "main activity." Examples include listening to the radio while cooking or keeping an eye on a child while doing the laundry. Secondary time-use is particularly relevant to the analysis of child care, which is often combined with other activities. Estimates suggest that somewhere between one-half and three-quarters of all time spent in child care may be accompanied by another activity.[33] These forms of joint production greatly complicate valuation of nonmarket activities.

The entire exercise of imputing market values is based on the notion that there is easy substitutability between home-produced goods and services and market substitutes. This is almost certainly the case for most material goods, and it may even be the case for many services. It matters little to most people, for instance, who vacuums their floors or cleans their toilets. But purchased services are only partial substitutes for personal services in which the identity of the care-provider and the continuity of the care relationship matter. Purchased care can be a good substitute for the custodial and educational component of child care, and for some portion—but not all—of the emotional component. Even parents who rely on paid care during the work day spend significant amounts of time with their children, and the quality of this time is extremely important.

As families purchase more services, they probably reallocate their nonmarket time and effort away from material production toward the personal and emotional dimensions of care. In an analysis of historical time-use data, for instance, Keith Bryant and Kathleen Zick show that parents may actually have increased the amount of time they spend in primary and secondary child care time *per child,* implying that paid child care may largely have displaced secondary or "on-call" time when most of parental attention was actually elsewhere—cooking dinner, for instance, while kids played in the yard next door.[34] Thus, the overall quantity of family care time has declined—but its quality has probably increased. Increased freedom to explore work opportunities outside the home means that the time that women spend on home care is more freely—and perhaps more joyously—given than before.

Whether improvements in quality of nonmarket work have been sufficient to compensate for declines in quantity we cannot say. But the greater the role that personal and emotional care play in non-market work, the greater the downward bias in market-based esti-mates of its value. There are some things you cannot buy perfect substitutes for. Nowadays the personal and emotional content of home life is becoming more and more concentrated in a relatively small number of activities—such as sharing meals or telling bedtime stories. Past a certain point—which we have yet to carefully define or negotiate—family time cannot be reduced without adverse conse-quences for all family members.

THE GROWTH OF THE SERVICE SECTOR

The growth of service jobs is a much-remarked-upon feature of mod-ern economic development, associated with the expansion of women's labor force participation. Services vary considerably along the dimension of personal contact. Some involve working purely with information, and some involve working purely with people, with many permutations in between.

Women tend to move into jobs that resemble their traditional responsibilities for family care, a factor that contributes to occupa-tional segregation. By one recent estimate, 53 percent of workers in the United States would need to change jobs to equalize the occupational distribution by gender.[35] That women are for the most part segregated in lower-paying jobs than men accounts for as much as 40 percent of the gender gap in earnings.[36]

The exact distribution of workers in jobs that involve care is difficult to specify. Hochschild estimates that about one-third of American workers have jobs that demand emotional labor.[37] But not all emotional labor is caring labor—some simply requires relatively shallow affective performance. Such performance may be stressful for workers but does not have serious consequences for consumers. It matters less—and is more difficult to ascertain—if an airline attendant is faking cheerfulness than if a nurse is faking concern for patients.

The two high-skilled occupations that most distinctly require care are nursing and teaching, two subcategories within the Professional, Technical, and Related category that are poorly paid, considering the amount of education they require. In the United States in 1991, almost half of all women in professional and technical work were either nurses or teachers. Throughout the world professional women are overrepresented in these two occupations.[38] Among occupations with lower education requirements there are two within the category of Service Workers that clearly embody care—child care workers and elderly care workers. The percentage of the labor force in these occupations tends to increase in the course of economic development, and working conditions within them are a particular cause of concern in the OECD countries.[39]

But caring responsibilities are not limited to the most explicitly caring occupations. Ethnographic studies of work show that secretaries are expected to protect their bosses from stress and construct a supportive and reassuring environment.[40] Waitresses are encouraged to be kind as well as personable.[41] Airline attendants are expected to be heroic in crises as well as cheerful in serving beverages.[42] Paralegals are expected to mother the lawyers engaged in tough-guy litigation.[43] Conventional categories cannot be used to tally up the exact percentage of jobs that fit the profile of caring labor.

Furthermore, the forms of personal contact involved in jobs are strongly affected by technological innovation and industrial organization. Both urbanization and increased geographic mobility probably reduce the likelihood that employers form personal relationships with workers or workers with consumers. But in the market as well as in the family the reduction of opportunities for personal interaction may heighten the importance of those opportunities that remain. Relationships among workers may acquire increased significance. Services requiring relatively long-term relationships, such as those provided by psychotherapists and personal athletic trainers, become conspicuously sought-after luxuries.

The nature of caring work is often defined by professional standards or by cultural norms that esteem and reward intrinsic values of care. Just because work is paid for doesn't mean that it is not also motivated by genuine concern.[44] As competitive pressures intensify, however, employers may be forced to reduce expenditures on the least profitable forms of care. The particular features of care discussed here, particularly the difficulty of monitoring and measuring its effects, mean that the negative effects of cost-cutting may not be immediately apparent.

3. Cutting Care Costs

Karl Polanyi argued long ago that economic development tended to "disembed" companies from the communities in which they operate.[45] Over the last twenty years it has become increasingly apparent that the intensification of global competition imposes harsh penalties on companies that are not strict profit-maximizers. Privatization of services previously provided by the public sector has a similar effect. Especially when defined in ways that include emotional well-being, quality of care is far more difficult to measure than out-of-pocket cost.

A process that can be termed "the commodification of care" is under way in virtually all countries. Clearly, this process has some good features, beyond the obvious possibilities for increases in efficiency. But we need to pay closer attention to the ways in which emphasis on "fee for service" affects quality. As Clare Ungerson puts it, "the social, political, and economic contexts in which payments for care operate and the way in which payments for care are themselves organized are just as likely to transform relationships as the existence of payments themselves."[46]

The National Income and Products Accounts are not designed to study these issues, and their strict separation between private industry and government makes it difficult to measure expenditures on care services as a whole. However, a good approximation of the value of private market services can be derived by adding expenditures on Personal Services, Health, Education, Social, Other and Miscellaneous, and Private Households. These have increased from about 4.3 percent of Gross Domestic Product in 1959 to about 10.6 percent in 1997.[47] Clearly, care services represent a growing sector of the market economy.

Good illustrations of the negative impact of competitive pressure on quality emerge from even a brief consideration of health care, child care, and elder care. Expenditures in these areas have risen significantly over the past thirty years, while institutional restructuring has created new openings for profit-oriented providers. There can be little doubt that the introduction of profit-based competition helps reduce the escalation of costs. What is at issue is whether it also reduces the quality of services in ways that consumers may be slow to recognize and even slower to act upon.

HEALTH CARE

The reorganization of the health care industry in the United States has significantly reduced the escalation of health costs. But the overall quality of care is threatened. Health maintenance organizations (HMOs) charge their members a fixed amount, creating obvious pecuniary incentives for them to cut costs and to discourage unhealthy applicants. Most of their cost savings come from lower rates of hospitalization.[48] In recent years, many HMOs have eliminated coverage for senior citizens on Medicare.[49] A recent study published in the *Journal of the American Medical Association* found that several measures of the quality of care are significantly lower in for-profit than in nonprofit HMOs.[50]

Hospitals have dramatically reduced the length of stays by sending patients home more quickly than ever before, offloading care costs onto family members and friends. Measures of cost-effectiveness do not take these hidden costs into account. Nor have the health effects been closely scrutinized.[51] Forced cutbacks in hospital stays created so much bad publicity that Congress passed legislation in 1996 prohibiting so-called drive-by deliveries, and requiring insurance companies to reimburse at least two days of hospital care for a normal childbirth. A recent article in *Forbes* magazine noted that hospitals are increasingly reusing medical devices that were designed to be disposable—and advised their readership not to sign surgical consent forms without specifying a ban on "unapproved re-use."[52] Even congressional Republicans voted recently in favor of a patients' bill of rights (in an effort to forestall stronger regulation by Democrats).[53]

These well-publicized issues, however, are less troubling than the less visible deterioration in the emotional dimensions of care. As a recent *New York Times* article put it, critics say "hit and run nursing has replaced Florence Nightingale."[54] Bedside nurses have been replaced by unlicenced "care technicians." A survey of over 7,500 nurses released in 1996 reported that 73 percent felt that they had less time to comfort and educate patients.[55] At the same time, reimbursements to home health care workers have been cut back. Deborah Stone, who has extensively interviewed home health care workers, reports, "The more I talked with people, the more I saw how financial tightening and the ratcheting up of managerial scrutiny are changing the moral world of caregiving, along with the quantity and quality of care."[56] These are not changes for the better.

CHILD CARE

Paid child care can serve as a very good complement for parental time. Although there is some controversy over the amount of time very young children should spend away from their parents, there is no evidence that paid child care per se has negative effects. The *quality* of both custodial and parental time is paramount. But experts and parents differ widely in their assessments of quality of paid care (children themselves are seldom consulted!). The time and effort required to monitor quality is quite costly, especially for parents constrained by a tight budget. A recent comprehensive survey argues that the physical and emotional environment in many child care centers remains relatively poor, partly because of poor regulation in many states.[57] Pay levels for child care workers are seldom much above minimum wage, and high turnover rates in the child care industry, averaging about 40 percent per year, preclude the development of long-term relationships between caregivers and young children.

Voluntary accreditation by the National Association for the Education of Young Children tends to improve quality. A recent California study, for instance, rated 61 percent of accredited centers as good in 1997, compared to only 26 percent of those seeking accreditation the previous year. Nationwide, however, only 5,000 out of the nation's 97,000 child care centers were accredited.[58] Furthermore, many children in paid child care are in small, informal family settings, where quality is even more variable than it is in centers. In the rush to expand child care slots to accommodate the exigencies of welfare reform, some states have provided child care vouchers that can be used virtually anywhere and may actually have a negative effect on quality.

The links among regulation, industrial organization, and quality of care are just beginning to be explored. In general, for-profit child care centers do not seem to emphasize "curbside appeal" at the expense of more difficult-to-monitor aspects of quality. However, for-profit child care centers that are part of national chains do seem to follow this strategy.[59] What looks attractive to the parent is not necessarily what is best for the child—shiny new toys matter less than skill and commitment levels of the workers providing care.

ELDER CARE

Quality issues are still more salient, even shocking, in elder care. Nursing homes now employ more U.S. workers than the auto and steel industries combined. Almost 95 percent of these homes are privately run, though most are subsidized with public dollars. Turnover rates among workers are high, amounting to almost 100 percent within the first three months. According to *Consumer Reports*, about 40 percent of nursing homes repeatedly fail to pass the most basic health and safety inspections.[60] In 1999, the General Accounting Office reported that government inspections of nursing homes across the country each year show that more than one-fourth cause actual harm to their residents.[61]

Given their poor track record at meeting even basic needs, it is chilling to consider how poorly nursing homes meet the emotional needs of the elderly. Susan Eaton describes the things companies "can't bill for, but that make all the difference if you're living in a nursing home: time to listen to somebody's story, time to hold their hand, time to comfort somebody who is feeling troubled. And you can't exactly put that on your bill; imagine finding 'holding hands' on the bill. You have to have a 'treatment,' you have to have some formal procedure."[62]

What we really need is some radical treatment for our larger problems of care.

4. CONCLUSION

Our diagnosis begins with the observation that traditional patriarchal laws and norms in the United States provided a partially effective device for assuring a supply of caring labor. They made it very difficult for women to do anything but care for family members, a form of coercive specialization that lowered women's bargaining power and guaranteed that the costs of care would remain relatively low— at least for men. With the weakening of patriarchal control over women in this country, the price of care has gone up. The impulse to make somebody else pay for care, or to cheapen it by lowering its quality, has shaped the emergence of new market-provided services. Intensified competition and privatization are worsening these trends, with traumatic results for individuals who are too poor, too weak, or too sick to effectively demand the care they require.

The solution to this problem is not to send women back home. Strict forms of patriarchal control are unacceptable—as well as unfair. Nor is the solution to find cheap market substitutes that inevitably lower the quality of care. There are alternatives between the devil and the deep blue sea. We need to forge a new social contract that shares responsibilities for care between men and women. We also need to support and protect caring work in a number of ways—by reducing the pressures of paid employment on family life, by setting strict quality standards for the provision of market care, and by fostering the development of new levels of skill and commitment among paid care workers. This will require rethinking the organization of work in both the private and the public sectors.

The supply of caring labor to the market economy resembles the supply of unpriced natural resources such as air and water. None of these resources appear to have much value until their quality deteriorates to the point that they threaten to become scarce. By that time, however, it may be too late to replenish them.

Efficiency in the use of easily measurable inputs is achieved by displacing costs into an arena in which they are not so easily monitored, sweeping the dirt under the rug. Sooner or later, however, negative externalities such as pollution become apparent—and costly.

The environmental metaphor is compelling. By the time we realized that an invisible ozone layer was protecting us from ultraviolet rays our chemical emissions had already put a hole in it that is impossible to repair. By the time we fully realize what is happening to our social environment, it too may be hard to patch back together. The Humpty-Dumpty of children's storybooks is a fragile, egg-shaped creature. When he falls off a wall, all the king's horses and all the king's men try—but fail—to put Humpty together again.

4

HIGH RETURNS ON PUBLIC SPENDING

Eric Beshers

THE ROLE OF GOVERNMENT

In a free-enterprise economy, most spending decisions are made by private agents: households and firms. Individuals (households) decide what to consume and businesses (firms) decide what facilities and equipment to build and buy in order to make a profit from supplying the goods and services that people consume. Individuals seek to maximize the satisfaction or pleasure they can get with their incomes, and firms seek to maximize their profits. The details of implementing these principles in the real world are complicated, but the basic concepts are simple.

Households and firms are not the only agents in the economy, however. There is also government—in the United States, many kinds of government: federal, state, local. Governments act in the economy in three basic ways: they tax, spend, and regulate. One may be inclined to a restrictive view of what government ought to do (I am), but however minimalist one is, it is difficult to deny that governments must levy some taxes, must make important spending decisions, and must engage in some regulation of the conduct of both people and businesses.

One fundamental economic responsibility of government is investment in the basic physical infrastructure of society. Basic infrastructure is a somewhat elastic concept, but at the very least it includes the water and sewer facilities essential for urban life. It also includes major transportation facilities. In the public sector are airports and the

49

air traffic system, ports, inland navigation (mostly the Mississippi system), some urban rail-passenger systems, and—by far the largest commitment of resources—roads and highways. There is continual discussion about privatization of some parts of the transport system that are now public. Privatization of some types of facilities may be a good idea, and some of it may actually occur. But it is a good guess that, for reasons set out in this chapter, streets and highways will remain in the public domain for the foreseeable future.

In my view, the level of investment in the highway system is and should remain a national concern, and the federal government should have a leading role in choosing the amount. Some sensible, intelligent people vigorously challenge this notion. They point out that the great preponderance of road travel is local travel, which is true both for the Interstate highway system and for local networks. Among people who pay serious attention to transportation policy there is a near-total consensus that highway *project* decisions—repaving segments, widening shoulders, adding new lanes, for example—should be made by state or local governments. The argument is that these must be undertaken by agencies and people close to the scene. There is little role here for federal officials.

There is, nonetheless, a persuasive case to be made that total highway investment is a legitimate and even crucial national policy issue and a proper concern for the federal government. Roads and streets are essential elements of our social and economic fabric. We simply could not function without them. (This has been true since long before the advent of the automobile; the Romans well understood the value of good roads.)

As will be shown in this chapter, investments in highways also generate high economic returns for society. (This may also be true for other kinds of transportation projects, but this chapter will stick to a discussion of highways.) And the highest returns come from the major roads that connect cities and the principal routes carrying traffic within urban regions—the roads that tie the nation together and underpin the workings of our cities. That which ties us together and is required for the working of our cities is of national concern.

The public sector will continue to have the dominant role in highway investments. The reasons are primarily political and institutional. The system is almost entirely in the public sector now. Changing this would be very difficult as a practical matter, and the political will to do so is nowhere to be seen. There are obvious issues of both fairness and practicality in collecting tolls for use of the local network. Are we going to slap tolls on a soccer mom every time she ferries her progeny to the local junior high school? I doubt it. An economic case could be made for allowing private firms to make major new investments in roads, but I don't think it will happen very often. I believe the body politic would simply not tolerate the notion. The American people expect their governments to provide good roads and take good care of them.

In sum, the road system is vital to our society, highway investments can generate high returns that reach all members of society, and the public sector must make most of those investments: good enough reasons to make the level of road-improvement spending a national policy issue.

In this chapter, I will show that the economic return on highway investment is high enough to justify a strong program of road improvement and that the consideration of environmental costs does not reverse this conclusion. The level of investment in roads is a legitimate issue of national policy, and the right national policy is a robust investment program.

THE ROLE OF THE HIGHWAY SYSTEM

The total network of highways, roads, and streets is ubiquitous, pervasive, complete in its connectedness, and absolutely fundamental to transportation in our country—and will remain so. A fact we know but rarely think about is that, with only trivial exceptions, every dwelling and business place in the nation is on the road network and is connected by it to every other dwelling and business place in the nation. No other element of our transportation system has anything like the ubiquity and seamless connectivity of the road network. No stops at terminals or transfers are required to move from local roads to feeders to main arteries and back again.

Most of the traffic moving on the road network is passenger transportation in private autos, but that is by no means all the traffic. Most public transportation (buses, school buses, and taxis) is over roads, as is most of the nation's freight transportation. Manufacturing firms could neither get their goods to market nor receive materials and components without highway-borne freight.

The private automobile is, by far, the dominant mode of transport for individuals in America. Some people argue over the reasons why this has come to be the case. But the central point here is that it is the case, and that is a critical fact of American life today. One way to see this is to look at person-trips (one person making one trip) by transport mode, as shown in Table 4.1. Auto, walk, and transit (bus and rail) do not require explanation or definition. "Other" comprises all other modes: taxis, school buses, and intercity public transportation such as aviation, rail passenger service, and buses.

For people, travel is predominantly local travel; the average length for a person-trip in 1995 was 9.1 miles.[1] If we look at intercity travel separately, the relative role of the private auto is probably slightly greater, largely because we eliminate walking. I am not aware of a direct source of information on intercity person-trips in autos, but I can assert with confidence that it is over 90 percent of the total, the rest being air or intercity bus service; in the context of the national totals, rail passenger service is negligible.[2]

Freight movement, however, is not dominated by the highway mode of transport in the same way people movement is. For local and short-haul service, trucks are virtually the exclusive means of goods movement, but other modes play a major role in long-haul freight. Table 4.2 shows intercity freight ton-miles by mode share.

A ton-mile means one ton moved one mile; if it moves two miles, then it's two ton-miles. When we measure traffic this way, railroads are at the top of the heap, because rail hauls are longer than truck

TABLE 4.1. PERSON-TRIPS BY MODE (1995)

MODE	PERCENT
Auto	86.4
Walk	5.4
Transit	1.8
Other	6.5

Source: U.S. Department of Transportation, *Summary of Travel Trends, 1995 Nationwide Personal Transportation Survey*, draft prepared by Patricia S. Hu, Center for Transportation Analysis, Oak Ridge National Laboratory, and Jennifer R. Young, Systems Development Institute, University of Tennessee, January 8, 1999, p. 14.

TABLE 4.2. MODE SHARES OF INTERCITY FREIGHT TON-MILES IN 1997

MODE	PERCENT
Railroads	39.2
Trucks	29.1
Pipelines	17.3
Inland Waterways	11.4
Great Lakes	2.6
Air	0.4

Source: Rosalyn Wilson, *Transportation in America 1998* (Washington, D.C.: Eno Transportation Foundation, 1998), p. 44.

hauls. Railroads' cost advantage over trucks increases with distance. But if we remove distance from the calculation and look only at tons of freight moved, then trucks predominate, as shown in Table 4.3.

Some goods movements go part by highway and part by rail, but often the entire movement is by rail. This latter is true, for example, of most coal shipments, most bulk chemical movement, ores, much of paper shipments, and all auto parts going into assembly plants by rail. As well as all-rail moves, there are also some all-barge moves and some rail-barge moves (common for coal).

Large volumes of goods do, thus, move without ever being on a highway. But virtually all of these movements are between producers of one kind or another: coal going from mines to power plants, bulk

TABLE 4.3. MODE SHARES OF INTERCITY FREIGHT TONNAGE IN 1997

MODE	PERCENT
Railroads	25.9
Trucks	49.1
Pipelines	15.0
Inland Waterways	8.2
Great Lakes	1.6
Air	0.2

Source: Rosalyn Wilson, *Transportation in America 1998* (Washington, D.C.: Eno Transportation Foundation, 1998), p. 46.

chemicals from petrochemical plants to industrial users, paper from mills to printing plants, and so forth. And for the most part, these are bulk commodities: coal, chemicals, and the like.

Aside from the special cases of autos and auto parts, most high-value goods that move by rail do so in intermodal service where containers or trailers are trucked to special rail terminals, go most of the way by rail, and complete their journeys by truck. Finished goods cannot reach retail outlets without moving over roads, and, for the most part, cannot reach distribution centers without a truck movement. For high-value goods, whether components or finished articles, the entire move will often be by truck, because trucking firms provide flexibility, speed, and reliability that rail service simply cannot match.

Highways are thus not the whole show for long-haul freight, but they're a major—and vital—component of the intercity goods movement system. The highway system, in short, serves the great preponderance of people movement in the United States, and is a large and essential piece of the freight-movement system. The quality of our roads has a direct effect on the cost and quality of goods and services produced in the United States.

THE CONDITION OF THE HIGHWAY SYSTEM

Our interest here is not really in the physical condition of our roads in the sense of state of repair, surface roughness, or the like. In that regard, our principal roads are not in particularly bad shape and are getting steadily better. The interesting questions relate to the growth of the road system and its performance in terms of levels of congestion, travel speeds, and similar characteristics.

If we compare the growth of vehicle travel with the growth of the road network, we see that travel on the highways has been increasing considerably faster than the highways themselves. The standard measure for travel is vehicle-miles of travel (VMT). If you drive your vehicle one mile, that's one VMT. I have chosen total miles of paved road as the measure of the road system.[3]

Let's look at 1941, the last year before we were engaged in World War II, and 1997, which is the most recent year for which we have data.

The midpoint of this fifty-six-year period is 1969. Two points are clear from Table 4.4. One is that vehicle travel has, indeed, been growing faster than the extent of the road network. The second is that growth of both travel and the highway system slowed over this period, but travel continued to grow faster than did the capacity of roads. These same trends persist in more recent periods; rate of growth of travel and roads continues to slow, but travel still grows faster than roads.

Using miles of paved road as a proxy for capacity, these trends would lead us to expect a steady increase in congestion. The available evidence, however, surprisingly suggests that there is not a tendency in this direction. Table 4.5 (see page 56) shows both length and speed of work trips by auto to be increasing somewhat, so that the increase in trip time is disproportionately less than the increase in trip length. We also note that the changes from 1990 to 1995 are barely notice-able. Other data show us that daily traffic per lane on Interstate highways in urban areas is increasing even as the percentage of peak-period travel in heavy congestion has been holding fairly steady.[4] This suggests that increases in *average* travel/capacity ratios in urban areas do not necessarily mean more travel in congested conditions.

These data seem contrary to much of the anecdotal evidence one hears. I can think of two explanations (and there may well be others). One is that changes in driver behavior have effectively generated new highway capacity. Maximum vehicle flow per freeway lane has gone up by 10–15 percent or more since the mid-1980s, because people are driving closer to the car in front of them.[5] (Fatality and injury rates have been coming down despite this.[6])

The other reason is that growth in work trips is happening in the suburb-to-suburb trips on the urban periphery, not on the radial corridors carrying workers from suburbs to central cities. If we think

TABLE 4.4. HISTORICAL COMPARISONS:
PAVED ROADS AND VMT

RATIOS	PAVED-ROAD MILEAGE	VMT
1997 to 1941	4.0	7.7
1969 to 1941	2.7	3.2
1997 to 1969	1.5	2.4

Source: Federal Highway Administration, United States Department of Transportation, *Highway Statistics Summary to 1995*, July 1997, p. V-5 for paved roads and pp. V-12–V-13 for VMT; *Highway Statistics 1997*, November 1998, p. V-10 for paved roads and p. V-89 for VMT.

TABLE 4.5. RECENT DATA ON WORK TRIPS BY AUTO: LENGTH, TIME, AND SPEED

Year	Trip Length (miles)	Trip Time (minutes)	Speed (MPH)
1983	8.9	17.6	30.2
1990	11.0	19.1	34.7
1995	11.8	20.1	35.4

Source: Federal Highway Administration, U.S. Department of Transportation, *Summary of Travel Trends, 1995 Nationwide Personal Transportation Survey,* draft prepared by Patricia S. Hu, Center for Transportation Analysis, Oak Ridge National Laboratory, and Jennifer R. Young, Systems Development Institute, University of Tennessee, January 8, 1999, p. 42.

of a metropolitan area as central city and suburbs, we have five basic commuting flows, as seen in Table 4.6.

The suburb-to-suburb flow is much the fastest growing of these as well as the largest.[7] And the auto trip times are much lower for the suburb-to-suburb commute than for the suburb-to-city commute (they are lowest for work trips within the city).[8]

Media perception of congestion may be affected by the fact that a large share of the nation's journalists, commentators, and the like work in the central parts of New York and Washington. These two metropolitan areas lead the nation both in relative share of jobs in the central city and in long commuting times.[9]

The foregoing discussion of travel times is in the context of work trips, because, more than any other kind of trip, they tend to occur in peak periods when highway travel conditions are worst. Work trips account, however, for less than one-third of households' auto travel

TABLE 4.6. METROPOLITAN WORK TRIPS BY FLOW PATTERN

Pattern	Percent
Within Central City	27.1
Suburb to Central City	17.0
Suburb to Suburb	39.4
Central City to Suburb	6.7
Out of Metropolitan Area	9.7

Source: Alan Pisarski, *Commuting in America II: The Second National Report on Commuting Patterns and Trends* (Washington, D.C.: Eno Transportation Foundation, 1996), p. 71.

(31 percent) and less than one-fourth of households' vehicle trips (24 percent). (The fraction is higher for travel than for trips because the average work trip is longer than the average of all trips—twelve miles compared to nine.)[10]

Table 4.6 tells us that about 44 percent of metropolitan work trips have central-city destinations. If all these trips were by auto, commuting to city jobs would be 11 percent of total auto trips. But some of them are not by auto, so less than 10 percent of all household auto trips are work trips to the central city.

I may seem to belabor this point, but people unfamiliar with transportation issues tend to think in terms of commuting flows on radial highways, and these account for a small fraction of total auto travel. Today's city is a sprawling, polycentric metropolitan region—and it is going to stay that way for quite a while. So-called smart-growth policies will have, at most, a marginal effect on the urban form that has been evolving over the past fifty years. Even where old centers are vibrant and strong (and they often are), they are no longer economic centers of gravity drawing in most jobs and shops and services. Though many types of businesses are attracted to the center, many others are not.

Within metropolitan areas, transportation issues that arise in the future will often be about circumferential movement among low-density fringes and peripheral subcenters rather than about movement along the radials that serve the high-density core.

In sum, both nationally and for urban areas generally, traffic volume is rising relative to road capacity. Despite this truth, average vehicle speeds have not fallen, indeed have risen slightly. The evolution of the sprawling, many-centered city has led to longer home-to-work trips while other types of trips have become shorter and increased in number. Ever-spreading gridlock is not the fate of all motorists or of all urban regions. Congestion, nonetheless, is a permanent feature of everyday life for the preponderance of motorists who use major urban arteries during rush hours.

ECONOMIC ANALYSIS OF HIGHWAY INVESTMENT

A fair amount has been written, and a great deal more said, about whether it is a good idea or a bad idea to invest in highways. Unfortunately, a lot of the writing is advocacy work from one viewpoint or another, and not very useful for informing public debate. Perhaps worse, there is very little work that attempts direct, original estimates of benefits or costs in quantitative terms. Most of what might be called the objective, scholarly writing is theoretical or conceptual; some of it is very good, but it rarely gets down to actual numbers.

There are several surveys of costs of highway travel that attempt to capture external costs such as air pollution, congestion, and other negative effects. These studies are of varying quality and do not take account of the benefits of the roads system. A good review and critique of these efforts has been written by Jose Gomez-Ibanez of Harvard University.[11] In general, he finds the economics fairly sloppy and the negative effects overstated.

The best analysis of such costs, by Mark Delucchi of the University of California, Davis—not reviewed in the Gomez-Ibanez paper just cited—is, indeed, notable for its original research, exhaustive treatment (twenty separate reports on different aspects of costs), and rigorous adherence to the canons of economic analysis.[12]

Delucchi, however, makes no effort to quantify benefits, although he does offer a useful theoretical discussion along with his opinion that the total social benefits of motor-vehicle use far exceed the total social costs.[13] I agree with Delucchi's assertion in this regard, but that does not tell me much about the gains from highway investment. We could be at just the right level of spending on better roads, or we could be spending too little, or too much.

The work that has directly addressed gains from highway investment in recent years is of two types: statistical analysis at the national level and project-specific benefit-cost analysis. In the former category, there is one excellent piece of work extant: that of Ishaq Nadiri of New York University.[14] Nadiri has used statistical analysis (multiple regression) to estimate the effect of highway investment on businesses' costs. Regarding the second type of analysis—benefit-cost analysis—there is, as already noted, far more conceptual work than actual calculation of real-world benefits. In the last few years, a number of people have developed computer models for this purpose, but for the most part systematic application of these models is not yet widespread.

The California Department of Transportation (Caltrans) routinely applies benefit-cost analysis to road projects; not many state transportation departments follow this practice.[15] The Federal Highway Administration, an element of the U.S. Department of

Transportation, has developed a fairly elaborate model called Highway Economic Requirement System (HERS), which is capable, perhaps with some modification, of estimating gains from a given level of national investment in road projects. HERS is interesting because it has been modified to include an estimate of air-pollution costs in its calculations. It has not, however, been used for this purpose.[16]

STATISTICAL ANALYSIS

Let us begin, then, with the statistical analysis. The regression analyses explore correlations[17] between sets of data to see if there is any connection between variations in the two sets. If, for example, one has two series of data over time, series A and series B, such a statistical analysis might show that the variations in the two series over time were closely related and that, in some sense, a very high percentage of the variation in B could be "explained" by the variation in A. Such findings can be very useful, but they do not conclusively demonstrate causality and they offer no information on the nature of the connection between A and B; they tell no "story" about why there is a connection.

The inference of causality is, as much as anything, a matter of common sense. Ishaq Nadiri conducted his regression analyses and found a strong statistical link between highway investment and firms' costs: the more highway investment, the lower the costs. Intuition tells us it's reasonable to suppose the cost and quality of transportation will affect the costs of operating businesses. High-quality transportation reduces delivery times and makes managing inventories more efficient, for example. In Nadiri's findings, the statistical relationship is robust, and the causal link makes sense. A particular strength of such statistical analysis is that on a national scale it will capture all sorts of indirect effects on business operations and costs that we may understand only dimly. By contrast, analysis of the benefits of a specific local project tells us only about direct effects on or closely related to that particular stretch of road.

It's useful to have an idea of the types of highway improvements we're talking about. Table 4.7 (see page 60) shows the breakdown of states' 1997 highway construction expenditures by improvement type; these expenditures include the federal highway money that is allocated among the states.

Table 4.7. 1997 Highway Construction Expenditures, Interstates and Other Arterials, by Improvement Type (Percentages)

New Roads	Wider Roads	Rebuilt Roads	Bridges	Other
20.4	7.5	45.5	18.1	8.5

Source: Federal Highway Administration, U.S. Department of Transportation, *Highway Statistics 1997*, November 1998, pp. IV-81–82.

"New Roads" means entirely new right-of-way, either a new road or a relocation of an existing road. "Wider Roads" means additional lanes on existing roads. "Rebuilt Roads" is a broad category; it could include anything from resurfacing (replacement of the top three or four inches of pavement) to complete reconstruction. In the latter case it could include improvements in curvature and grade, widening of lanes and shoulders, and other major improvements, but not new lanes.

"Bridges" includes new bridges, wider bridges, and bridges rebuilt or improved in other ways. "Other" includes a variety of improvements—related to safety, environmental protection, or traffic flow—that are not part of the road structure; guard rails would be one example.

On the valid assumption that most of the bridge spending is for rebuilding, we can say that over 60 percent of investment in major highways is for rehabilitation or improvement of existing facilities *without* significant capacity expansion.

Statistical Analysis: The Recent Work

We should have an idea of the context in which Nadiri undertook his effort; it was not the first attempt to find a relationship between public sector investment and economic performance. Economists have been working in this area for some time. Discussions among scholars broke into a wider public argument in 1989, with publication of a paper by David Aschauer, of Bowdoin College.[18]

Aschauer's findings were startling. He had conducted an analysis of the relationship between Gross Domestic Product and public capital. Skipping past the technical detail, we can say his results implied that an increase in government capital would pay for itself in one year in higher output in the economy, a return of 100 percent.[19] Similar work, published the following year by Alicia Munnell, seemed to support Aschauer.[20]

Many economists were skeptical; they saw such high returns as unrealistic. The reaction led to a line of research that culminated in Nadiri's effort.[21] One line of criticism was that Aschauer had the causality backwards: robust economic growth generated the tax revenues that allowed an increase in public investment. A related point of attack was more technical; the argument was that Aschauer had aggregated too much. In other words, with U.S. GDP as a single number and government capital as a single number, the relationship was oversimplified. We might not be seeing the effects of public capital on GDP; we might be seeing the effect of other forces on both public capital *and* GDP.

Some researchers sought to fix this by looking at outputs by types of industry and public investment across states and produced a lesser impact for government investment but a stronger statistical relationship. Munnell, for example, having done an analysis on an aggregated basis with results similar to Aschauer's, repeated the work with separate values for states and got a much lower value for the increase in output due to public investment.[22]

Mindful of the questions raised by these efforts, Arthur Jacoby, an economist at the Federal Highway Administration, arranged to commission Nadiri's study. The project that Jacoby and Nadiri developed was different from its predecessors in several ways. For one thing, the project was focused on highway capital only, not all public capital. Furthermore, Nadiri looked at the effects of highway capital on costs, not output.[23] For a variety of technical reasons, this led to a stronger analysis. Nadiri measured costs across thirty-five industry sectors[24] covering all types of private firms. He compared changes in these costs to changes in the capital stock of highways. (In any given year, the change in capital stock is new investment minus depreciation of the existing system.)

Basically, Nadiri found that investment in highways had a strong downward effect on business costs, and he was able to express this effect as a return to society from highway investment. The gains to society are the cost reductions of firms. Circumventing some technical details, we can say that Nadiri compared the cost reductions over time with the changes in highway capital stock to get his rate-of-return estimate.

Nadiri estimates returns on total highway investments and on investments in what he refers to as the "non-local road system" (NLS). The
NLS represents approximately 935,000 route miles (just under 25 percent of total road mileage in the nation) and is roughly congruent with
the system of roads eligible for federal aid. The rate of return estimated
for the NLS can, then, be taken as an approximation of the average
return on the federal government's investments in highways.

As would be expected, the NLS returns are higher than those for
all roads. Generally, returns on investment in higher-level roads are
higher than returns for lower-level roads. Virtually by definition,
major arterials carry larger volumes of traffic and are more prone to
congestion than lower-level roads.

Here then are Nadiri's specific results for the return on investment in the NLS over the period 1950–89. His estimates show a very
high annual return, about 48 percent, in the period 1950–69, reflecting the initial impact of the Interstate system on freight movement and
other costs to firms. As the cost reductions caused by the Interstate
work their way through the economy, returns decline; the average
return for the period 1980–89 is 16 percent.[25] For the last year, 1989,
the return on investment in NLS roads is, by Nadiri's analysis,
approximately 9 percent.[26]

If we were to take 9 percent as a good estimate of the social
return on highway investments, we would conclude that the level of
investment in 1989 was at about the right level. Many economists
believe the return on marginal investment in the private sector is
around 9 or 10 percent. (Nadiri thinks it's around 9 percent.[27]) If
public-sector investment in highways has the same rate of return as
marginal investments in the private sector, then there's no reason to
increase the rate of highway investment. And, also, no reason to
decrease it.

It is important to note, however, that Nadiri's estimate of return
is based on a partial analysis; only some user benefits are counted
and external costs are omitted as well. Benefits to nonbusiness highway travelers in terms of time savings, accident reductions, or other
impacts are not counted at all. I don't have an exact number, but I do
know that nonbusiness travel on the roads is much greater than business travel or freight movement. Put another way, look at any typical
stretch of road, and vehicles carrying business travelers or freight will
be in the minority. Most of the vehicles you see will contain private
persons traveling for their own purposes. Whatever benefits accrue to

businesses from highway investment must also, to some degree, accrue to individuals. Since personal vehicle travel is much greater than business vehicle travel, I have no problem in asserting that the benefits for households are at least as great as those Nadiri finds for businesses. This being the case, the rate of return to society would be at least double what Nadiri has found. Thus, the 9 percent estimated by Nadiri for the NLS in 1989 might have reflected a total return of 20 percent or higher.

But we should also note that the NLS includes a high proportion of lightly used, two-lane rural highways. If the investment is limited to large roads, this suggests that returns would be higher. The National Highway System (NHS) includes only large, high-level roads; it is 163,000 miles of highway, compared to 935,000 miles for Nadiri's NLS. The return on NHS investments is virtually certain to be higher than the return on NLS investments. This reinforces my comfort in asserting that Nadiri's analysis tells us that society's annual return on improvements in NHS roads is at least 20 percent.

The foregoing is based on data through 1989. At the request of FHWA, Nadiri extended the analysis using data through 1991 and obtained essentially the same results. He found return on investment in all roads of 9 percent in 1991, compared to 9 percent for the NLS in 1989, implying a somewhat higher return for the NLS in 1991 (the extended analysis did not include separate treatment of the NLS).[28]

We have to note, however, that Nadiri's analysis does not consider any of the external costs of highway use, such as air pollution and noise. This point is addressed in the following section, which focuses on highway benefit-cost analysis undertaken by the state of California.

Analysis from California Department of Transportation

Benefit-cost analysis is concerned with the future effects of a specific improvement project. Conceptually, the procedure is simple. The costs are the up-front capital plus any change (up or down) in the future stream of maintenance costs. Benefits come from future reductions in travel time, accidents, and vehicle operating costs. The value of increases in air pollution (if estimated) is subtracted from benefits; value of decreases in pollution would be added to benefits. A strength of benefit-cost analysis is that the causal links are clear. We know *how* an improvement causes benefits: straightening a curve or widening lanes reduces accidents, adding lanes would increase speed, and so forth. The California Department of Transportation is one of the few that subjects highway projects to benefit-cost analysis on a systematic basis. Further, California is a big state with a wide range of types of highway projects, and the results they obtain give us useful information.

Caltrans's transportation improvement program (TIP) for 1998 included seventy-seven highway improvement projects. The average benefit/cost ratio for the entire set was 2.5. That is, benefits were two-and-a-half times cost over twenty years. The average annual rate of return was 13.7 percent. Of the seventy-seven projects, twenty-seven had benefit/cost ratios in excess of 2.0; thirty-three had rates of return in excess of 10 percent.[29]

I believe that Caltrans employs a sound methodology, as far as it goes, and applies it to potential projects in a competent and objective manner. Nonetheless, I do not have to be completely certain that each of these seventy-seven projects is a worthwhile investment (or even that each of the twenty-seven with benefit/cost ratios above 2.0 is a good idea) to reach the following inference from the Caltrans analyses. These high rates of return suggest there is no lack of economically desirable highway investments out there.

But we need to consider what happens when we introduce negative environmental impacts of these road projects. We are largely concerned with health effects of air pollution. If we look at the available estimates of external costs of operation of highway vehicles, we find that the dominant numbers are associated with three effects: congestion costs, accident costs, and health effects of air pollution.[30]

The benefit-cost analyses we are looking at include all travel-delay and accident costs, whether internal or external to a particular motorist; congestion and accident costs are already included in the Caltrans numbers. Air-pollution costs are not included, although people are starting to do this work. But we can use some indirect evidence to put the scale of air-pollution costs in perspective with the other costs and benefits we are considering.

I selected four of the seventy-seven projects as test cases for this purpose, projects with benefit/cost ratios ranging from 2.0 to 5.3.

The projects were in a rural county, in the San Francisco metropolitan area, and one each in the Los Angeles and San Diego areas. I used emissions rates (grams per vehicle mile) and air-pollution costs that have been recommended to Caltrans in a recent study.[31] The emissions covered are carbon monoxide, oxides of nitrogen, PM-10 (particles less than ten microns in diameter), and hydrocarbons.

Health costs are estimated in dollars per short ton of emissions. They vary with type of emission. They also vary with location—highest in Los Angeles, lowest in rural areas, and in between in other cities. And they vary with speed.

For the four projects I looked at, I estimated the *total* air-pollution cost on these road segments for the twentieth year after the improvement and compared that cost with the value of time savings estimated for that year. I chose the twentieth year, because that allows time for traffic build-up and some erosion of speed gains.

The time savings are those attributable to the project. Some of the emissions would have occurred with or without the project—indeed, some projects may reduce emissions. One of the four projects (the one in Los Angeles) had no time savings in the twentieth year. For the other three, the total emissions cost ranged from 13 percent to 29 percent of the value of time savings.

Let's assume that half the total emissions were caused by the projects. So, in these three cases, the benefits should be reduced by 6.5 to 14.5 percent of the time savings. If you have a benefit/cost ratio of, say, 2.5, a 15 percent reduction in benefits makes it 2.1. If it were 3.5, it would be reduced to 3.0.

What we can safely draw from this crude analysis is that a large proportion of highway projects will show good returns to society even when one allows for environmental effects. A few years ago, some colleagues and I tried to bring air-pollution costs into FHWA's HERS model and got similar results; the effect was small.[32]

It would be absurd to leap from these results to a conclusion that air-pollution costs never matter. They may matter quite a lot for some projects and should always be included in the analysis. But the exercise I have gone through here establishes the point that we can bring environmental costs into the analysis and still find that a great many, although certainly not all, highway improvement projects are fully justified.

SUMMING UP

We have been walking across some fairly arid analytical ground. What do we have to show for it? I think we can say two useful things:

1. Highway investment, in general, is a sound use of society's resources.

2. We are probably underinvested in highways; the available evidence says there are highway improvement projects out there that will pay a higher return than the marginal investment in the private sector.

The second point is a strong one. It means road investments should stay high on state and local governments' lists of capital projects. We have seen that inclusion of environmental effects does not invalidate this finding. This does not mean that every project on every state transportation department's list is a good idea. This does not mean there are no road projects with excessive environmental impact. But it does mean that highway improvement projects should not be regarded as guilty of excess environmental damage until proven innocent.

Individual road projects, or whole groups of projects, are often attacked on the grounds they will perpetuate sprawl, and that, it is alleged, is a bad thing. The whole issue of sprawl and changing forms of urban land use is large, complicated, and deserves more careful analytical treatment than it usually gets.

I noted earlier in the chapter that the sprawling, polycentric urban region is today's city in a functional sense. Parts of it resemble cities of the past, and parts of it don't. I am convinced it is here to stay. Reduced transportation and communications costs allow dispersal. Sprawl wouldn't happen if it didn't bring benefits as well as costs. In my view, cutting back on suburban road projects is not going to drive American life back into pre–World War II patterns. I don't think the genie can be put back in the bottle.

This is not to say that sprawl can't get out of control. And, without question, it is often ugly. The aesthetic cost may be the biggest economic cost of sprawl. In any event, my central point is that sprawled living and working are going to continue, and there are road projects that will make the new urban form work better.

One of the most frequently heard arguments against urban road projects is that they are self-defeating because they never really relieve congestion. Build or expand a road, it is said, and people will take advantage of the new capacity and eventually fill it up.

There is not room here to explore thoroughly the issues surrounding the notion of "induced travel." Without doubt, anything that reduces the cost of road travel is going to cause *some* increase in travel; whether it's a lot or a little is something we aren't going to resolve here. But it is economically beneficial when people find a way to take advantage of the new capacity. This is often lost sight of. If a private businessman expands his plant and finds he is soon using all the additional capacity, he is not going to think he made a terrible mistake; he's going to think he made a good decision. In fact, I would argue strongly that if you built a new urban road and *did* eliminate peak-period congestion you obviously overinvested. Peak-period congestion is the equilibrium condition in an urban setting. It is to be expected that people will rearrange job and dwelling patterns to take advantage of road capacity and fill it up.

Where does this take us in terms of public policy? Regarding the federal government, the current highway program provides abundant funds. A number of states have raised fuel taxes recently to increase highway investment, and others are thinking of following suit.

There are two significant policy points here. At the federal level, investments in highways have strong positive returns for the nation. At the state and local level, it means proposals for road improvements should be tested on the merits of each project.

Sensible road investments will improve people's lives. That is really what the economic analysis is telling us. And this is something that governments have to do.

5

MYTHS AND MISINFORMATION ABOUT AMERICA'S PUBLIC RETIREMENT SYSTEM

Teresa Ghilarducci

AMERICA'S LOST CONFIDENCE IN SOCIAL SECURITY

One of the most startling about-faces in American politics occurred in 1994: the sacred became unsacred. Inside and outside the Beltway, and especially after President Nixon agreed to index benefits to inflation in 1972, Social Security was seldom challenged—from its inception as a 1935 New Deal program it enjoyed almost six decades of unquestionable status. Opinion polls, policymakers, and economists agreed Social Security fostered social stability and a sense of national community, served the deserving and needy, and was so popular its basic structure remained sacrosanct. Politicians only occasionally mused that it could be altered; for example, President Reagan mentioned to reporters in 1982 on a Los Angeles runway that Social Security could be made voluntary. The public quickly detected and rejected this trial balloon. *Time* magazine declared it was President Reagan's first setback and he immediately called for a bipartisan commission—the Greenspan Commission (named after its now famous chairman, Alan Greenspan)—to solve a real financial shortfall. Social Security was going to run out of money in a matter of months.

Ironically Social Security is now financially healthier than it was in 1983, but the public's view of the system is more dismal and uncertain. A 1998 poll shows that only 20 percent of adults expect to receive benefits at current levels.[1] In contrast, 46 percent of adults surveyed in 1983 felt Social Security would have the money to pay benefits when they needed them.[2]

Another concrete sign of a political change of heart was an unprecedented split in the report of the fifty-year-old Quadrennial Social Security Advisory Council released in January 1997. (The president appoints an Advisory Council every four years to review the system's finances and effectiveness and issue a partially political report. The council contains three representatives from business, three from labor, one self-employed, and five from the general public. The Social Security system's trustees, on the other hand, issue an annual technical financial report.) This time a substantial minority of the 1994–96 Social Security Advisory Council floated the privatizing trial balloon. The council divided between proposals to maintain the system's fundamental social insurance structure and those that carved out private individual accounts by diverting payroll tax revenues from the Social Security system. *Privatization* is the term generally used to describe such plans, in which individuals themselves manage all or a portion of the funds dedicated to their own retirement. The economists from Watson-Wyatt (a pension consulting firm) and the American Enterprise Institute (a Washington think tank that advocates market-based solutions) led the privatization group. Those advocating raising revenues and trimming benefits so as to maintain the current program were the three labor representatives and two of the public members, including Robert Ball, a chief spokesperson for maintaining the system and a former Social Security chief commissioner.[3]

The Social Security debate has not been about economic and wage growth, demographics, or inflation. The two sides of the debate accept the Social Security trustees' basic projections that the system faces a deficit in thirty-three years. Rather, the Social Security debate is based on political and economic ideology. There is a distinct dichotomy between those who oppose and those who favor privatization. Generally speaking, organized labor, women's and civil rights groups, and organizations of the aged favor maintaining the system as it is. They claim government's function is to spread the cost of a retirement program across the working population and that privatization would erode such a program for most workers. On the other side generally stand the financial industry and well-funded conservative think tanks and lobbying groups, who champion individual control and self-reliance. They want to reduce government, enhance private finance markets, increase individual autonomy, and boost work effort among the aged. There is a large group of relatively undecided Americans in between. When Americans are polled over two-thirds want Congress to strengthen the system's finances, while at the same time, 62 percent of the respondents in the same poll want money to be diverted from the system to create private accounts.

There is an evident contradiction here. Americans can't both strengthen the system and divert money away from it. This contradiction reflects the confusion and misinformation, and arguably the disinformation, that has characterized the debate and in which political leaders have not distinguished themselves. On the other hand, the poll findings also reveal a wisdom that can't be easily dismissed. Americans want government to protect them against risk, but they also want improvement. The fact that real wages have barely risen in the last two decades, while the stock market and profits have soared, suggests that workers correctly believe they have been left out of the American prosperity and want a piece of the action.

An example of how ill-informed people are about Social Security is that few people are familiar with its main benefits. Over 50 percent cannot name any other benefit provided by the system other than conventional retirement benefits, ignoring completely the important disability and dependent benefits of the system. Instead, most Americans view Social Security as a retirement fund into which they pay to buy future benefits. Extending that idea, they think they should judge the system on its ability to provide "high rates of return" so that they get their "money's worth." But the comparison is wrong. Social Security is *insurance*, not an asset that generates rates of return. The false comparison, which was so seductive at first because the early cohorts got much more in benefits than they paid in, laid an intellectual but misleading foundation for current privatization proposals. It may well be the main source of confusion.

SOCIAL SECURITY IS SOCIAL INSURANCE

The Social Security program, like most insurance programs, requires defined benefits to be paid when certain contingencies occur. For instance, fire insurance pays a defined benefit when a house burns.

Thus fire insurance insures against one of the risks of owning a home. The Social Security system insures against the risks of having inadequate funds on retirement, of being disabled before retirement, and of paying for dependents if the insured worker dies. Without such insurance, capitalism itself would assuredly be less popular. Political commentator E. J. Dionne makes this point very well: "Social insurance was a wise admission on the part of supporters of competitive economies that citizens would take the risks such economies require only if they are provided with a degree of security against old age, unemployment, the sudden death of a spouse or the vicissitudes of health."[4]

Social Security actuaries estimate that the values of Social Security's disability insurance and dependent and survivor life insurance policies for a twenty-seven-year-old average-wage worker with two children are each $203,000 and $295,000, respectively.[5] The system now pays benefits to 30 million retired workers. Meanwhile, 6 million younger people receive disability benefits, and another 7 million children and older dependents of beneficiaries receive Social Security income. In addition, the Social Security retirement benefit is an annuity indexed to inflation, which is simply not affordable or available in private markets. To the contrary, private annuities are unusually expensive because people who predict they will live a long time (insurance companies find that people know their own health status better than any actuary can predict) buy annuities—a guaranteed income for life—rather than invest in a mutual fund or bank account. Annuity companies charge more to protect themselves against this "moral hazard." As noted, annuities indexed to inflation, like Social Security, simply do not exist in private markets because of the excessive cost.

All these benefits are paid for by payroll taxes on current workers. Most of the benefits are determined by the amount earned and the number of years worked. Workers who retire with substantial assets are not penalized; the benefits are not means tested. In 1962, 69 percent of Americans over sixty-five received some Social Security income; in 1994, over 92 percent of the aged received Social Security.

The Social Security system has a variety of interesting characteristics. It has reduced poverty among the elderly from nearly 50 percent in 1935 to just 8 percent today. The progressive benefit structure is responsible for much of the poverty-fighting success of the program. Low-income workers obtain 70 percent of their preretirement earnings and higher-income earners average a 25 percent replacement rate.

Since the 1970s these rates have been constant in real terms (after adjusting for inflation). Horizontal equity is achieved since the rules are national and workers with the same work history, mortality, morbidity, and marital and dependent situation receive the same benefits. And the system is highly efficient. The question of efficiency can hardly be challenged. Administration costs are low—0.01 percent of contributions—and payments are reliably sent or automatically deposited.

A MAJOR SOURCE OF CONFUSION: MIXING METAPHORS

A great source of confusion about Social Security is its terminology. Although it is an insurance program, the payroll tax funding the program is called a "contribution" and what most workers get from the system are "pensions." These are the same terms used and results experienced under popular savings-account programs—defined-contribution pension plans such as 401(k) plans, for example. Social Security is not a savings program, but to most people it looks like one. Why the confusion? Ironically, the original framers intended to be ambiguous.

Back in 1935 politicians adopted the word *contributions*—FICA stands for the Federal Insurance Contributions Act—to describe payroll taxes. President Roosevelt said many times that the terminology was meant to protect the system, making payers act like owners.[6] In fact, the system flourished because an increasingly prosperous workforce paid into an old age, survivors, and disability fund from which could thus be paid ever-increasing benefits. Current benefits to the aged and other recipients are paid from what current workers pay in each year—known as "pay as you go," or a PAYGO-designed program. (Between 1983 and 2016, workers are paying more than benefits provided, and the trust fund is growing. Over this period, the system is a PAYGO and advanced funded program.)

The public was sold on a savings metaphor, however. They were told that as workers and owners they got a good return on their "contributions." The metaphor of savings has obscured the system's function and blurred debate, and ironically it has in the last decade done the opposite of what President Roosevelt intended. It is supporting a radical reform of the system that probably would have appalled him. The savings metaphor has also been promoted and extended by economists, as we shall see.

Despite the widespread sense that Social Security is a pension system, it has been expanded and updated dramatically over the years. The retirement portion of the system, the old age insurance (OAI), was established in 1935, and survivor's and dependent's benefits only four years later. The industries and occupations covered by the program were extended significantly in 1950. Disability insurance (DI) was introduced in 1956. Social Security refers to the Old Age, Survivors, and Disability Insurance (OASDI) program—not Medicare. (Medicare is an important source of security to the elderly; it was implemented in 1965.) Social Security benefits were gradually raised and expanded. In 1972 and 1977, President Nixon and Congress significantly improved the system by increasing benefits by 20 percent, indexing earnings used in the formulas to wage increases so replacement rates stabilized, and indexing benefits to price inflation.

These valuable provisions enabled the system to compensate for economic fluctuations—such as when inflation exceeded wage growth during periods of chronic stagflation, and later when real wages lagged behind productivity growth. Thus, Social Security evolved to cover more "risks" as the risks appeared. The upgrades naturally involved an increase in payments. Taxes, or the more palatably termed "contributions," started out at 2 percent of covered payroll in 1940 (paid equally by employers and workers) and have climbed to 12.4 percent in 1999. (The current rate is relatively low compared to 18–25 percent payroll tax rates in OECD nations.)

Economists grabbed onto the savings metaphor in academic attempts to explain the system in their own terms. Nobel laureate Paul Samuelson used the rate of return metaphor to describe PAYGO systems.[7] The cottage industry of "overlapping intergeneration models" developed after Samuelson's paper showed that the worker/contributors' "rates of return" are dependent on labor force growth and productivity (assuming pay matches productivity growth) of the younger cohort. The model simply wanted to estimate what workers could pay for benefits to nonworkers. But the shorthand was the computation of a number that looked like an investment rate of return. Samuelson clearly wanted to show that pay-as-you-go systems could clearly work as long as labor force and productivity growth are strong. Social insurance advocates framed their arguments in Samuelson's terms to show the system was solvent. But the rate of return metaphor is clearly wrong in describing insurance. Comparing "rates of return" on fire insurance against the Dow Jones index would

be ludicrous. The strong postwar economy accommodated the intellectual sloppiness.

The benefit upgrades and tax increases also explain how privatization advocates can describe the system as a system gone wrong. As
the system evolved, an inescapable development haunted system advocates who took public support for granted. A maturing pay-as-you-go
system means that, over time, more recipients will have paid taxes
throughout their working lives. Therefore, the "return" on taxes paid
in terms of benefits received falls dramatically, especially in comparison to the first cohort of beneficiaries who received lifetime benefits
after only a few years of paying taxes. Ida Fuller, the first recipient,
started collecting in 1940 after paying in for just four years—and she
lived to the age of one hundred.

Furthermore, the "rate of return" argument is used to pit generations against each other. Cross-country comparisons show a positive
relationship between high tax rates and large ratios of beneficiaries to
the total number of workers. And in any one nation, younger cohorts
do pay more taxes for benefits received than the earliest generations
did—the Ida Fullers.[8] This fact about maturing PAYGO systems is
used to argue that Social Security lets the "old eat the young."
Americans retiring between 1960 and 1968 (those who started work
at about the inception of the U.S. system) received a 12.5 percent
"return" while individuals who are twenty years younger received a
5.9 percent "return."[9]

The declining "money's worth" argument is a starting point for
advocates of transforming the system into private individual accounts.
A typical example can be found on the Cato Institute's Web page.[10] In
an article in the youth magazine *Rolling Stone,* Cato research fellow
P. J. O'Rourke argues for privatization by complaining that eighty-
two-year-olds get a 16.5 percent return, sixty-seven-year-olds get 1.4
percent and "if we are age twenty-four to sixty-two, we can expect a
return of between –.034 percent and –1.7 percent, and might be better off leaving the money in our old jeans and going through the
closet when we retire."[11]

In 1994 and 1995 an Internet search for the term *Ponzi scheme*
would have found hundreds of articles and op-eds linking such an
accusation with Social Security. Just like a Ponzi scheme, Social
Security, critics claim, has no real assets backing the promised Social
Security benefits. But the rascal Ponzi had no assets; the U.S. government and Social Security trust fund do. In fact, the same assets

the Social Security trust fund owns, U.S. Treasury securities, are the most coveted assets in the world. Not so Charles Ponzi's promises. The major asset of the Social Security system is the U.S. workforce.

IS THERE A SOCIAL SECURITY CRISIS?

The calls for radical reforms to the system have generally started with claims that there is a Social Security crisis. The actuaries and staff of the Social Security Administration project how different scenarios—dismal, intermediate, and rosy—would affect the system. The scenarios are created by simulating what would happen to the system under different assumptions about fertility, immigration, wages, employment, disability, and retirement trends. The U.S. Social Security actuaries are unusually conservative, because they project out to seventy-five years, whereas most nations project out to fifty years.

The 1994 edition of the annual Social Security Trustees Report projected an unexpected future-funding shortfall, which is expressed as the difference between the current tax rate and what the tax rate would have to be to keep the system solvent for seventy-five years. The predicted shortfall in 1998 is 2.17 percent under the intermediate assumptions. That means that an additional 1.08 percent of payroll would have to be paid by both employers and employees to keep the system solvent for seventy-five years, or a 17 percent increase in taxes. If nothing is done, the Social Security trust fund would be exhausted by 2034, according to the 1998 projections. But this is a projected problem based on conservative growth assumptions.

Bear in mind that—as noted earlier—a far more serious unexpected shortfall was reported in a very different economic environment in 1982. The stock market barely beat inflation and schoolchildren learned a new economic term—stagflation. President Reagan responded by retreating on privatization proposals being discussed then and appointed the National Commission on Social Security to maintain the system in the face of soaring inflation and unemployment. In 1983, the president and Congress approved the Greenspan Commission's recommendations to fix half of the financial balance by raising revenues and the other half by cutting benefits. Most of the benefit cuts consisted of raising the age at which workers can collect full benefits from sixty-five to sixty-seven in 2027, starting gradually in 2004. The payroll tax was raised by 42 percent. There was nary a peep of protest because the tax increase eliminated the expected deficit and created a substantial trust fund for the first time. The tax increase was seen as helping a trusted and favorite program.

The 1983 reforms marked the first time benefits were cut. It also marked the first time the surplus of contributions over liabilities became significant. The 1983 reforms raised taxes far beyond what was needed to pay for current benefits. It made baby boomers partially fund their own retirement by paying more Social Security tax than required to pay current benefits. Social Security thus became a mandatory savings program. The Social Security trust fund is now over $600 billion, with an annual surplus of approximately $110 billion a year. By comparison, personal savings, in 1998, were $260 billion per year.

How does a system with a $600 billion reserve get described as having a financial problem? One reason is that people do not think the trust fund is real. The same poll that showed most workers want Congress to fix Social Security also reveals that 61 percent of Americans think the trust fund is being used for purposes other than Social Security. The Social Security tax revenues do enable the federal government to avoid borrowing more money on the open market to meet other budget needs, but the trust fund holds Treasury bonds. These bonds pay a rate equivalent to approximately 7 percent in the open market because they are indexed to inflation and can be redeemed at any time at par. They are, however, not traded on the open market. The Social Security framers thought doing so would leave the government open to criticism for trying to alter private bond markets.

Thus the Social Security financial problem is a projected and not a current financial problem. As with all forecasts of the future, the projection will not be precisely accurate. The actual shortfall will be larger or smaller depending on the course of economic events.

As of 1998, the projection shows the system will start spending the interest on the trust fund assets in 2013. This will require an outlay from taxpayers, if there is no general budget surplus, or deficit financing by the government. In about 2021, the system redeems the Fund's Treasury notes. This means that the system will no longer show a surplus, but will start selling the notes back to taxpayers. If the mechanisms work as they were intended, the Social Security trust fund will act like any pension fund—eventually selling assets to pay benefits. The trust fund will be worth approximately $2.87 trillion in Treasury notes in 2018 and is projected to sell all the notes by 2032.

If tax rates are not increased, or the economy and wages do not grow further, only 73 percent of the benefits can be paid. But note that the Social Security system does not disappear. Three-quarters of benefits will still be paid.

Let us remind ourselves that the original Greenspan solution of 1983 was designed to keep the system solvent for the next seventy-five years. Yet eleven years later, in 1994, the system showed more short-fall than expected according to the intermediate scenario.

Where did the surprise deficit come from? Much of it comes from the intermediate scenario's assumption that GDP will grow only about 2 percent a year over the next thirty years. The Congressional Budget Office, the Council of Economic Advisers, and many private financial firms traffic in projections—and the Social Security trustees come in with the lowest assumed rate. They predict real wage growth to be just 1.2 percent a year—slower than the predicted rate of pro-ductivity growth.

These assumptions, of course, produce a low revenue projection. The Congressional Budget Office's long-term GDP growth forecast is 2.2 percent and Wall Street firms have routinely predicted over 3 per-cent growth. The so-called shortfall in Social Security is very sensitive to this assumption. For example, if the economy continues to grow at its average rate for the last twenty years, that is, at 2.5 percent per year instead of the projected 2 percent, the Social Security shortfall is less than 0.7 percent of payroll. If long-term GDP growth averages out to an unlikely 3.5 percent, there would be no projected shortfall.[12]

One myth should be clarified—the shortfall compared to the early Greenspan projections is not the result of the baby-boomer bulge. The expert Social Security actuaries easily foresaw these demo-graphic changes. Paying for them is already figured in the tax rate and trust fund accumulation established by the Greenspan commission. In fact, workers have supported more dependents in the past than they ever will in the foreseeable future. In 1965 moms and their little baby boomers stayed home and went to school while one dad supported them—a hundred workers supported eighty-five dependents, both children and the elderly. As discussed earlier, at the peak of the baby boomers' retirement in 2030, the rate will be a hundred workers for just seventy-nine dependents, up from a rate of a hundred to seventy-two recently. The basic culprit was the slow growth of wages. Fully half of the projected deficit would not exist if wages had grown as fast as the Greenspan Commission predicted.

In sum, the Reagan administration responded to a much worse financial problem by shoring up the basic social insurance structure. Yet at the end of the millennium, when we face a less significant financial deficit, the basic structure of Social Security is under attack.

Is Class Warfare Going to Be Fought on Social Security Territory?

There are powerful interests who would like to see the Social Security system changed. Whether or not these interest groups are explicitly aware of their motivations or are generous and well meaning does not matter. The consequences are the same. These groups almost all benefit financially from radical reform. The privatizers want to make retirement something less than an entitlement and more like a commodity. The ability to pay for that commodity will be borne by workers; if they can't accumulate enough to retire then older people will have to work longer.

It should be clearly noted that employers may gain if older workers flood labor markets because surplus labor will keep wages down. Similarly, the financial industry gains when millions of new individual investment accounts are created. The contested future of the Social Security system is about the future of retirement in America. The debate can be seen in part as a question about assuring the resources for retirement and about U.S. economic growth. But it also can be seen in part as a clash of vested interests. The current debate about Social Security cannot be fully understood unless it is realized that America's retirement insurance program was a hard-won victory for labor.

As noted, Social Security expanded to cover over 90 percent of workers by 1995 (from 16 percent at its inception), making it a universal pension system. The expansion of total coverage was not simply organic or inevitable. Political battles and coalitions between labor (those that paid into the system) and the aged (those that got benefits) supported Social Security upgrades.[13] In 1999, almost all union members are covered by Social Security (except some state and local workers) and 79 percent of union members are covered at work by a collectively bargained pension plan. In contrast, only 38 percent of nonunion workers have a pension from the employer.

The importance of Social Security as a middle-class pension is clear when we look at its share of middle-class retirement income.

Most workers become "middle-class" retirees with family income between $17,000 and $29,000 (in 1990 dollars).[14] Middle-class retirees received under 40 percent of their income from Social Security in 1980. However, because of the erosion in private pension benefits and coverage, wealth, and wages, Social Security made up 60 percent of retirement income to this group by 1990. This is a rarely observed fact. Though a common image of the sources of retirement income is a three-legged stool for the middle class—with Social Security, company pensions, and personal savings as the three legs—in fact, the more accurate image is a pyramid because Social Security is far more than simply one of three legs of the stool. Social Security is the base of the pyramid, employer pensions make up the smaller middle, and individual wealth and savings are the smallest component at the top.

If Social Security benefits are reduced or delayed, the evidence strongly suggests that those over sixty-five will increasingly look for work, providing business with more labor. Unlike the vast majority of the world's workers whose nations have forced retirement at a specified age—in France it is sixty, in most other OECD nations the age is close to sixty-five—American workers can choose their retirement age. The uniquely American 1978 Age Discrimination Employment Act prevents disparate treatment in wages, employment, and promotion when workers are over the age of forty. The evidence suggests that male workers choose to retire when they have sufficient retirement income.[15] In 1950, more than 45 percent of men over the age of sixty-five were in the labor force. By 1980, as retirement benefits increased, 19 percent of males over sixty-five were working or looking for work, and by 1994, that percentage dropped to 16.9 percent.[16] One of the ways post–World War II prosperity was divided between labor and capital was that workers were granted leisure after sixty-five. Privatizing would reduce retirement savings for a significant proportion of retirees and maybe for the majority. They would most likely seek work.

The gap between death and retirement clearly shows a potential labor force ready to work if other sources of income—like Social Security and pensions—are made less certain and generous. In the year 2000, approximately 4.2 million Americans over the age of sixty-five are expected to be in the labor force. If labor force participation rates rise to the 1950s level because of smaller Social Security benefits, the number of jobs created for the elderly would have to triple or unemployment will soar.

FIGURE 5.1. LONGEVITY AND WORK EFFORT: MALES OVER SIXTY-FIVE, 1950–93

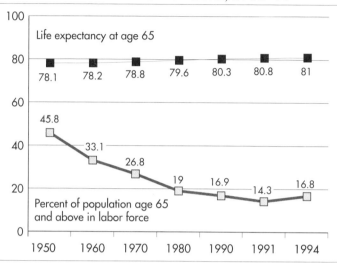

Source: Eugene Steuerle and Jon Bakija, *Retooling Social Security for the Twentieth Century* (Washington, D.C.: The Urban Institute, 1994).

If there are vested interests in favor of privatization, there are ample new opportunities to create wedges between workers and retirees. In particular, the U.S. Social Security system indexes benefits to prices in order to maintain pension adequacy. This feature has significant political consequences when real wage growth is negative and inflation is positive, as occurred in the 1970s. By the 1980s and early 1990s, U.S. Social Security pensions were growing faster than wages, as wages stagnated but inflation continued. Old people were not sharing equally in economic decline—or rather in the decline in workers' living standards. The old seemed to be eating the young. Thus, ironically, the erosion of workers' pay led to an attack on what was originally a workers' program, probably the most successful of all such programs.

Social Security detractors argue the system is unfair because the FICA is regressive. High-income workers pay a smaller share of their earnings because the earnings subject to FICA tax are capped. However, the regressive structure is mitigated by the earned income tax credit, which pays a credit to workers who earn less than $25,000 per year.[17] In addition, half of Social Security benefits are subject to ordinary income tax for beneficiaries with incomes over $25,000

($32,000 for couples)—the claw-back, paying a benefit and then tax-
ing it—makes it somewhat proportional.

In contrast, real wage indexation means that the elderly share in
the productivity gains of the current generation. (Austria and Mexico
index pensions to wages and Japan and Germany index pensions to
net-of-taxes wages, so pensioners bear the brunt of a rising tax burden.) A nation may want to spend productivity gains in ways other
than keeping the elderly at the same relative position. Switzerland
compromises and uses a fifty-fifty combination of wage and price
growth to index pensions. Sweden is also indexing pensions by average longevity, so that the elderly will stay in the same relative position
as the definition of who is old becomes stricter.

Freeman argues that older workers have more political power in
unions and therefore their preferences dominate the tradeoffs made in
collective bargaining negotiations.[18] Others argue that union employers want pensions to complete implicit contracts[19] that encourage
workers to invest in specific skills or settle contracts with least costs.[20]

SOCIAL SECURITY HELPS BOOST SAVINGS
AND STABILIZE STOCK MARKETS

Another and perhaps even stronger "old-eat-the-young" argument is
made by the World Bank,[21] among others. The organization makes the
point that PAYGO systems shift resources away from the young by
inhibiting economic growth. Therefore, the World Bank argues, the
effect of public pension systems on economic growth and savings is an
issue of intergenerational equity.

The macroeconomic argument that Social Security inhibits
growth is based on the assertion that the Social Security system lowers the savings rate. Since workers have a guaranteed source of retirement income, the argument goes, they are less likely to save for
retirement. Since pensions are financed by taxes and not returns on
accumulated savings, advocates for diminishing Social Security argue
that lower savings reduces investment and therefore productivity.[22]

Ironically, some evidence on Social Security's effect on savings
could lead to the opposite conclusions. When Social Security passed in
1935, the insurance industry argued that the new system would cause
people to stop buying private annuities from the insurance industry. A
year later, when friendly senators asked industry representatives

whether the insurance companies wanted legislation to make Social Security voluntary, the industry said no. The insurance industry was thrilled with the new system. People began to plan for retirement and used the industry products more than they had when Social Security was established!

In addition, in the post–World War II period pensions emerged as a key union bargaining issue, in part because a decent Social Security system provided a floor of retirement income and planted the idea that retirement can extend to the working class. Social Security thus created a retirement savings motive. Further evidence to support the argument that Social Security "crowds in" savings are in one survey about people's savings attitudes. The Public Agenda Foundation and the Employee Benefit Research Institute found that 34 percent of people claim they do not save because of low earnings; 37 percent do not save because they underestimate what they need in retirement.[23] The rest are split between those who plan their future and save and those who figure they will work until they die. People did not report they lowered their savings because they thought Social Security would provide enough in retirement.

Further, if people acted in accordance with the life cycle behavior model assumed by economist Martin Feldstein, then savings would go up as reports of the Social Security deficit circulate. However, the opposite has occurred. Consumer debt is at an all-time high when fears over Social Security's solvency are also high,[24] and official savings rates have turned negative.

In sum, three pieces of evidence support the argument that Social Security does not inhibit savings and can even encourage more retirement savings: one, historical evidence that individuals and labor unions supplement Social Security with insurance annuities and employer pensions; two, surveys on retirement savings do not show excessive reliance on Social Security to fund planned retirement; and three, econometric evidence on cross-section and time series of individual savings behavior show no correlation between Social Security wealth and savings.

There is some evidence that workers use collective programs such as Social Security and mandatory pensions as self-disciplinary devices against overconsumption and myopic financial planning. In other words, without such programs they would spend more and save less. One way to see this is that workers, when negotiating in a group, reveal different preferences for future and current consumption than workers exhibit acting as individuals. Workers choose to save more when the whole group must save than they do when making individual and voluntary savings decisions. Union employers pay a much larger percentage of total compensation on pensions than nonunion employers, for example. The rate of increase in unionized employers' pension expense outpaced union wage growth between 1980 and 1990. In the same time period, nonunion employers' pension costs fell as a share of pay while nonunion workers' rate of pay outpaced union wage increases.[25]

There is another irony worth considering. Privatizers argue that the increase in the number of retirees as compared to workers necessitates abandoning the current PAYGO system. But in fact it may be a reason to have a PAYGO system. Baby boomers will start retiring in twelve years, and by 2030 each hundred workers will support thirty-six retirees, up from twenty-one in 1995. Privatizing advocates argue that people should save for their own retirement so that smaller generations do not have to support large retired ones. Instead, they want workers to invest their deferred consumption—rather than put it into current Social Security benefits—and sell assets when they retire. However, just as the baby boomers' demand for financial assets lifted stock and bond prices in the 1980s and 1990s, their sell-off, starting in the year 2020, will lower asset values.[26] This de-accumulation may cause asset values to fall, potentially destabilizing markets and reducing pensions. The financial industry's response has been an expressed hope for a source of demand to buy the surplus assets in 2020–2035: perhaps the young populations of Mexico, Brazil, and China and India.[27] This works if these nations have private pension systems that invest in foreign assets. This may explain why the World Bank's effort to privatize pension systems spans the globe. Therefore, there is a second reason in addition to the "crowd in" reason Social Security helps boost private finance markets. Social Security (or any PAYGO system) helps smooth out the demographic effects in finance markets.

In sum, Social Security eliminates poverty, is the main source of middle-class pensions, is indexed to inflation, provides disability and survivors insurance, diversifies retirement wealth portfolios, and helps stabilize financial markets and possibly increases savings. If it works well, why are there so many proposals to privatize? The projected shortfall is surely not imminent. it is not even large enough to explain the attraction for privatizing. More recently, the decade of the 1990s has been blessed with an unusual and glittering prosperity. As I write this, inflation and unemployment rates are minuscule and the financial sector is riding an unprecedented sixteen-year bull market.

On the other hand, most workers' real wages were not increasing and the stock market was passing them by. Some have suggested workers' interest in changing the system may be rooted in such a buyer's remorse—they wish someone had forced them to buy stocks in the late 1980s. The next section explores the arguments made by, and the nature of, the interest groups in favor of privatization.

THE PRIVATIZERS' WORLDVIEW

Advocates of Social Security privatization basically advance three arguments to support their view. First, as noted, people are not getting their "money's worth" because the system is outdated. Increases in longevity, the immense size of the baby boom generation, and the so-called obvious ability of people to work later in their lives in an age of white-collar work, make the system outdated. The implication is that the system can work if the beneficiary-to-worker ratio is sixteen to one (as it was at inception) but fails if the ratio of workers to retirees falls to two to one as projected in twenty years.

In fact, the irrelevance of these ratios is the main lesson from intergenerational models. The models point out that quality, not quantity, is what matters. A healthy Social Security system depends on rising contributions from rising wages and full employment more than on maintaining the dependency ratio at some mythical level.

The second argument for privatization is that it is better for the economy. But this is based on two faulty assumptions about economic behavior. One is that private investment in industry and business is invariably more productive than public investment in education, transportation, and social programs. So, by this logic, privatizing Social Security is good for us all. Transferring Social Security taxes from public hands to private ones will increase returns and result in faster growth.

Furthermore, it is presumed that advance-funding pensions through private accounts will increase savings. Individuals will have to set aside more money rather than spend. Moreover, a public retirement program encourages people to spend now rather than save for their old age. Actually, as we discussed, Social Security may give Americans a motive to save for retirement because retirement is expected and within reach. Moreover, privatizing Social Security could flood financial markets with new demand for equities and subject financial markets to a new source of volatility unrelated to economics and due only to swings in the nation's age structure.

Third and last is the idea that the trust funds do not have real assets and that the government is using Social Security money for purposes other than its intent. The argument here is that workers would be better off directly owning and managing their own accounts, and keeping the money out of the hands of the government, which might spend it on other programs.

But if we examine more closely how privatization works, we will see that the odds are significant that only higher-income individuals will be better off on average with privatization. This is because of the increased risk and variability of private investing as well as increased costs of managing money privately and of funding a transition from the old system to the new.

How Privatizing Would Work

As discussed earlier, the idea of making Social Security optional and voluntary, first proposed back in 1935, has evolved into converting a portion of the system into individual private accounts (IPAs). Various proposals exist—the modern ones began to appear in 1995.[28] The latest (as of this writing) was proposed in May 1999 by three Republican senators and one Democrat—Senator Robert Kerrey (D.-Neb.). It would divert 2 percent of the payroll taxes now going into the Social Security system (2 percent of the 6.2 percent) into private individual accounts to be managed by individuals. This will reduce revenues for the Social Security system. Advocates propose to reduce Social Security benefits principally by raising the retirement age. Individuals are assured that the increased rate of return in the individual accounts would more than make up for the loss in benefits.

The projections of future benefits require four sets of assumptions: assumptions about the returns on privately traded financial assets, the typical investing patterns of certain groups, the size of administrative fees, and the effect of the increased flow of funds into the stock and bond markets. The latter point is particularly important, as the projections stay favorable only if the increasing flow does not cause stock and bond prices to increase and rates of return to fall.

One simulation showed that the privatization plan advanced by the business faction of the Advisory Council, which is practically identical with the Kerrey plan, would require raising payroll taxes 12.5 percent between 1998 and 2069. This assumed that spouses' benefits would be cut by one-third and the age at which full benefits can be collected raised from sixty-five to sixty-nine by 2059. Furthermore, Social Security retirement benefits for those between ages sixty-two and sixty-five would be eliminated by 2012. As with all privatization schemes, a transition tax would be required to pay for current benefits to retirees and those nearly retired while the privatized accounts are being phased in. Estimates of new taxes required to pay for the transition range from 3 percent of payroll each year for the next thirty-five years to 1.5 percent for the next seventy-two years.[29]

PRIVATIZING EXACERBATES INEQUALITY

In my view, the transition from the current system to one based on individual private accounts would increase the gap between higher-income workers and others. The majority of workers would generally be better off under the defined-benefit insurance structure of the current system—even if payroll taxes are raised—for several reasons. First, lower- and middle-class workers would earn lower returns on IPAs than would higher-income workers because they invest more conservatively. Despite the rhetoric that more financial education will encourage people to take more risk, financial education also teaches that those with less money to lose *should* take fewer risks. There will also be more variation of returns around the mean, even at lower levels of risk. Many investors will inevitably do very poorly.

In addition, most workers reasonably fear they will outlive their savings and will instead want to buy an annuity like current Social Security benefits (a guaranteed stream of income for life). The problem is that, as we noted, in open markets annuity sellers presume that people who expect to live for a long time are more likely to buy annuities. This raises the costs of annuities. In other words, the private and voluntary annuity will be smaller than an annuity paid in a mandatory and universal system. Moreover, unlike Social Security, affordable annuities are not indexed to inflation, and low inflation rates can lead to dramatic decreases in living standards. A mild 3 percent annual inflation cuts real income in half in twenty years. Since women, on balance, live longer, losing the inflation protection hurts women more.

Raising the retirement age also increases inequality. Millions of Americans, particularly those with physically demanding jobs, are more likely to suffer health problems that will require them to retire earlier than white-collar employees.[30] Raising the age at which one can collect full benefits by one year is an effective 7 percent decrease in benefits.[31] Lower-income workers in blue-collar jobs will likely experience a disproportionate share of these lower benefits.[32]

In sum, in the switch to private accounts from a PAYGO system workers lose the security of an indexed annuity and bear all the risks of financial downturns, inflation, living too long, and being disabled. Since the transition probably requires cutting benefits and raising the retirement age, blue-collar workers bear the brunt. The transition winds up costing more than what it would take to put the current system in balance.

In addition to the high cost of the transition and the attendant increase in inequality, privatizing involves arguments that are disturbingly inconsistent. The same assumptions that forecast a large deficit for Social Security also doom the privatizing plan. A low GDP growth rate would negate the privatizers' claim that investing in private financial markets will yield an average return of 7 percent. If the economy is what makes privatizing attractive because of high GDP growth rates, then the current system's future is rosy and not in deficit.[33]

Martin Feldstein, former chair of the Council of Economic Advisers under Ronald Reagan and chief economic adviser to George W. Bush's presidential campaign, has proposed a privatizing scheme that he claims will markedly raise the rate of economic growth. Feldstein does not bother to propose cutting benefits even as he would divert the FICA tax to individual private accounts. Feldstein presumes that the cost of such a plan will be held down because the economy will grow by close to 5 percent a year due to the infusion of private capital through the individual accounts. This is supply-side economics redux. It is based on the neoclassical assumption that private financial capital induces private productive investment, which leads to economic growth. This belief ignores the evidence that business confidence about future profits induces investment—not the mere supply of capital—and that both public and private investment are needed for economic growth.

One last point. Social Security privatization may place more focus on short-term profits than on long-term growth. Under a private personal account, a retiree's pension depends on the stock market and not the growth in wage income. The benefits of the current PAYGO Social Security system depend on rising wages. A political split could develop in the United States that would jeopardize long-term growth. Retired workers may want to reduce wages and employment to boost profits and indirectly their pensions. If the capital market consistently outperforms the rest of the economy, it represents a transfer from workers to capital. Over time, however, neither wages nor returns to the capital market would be optimized by such a strategy.

OPTIONS TO SHORE UP THE CURRENT SOCIAL SECURITY SYSTEM

The projected deficit in Social Security can be closed by adopting a variety of measures to reduce benefits or raise revenues without undermining the basic advantages of the PAYGO system we now have. But the most frequently offered solutions are rather mundane, which may help explain why the privatizers have gotten so much more attention. Some Social Security advocates have ventured out of the bounds of the traditional Social Security system with an idea that starts from the observation that the nation's better-off households obtain a substantial amount of income from nonlabor sources—capital gains and interest income. Wage and salary income accounts for relatively little of the new wealth in the last ten years. There is a cap on the taxable amount of earnings, which as of this writing stands at $72,600. If we lifted the cap completely for OASDI, as we do for Medicare, and thereby taxed all earnings, all Social Security projected deficits would disappear.

This is probably politically impracticable. The oft-cited drawback is wealthy CEOs and others receive so little from Social Security benefits compared to their salaries that their "money's worth" would fall to a very low level. This, it is argued, would reduce the top-paid workers' support for the system. Politically speaking, however, the argument might be appealing. Seventy-five percent of the members of the National Association of Manufacturers (one of the few polls of corporate thinking on Social Security privatization) revealed that executives want privatized accounts, anyway. Upper-middle-income workers would experience a reduced "return" on premiums—12 percent or so of male workers make over the cap and below $110,000. They probably would not support the system even if their taxes were raised dramatically.

In the appendix to this chapter I have assembled some of the most popular options to amend Social Security and have ranked them by desirability. I chose the proposals that achieve solvency with the least cost, disruption, and inefficiency. Almost all the options require trade-offs between raising revenues and reducing benefits. In some cases, women are clearly penalized more than men. For example, if the typical benefit is averaged over the highest thirty-eight years of earnings rather than thirty-five, women will be hurt more than men because they usually work fewer years. I am also opposed to raising the retirement age to reduce benefits unless there is some accommodation for those who do physical blue-collar work.

CONCLUSION:
PRIVATIZATION'S WINNERS AND LOSERS

Well-meaning people advocate privatizing the Social Security system. Many are motivated by the determination to reduce government control over our lives. But there are also clear winners and losers. The financial industry clearly wins from privatizing Social Security. Employers in general will also win if more people are forced to work after age sixty-five. Most workers lose. On average, they would receive lower benefits. They may also lose as the nation generally supports promoting strong and rising financial markets rather than strong and rising wages.

If the Social Security system goes on the way it has, with no reduction in benefits, how much will it eventually cost? The answer is 6.6 percent of GDP in 2040, up from 4.78 percent of GDP in 1993.[34] Is that too much? The current system efficiently pays for what most workers want—leisure at the end of their lives and insurance against the risk of not being able to work. The system also most likely stimulates savings and economic growth. Is 6.6 percent of GDP too much to pay for all of that? Economists can't answer that, thank goodness. In a democracy, voters do.

APPENDIX: SOLVING THE 2.19 PERCENT PAYROLL DEFICIT IN SOCIAL SECURITY'S SEVENTY-FIVE-YEAR FORECAST

PROPOSAL	% OF DEFICIT SOLVED
Best Options	
Eliminate cap on employer contributions to cover 90 percent of all income (cap goes to $97,000 from $68,400)	25
Raise payroll tax by 0.04 percent per year while indexing the earned income tax credit	64
Use the CBO projections on growth (SSA uses a 2 percent growth assumption; the CBO uses 2.3 percent)	33
Acceptable Options	
Correct CPI by BLS criteria (impacts long-livers)	14
Give Social Security revenue to Social Security—now it goes to Hospital Insurance (this option would hurt Medicare)	10
Raise normal retirement age to sixty-seven in 2011 only if disability criteria loosened to include sector unemployment (this costs 0.004 percent)	22
Unacceptable Options (which violate fairness, portfolio diversity, and efficiency criteria)	
Privatization (too costly, disruptive, and violates diversity)	N/A
Shift 40 percent of trust funds out of government bonds to stocks by 2014 (puts too much of retirement income assets in the financial markets)	12
Diversionary Options (which are not worth the fight or too vague)	
Extend coverage to state and local employees	10
Divert the federal budget surplus to Social Security (too vague—the surpluses might not materialize)	64
Tax unearned income, including capital gains and interest (which invites class warfare and moves away from the pension-for-work model)	145

Note: In preparing this table, I depended to a great extent on my own papers and congressional testimony and on Dean Baker's calculation of the revenue contribution of surpluses and tax increases in his latest Economic Policy Institute paper, "Saving Social Security in Three Steps" (November 1998); The Report of the 1994–95 Advisory Council on Social Security; the Bipartisan Commission Final Report on Entitlement and Tax Reform, 1995; and Robert Ball's many communications. Estimates about the revenue impact of taxing unearned income comes from the AFL-CIO in Washington, D.C.

6

THE SOCIAL AND ECONOMIC DETERMINANTS OF HEALTH

Peter S. Arno and Janis Barry Figueroa

INTRODUCTION

If you are a man between the ages of twenty-five and sixty-four, and your family income is $50,000 or more, your chance of dying this year is less than one-third that of a man whose income is $5,000 or less.[1] Conversely, if you are at the bottom of the distribution in terms of education, income, or occupational standing, your risk of death is two to three times higher than it would be if you were at the top of such distributions.

Such mortality figures are not the only evidence of dramatic inequality. By other definitions of health as well—including measures of morbidity, disability, and pain—people are less healthy if they are closer to the bottom of the social and economic spectrum than to the top.

Disparities in health outcomes have increased over the last three decades, according to several reports.[2] Yet insufficient attention has thus far been paid to these findings. To the contrary, analysts have typically emphasized two pieces of good news: life expectancy at birth for Americans has increased to an all-time high, and infant mortality has fallen to a record low.[3] Where disparities have been noted, they are generally attributed to racial differences. For example, age-adjusted death rates for blacks are still 50 percent higher than for whites; for black infants, the difference is more than 100 percent.[4] Where solutions have been sought, they have generally focused on improving access to high-quality medical care or making requests to change individual lifestyles or behaviors rather than on attributing poor health outcomes to socioeconomic status.

These access or lifestyle approaches fail to recognize the many complex and interrelated influences of economic factors on health. One reason is that far more research is needed, at both the individual and the population level, to appreciate the role that socioeconomic status plays in determining health outcomes. By more fully understanding this process, policymakers can better address some of the key barriers to improving health.

The fierce heat wave that swept across much of the United States in the summer of 1999 illustrates the neglect of this perspective. Between July 19 and July 31, 1999, at least two hundred persons around the country died from the heat, mostly poor and elderly people who lacked fans or air-conditioning systems. Some met their demise because they chose to keep their windows shut rather than risk their safety in areas where criminal activity was routine. These unnecessary deaths were portrayed as tragic human-interest stories in which the irrational behavior of the deceased was the news. The link between the higher-than-expected mortality rates of this vulnerable population and their economic and social disadvantage went almost unmentioned. There was no angry public response, nor any recognition that broad-based initiatives might address the problem at its roots.

This paper takes as its premise that documenting the links between socioeconomic status and health disparities would have a large impact on public policies. In Canada and Western Europe, procedures for assessing the health impact of new economic or social initiatives are being developed. But in the United States, the health consequences of public policy are virtually absent from the debate. Recent discussions of important social policies such as raising the minimum wage or revamping the Social Security system rarely mention the potential health impact.

We focus here on three key areas, and since elements of this analysis are controversial and have not been widely accepted by economists, we offer substantial documentation in the international literature on socioeconomic status and health inequalities:

- ♦ First, we review some of the basic findings from the social determinist health perspective, illustrating the importance of socioeconomic conditions in explaining patterns of population health.

◆   Second, we examine traditional explanations of the link between socioeconomic status and illness. Most notably, we look in greater depth at the so-called health selection effect and the assertions that poor health is the result of limited access to medical care. We find these analyses are too narrow and divert attention away from the underlying social and economic conditions that have a larger impact on our health.

◆   Finally, we consider the implications of requiring health impact assessments of both existing and new economic and social initiatives and review how this is already being done in England, Canada, and other industrialized countries.

UNDERSTANDING THE PROBLEM

Socioeconomic status (SES) as a major determinant of health inequalities has been documented for most countries, including the United States, for many years. Low socioeconomic status, measured variously in terms of poverty, income, wealth, education, or occupation, has been repeatedly linked to a greater burden of disease and death.[5] Although this has been one of the most consistent findings in social epidemiology for decades, neither the general public nor the mainstream of the economics profession has generally accepted it.

Overall, life expectancy increases as income rises.[6] In fact, the relationship between socioeconomic status and mortality appears graded such that each increment in level of income, education, and occupational status is associated with a reduced risk of death.[7] However, the relationship between income and health does not appear to be linear—large improvements in health are seen when moving up the income ladder from low to average or median levels, with increasingly diminishing returns to health from gains at the upper end of the income distribution. One likely explanation is that higher income groups reach a "health ceiling" in which good health is enjoyed into later life and thus the ability to make further health improvements in adulthood are small.[8] If true, policies that improve the social and economic status of lower-income populations can dramatically improve their health without worsening the health of higher-income groups, thereby enhancing the overall health of the population.

While the precise pathways between social factors and health status remain elusive and a fertile area for research, empirical studies in the United States confirm that specific populations bear a disproportionate burden of poor health. Blacks have higher mortality rates than whites for nearly every cause of death.[9] In a report published by the federal government in 1985, a few causes of death were identified as being responsible for 80 percent of the excess deaths: cancer; heart disease and strokes; chemical dependency; diabetes; homicide, suicide, and unintentional injuries; and infant mortality and low birth weight.[10] In some impoverished inner cities, more than one-third of African-American girls and nearly three-quarters of boys who reach their fifteenth birthday do not live to see their sixty-fifth.[11] And those that do survive have three times the rate of health-induced disability as do their white counterparts nationwide. A widely publicized paper published in 1990 reported that black males in Central Harlem between the ages of twenty-five and forty-four are six times more likely to die than white males in that age group, and the life expectancy of adult males in Harlem is lower than that of men in Bangladesh.[12]

Despite these dramatic differences in health outcomes, when researchers adequately control for socioeconomic status, the racial disparities in health are considerably (though not entirely) reduced.[13] This is not say that other factors are not extremely important. The impact on health of social and cultural pressures related to racism, residential and occupational segregation, and environmental exposures is beginning to draw increasing attention among researchers.[14] While the complex ways in which race, ethnicity, and socioeconomic status are associated are not fully understood, it is evident that social and economic disadvantage has been uniquely reproduced for certain populations along racial and ethnic lines. David Williams from the University of Michigan argues that "culture, biology, racism, economic structures, and political and legal factors are the fundamental causes of racial differences in health."[15] Without a more sophisticated analysis of these factors and their historical interplay, policymakers and the public at large will remain narrowly focused on the medical model in which access to services and exposure to individual risk factors are perceived as the key to understanding the etiology of disease.

THE HEALTH SELECTION EFFECT

To the extent that mainstream economists have considered disparities in health at all, they generally have focused their attention on what is known as the "healthy worker" or "health selection" effect. At its most basic, this means that healthy workers are more likely to be employed than sick workers and therefore are more likely to earn higher incomes. Certainly, there is some truth to this commonsense notion—numerous economic studies document the magnitude of income loss that results when individuals are in poor health and are able to work less or not at all.[16] But the proponents go too far in arguing that the direction of causality moves from health to income, rather than from income (or socioeconomic status) to health. In advancing this position, they undermine the past fifty years of social epidemiology and public health, which argues that socioeconomic status and the social and economic conditions under which people live are primary determinants of health status.

The real question is not whether a health selection effect exists, but how powerful it is and whether it can explain the dramatic socioeconomic differences in health outcomes. A growing body of research has shed considerable doubt on the large-scale impact of the health selection effect. These studies suggest that income remains strongly associated with health outcomes even after controlling for baseline differences in health status; excluding persons with chronic conditions or disabilities; and particularly when the results are based on long-term follow-up.[17] While these studies have generally found some evidence that those who are most healthy have higher incomes, they also suggest that this phenomenon explains only a small part of the overall mortality differentials between socioeconomic or racial groups.[18]

WILL ACCESS TO CARE ELIMINATE HEALTH DISPARITIES?

Improving access to care has been embraced by health service researchers as a strategy for eliminating health disparities and has been the primary focus of health care policy reform for the past thirty

years. Certainly, access to medical care makes a difference, particularly at the individual level, and wider insurance coverage is one tool
for achieving this. To a degree, this notion has gained even more
poignancy as the number of uninsured Americans has grown to nearly
45 million. Social justice dictates that in the United States the availability of affordable health care for everyone should certainly be a
national goal. But we want to emphasize strongly that the debate
should not end there.

At the population level, there is no guarantee that greater access
would significantly reduce the disparity in health outcomes among different groups.[19] For example, despite the improved access to medical
care that exists in countries with national health insurance programs,
findings from many European countries demonstrate that health disparities persist.[20] Moreover, these disparities exist both among people
with medical conditions that are amenable to medical intervention—
where one might reasonably expect improved access to make a difference—and those that are not.[21] Further, those conditions that are
sensitive to medical intervention comprise a much smaller component of overall mortality than conditions that are less amenable to
treatment. As a result of such findings, a number of researchers conclude that death rates are more closely related to social and economic
factors than to the provision of medical care.[22]

One of the problems in the debate is that access tends to be considered from a narrow perspective. Access involves more than the
simple ability to afford care. It also requires that adequately funded
health services be available in a nonthreatening environment.[23] For
many rural and urban populations, significant access barriers exist in
the form of cultural and racial discrimination and the lack of convenient health care services, and these barriers will not be entirely eliminated even by more readily available insurance coverage.[24]

Another assumption underpinning discussions of access is that
allocating more resources toward the health care system within the
United States would inevitably improve health outcomes for most
people. Yet the United States already outspends all twenty-nine
members of the Organization for Economic Cooperation and
Development (OECD) on health care services. This has not resulted
in achieving better, or even comparable, health outcomes based on
a number of major indicators. For example, despite dramatic increases
in health care spending over the past few decades, U.S. infant
mortality rates—though they have decreased absolutely—have

slipped significantly in international comparisons, from twelfth place in 1967 to twenty-fourth in 1996.[25]

Unfortunately, discussions of rankings on these and other major health indicators have been largely absent from the debate over health disparities. This poor performance suggests that reforming the medical system may not be the only, or even the best, route to improving the nation's health.[26] It adds more evidence to the claims that the genesis of disease and illness lies outside the medical domain and in the social and economic nexus of everyday life, involving issues such as employment, education, housing, nutrition, and environmental exposure.

Individual risk factors such as health-related behaviors including diet, exercise, and alcohol and tobacco use show clear differences by income and socioeconomic status. But the relative importance of behavioral explanations (lifestyle issues) in determining health outcomes continues to be debated.[27] Whatever the precise role that individual risk factors play in disease etiology, perhaps the more fundamental issue is that the pattern of risk factors in different population groups at different moments in history are shaped by political, economic, and social conditions.[28] For example, Michael Marmot from the University of London and Fraser Mustard, founder of the Canadian Institute for Advanced Research, trace the incidence of coronary heart disease from its being thought of as a "disease of affluence" in the first half of the twentieth century to its more recent association with lower-income and less-educated populations.[29] They find convincing evidence to support the notion that biological processes respond to the social and physical environment. From a public health perspective this implies that focusing mainly on targeted, individual-based health behavior interventions may be misguided. Such findings strongly suggest the need to move beyond questions of individual risk factors and improved access to care to consider structural and institutional factors that are militating against health equity in the United States.

CONCEPTUALIZING THE RELATIONSHIP BETWEEN INCOME INEQUALITY AND HEALTH

Although the association between socioeconomic status and health has been known for decades, the notion that economic inequality, or the relative difference between the rich and the poor, is itself a health risk factor has received increased attention in just the past few years.[30] Many studies have explored the relationship between levels of income inequality and health status both across nations and within nations.[31] These studies, which remain controversial, suggest that regions with greater levels of income inequality experience higher mortality and morbidity rates.

While further research needs to be done to confirm and explain these findings, they are especially troubling given the dramatic growth of income inequality in the United States and the world. According to the 1996 United Nations Development Report, the poorest 20 percent of the world's population experienced a drop in their share of global income from 2.3 percent to 1.4 percent during the past thirty years. At the same time the richest 20 percent saw an increase in their share from 70 percent to 85 percent.[32] Studies in the United States conducted by the Census Bureau indicate that the level of income inequality fell by approximately 9 percent from 1947 to its postwar low in 1969, but has since grown by at least 25 percent, reaching a postwar high in 1993 and 1994 and remaining stable since then.[33] As a result, income inequality in the American economy now surpasses that of any other advanced industrial country.[34]

In 1997, the top fifth of all families in the United States received approximately 47 percent of the nation's total income while the bottom fifth received about 4 percent.[35] This growing income dispersion has been accompanied by absolute declines in real income among individuals at the bottom of the income distribution and by real gains at the top. Lynn Karoly of the RAND Corporation has demonstrated that in 1995 the poorest 25 percent of the U.S. population had a lower real family income than it had more than twenty years earlier, in 1973.[36] Wealth is even more dramatically skewed: In 1995, 39 percent of total household wealth was controlled by the top 1 percent of wealth holders, while the bottom 80 percent controlled just 16 percent of the nation's wealth.[37] This is the highest concentration of wealth amassed in the United States since the Great Depression.

Most of the studies relating economic inequality to adverse health outcomes have done so at the population level using large, unlinked datasets. In other words, economic and health conditions have been measured not at the individual level but over broad geographical categories—nations, states, or standard metropolitan areas. Thus they have been subject to criticism that findings that link the two are based on aggregate data that are not necessarily applicable to individuals residing in those areas. However, the most recent studies have attempted to address this issue by combining data at the individual and aggregate levels. They have used individuals' specific income and health status along with more geographically based measures of economic inequality. With only a few exceptions,[38] these studies tend to support the view that income inequality has an independent adverse effect on health outcomes, but its impact is most acutely felt at the lower end of the income distribution.[39]

Thus, the empirical work to date provides fairly consistent evidence of a statistical relationship between economic inequality and health. The greater degree of economic inequality found in a region, the worse the health outcomes are in that area. But discussions of the precise pathways or mechanisms through which disparities in income or socioeconomic status influence health are still in an exploratory stage. A number of competing hypotheses have been advanced. Hugh Gravelle from the University of York has argued that the association between income inequality and mortality in a geographic area is merely a reflection of the inverse relationship between income and mortality risk at the individual level. In other words, in areas of high inequality there are more poor people who are at greater risk of dying in the near future and therefore inequality itself is not causally linked to adverse health.[40] This suggests that the more skewed the distribution of income in a society, the more likely that the mortality rates of the poor will outweigh the mortality rates of the affluent, leading to a rise in average mortality rates.

Other researchers, however, believe there are more complex factors at play. Richard Wilkinson from the University of Sussex, one of the world's leading proponents of the inequality-health dynamic, argues that psychosocial factors related to deprivation explain the relationship between income distribution and health. He claims it is "less a matter of the immediate physical effects of inferior material conditions than of the social meanings attached to those conditions and how people feel about their circumstances and about themselves."[41] Thus people's perception of their place in the social hierarchy rather than the underlying material conditions they experience can explain the relationship between inequality and health. Ichiro Kawachi, Bruce Kennedy, and other colleagues at Harvard have applied the concept of social capital—measured crudely as voluntary membership in groups and levels of social trust—to link the characteristics of communities to the health experiences of individuals.[42] John Lynch and George Kaplan from the University of Michigan add a more materialistic explanation: "Inequitable income distribution may be associated with a set of social processes and policies that systematically underinvest in human, physical, health and social infrastructure, and this underinvestment may have health consequences."[43]

None of these conceptual approaches as yet adequately explains the nature of the relationship between economic inequality and health. Yet it is useful to remember that it took decades after cigarette smoking was widely recognized as a health hazard before scientists were able to articulate the pathways by which smoking caused disease. It hardly seems too early to acknowledge that economic and social policies that exacerbate economic inequality may have important health consequences.

POLICY IMPLICATIONS AND DIRECTIONS

Documenting the links between socioeconomic status and health disparities has the potential for an enormous public policy impact. This is suggested by one of the principles of the Charter on Environment and Health, which was initiated by the World Health Organization's European Regional Office in 1989 and eventually adopted by all member states and the Commission of the European Union. The document asserts that, "The health of the individual and communities should take precedence over consideration of economy and trade."[44]

Requirements that governmental agencies consider potential health consequences when they construct long-term plans involving employment opportunities, tax and income transfer policies, monetary policy, or the size and quality of the social safety net can have a major impact on population health. In general, however, there has been a greater willingness among industrialized countries outside the United States to include health impact assessments as part of the process of introducing new economic and social initiatives.

In England, there has been a resurgence of research in this area following the release of the *Black Report* in 1980 and more recently the *Acheson Report* of 1998.[45] These reports, commissioned by the government, provided solemn assessments of the state of health disparities in England, discussed their potential causes, and outlined a framework for remediation. Likewise, the Canadian government has taken an active role in studying inequalities in health, grouping the determinants of health into nine categories for policy research: health and child development, education, income and social status, employment and working conditions, social support networks, the physical environment, biological and genetic endowments, personal health practices and coping skills, and access to health care services.[46]

The decline of tuberculosis from the late nineteenth century through most of the twentieth century in the United States provides a good case study in how investing in the social and physical environments in which people live, including housing, water systems, proper ventilation, and the maintenance of higher standards of nutrition, can yield a much larger health payoff than short-term governmental or medical interventions targeted at the individual.[47] While there is a time lag between public expenditures for such goods as quality housing, clean environmental conditions, and protection from occupational safety and health hazards, the size of the investment ultimately helps determine the level of public health.

There are some encouraging signs on the American scene. The United States has taken a step in the right direction in the drafting of *Healthy People 2010 Objectives*.[48] This lengthy document, assembled by the U.S. Department of Health and Human Services, is designed to help guide government, provider, and voluntary community efforts to improve the nation's health over the next decade. But although it laudably calls for the elimination of health disparities for low-income populations and people of color, its approach is based largely on improving access to care and modifying individual behavior.

We have already discussed the limitations of such an approach. It has strong and multiple roots in the United States. At one level, everyone experiences their own health as an individual, and therefore individual risk factors (such as smoking, poor diet, excessive drinking, and lack of exercise) rather than poverty or income inequality have a strong intuitive appeal as direct causal factors of poor health. Second, the biomedical model, which has dominated medical research in the United States, has fostered an almost exclusive focus on individual risk factors as the key to disease etiology, at the expense of social conditions. And finally, pointing the finger of blame at individuals for their "bad" choices is always an easier political response to health issues than questioning the underlying social and economic conditions that may promote poor health for the public at large.

Uncertainty over how to control or reduce health disparities that have their origins in the social and economic mix remains a serious political obstacle. Lacking a universal health care system in which population data is routinely collected and monitored, researchers in the United States have not developed a common protocol for incorporating health equity concerns into regional and local health plans.

This is an unfortunate knowledge gap because exploring the health implications of our social policies would almost surely alter the dimensions of the public discourse. For example, as noted, the health impact of raising the minimum wage has rarely been raised in the ideologically charged public debate during the past few years. Yet a number of studies have shown that the decline in the real value of the minimum wage contributed to wage stagnation experienced by the majority of Americans and to the increase in economic inequality during the 1980s.[49]

A more comprehensive model of health determinants would include not only conventional information on an individual's biologic and genetic endowment but also measures of the physical and social environment as well. If more rigorous data becomes available in the United States and the health consequences of economic policies are better understood, they could be incorporated into the public debate and perhaps change its character. Entrenched economic and political interests in Congress are constantly attempting to repeal the estate tax and diminish tax rates for the top income earners within the United States. Policymakers should give careful thought to possible lag structures and how the rising inequality and diminished social cohesion that such tax policies could promote would affect population health.

Just as environmental impact statements have become part of the routine process of developing policy, so too should matters vital to the public health be considered. Understanding the health consequences of economic and social welfare policies likely to affect levels of economic inequality would surely enhance public debate. When policies involving welfare reform, higher educational subsidies, the minimum wage, capital gains taxes, earned income tax credits, and changes in Social Security come before the American public and their elected officials, for example, they should be accompanied by "health impact statements" that examine the social, economic, and human costs and benefits of such policies. If public health interests are factored into the development of our economic and social policies a consensus may emerge that a more egalitarian and healthier society is not only possible but also prudent.

II

THE STATE OF AMERICA

7

WHY STOCKS WON'T SAVE
THE MIDDLE CLASS

Edward N. Wolff

The recent run-up in stock prices has created the impression that all families are doing well in terms of household wealth accumulation. This is emphatically not the case. Indeed, as I shall demonstrate, most American families have seen their net worth stagnate since 1989.

This chapter will document and attempt to explain the rather startling collapse of financial reserves among low- and middle-income households. This is an important issue because the existence of financial liquidity serves as the safety blanket or buffer that allows families to weather sharp drops of income, occasioned, for example, by job loss, marital divorce or separation, sickness or disability, and the like. The veritable "savings for a rainy day" permits families to maintain their consumption (or some fraction of their normal consumption) during periods of low income. The failure of a large portion of the population to accumulate financial reserves of any meaningful level thus increases the financial fragility of the poor and near-poor. Indeed, one reason why labor today may not be willing to push very hard for higher wages is that the potential job loss that might result is no longer cushioned by a financial reserve. Moreover, in a direct way, the recent upsurge in personal bankruptcies is one of the implications of this trend.

I begin the chapter with a brief discussion of what wealth is and why it is important over and above the income that it generates (Section 1). Section 2 presents the disturbing finding that despite the stock market boom, average family wealth holdings were still lower as of 1997 than in 1989. Section 3 further documents the disastrous collapse of financial reserves among the middle class. The next section presents evidence of the dramatic rise in wealth concentration that has occurred since the early 1980s. Only a small proportion of American families reaped the benefits of the remarkable economic growth of the 1980s and 1990s.

Section 5 investigates changes in the composition of household wealth. Several key findings are highlighted, including the continued high concentration of stock ownership in this country despite the spread of mutual funds and pension-type assets like 401(k) plans, and the growing indebtedness of the middle class. Section 6 examines some of the factors responsible for the declining wealth of the average American since the early 1980s. The last section of the chapter considers some of the broader political and social implications of falling family wealth in our country and possible policy remedies.

1. WHAT IS WEALTH AND WHY IS IT IMPORTANT?

In this study, I use the term *marketable wealth* (or *net worth*), which is defined as the current value of all marketable or fungible assets less the current value of debts. Net worth is thus the difference in value between total assets and total liabilities or debt. Total assets are defined as the sum of (1) the gross value of owner-occupied housing; (2) other real estate owned by the household; (3) cash and demand deposits; (4) time and savings deposits, certificates of deposit, and money market accounts; (5) government bonds, corporate bonds, foreign bonds, and other financial securities; (6) the cash surrender value of life insurance plans; (7) the cash surrender value of pension plans, including IRAs, Keogh plans, and 401(k) plans; (8) corporate stock and mutual funds; (9) net equity in unincorporated businesses; and (10) equity in trust funds. Total liabilities are the sum of (1) mortgage debt, (2) consumer debt, including auto loans, and (3) other debt.

This measure of wealth is used because the primary interest here is in wealth as a store of value and therefore a source of potential consumption. I believe that this is the concept that best reflects the level of well-being associated with a family's holdings. Thus, only assets that can be readily converted to cash (that is, *fungible* assets) are included. As a result, consumer durables like cars and retirement wealth (that is, the discounted present value of future private pension benefits from defined benefit pensions plans and future Social Security benefits), which are sometimes included in broader concepts of wealth, are excluded here.

I also use a more restricted concept of wealth, which I call *financial wealth*. This is defined as net worth minus net equity in owner-occupied housing. Financial wealth is more liquid than marketable wealth, since one's home is difficult to convert into cash in the short term. It thus reflects the resources that may be immediately available for consumption or various forms of investment.

The primary data sources used for this study are the 1983, 1989, 1992, 1995, and 1998 Survey of Consumer Finances (SCF) conducted by the Federal Reserve Board. Each survey consists of a core representative sample combined with a high-income supplement, which is drawn from the Internal Revenue Service's Statistics of Income data file. The survey questionnaire consists of hundreds of questions on different components of family wealth holdings. Though there are other data sources available for analyzing household wealth in the United States, the SCF is the best one for capturing both the wealth at the top of the distribution and the complete wealth portfolio of households in the middle.[1]

Family wealth by itself is also a source of well-being, independent of the direct financial income it provides. There are four reasons. First, owner-occupied housing provides services directly to its owner. Second, wealth is a source of consumption, independent of the direct money income it provides, because assets can be converted directly into cash and thus provide for immediate needs. Third, the availability of financial assets can provide liquidity to a family in times of economic stress, such as occasioned by unemployment, sickness, or family breakup.

Fourth, in a representative democracy, the distribution of power is often related to the distribution of wealth. Indeed, for the very rich, large fortunes can be a source of tremendous economic and social power. A large accumulation of financial and business assets can confer special privileges on their holders. It can enable them to influence the political process through large donations to candidates running for public office. In some cases, it gives them a special advantage in seeking public office, as the Kennedys, Rockefellers, Ross Perot, and, most recently, Steve Forbes have demonstrated. Large fortunes are often transmitted to succeeding generations, creating family dynasties.

2. Have Average Wealth
Holdings Grown Since 1983?

Perhaps the most striking result from Table 7.1 is that *median wealth* (the wealth of the household in the middle of the distribution) was only 4 percent greater in 1998 than in 1989. After rising by 7 percent between 1983 and 1989, median wealth fell by 17 percent from 1989 to 1995 and then rose by 24 percent from 1995 to 1998. One reason for the slow growth in median wealth is evident from the third row of Panel A, which shows that the percentage of households with zero or negative net worth increased from 15.5 percent in 1983 to 18.0 percent in 1998. The share of households with net worth less than $5,000 and less than $10,000 (both in 1995 dollars) also rose over the period.

Table 7.1. Mean and Median Wealth and Income, 1983–98 (in thousands, 1998 dollars)

	1983	1989	1992	1995	1998	Percent Change 1983–98
A. Net Worth						
1. Median	54.6	58.4	49.9	48.8	60.7	11.1
2. Mean	212.6	243.6	236.8	218.8	270.3	27.1
3. Percent with net worth						
a. Zero or negative	15.5	17.9	18.0	18.5	18.0	
b. Less Than $5,000[a]	25.4	27.6	27.2	27.8	27.2	
c. Less Than $10,000[a]	29.7	31.8	31.2	31.9	30.3	
B. Financial Net Worth						
1. Median	11.8	13.9	11.7	10.6	17.8	51.0
2. Mean	154.3	181.8	180.5	167.9	212.3	37.6
3. Percent with zero or negative financial wealth	25.7	26.8	28.2	28.7	25.7	
C. Income						
1. Median	33.1	31.6	30.3	32.1	33.4	0.8
2. Mean	46.9	49.0	49.7	46.6	52.3	11.4

[a] Constant 1995 dollars

Mean wealth is much higher than the median—$270,000 versus $61,000 in 1998. This implies that the vast bulk of household wealth is concentrated in the richest families. Mean wealth also showed a sharp increase from 1983 to 1989 followed by a rather precipitous decline from 1989 to 1995, and then, buoyed largely by rising stock prices, another surge in 1998.[2] Overall, it was 27 percent higher in 1998 than in 1983, and 11 percent larger than in 1989.

Median financial wealth was less than $18,000 in 1998, indicating that the average American household had very little savings available for its immediate needs. The time trend for financial wealth is similar to that for household net worth. Median financial wealth rose by 18 percent between 1983 and 1989, plummeted by 24 percent from 1989 to 1995, and then climbed in 1998 for a net increase of 51 percent. Between 1983 and 1995, the fraction of households with zero or negative financial wealth expanded from 26 to 29 percent and then fell back to 26 percent, partly explaining the trend in median financial wealth.

Mean financial wealth, after increasing by 18 percent from 1983 to 1989, declined by 8 percent between 1989 and 1995, and then jumped in 1998 for a net gain of 38 percent. The bull market was largely responsible for the sharp growth in financial wealth between 1995 and 1998. Median household income, after falling by 5 percent between 1983 and 1989, grew by 6 percent from 1989 to 1998, for a net change of only 1 percent. Mean income rose by 4 percent from 1983 to 1989, declined by 5 percent from 1989 to 1995, and then jumped by 11 percent in 1998, for a net change of 11 percent.

In sum, the results point to stagnating living conditions in the 1990s for the average American household, with median net worth growing by only 4 percent and median income by 5 percent between 1989 and 1998.

3. ARE FINANCIAL SAVINGS FALLING FOR THE MIDDLE CLASS?

Another way of viewing the resources of the middle class is in terms of the number of months its financial reserves can be used to sustain its normal consumption. In this case, I divide households by income class (not wealth class) and I use financial wealth as the basis of the calculation, since families still require a place to reside even if their income falls to zero. Annual consumption expenditures by income class are derived from the Consumer Expenditure Survey published by the Bureau of Labor Statistics for 1983, 1989, 1995, and 1998.

As shown in Table 7.2, middle-income families headed by individuals between twenty-five and fifty-four years of age in 1983 had accumulated, on average, only enough financial wealth to sustain their normal consumption for a period of 2.3 months in case of income loss and to sustain consumption at 125 percent of the poverty standard for 4.6 months. Indeed, the financial resources of the upper-middle-income class (the fourth quintile) were sufficient to maintain their normal consumption for only 5.7 months and consumption at 125 percent of the poverty line for 14.6 months. The lower-middle-income class and the low-income class had accumulated virtually no financial reserves.

The situation improved somewhat between 1983 and 1989, with the middle class able to sustain its normal consumption for 3.6 months (up from 2.3 months) and consumption at 125 percent of the poverty standard for 9.0 months (up from 4.6 months). However, by 1998 the situation was even more dire than in 1989. The bottom 40 percent of households in this age group as ranked by income still had not managed to gather any financial savings. The middle-income class was now in even worse straits, with enough financial reserves to sustain their normal consumption for only 2.2 months (compared to 3.6 months in 1989) and consumption at 1.25 times the poverty threshold for only 3.4 months (compared to 9.0 months in 1989). On the other hand, the financial resources of the upper-middle-income class (fourth quintile) increased relative to their normal consumption and to consumption 25 percent above the poverty threshold.

Suppose one considers the possibility of establishing an Asset Poverty line that, like the official income poverty measure, would set a minimum standard as a national benchmark. A reasonable standard might be that families should have an asset cushion that allows them to meet a minimum consumption level for six months on their own, should all other sources of support fail. Such a minimum consumption standard might be the official, family-size specific needs standard that underlies the official income poverty measure, or even 125 percent of this level. With this latter standard, a four-person family that had net financial assets of less than $10,300 would be declared

TABLE 7.2. ACCUMULATED FINANCIAL RESERVES OF MIDDLE-AGED FAMILIES BY INCOME QUINTILE IN TERMS OF NUMBER OF MONTHS RESERVES CAN SUSTAIN CONSUMPTION, 1983–98[a]

Income Quintile	Number of Months Current Consumption Can be Sustained[b]	Number of Months Consumption at 125% of Poverty Standard Can be Sustained[c]
A. 1983		
Top Quintile	16.5	51.4
Fourth Quintile	5.7	14.6
Third Quintile	2.3	4.6
Second Quintile	0.9	1.3
Bottom Quintile	0.0	0.0
B. 1989		
Top Quintile	18.7	72.6
Fourth Quintile	4.7	14.6
Third Quintile	3.6	9.0
Second Quintile	0.5	0.9
Bottom Quintile	0.0	0.0
C. 1995		
Top Quintile	19.0	61.3
Fourth Quintile	3.5	7.9
Third Quintile	1.2	1.8
Second Quintile	0.1	0.1
Bottom Quintile	0.0	0.0
D. 1998		
Top Quintile	25.2	81.5
Fourth Quintile	8.2	18.4
Third Quintile	2.2	3.4
Second Quintile	0.1	0.1
Bottom Quintile	0.0	0.0

[a] For households with age of householder between 25 and 54. Calculations based on data from the "Survey of Consumer Finances" and the "Consumer Expenditure Survey."

[b] Defined as the ratio of median financial wealth (total net worth less the equity in owner-occupied housing) to the median consumption expenditures for the income group.

[c] Defined as the ratio of median financial wealth of the income class to 125 percent of the poverty standard for a family of four.

"asset poor," which would be the analogue of being income poor. Similarly, a one-person family with assets below $5,000 or a six-person family with assets below $13,800 would likewise fall below the asset poverty line.

The results of such a calculation show that in 1983, 48 percent of Americans lived in families that were asset poor; things had improved to 45 percent by 1989, but by 1995 the rate had risen to 49 percent. About 80 percent of black Americans were asset poor in 1995. These results accentuate the argument that one likely reason for the "growing anxiety" of the middle class is its falling financial reserves.

4. HAS THE CONCENTRATION OF WEALTH INCREASED SINCE 1983?

The calculations shown in Table 7.3 indicate an extreme concentration of wealth in 1998. The top 1 percent of families (as ranked by marketable wealth) owned 38 percent of total household wealth, and the top 20 percent of households held 83 percent. Financial wealth is even more concentrated, with the richest 1 percent (as ranked by financial wealth) owning 47 percent of total household financial wealth and the top 20 percent owning 91 percent. The top 1 percent of families (as ranked by income) earned 17 percent of total household income in 1997 and the top 20 percent accounted for 56 percent—large figures but lower than the corresponding wealth shares.

The figures also show that wealth inequality, after rising steeply between 1983 and 1989, increased at a slower pace from 1989 to 1998. The share of wealth held by the top 1 percent rose by 3.6 percentage points from 1983 to 1989. Between 1989 and 1998, the share of the top percentile grew by a more moderate 0.7 percentage points but the share of the next 9 percentiles fell by 0.4 percentage points and that of the bottom two quintiles grew by 0.9 percentage points.

The trend is similar for the inequality of financial wealth. The share of the top 1 percent gained 4.0 percentage points between 1983 and 1989. In the ensuing nine years, the share of the richest 1 percent grew by another 0.4 percentage points but the share of the next 19 percentiles declined, as did the share of the second quintile, and that of the

TABLE 7.3. THE SIZE DISTRIBUTION OF
WEALTH AND INCOME, 1983–98

	PERCENTAGE SHARE OF WEALTH OR INCOME HELD BY:							
	TOP 1%	NEXT 4%	NEXT 5%	NEXT 10%	TOP 20%	2ND 20%	3RD 20%	BOTTOM 40%
A. Net Worth								
1983	33.8	22.3	12.1	13.1	81.3	12.6	5.2	0.9
1989	37.4	21.6	11.6	13.0	83.5	12.3	4.8	−0.7
1992	37.2	22.8	11.8	12.0	83.8	11.5	4.4	0.4
1995	38.5	21.8	11.5	12.1	83.9	11.4	4.5	0.2
1998	38.1	21.3	11.5	12.5	83.4	11.9	4.5	0.2
B. Financial Wealth								
1983	42.9	25.1	12.3	11.0	91.3	7.9	1.7	−0.9
1989	46.9	23.9	11.6	11.0	93.4	7.4	1.7	−2.5
1992	45.6	25.0	11.5	10.2	92.3	7.3	1.5	−1.1
1995	47.2	24.6	11.2	10.1	93.0	6.9	1.4	−1.3
1998	47.3	21.0	11.4	11.2	90.9	8.3	1.9	−1.1
C. Income								
1982	12.8	13.3	10.3	15.5	51.9	21.6	14.2	12.3
1988	16.6	13.3	10.4	15.2	55.6	20.6	13.2	10.7
1991	15.7	14.8	10.6	15.3	56.4	20.4	12.8	10.5
1994	14.4	14.5	10.4	15.9	55.1	20.6	13.6	10.7
1997	16.6	14.4	10.2	15.0	56.2	20.5	12.8	10.5

Note: For the computation of percentile shares of net worth, households are ranked according to their net worth; for percentile shares of financial wealth, households are ranked according to their financial wealth; and for percentile shares of income, households are ranked according to their income.

bottom two quintiles grew by 1.3 percentage points. However, financial wealth was still more unequally distributed in 1998 than in 1983.

Income inequality increased sharply between 1982 and 1988. However, there was very little change between 1989 and 1997. While the share of the top 1 percent remained at 16.6 percent of total income, the share of the next 19 percent increased by 0.6 percentage points and the share of the other quintiles lost.

Table 7.4 (see page 116) highlights how uneven gains in wealth were over the years from 1983 to 1998. The largest increases in relative

TABLE 7.4. MEAN WEALTH HOLDINGS BY WEALTH
CLASS, 1983–98 (IN THOUSANDS, 1998 DOLLARS)

	Top 1%	Next 4%	Next 5%	Next 10%	Top 20%	2nd 20%	3rd 20%	Bottom 40%	All
A. Net Worth									
1983	7,175	1,187	516.2	278.7	864.5	133.6	55.5	4.7	212.6
1998	10,204	1,441	623.5	344.9	1126.7	161.3	61.0	1.1	270.3
% change	42.2	21.4	20.8	23.7	30.3	20.7	10.0	-76.3	27.1
% of gain[a]	52.5	17.7	9.3	11.5	91.0	9.6	1.9	-2.5	100.0
B. Financial Wealth									
1983	6,187	906	354.0	158.7	658.3	57.0	12.3	(6.3)	144.2
1998	10,044	1,114	485.8	237.6	965.3	88.0	19.9	(5.9)	212.3
% change	62.3	23.0	37.2	49.7	46.6	54.4	62.7	0.0	47.2
% of gain[a]	55.6	12.0	9.5	11.4	88.6	8.9	2.2	0.3	100.0

Note: For the computation of percentile shares of net worth, households are ranked according to their net worth; and for percentile shares of financial wealth, households are ranked according to their financial wealth.

[a] The computation is performed by dividing the total increase in wealth of a given group by the total increase of wealth for all households over the period, under the assumption that the number of households in each group remains unchanged over the period. It should be noted that the households found in each group (such as the top quintile) may be different in each year.

terms were made by the wealthiest households. The top 1 percent saw their average wealth (in 1998 dollars) rise by $30 million or by 42 percent. The remaining part of the top quintile, as well as the second quintile, experienced increases from 21 to 24 percent, while the middle quintile gained 10 percent, and the poorest 40 percent lost 76 percent.

Another way of viewing this phenomenon is afforded by calculating the proportion of the total increase in real household wealth between 1983 and 1998 accruing to different wealth groups. This is computed by dividing the increase in total wealth of each percentile group by the total increase in household wealth, while holding constant the number of households in that group. If a group's wealth share remains constant over time, then the percentage of the total wealth growth received by that group will equal its share of total wealth. If a group's share of total wealth increases (decreases) over time, then it will receive a percentage of the total wealth gain greater (less) than its share in either year. However, it should be noted that in these calculations, the households found in each group (say, the top quintile) may be different in the two years.

The results indicate that the richest 1 percent received 53 percent of the total gain in marketable wealth over the period from 1983 to 1998 (also see Figure 7.1). The next 19 percent received another 39 percent, so that the top quintile together accounted for 91 percent of the total growth in wealth, while the bottom 80 percent accounted for 9 percent.

The pattern of results is roughly similar for financial wealth. The average financial wealth of the richest 1 percent grew by 62 percent, that of the next-richest 4 percent by 23 percent, and that of the next-richest 5 percent by 37 percent. However, in the case of financial wealth, the second and third quintiles also showed substantial gains, of 54 and 63 percent, respectively, and the bottom quintiles also showed positive gains. Of the total growth in financial wealth between 1983 and 1998, 56 percent accrued to the top 1 percent and 89 percent to the top quintile, while the bottom 80 percent collectively accounted for only 11 percent.

FIGURE 7.1. PERCENTAGE SHARE OF TOTAL WEALTH
GAIN BY WEALTH CLASS, 1983–97

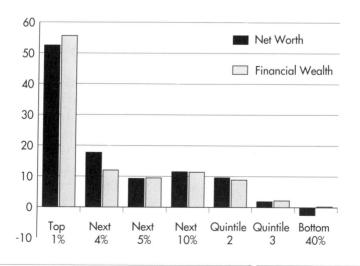

These results indicate rather dramatically that the growth in the economy during the period from 1983 to 1998 was concentrated in a surprisingly small part of the population—the top 20 percent, and particularly the richest 1 percent.

5. Is the Composition of Household Wealth Changing?

Further evidence of the stagnating financial condition of the middle class can be seen by looking at the change in the composition of household wealth. I begin with the overall portfolio composition of household wealth, which shows where households, on average, put their savings. In 1998, owner-occupied housing was the most important household asset in the breakdown shown in Table 7.5, accounting for 29 percent of total assets. Real estate other than owner-occupied housing comprised 10 percent, and business equity another 18 percent. Liquid assets, including demand deposits, time deposits, money market funds, CDs, and the cash surrender value of life insurance made up 10 percent; pension accounts amounted to 12 percent; and bonds and other financial securities, corporate stock and mutual funds, and trust equity added up to 20 percent. Debt as a proportion of gross assets was 15 percent, and the debt/equity ratio (the ratio of total household debt to net worth) was 0.18.

There have been some significant changes over time in the composition of wealth. The most disturbing trend is the rising indebtedness of American families, with the debt/equity ratio leaping from 15.1 to 17.6 percent between 1983 and 1998. Moreover, as we saw above, the fraction of households recording zero or negative net worth grew from 15.5 percent in 1983 to 18.0 percent in 1998. The principal source of these increases, contrary to popular wisdom, is not rising consumer debt—credit card balances and the like. In fact, non-mortgage debt as a fraction of total assets fell from 6.8 to 4.2 percent over the period from 1983 to 1998.

Rather, the primary source is rising mortgage debt, including home equity loans and second mortgages, which climbed from 6 to 11 percent of total assets. Indeed, mortgage debt as a share of the value of

TABLE 7.5. COMPOSITION OF TOTAL HOUSEHOLD WEALTH, 1983 AND 1998 (PERCENT OF GROSS ASSETS)

	1983	1998
Principal residence (gross value)	30.1	29.0
Other real estate (gross value)	14.9	10.0
Unincorporated business equity[a]	18.8	17.7
Liquid assets[b]	17.4	9.6
Pension accounts[c]	1.5	11.6
Financial securities[d]	4.2	1.8
Corporate stock and mutual funds	9.0	14.8
Net equity in personal trusts	2.6	3.8
Miscellaneous assets[e]	1.3	1.8
Total	100.0	100.0
Memo:		
Debt on principal residence	6.3	10.7
All other debt[f]	6.8	4.2
Total debt	13.1	15.0
All stocks/total assets[g]	11.3	22.6

[a] Net equity in unincorporated farm and non-farm businesses and closely-held corporations.
[b] Checking accounts, savings accounts, time deposits, money market funds, certificates of deposit, and the cash surrender value of life insurance.
[c] IRAs, Keogh plans, 401(k) plans, the accumulated value of defined contribution pension plans, and other retirement accounts.
[d] Corporate bonds, government bonds, open-market paper, and notes.
[e] Gold and other precious metals, royalties, jewelry, antiques, furs, loans to friends and relatives, future contracts, and miscellaneous assets.
[f] Mortgage debt on all real property except principal residence; and credit card, installment, and other consumer debt.
[g] Direct ownership of stock shares and indirect ownership through mutual funds, trusts, and IRAs, Keogh plans, 401(k) plans, and other retirement accounts.

homeowner's property increased from 21 to 37 percent (see Table 7.6, page 120). Whereas the total market value of homes remained almost constant as a share of total assets over this period, net home equity— the value of the house minus any outstanding mortgages—plummeted from 24 to 18 percent of total assets. This is true despite the fact that, according to the SCF data, the homeownership rate (the percentage of households owning their own home) rose from 63.4 percent in 1983 to 66.3 percent in 1998.

TABLE 7.6. AVERAGE HOUSEHOLD
INDEBTEDNESS, 1983 AND 1998

	1983	1998
Debt/equity ratio	15.1	17.6
Net home equity/total assets[a]	23.8	18.2
Principal residence debt/house value	20.9	37.0

[a] Ratio of gross value of principal residence less mortgage debt on principal residence to total assets.

One popular argument is that home equity loans have been used by families to borrow against their rising stock values and that the recent surge in consumption has been financed with mortgage debt. However, according to Federal Reserve Board national balance sheet figures, the big jump in mortgage debt occurred between 1983 and 1995, predating the stock market boom, and has actually leveled off recently. The ratio of mortgage debt to total household assets grew from 6.3 percent in 1983 to 11.0 percent in 1995 and then fell off to 10.7 percent in 1998, while the ratio of mortgage debt to home values increased sharply from 20.9 to 36.0 percent between 1983 and 1995 and then slightly to 37.0 percent in 1997.

Moreover, examining the 1995 Survey of Consumer Finances, I find that it is just not true that families with mortgage debt (or home equity loans) are major stockholders. The average stock holdings of mortgage holders in 1995 was $49,000, compared to $72,000 among homeowners without mortgage debt. Even families with second mortgages and home equity loans had lower stock values than non–mortgage holders. Furthermore, the correlation between stock holdings and total mortgage debt is only 0.07 (and that between stock values and home equity plus second mortgage debt is even smaller, 0.03). So it is true that mortgage debt has been used to fuel consumption over the last fifteen years or so—but not as a way of drawing equity out of the stock market. Rather, on the surface, at least, it appears that families are now using tax-sheltered mortgage loans to finance normal consumption rather than more normal consumer loans and other forms of consumer debt. However, in so doing, they are eroding the value of their home equity.[3]

A second notable change is that pension accounts rose from 1.5 to 11.6 percent of total assets between 1983 and 1998 (see Table 7.5). However, this increase almost exactly offset the decline in liquid assets, from 17.4 to 9.6 percent. As a result, the explosion in the use of various pension-type accounts such as IRAs, 401(k) plans, and other thrift plans, rather than increasing overall family savings, appears instead to have allowed households to substitute tax-free pension accounts for taxable savings deposits.

A third important change is the sharp rise in the share of corporate equities in total assets, from 9.0 to 14.8 percent, reflecting the bull market in corporate stocks. However, this result does not reflect the full extent of the growth in corporate stock holdings, because stocks are also indirectly held in mutual funds, pension accounts, and trust funds. If we include these, then corporate stocks, both directly and indirectly owned by households, doubled, from 11.3 to 22.6 percent of total assets.[4]

ARE THERE IMPORTANT CLASS DIFFERENCES IN WEALTH COMPOSITION?

The tabulation in Table 7.5 provides a picture of the average holdings of all families in the economy, but there are marked class differences in how middle-class families and the rich invest their wealth. As shown in Table 7.7 (see page 122), the richest 1 percent of households (as ranked by wealth) invested almost 80 percent of their savings in investment real estate, businesses, corporate stock, and financial securities in 1998. Corporate stocks, either directly owned by the households or indirectly owned through mutual funds, trust accounts, or various pension accounts, comprised 29 percent by themselves. Housing accounted for only 8 percent of their wealth, liquid assets another 5 percent, and pension accounts 7 percent. Their ratio of debt to net worth was 3 percent and their ratio of debt to income was 49 percent.

Among the next-richest 19 percent of U.S. households, housing comprised 29 percent of their total assets, liquid assets another 11 percent, and pension assets 15 percent in 1998. Forty-three percent took the form of investment assets—real estate, business equity, stocks, and bonds—and 24 percent was in the form of stocks directly or indirectly owned. Debt amounted to 13 percent of their net worth and 90 percent of their income.

In contrast, about 60 percent of the wealth of the middle three quintiles (60 percent) of households was invested in their own home

TABLE 7.7. COMPOSITION OF HOUSEHOLD WEALTH BY WEALTH CLASS, 1983 AND 1998
(PERCENT OF GROSS ASSETS)

	TOP 1%		NEXT 19%		MIDDLE 3 QUINTILES	
	1983	1998	1983	1998	1983	1998
Principal residence	8.1	7.8	29.1	28.8	61.6	59.8
Liquid assets (bank deposits, money market funds, and cash surrender value of life insurance)	8.5	5.0	21.4	11.3	21.4	11.8
Pension accounts	0.9	6.9	2.0	14.9	1.2	12.3
Corporate stock, financial securities, mutual funds, and personal trusts	29.5	31.6	13.0	20.0	3.1	5.5
Unincorporated business equity and other real estate	52.0	46.9	32.8	23.2	11.4	8.8
Miscellaneous assets	1.0	1.8	1.6	1.8	1.3	1.8
Total assets	100.0	100.0	100.0	100.0	100.0	100.0
Memo:						
Debt/equity ratio	5.9	3.3	10.9	12.9	37.4	51.3
Debt/income ratio	86.8	49.4	72.8	90.2	66.9	101.6
All stocks/total assets[a]	21.2	28.7	9.1	24.1	2.4	11.2

[a] Direct ownership of stock shares and indirect ownership through mutual funds, trusts, and IRAs, Keogh plans, 401(k) plans, and other retirement accounts.

in 1998. Another 24 percent went into monetary savings of one form or another and pension accounts. Together, housing, liquid assets, and pension assets accounted for 84 percent of the total assets of the middle class. The remainder was about evenly split among non-home real estate, business equity, and various financial securities and corporate stock. Stocks directly or indirectly owned amounted to only 11 percent of their total assets. The ratio of debt to net worth was 51 percent, much higher than for the richest 20 percent, and their ratio of debt to income was 102 percent, also higher than the top quintile.

There is remarkable stability in the composition of wealth by wealth class between 1983 and 1998. The most notable change is a substitution of pension assets for liquid assets—a transition that occurred for all three wealth classes but was strongest for those in percentiles 80 to 99. The share of stocks directly or indirectly owned in total assets increased by eight percentage points among the richest 1 percent, fifteen percentage points among the next-richest 19 percent and by nine percentage points for the middle three quintiles.

Another way to portray differences between middle-class households and the rich is to compute the share of total assets of different types held by each group (see Table 7.8). In 1998 the richest 1 percent of households held half of all outstanding stock, financial securities,

TABLE 7.8. THE PERCENT OF TOTAL ASSETS HELD BY WEALTH CLASS, 1998

	Top 1%	Next 9%	Bottom 90%	All	Share of Top 10% 1983	Share of Top 10% 1998
Investment assets						
Stocks and mutual funds	49.4	35.7	14.9	100.0	90.4	85.1
Financial securities	50.8	33.2	15.9	100.0	82.9	84.1
Trusts	54.0	36.8	9.2	100.0	95.4	90.8
Business equity	67.7	24.0	8.3	100.0	89.9	91.7
Non-home real estate	35.8	39.1	25.1	100.0	76.3	74.9
Total for group	54.1	32.1	13.8	100.0	85.6	86.2
Stocks, directly or indirectly owned[a]	42.1	36.6	21.3	100.0	89.7	78.7
Housing, liquid assets, pension assets, and debt						
Principal residence	9.0	26.2	64.8	100.0	34.2	35.2
Deposits[b]	19.5	31.5	49.0	100.0	52.9	51.0
Life insurance	11.3	41.5	47.2	100.0	33.6	52.8
Pension accounts[c]	19.7	40.2	40.2	100.0	67.5	59.8
Total for group	13.0	31.0	56.0	100.0	41.0	44.0
Total debt	7.1	19.9	73.0	100.0	31.8	27.0

[a] Direct ownership of stock shares and indirect ownership through mutual funds, trusts, and IRAs, Keogh plans, 401(k) plans, and other retirement accounts.
[b] Demand deposits, savings deposits, time deposits, money market funds, and certificates of deposit.
[c] IRAs, Keogh plans, 401(k) plans, the accumulated value of defined contribution pension plans, and other retirement accounts.

and trust equity, two-thirds of business equity, and 36 percent of investment real estate. The top 10 percent of families as a group accounted for about 90 percent of stock shares, bonds, trusts, and business equity, and about three-quarters of non-home real estate. The richest 10 percent of households also accounted for 79 percent of the total value of stocks directly or indirectly owned, only slightly less than its 85 percent share of directly owned stocks and mutual funds.

In contrast, owner-occupied housing, deposits, life insurance, and pension accounts were more evenly distributed among households. The bottom 90 percent of households accounted for about two-thirds of the value of owner-occupied housing, almost 50 percent of deposits and life insurance cash value, and 40 percent of the value of pension accounts. Debt was the most evenly distributed component of household wealth, with the bottom 90 percent of households responsible for 73 percent of total indebtedness.

There was again relatively little change in the concentration of asset ownership between 1983 and 1997. The richest 10 percent held 86 percent of all investment assets in both 1983 and 1998 and 41 percent of housing, liquid assets, and pension assets in 1983 and 44 percent in 1998. The most significant change is that the share of total stocks directly or indirectly owned was somewhat watered down over this period, from 90 to 79 percent.

Who Has a Stake in the Stock Market?

There have been numerous reports in the media that stock ownership has substantially widened in the United States, particularly during the 1990s. There is some truth to these reports. The proportion of households that own some stock either outright or indirectly through mutual funds, trusts, or various pension accounts increased from 24.4 percent in 1983 to 48.2 percent in 1998 (see Table 7.9). Much of the increase was fueled by the growth in pension accounts like IRAs, Keogh plans, and 401(k) plans. Indeed, between 1983 and 1989, direct stock ownership declined somewhat (from 13.7 to 13.1 percent)—likely, a result of the 1987 stock market plunge. However, the share of households with pension accounts nearly doubled over this period, from 11 to 23 percent, accounting for the overall increase in stock ownership. Between 1989 and 1998, the direct ownership of stocks grew rather modestly, by six percentage points, while the share

TABLE 7.9. PERCENT OF HOUSEHOLDS OWNING STOCK DIRECTLY OR INDIRECTLY, 1983–98

	1983	1989	1992	1995	1998
Any stock holdings	24.4	31.7	37.2	40.4	48.2
Stock worth $5,000 or more[a]	14.5	22.6	27.3	29.5	36.3
Stock worth $10,000 or more[a]	10.8	18.5	21.8	23.9	31.8

Note: Includes direct ownership of stock shares and indirect ownership through mutual funds, trusts, and IRAs, Keogh plans, 401(k) plans, and other retirement accounts.

[a] 1995 dollars

of households with a pension account again doubled, accounting for the bulk of the overall increase in stock ownership.

Despite the overall gains in stock ownership, less than half of all households had any stake in the stock market by 1998. Moreover, many of these families had only a minor stake. In 1998, while 48 percent of households owned some stock, only 36 percent had total stock holdings worth $5,000 or more and only 32 percent owned $10,000 or more of stock.

Stock ownership is also highly skewed by wealth and income class. As shown in Table 7.10 (page 126), 93 percent of the very rich (the top 1 percent) reported owning stock either directly or indirectly in 1998, compared to 46 percent of the middle quintile and 19 percent of the poorest quintile. While over 91 percent of the very rich also reported stocks worth $10,000 or more, only 26 percent of the middle quintile and less than 2 percent of the bottom quintile did so.

Stock ownership also tails off by income class (see Table 7.11, page 126). Whereas 93 percent of households in the top 1 percent of income recipients (those who earned $250,000 or more) owned stock in 1998, 52 percent of the middle class (incomes between $25,000 and $50,000), 29 percent of the lower-middle class (incomes between $15,000 and $25,000), and only 11 percent of poor households (income under $15,000) reported stock ownership. The comparable ownership figures for stock holdings of $10,000 or more are 92 percent for the top 1 percent, 27 percent for the middle class, 13 percent for the lower-middle class, and 5 percent for the poor. Moreover, about three-fourths of all stocks were owned by households earning $75,000 or more (the top 16 percent) and 88 percent by the top third of households in terms of income.

TABLE 7.10. CONCENTRATION OF STOCK OWNERSHIP BY WEALTH CLASS, 1998

WEALTH CLASS	PERCENT OF HOUSEHOLDS OWNING STOCK WORTH MORE THAN		
	ZERO	$4,999	$9,999
Top 1 percent	93.2	92.9	91.2
Next 4 percent	89.0	87.0	86.1
Next 5 percent	83.9	80.4	78.9
Next 10 percent	78.7	74.0	71.6
Second quintile	58.9	49.8	45.4
Third quintile	45.8	32.7	25.9
Fourth quintile	35.1	15.1	8.6
Bottom quintile	18.6	4.6	1.8
All	48.2	36.3	31.8

Note: Includes direct ownership of stock shares and indirect ownership through mutual funds, trusts, and IRAs, Keogh plans, 401(k) plans, and other retirement accounts.

TABLE 7.11. CONCENTRATION OF STOCK OWNERSHIP BY INCOME CLASS, 1998

INCOME LEVEL	SHARE OF HOUSEHOLDS	PERCENT OF HOUSEHOLDS OWNING STOCK WORTH MORE THAN			PERCENT OF STOCK OWNED	
		ZERO	$4,999	$9,999	SHARES	CUMULATIVE
$250,000 or more	1.6	93.3	92.7	91.9	36.1	36.1
$100,000–$249,999	6.9	89.0	85.5	82.8	27.7	63.9
$75,000–$99,999	7.7	80.7	70.4	66.5	10.8	74.7
$50,000–$74,999	17.4	70.9	55.6	48.8	13.1	87.8
$25,000–$49,999	29.0	52.0	34.3	27.4	8.5	96.3
$15,000–$24,999	16.1	29.2	16.9	12.9	2.6	98.9
Under $15,000	21.3	10.6	5.2	4.5	1.1	100.0
All	100.0	48.2	36.3	31.8	100.0	—

Note: Includes direct ownership of stock shares and indirect ownership through mutual funds, trusts, and IRAs, Keogh plans, 401(k) plans, and other retirement accounts.

Thus, in terms of wealth or income, substantial stock holdings have still not penetrated much beyond the reach of the rich and the upper middle class. The big winners from the stock market boom of the last few years have been these groups, while the middle class and the poor have not seen sizable benefits from the bull market. It is also apparent which groups benefit from the preferential tax treatment of capital gains.

6. What Are the Reasons for Declining Household Wealth?

Why has median wealth declined since 1989? There appear to be two major factors. The first is that savings for middle-income families was actually negative over this period. The second is that their assets were heavily concentrated in housing and bank deposits, and these assets experienced low real rates of return over these years.

The results are documented in Table 7.12 (page 128). Over the period from 1989 to 1998, median household income, based on the Current Population Survey, increased by about $900. Consumption expenditures remained virtually unchanged for this group. However, in every year throughout this period, household savings among middle-income households was negative, though it became slightly less negative over time. Moreover, in 1989, 69 percent of the assets of the middle-income quintile were in housing and another 15 percent in liquid assets. Over the 1989–98 period, the real rate of return on housing was very low (0.4 percent per year), while that on liquid assets (principally, savings accounts and money market funds) was a modest 1.4 percent per year. Altogether, the real rate of return on the portfolio of the middle-income quintile was a dismal 1.2 percent per year, despite the surge in stock prices. This compares to a historical average of 2.9 percent per year over the period 1962 through 1992.

The bottom panel of Table 7.12 decomposes the change in median household wealth, which amounted to about $2,200 in 1998 dollars, into three components. First and foremost is that the present value of household savings, accumulated over the period, amounted to –$11,500. Second, this was offset by capital gains of $13,100.

TABLE 7.12. CHANGE IN MEDIAN WEALTH AND CONTRIBUTORY FACTORS, 1989–98 (IN THOUSANDS, 1998 DOLLARS)

	1989	1998	CHANGE, 1989–98
Median household wealth	58.4	60.7	2.2
Median household income	38.0	38.9	0.9
Consumption expenditures at median income level	40.1	40.3	0.1
Savings rate at median income level (percent)[a]	−5.4	−3.7	1.7

	PERCENT PER ANNUM, 1989–98
Real rate of return on portfolio of middle quintile household	1.15

FACTORS CONTRIBUTING TO CHANGE IN MEDIAN HOUSEHOLD WEALTH	CHANGE, 1989–98
Present value of household savings, accumulated annually over the period	−11.5
Change in value of portfolio of middle wealth quintile resulting from asset price changes	13.1
Other factors (residual)	0.6
Total change in median household wealth	2.2

Sources: U.S. Bureau of the Census, "Current Population Surveys," http://www.census.gov; Bureau of Labor Statistics, Consumer Expenditure Surveys, years 1989–95, http://stats.bls.gov; Council of Economic Advisers, *Economic Report of the President* (Washington, D.C.: U.S. Government Printing Office, February 1998); U.S. Bureau of the Census, *Statistical Abstract of the United States, 1997* (Washington, D.C.: U.S. Government Printing Office, 1997).

[a] Ratio of household income less household consumption expenditures to household income.

Other factors (the residual) contributed the remaining $600 to the change in median net worth. Interestingly, if the real rate of return on household assets in the 1989–95 period had remained at its historical average of 2.9 percent per annum then median household wealth would have increased over this period by about $16,000 instead of by $2,200.

7. SOCIAL AND POLITICAL IMPLICATIONS

This chapter has documented that median net worth (in constant dollars), after growing strongly from 1983 to 1989, rose very modestly between 1989 and 1998. Median financial wealth did improve from 1989 to 1998. Median income did recover a bit between 1989 and 1998 but was still about at its 1983 level at the end of the period. The main reason for slow growth in median wealth over the 1989–98 period is that middle-class households dissaved over this period. A secondary reason is that while the middle class experienced positive capital gains (in real terms) on their portfolio over this period, the gain was considerably smaller than in the preceding two decades.

What is also clear is that the financial resources accumulated by families in the bottom three income quintiles is very meager relative to their normal consumption and even to consumption at 125 percent of the poverty threshold, and these resources have dwindled over time, between 1989 and 1998, particularly for middle-income families.

Wealth inequality also continued to rise in the United States since 1989 but at a more muted pace than during the 1980s. While the share of the top 1 percent of wealth holders rose by 3.6 percentage points from 1983 to 1989, it grew by only 0.7 percentage points between 1989 and 1998. As a result, the strongest growth in net worth between 1983 and 1998 occurred in the top 20 percent of the wealth distribution and the gains were particularly strong for the richest 1 percent. Indeed, 53 percent of the gains in wealth over this period accrued to the top 1 percent and over 90 percent of the gains to the top 20 percent of households.

The new figures also point to the growing indebtedness of the American family. The overall debt/equity ratio has climbed sharply since 1983, from 0.15 to 0.18 in 1998. Moreover, the proportion of households reporting zero or negative net worth jumped from 15.5 percent in 1983 to 18.0 percent in 1998. Net equity in owner-occupied housing as a share of total assets fell sharply over this period, from 23.8 percent in 1983 to 18.2 percent in 1998, reflecting rising mortgage debt on homeowner's property, which grew from 21 to 37 percent. The debt/equity ratio was also much higher among the middle three quintiles of households in 1998, at 0.51, than among the top 1 percent (0.03) or the next 19 percent (0.13). For the middle class, in particular, indebtedness grew sharply since 1983, with the debt/equity ratio rising from 0.37 to 0.51.

Since the early 1980s, households have shifted their assets toward corporate stocks. This change has been particularly marked over the last few years as a result of the recent surge in stock prices. Moreover, because of the spread of mutual funds and pension assets like 401(k) plans, by 1998, 48 percent of households owned stock shares either directly or indirectly through mutual funds, trust funds, or pension plans, up from 24 percent in 1983. Yet despite this growth in stock holdings, stock shares still remain heavily concentrated in the hands of the rich, with the richest 10 percent still accounting for 79 percent of the total value of these stocks in 1998. Moreover, the middle class still has a small stake in the stock market, with only about a fourth owning even a moderate amount of stocks ($10,000 or more). These results, in particular, indicate that stock ownership has not penetrated deeply enough into the middle class to lift its wealth substantially or to salvage its fortunes.

These results suggest some of the sources of the "growing anxiety" of the middle class in this country over the last decade. Between 1989 and 1998, real incomes have grown slowly for households at all levels except the top 20 percent of the income distribution. Median net worth was also up slightly in 1998 as compared to 1989. The average indebtedness of American families relative to their assets continued to rise, as did mortgage debt on the value of owner-occupied housing. There has been almost no trickle down of economic growth to the average family: almost all the growth in household income and wealth has accrued to the richest 20 percent. The finances of the average American family are more fragile in the late 1990s than in the early 1980s. It is not surprising that the fraying of the private safety net as well as the public safety net has led to a growing sense of economic insecurity in the country.

These results also point to the growing divide between the rich and the poor and provide some urgency to a consideration of potential policy remedies. On grounds of equity, can a society in which the gains of economic growth are concentrated in a diminishing share of the population long endure without increasing political divisiveness? Will the increasing wealth concentration in this country further exacerbate the tilt of political power toward the rich? These appear to be the policy challenges the United States faces in the years ahead.

How can we reverse the rising inequality of recent years? Insofar as rising inequality in our country is a result of structural shifts of market forces in the labor market—shifts in relative demand toward skilled labor and away from semiskilled and unskilled workers—there may be little the government can do to reverse the underlying causes. However, the experience of European countries as well as our neighbor, Canada—all affected by the same market forces—suggests that one effective mechanism is to place more of the tax burden on the rich and less on the middle class. In the United States, the 1980s witnessed falling marginal tax rates, particularly on the rich and very rich. Though the federal government raised the marginal rates on the very rich in 1993, they are still considerably lower than in 1980 and in comparison to Western European countries.

Should we think about direct taxation of the wealth holdings of households? Almost a dozen European countries have such a system in place, including Denmark, Germany, the Netherlands, Sweden, and Switzerland. On the grounds of equity, a combination of annual income and the current stock of wealth provides a better gauge of the ability to pay taxes than income alone. Moreover, there is no evidence from other advanced economies that the imposition of a modest direct tax on household wealth has had any deleterious effect on personal savings or overall economic growth. Indeed, there are arguments to the contrary—that such a tax may induce a more efficient allocation of household wealth, away from unproductive and toward more productive uses. Finally, the possibility that such a levy might promote capital flight is not borne out by the facts—consider Switzerland, a net importer of capital.

I propose a very modest tax on wealth (a $500,000 exemption with marginal tax rates running from 0.05 to 0.3 percent). My calculations show that such a tax structure would yield an average tax rate on household wealth of 0.2 percent, which is less than the loading fee on most mutual funds, and would reduce the average yield on household wealth holdings by only 6 percent. Even the top marginal tax rate of 0.3 percent would reduce the average yield on personal wealth by only 9 percent. These figures suggest that disincentive effects on personal savings would be very modest indeed. Moreover, there are arguments as suggested earlier that personal savings might actually rise as a result of the imposition of a wealth tax.

I estimate that such a tax could raise $50 billion in additional revenue and have a minimal impact on the tax bills of 90 percent of American families. This is not a large amount, representing about 3 percent of total federal tax receipts. However, on the margin such additional revenue could be critical. In particular, it could help provide the fiscal latitude to enact more generous social transfers of a Canadian-type system, including a family allowance plan, which, if coupled with a rising minimum wage (indeed, even a *constant* minimum wage in *real* terms) and extension of the Earned Income Tax Credits, would do much to improve the financial well-being of the poor and the lower middle class.

We might also consider the development of mechanisms to promote asset ownership in the United States. These include Individual Development Accounts (IDAs), in which amounts set aside by eligible low-income families are partially matched by public funds. (The Universal Savings Accounts—USAs—proposed by President Clinton in his 1999 State of the Union address are similar in function.) The accounts draw interest, and the principal can be withdrawn to support schooling or training, to purchase a home, or to start a business. IDAs can be complemented in some places by subsidized home ownership programs for the poor. Indeed, the Ford Foundation has recently made its largest single grant, upwards of $50 million, to support a "national home ownership for the poor" initiative, and local community groups have warmed to the challenge. Restoring asset ownership to middle-income and poor families can contribute greatly to increasing their economic security, restoring their participation in the social life of the community, and reversing their political disenfranchisement.

8

INEQUALITY AND THE
NEW HIGH-SKILLED
SERVICE ECONOMY

Anthony P. Carnevale and Stephen J. Rose

In the past fifteen years, there have been hundreds of academic papers documenting the growing inequality of earnings among American workers. The typical approach to measuring income inequality is to examine how the relationship among high-, middle-, and low-income workers has changed over time. As can be seen in Figure 8.1 (page 134), workers whose earnings were higher than those of 90 percent of all other workers—that is, those in the 90th percentile—made 1.8 times as much in 1979 as the workers in the 50th percentile. But by 1997, the workers in the 90th percentile were earning 2.1 times as much as the workers in the 50th percentile. In Figure 8.2 (page 134), we compare well-off workers to poor workers by both income and sex. In 1979, male workers in the 90th earnings percentile earned 3.6 times as much as those near the bottom of the distribution (in the 10th percentile) and 4.5 times as much in 1997. Earnings inequality rose almost as rapidly for women. Female workers in the 90th percentile earned 2.7 times as much as those in the 10th percentile in 1979, compared to 4 times as much in 1997. Earnings inequality grows still greater as one moves higher up on the income ladder.

These growing differences in earnings contrast sharply with the experience of the preceding thirty years. During the 1940s, there was a compression in the earnings distribution as administered prices, an active government hand, and a rapidly growing economy raised wages for those at the middle and the bottom. In the years following the war, the commitment to avoid another depression fostered strong

FIGURE 8.1. RATIO OF HIGH- TO MIDDLE-INCOME EARNINGS

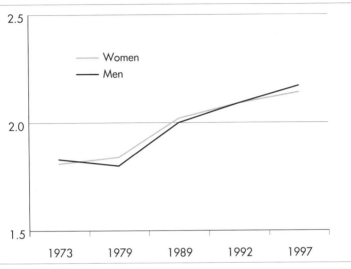

Source: Lawrence Mishel, Jared Bernstein, and John Schmitt, *The State of Working America, 1998–99* (Ithaca, N.Y.: Cornell University Press, 1999), pp. 132–33.

FIGURE 8.2. RATIO OF HIGH- TO LOW-INCOME EARNINGS

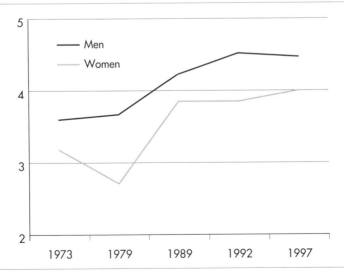

Source: Lawrence Mishel, Jared Bernstein, and John Schmitt, *The State of Working America, 1998–99* (Ithaca, N.Y.: Cornell University Press, 1999), pp. 132–33.

and persistent growth that was shared almost equally by Americans on every rung of the economic ladder. Feeling flush with prosperity, President Kennedy and President Johnson initiated a series of programs to address the needs of those "other Americans" who had been left behind in the postwar economic boom.

The golden years came to an end in the 1970s as economic growth slowed significantly—due to a variety of factors economists have yet to sort out, including increased international competition, a quadrupling of OPEC oil prices, and rising inflation. In an effort to wring double-digit inflation out of the economy, the new Federal Reserve Board chairman, Paul Volcker, embarked on a tight monetary policy in 1979 that led to a modest recession in 1980—to be followed by a severe recession in 1982. Following the turmoil of the preceding decade, companies used the recession to restructure their operations, which partly explains the expansion of wage inequality.

What economists soon discovered was that the earnings inequality that developed after 1979 was strongly correlated with educational attainment. The difference between the average income of a college graduate and a high school graduate grew markedly in the 1980s. Finally, in the early 1990s, the gap stabilized at levels of disparity not experienced since the end of the Great Depression and higher than in any country in the industrialized world.

Since 1995, a strong economy has lifted wages slightly for those on the bottom rungs of the economic ladder, suggesting to some that income differences may at last be shrinking. But it is still far too early to conclude that a new round of wage compression is under way. The ratio of the 90th to the 10th percentile among male wage earners increased from 3.59 in 1979 to 4.52 in 1993 before declining to 4.47 in 1997. In other words, the decline in the 1990s has been small and accounts for only a 6 percent reversal of the 1979 to 1993 increase.

Economists have developed two general explanations for the dramatic rise in earnings inequality. One view focuses on political changes such as declining unionization, deregulation, free trade agreements, and the failure of Congress to enact legislation increasing the minimum wage to keep up with inflation and economic growth.[1] Proponents of this view also argue that structural changes associated with the shift from manufacturing to services and to a more integrated world market undercut the bargaining power of workers. They assert that each of these has contributed to a general shift in political power toward business and away from workers, including away from middle-class workers who are now part of an "anxious class" that fears it will be left behind economically in the next century.

A second view argues that inequality grew out of skill differences among individuals that affect their ability to adapt to new technology requirements in the workplace. According to this approach, technological change has been biased in favor of those who can work best with new technological procedures—hence the phrase "skill-biased technology change."[2]

The two dominant explanations for growing earnings inequality resonate with the popular consciousness. Yet, on closer examination, neither completely aligns with the timing of the growing earnings inequality. Both corporate profit growth and computer usage were increasing slowly when inequality was rising fastest and increasing most quickly when inequality measures were stabilizing. For example, while the acceleration of income differentials occurred in the early 1980s, the real expansion in computer usage came after the price declines set off by widespread cloning of the IBM PC after 1985. Similarly, the share of corporate profits and net interest out of corporate domestic income dropped steadily from 21.3 percent in 1959 to 16.6 percent in 1979. This share rose slightly to 17.8 percent in 1989 and then increased sharply thereafter in the 1990s, reaching 20.5 percent in 1997. So in the 1990s, computer usage, stock prices, and corporate profits were all growing at their fastest pace when inequality measures were leveling off.

This is not to say that business power and technology do not matter but rather that they matter in ways other than the prevailing theories of earnings inequality claim. Let us explore this argument a little more closely. According to the technology explanation, high-tech workers who interact most directly with the new computer technology—from CAD/CAM machine operators to computer scientists—are increasing as a proportion of the workforce and also are earning increasing wages, compared to those who do not work with the new technology. This strong technology complementarity argument, however, is not supported by the data. The share of technicians and science professionals (for example, engineers, architects, chemists, and computer systems analysts) comprises less than 7 percent of the workforce, and this figure is only three percentage points higher than in 1959. This can hardly cause a major restructuring of the pay of the labor force.

Instead, the types of jobs that have had the largest increases in number and earnings are managerial and professional jobs in health care, education, and—especially—the headquarters of businesses. These changes are in many ways technologically driven, but not tied directly to the hands-on design, manufacture, or repair of technology. Instead, the focus in these jobs with the most growth is on the use, exploitation, or deployment of technology. Apparently, the job creation, value added, and wage benefits of technology have leapfrogged its very creators. College-educated managers and professionals, though not specifically technically skilled, are "empowered" by information technology that has become broadly distributed throughout all workplaces rather than sequestered in technical work settings.

EDUCATION AND INCOME DISPARITIES

Determining the causes of income inequality is not simply a matter of quibbling among academics. Knowing what causes inequality in earnings affects our choices of remedies. For example, in designing training and education programs, it is important to know that the contemporary economy apparently needs more of the general skills learned in college rather than technical, vocational, or job-specific skills.

There is little doubt that education levels have become highly correlated to earnings performance, and the differences in education levels account for the growing differences in earnings. As can be seen in Table 8.1 (page 138), the change in earnings from 1979 to 1995 varies directly with educational attainment.[3] Men with graduate degrees saw their real earnings increase by 26.2 percent between 1979 and 1997, while men with bachelor's degrees earned only 2.2 percent more.[4] For all men without bachelor's degrees, earnings were on average lower in 1997 than they had been in 1979. The decline ranged from 21.6 percent for high school dropouts to 16.7 percent for men with exactly a high school diploma to 8 percent for those with some college.

One way to see the rising importance of education in determining earnings levels is to look at those with exactly a high school diploma. As recently as 1969, prime-age men and women with this level of education earned slightly above average. But by 1997, those with only high school diplomas earned 22 percent less than average. Men with exactly a bachelor's degree earned 45 percent more than high school graduates in 1973 (only 36 percent more in 1979), but by

Table 8.1. Average Earnings of
Prime-Age Workers, 1979 and 1997

	1979	1997	Percent Change
All Men	$40,052	$40,507	1.1
H.S. Dropout	$28,619	$22,451	−21.6
H.S. Graduate	$37,893	$31,554	−16.7
Some College	$41,834	$38,478	−8.0
Bachelor's Degree	$51,704	$52,817	2.2
Graduate Degree	$55,427	$69,947	26.2
All Women	$17,548	$24,064	37.1
H.S. Dropout	$15,255	$12,085	−20.8
H.S. Graduate	$18,127	$18,509	2.1
Some College	$20,093	$23,212	15.5
Bachelor's Degree	$22,070	$31,812	44.1
Graduate Degree	$30,366	$43,281	42.5

Source: Author's calculations from U.S. Department of Commerce, Bureau of the Census, *Current Population Survey*, March 1980 and March 1998.

1997, they were earning 67 percent more. The premium for a graduate degree was still greater, rising from 50 percent in 1973 to 122 percent in 1997.

For women, only high school dropouts had lower earnings in 1997 than 1979. Overall, their average earnings were up 37 percent. Most of this rise was attributable to working more hours per week and more weeks per year, while hourly pay was up by less than 10 percent. As a result, men's earnings, which had been 128 percent higher than women's earnings in 1979, were only 68 percent higher than women's in 1997.

The educational pay differences among women grew over this period to levels that almost exactly equaled those of men. The difference in the earnings of women with bachelor's degrees, compared to those with high school diplomas, increased from 22 percent to 72 percent and the difference between females with graduate degrees and those with bachelor's degrees increased from 68 percent to 134 percent between 1979 and 1997.

The share of the prime-age workforce that attended college for at least some time increased from 20 percent in 1959 to 30 percent in

1973 and to 56 percent in 1997. Thus, the supply of college graduates was increasing at the same time their relative pay was rising. Based on simple supply-and-demand theory, prices (in this case the relative wages of college-educated workers) should be expected to fall as supply increases. Since the earnings of these workers (the price of their labor) went up, demand for educated workers must have increased even more than the rapidly growing supply. This, in fact, is the principal support for the skill-biased technology argument, which we will now explore in greater detail.[5]

In Search of Skill-Biased Technology Change

What could have caused the demand for skilled labor to outpace increasing supply? Many researchers believe that the most plausible answer is the technological changes associated with the explosive expansion of information technology. Jeremy Greenwood provides an interesting historical context for this argument.[6] He argues that inequality has risen during the implementation of all major new technologies because those able to utilize them most directly are rewarded for their unique abilities. But Greenwood and other researchers who support this approach offer no substantial proof of this proposition. Steven Davis and Robert Topel likened the acceptance of technology as the root cause of the new inequality to astronomers' projecting the existence of Pluto before their telescopes were powerful enough to observe it because the orbital paths of Neptune would not fit without the gravitational pull of a planet-sized object in its orbit.[7] Peter Gottschalk and Timothy Smeeding were a bit more blunt when they said that "technological change [may be] simply a label for our ignorance."[8]

Thus the technology-biased argument requires a firmer foundation than the mere observation that demand for educated workers is stronger than the supply. And indeed many economists have tried to provide more direct proof. In one of the earliest attempts, Alan Krueger found a 15 percent earnings premium for workers who used computers, compared to similarly qualified workers who did not.[9] But John Dinardo and Jorn-Steffen Pischke, using a German data set, cast doubt on those findings by showing that the earnings premium associated with those who used pencils was almost identical.[10] They concluded that there was something about those who used office tools, high-tech or not, that led to higher earnings than would be expected solely on the basis of their human-capital attributes.

A series of papers—including work by Eli Berman, John Bound, and Zvi Griliches;[11] Berman, Bound, and Stephen Machin;[12] and David Autor, Lawrence Katz, and Alan Krueger[13]—try to show that the share of skilled workers is rising fastest in industries that are most technologically advanced. These papers use the share of nonproduction workers in detailed manufacturing industries as a measure of the skill level of the labor force in that industry. They find that the ratio of skilled to unskilled labor increased dramatically in the 1980s, during the time of the fastest-rising inequality. Further, those sectors that have the largest-rising share of nonproduction workers—the allegedly more skilled—are closely correlated with their investment in computers.

Thus it would seem that changing technology in business and rising inequality are linked. But to us, this measure of skills is ambiguous. First, it is connected only to manufacturing industries that represent a relatively small share of total employment. Second, nonproduction workers are predominantly white-collar office workers—an important category, but not one that we would unambiguously describe as technically skilled. Indeed, it is implausible that nonproduction workers are more technically skilled than production workers on the modern factory floor, where many people work with computer-based technology that is much more complex than office PCs.

In contrast to these studies, Mark Doms, Timothy Dunn, and Kenneth Troske use a very detailed data source about individual firms and find that the level of a company's technology does not affect the share of nonproduction workers in its employ.[14] In other words, there is no increase in the proportion of skilled workers as defined earlier. These authors find that the most innovative firms actually used increasing numbers of skilled nonproduction workers both before and after they adopted new technologies. They speculate that Autor, Katz, and Krueger's findings on the importance of computer use are driven by the connection of computers with office work and not with factory automation in general.

It should also be noted that skill upgrading in most of these industries preceded the surge in computer investments. In the Autor, Katz, and Krueger study, for instance, industries that introduced computers more quickly in 1980s were the same ones that had increased the education levels of their workforces in the preceding decade. In addition, in evaluating their conclusions, David Howell finds that virtually all of the movement in the skill-intensity variable of the 1980s occurred between 1979 and 1983, a time of two recessions and massive organizational restructuring. But the largest increases in computer spending, on the other hand, occurred from 1985 onward. The slowdown in the growth of increased inequality and a parallel slowdown in the growth in the share of nonproduction workers during the 1990s also were troubling because that was a time of widespread computer expansion. Thus the timing seems off—the labor market changes that indicate "skill upgrading" and the investments in computer equipment do not closely correlate with the change in inequality.

In all of this discussion of technology-driven income disparities, it should be added, no one has yet specified the particular technical skills associated with using computers that would result in the substantial growth in earnings differences experienced after the 1980s. James K. Galbraith therefore understandably asks the following: "What exactly are the acquired skills, the educationally derived bits of human capital, whose productivity the use of the computers is supposed to enhance?"[15] Timothy Bresnahan makes a similar argument based on a careful analysis of specific companies and how they have introduced and used computers.[16] He finds that the increased demand for managers and professionals is not due to how they use machines, but rather due to organizational changes that result from the introduction of information and communication technologies. Thus it is not that computers complement the human capital of their users. Rather, they generally replace lower levels of blue-collar and white-collar workers, which increases the value of higher-level white-collar workers. This is, in our view, the key to understanding why incomes have become more unequal.

EARNINGS DISPARITY BY OCCUPATION AND INDUSTRY

The most obvious anomaly that casts doubt on both the high-tech and political explanations is that neither is much good for the specific changes in income disparity that they are meant to explain. As Galbraith points out, there is a level of specificity that is missing—we need to identify clearly the winners and losers.

According to the political power school, various changes in the economy have caused the number of "good jobs" to decline. From this point of view, the shift from primary agrarian production to secondary industrial production was successful. Although there were many bumps in the road, wages for industrial workers rose and the middle class grew. According to the political-power school, the transition to a tertiary service economy has not been as successful. Now the contention is that hamburger-flipper jobs and related low-skilled service and retail jobs have grown at the expense of unionized industrial jobs. Consequently, the number in the middle class has shrunk, leaving a polarized society of relatively few high-level managers and professionals and many low-skilled, low-paid service workers.

In the last several years, a number of researchers have attempted to assess the evolution of the quality of employment in the United States.[17] In each study, the share of high-quality, high-paying jobs has increased while the share of low-quality jobs has decreased. In our earlier research, we divided jobs into elite, good, and less-skilled positions. In 1959, 17 percent of jobs were in the top group and 47 percent were in the bottom. By 1997, the top group had grown to 28 percent while the bottom group had shrunk to 36 percent. In both years, approximately 36 percent were in the middle group. Clearly, as the workforce has become more educated, the quality of jobs has risen rather than declined.

On the other hand, the "good jobs" that have been growing have not been those that required the highest level of technological training. To demonstrate this claim, we have regrouped official government categories, an essential step because the normal way of reporting the data combines jobs of very unequal pay and educational quality—for example, the managers in fast food restaurants are included with corporate CEOs, police and firefighters are included with janitors as service workers, and financial and real estate brokers are included with salesclerks. Our categories are meant to be more consistent in terms of pay and educational requirements. Table 8.2 presents summary information on each of seven job clusters.

The first four categories are what we call *elite jobs*—those jobs that require the most education and receive the highest earnings. Medical doctors is a small outlier category that does not fit well anywhere else because their earnings and education levels are so high. Managers and business professionals are office workers who coordinate and promote the interests of the enterprise. They tend to wear suits and ties, or dresses, and entertain clients on company expense accounts. They earn more than high-tech workers and education and

TABLE 8.2. EMPLOYMENT AND EARNINGS OF PRIME-AGE WORKERS, 1997

TYPE OF WORK	SHARE OF JOBS	AVERAGE EARNINGS	SHARE WITH SOME POSTSECONDARY EDUCATION
Medical Doctors	0.8	$108,700	100
Managers and Business Professionals	18.1	$50,800	79
High-tech Workers	7.2	$45,300	86
Education and Health-care Professionals	11.3	$33,600	92
Supervisors and Skilled Blue-collar	19.3	$34,400	46
Clerical and Related Occupations	14.6	$23,000	52
Less-skilled Jobs	28.7	$19,400	28

Source: Author's calculations from U.S. Department of Commerce, Bureau of the Census, *Current Population Survey,* March 1998.

health-care professionals even though a smaller proportion have attended college.

High-tech workers include scientists and technicians (such as engineers, chemists, architects, and computer systems analysts) who do not work for universities. The education and health-care professional fields (teachers, college professors, nurses, clergy, social workers, musicians, and so on) have historically been dominated by women and combine high educational requirements and relatively low pay.

The next two categories are what we call *good jobs*—jobs that can command reasonable pay and working conditions without having to have a four-year degree. Supervisors and craft and repair workers are in predominantly male jobs that have average earnings that are slightly above that of the education and health-care professionals. Clerical jobs, by contrast, are normally held by women who earn considerably less than supervisors and skilled blue-collar workers even though they are more likely to have higher educational credentials.

The final group—less-skilled jobs—consists of salesclerks, janitors, guards, food-service workers, laborers, and factory operatives. These positions require the least education and, with the exception of some unionized factory jobs, have much lower earnings than the previous six job categories.

Using this breakdown, Table 8.3 tracks the changes in earnings and employment of male workers with bachelor's or graduate degrees between 1979 and 1997. If the technology argument is true, then there should be large gains in employment and pay among high-tech workers. But, as can be seen, this is not the case. First, the share of high-tech workers was basically unchanged—up slightly for those with graduate degrees and down slightly for those with just bachelor's degrees. In both educational categories and both years, this group never accounted for more than 20 percent of total employment.

Second, the earnings of high-tech workers did not perform better than those of other workers: The pay of workers with bachelor's degrees was unchanged, while the pay of those with graduate degrees

TABLE 8.3. TRENDS IN MALE COLLEGE GRADUATE EMPLOYMENT, 1979 AND 1997

	EXACTLY A BACHELOR'S DEGREE				GRADUATE DEGREE			
	EMPLOYMENT SHARE		EARNINGS (000s IN 1996$)		EMPLOYMENT SHARE		EARNINGS (000s IN 1996$)	
	1979	1997	1979	1997	1979	1997	1979	1997
All			51.7	52.8			57.1	69.9
Medical Doctors	0.0	0.0	0	0	7.4	10.0	86.7	114.0
Managers and Business Professionals	42.4	38.1	59.9	65.7	34.7	37.3	63.2	81.7
High-Tech Workers	19.3	17.5	56.9	56.9	14.5	16.0	59.6	65.7
Education and Health-Care Professionals	10.9	12.1	34.8	39.8	33.0	25.4	42.3	48.2
Supervisors and Skilled Blue-Collar	14.2	18.1	48.5	47.7	5.4	6.7	50.4	60.5
Clerical and Related Occupations	6.0	5.5	38.9	33.7	2.3	1.7	45.6	38.0
Less-Skilled Jobs	7.1	8.8	31.6	29.7	2.7	2.9	25.2	21.9

Source: Author's calculations from U.S. Department of Commerce, Bureau of the Census, *Current Population Survey,* March 1980 and March 1998.

increased by 10 percent. This last figure contrasts with a nearly 30 percent rise for male graduate degree holders who are managers and business professionals. This somewhat startling finding was confirmed when we looked at more finely graded occupations. For example, among college-educated engineers, earnings were 4 percent lower in 1997 than in 1979. Among computer systems analysts with bachelor's degrees, there was no change in earnings between 1979 and 1995 and then a 20 percent increase between 1995 and 1998.

By contrast, managers and business professionals—the nation's elite office workers—formed a much larger group. They combined the largest concentration of employment (over double the size of high-tech workers) with the highest average pay (except for medical doctors) and the largest increases in income over the last eighteen years. In fact, the movements of this group—growth of jobs, high level of pay, and fastest growth of pay—were responsible for most of the increase in the change in relative earnings of college-educated men. Most important, they do not readily fit into the scenario described by advocates of the technology argument. It is not directly the new technologies that made these workers more productive. Rather, as Bresnahan has argued, the new technologies simplified the tasks of some of the other workers within enterprises and allowed more value to be added by elite managers and business professionals.

Finally, it should be noted that the pay of male college-educated workers who were supervisors or skilled blue-collar workers, clericals, or in less-skilled jobs declined during these years. Although they were college-educated, their employment in nonmanagerial and nonprofessional positions undermined their ability to receive wage gains. Thus higher education alone is not sufficient to guarantee success in today's labor market. One must also get the right job. As we will show, earnings for men in less-skilled and even good jobs have been falling since 1979.

The same data on women are presented in Table 8.4 (page 146). Here the trends are quite different, with earnings gains of greater than 40 percent over this eighteen-year period. Once again, high-tech workers do not stand out. Fewer than one in sixteen female college graduates falls into this category. The major compositional change during this period was the move from the education and health care professions into managerial and business professions. For those with a bachelor's degree, there was a 14 percentage point reduction in the former category and a 14 percentage point rise in the latter. Among postgraduate women, there was a 13.5 percentage point loss among education and

TABLE 8.4. TRENDS IN FEMALE COLLEGE GRADUATE EMPLOYMENT, 1979 AND 1997

| | EXACTLY A BACHELOR'S DEGREE | | | | GRADUATE DEGREE | | | |
| | EMPLOYMENT SHARE | | EARNINGS (000s IN 1996$) | | EMPLOYMENT SHARE | | EARNINGS (000s IN 1996$) | |
	1979	1997	1979	1997	1979	1997	1979	1997
All			22.1	31.8			30.4	43.3
Medical Doctors	0.0	0.0	0.0	0.0	1.2	4.2	69.0	93.2
Managers and Business Professionals	12.2	26.4	31.8	41.7	14.0	25.0	38.8	55.3
High-Tech Workers	5.0	7.5	31.2	38.2	5.1	5.8	36.5	46.3
Education and Health-Care Professionals	50.7	36.3	22.6	30.1	67.6	54.1	29.9	36.3
Supervisors and Skilled Blue-Collar	3.8	7.2	20.2	35.2	2.0	2.8	25.2	42.8
Clerical and Related Occupations	20.3	14.5	17.2	21.9	6.7	5.5	16.1	27.1
Less-Skilled Jobs	8.0	8.1	11.6	16.4	3.3	2.6	11.7	19.9

Source: Author's calculations from U.S. Department of Commerce, Bureau of the Census, *Current Population Survey,* March 1980 and March 1998.

health-care professionals offset by an 11 percentage point rise in elite business jobs. For women college graduates, average earnings were up significantly in each occupational category. But the switch from relatively low-paying education and health-care work to managerial and business professional positions was responsible for one-quarter of the overall gain in average earnings for bachelor's-only women and one-third of the gain for those with graduate degrees.

THE U.S. "SERVICES" ECONOMY: MYTH VERSUS REALITY

Neither those who connect inequality to skill-biased technology nor those who focus on shifts in political power foresaw the growth of relatively high-wage service jobs, especially the college-level office jobs in the managerial and business professions discussed in the preceding section. In our view, both camps have been selective in their use of the evidence. Those who have argued for changing institutions and political power have focused more on low-skilled services and the impact of trade. Conversely, those who think that technology is the driving factor have been remarkably unspecific about how this process works. They give the impression that it is highly skilled engineers, scientists, technologists, and computer specialists who are the winners in the new high-tech economy. Yet, as we have shown, the number of workers in these jobs is small.

The deindustrialization prophesied by those who saw shifting political power at the heart of the new economy has not proved to be as damaging as many people feared because a smaller proportion of the net new jobs were low-skilled service jobs. In our earlier research, we found that low-wage service jobs accounted for less than 21 percent of all U.S. jobs in 1997, almost the same percentage as in 1959. Moreover, 30 percent of low-wage workers are under twenty-one years of age and are most likely to hold those positions only temporarily as they finish their education or make transitions to better career opportunities.

But neither are the better jobs being created in the United States in high technology. In fact, high-tech jobs have grown from only 3.4 to 6.6 percent of all U.S. jobs since 1959. So, in our view, the technology enthusiasts have overstated their case when they assume that information technology will create massive numbers of new technical jobs. This is even true inside technical companies. Consider Intel Corporation, the world's primary silicon chip producer, with $30 billion in annual sales and more than sixty thousand employees. Surprisingly, only about one in four Intel employees requires advanced technical training. So just what do Intel workers do? Fifteen percent of the company's employees are researchers. An additional 10 percent constitute a small share of the many Intel employees who are involved in chip production and facility maintenance and require advanced skills. The other production and maintenance workers (45 percent) use sophisticated machinery but perform relatively routine functions. An additional 30 percent of the Intel workforce are office workers—managers, administrators, and sales staff.

While the number of high-technology jobs was up by 3.2 percentage points since 1959 and low-skilled service workers were up by just 0.8 percentage points, employment in education and health care grew by 5.3 percentage points. And there were 36 million more white-collar office jobs than in 1959, an increase of 10.2 percentage points.

Marketers, lawyers, editors, accountants, salespeople, stockbrokers, and others now account for 54 million, or 41 percent of the economy's 133 million jobs. The workers in these two areas are highly educated: 74 percent of today's education and health-care workers and 66 percent of office workers have at least a partial college education.

THE SHIFT FROM SPECIFIC TO GENERAL SKILL

The shift just described in the occupational structure of the U.S. economy suggests that there has also been a general upgrading in skill requirements. The people who talk about the importance of technology often focus narrowly on technical and vocational skill development. But, in addition to more specific vocational skills and technical skills, there is a growing need for more general cognitive skills (mathematical and verbal reasoning ability), for a set of applied problem-solving skills, and for a set of "soft" interpersonal skills. Workers need to have higher levels of general cognitive skills in order to adapt successfully to changing job requirements. Delivering on a new set of standards for producing variety in products and customized services requires creativity as well as the ability to solve problems. As service functions grow in nearly every job and as the share of service occupations grows as well, increased human interaction demands a new set of interpersonal skills—the ability to work on a team, to work in complex institutional networks, or to communicate with customers, students, clients, or patients. Employers who set high standards for quality require conscientious workers who are able to take responsibility for a final product or service, regardless of their level in the organization.

We know a great deal about developing and assessing general cognitive skills, but little about how to develop and assess problem-solving and interpersonal skills in students and workers. Consequently, most employers use educational credentials, especially college-level study, as the best proxy for having these skills.

THE DOWNSIDE

But there is a downside to this high-skilled service economy. Slow growth combined with growing inequality means stagnating earnings for many American workers. As shown in Table 8.1, overall male earnings have barely changed since 1979, while average earnings for all but four-year college graduates and those with graduate and professional degrees have declined. Women's earnings are up across the board, but their earnings are still appreciably lower than men's earnings. In addition, the educational requirements in all jobs have gone up—so job opportunities at every educational level have been ratcheted downward. For example, 54 percent of prime-age managers and business professionals did not have any schooling past high school in 1959; by 1997, this figure had dropped to 21 percent. Even among less-skilled jobs, the share with some postsecondary education went from 5 percent in 1959 to 28 percent in 1997.

For the 44 percent of prime-age male workers who did not go past high school, job opportunities have narrowed and pay, even for those holding the same job, has fallen. Among those with exactly a high school degree in 1959, 22 percent were employed in some sort of managerial or professional position (the first four categories in Table 8.2). By 1997, this figure had fallen to 13 percent. In 1959, 31 percent of high school graduates were in less-skilled jobs with an average pay of $31,500. By 1995, 42 percent of these high school graduates were employed in less-skilled jobs and their pay was down to $25,800.

For those men with some college but no bachelor's degree, the share in elite employment fell from 40 percent in 1959 to 30 percent in 1997. Offsetting this decline was an increase in the share employed in less-skilled jobs, from 18 to 27 percent. During the years when earnings were falling after 1979, the pay of men with some college in less-skilled jobs fell from $31,000 to $27,000 in 1997. The pay of these men in good and elite jobs also declined, but only by 4 percent.

Overall, what is most noteworthy is that the pay of different types of jobs has moved in different directions for male workers. While earnings in elite jobs were rising by 5 percent, the earnings in less-skilled jobs declined by 16 percent. Even among such good jobs as supervisor, skilled crafts worker, police officer, and firefighter, earnings were down 5 percent from their peak.

As technology has changed the nature of our economy, changes in wage structure often come about through changes in social and political institutions. The political-power school is correct to point to policies affecting deregulation, international trade, immigration, minimum wages, and unionization as influences over inequality and wage determination. But what underlying forces created the new environment in which these new policies were adopted?

Sophisticated urban consumers led the movement from home-grown brand loyalty to global competition. Other "market-opening" initiatives were touted as efficiency gainers. The choice of better quality, reliability, and lower prices made international trade a boon for consumers but led to a decline in pay and employment for many blue-collar workers. There was a concern for equity, but the feeling was that the economy would perform best if it were not "coddled"; all actors were going to have to earn their position in the market. The bias toward global markets was accompanied by deregulation in the domestic economy. Thus the cause of the change was not some cabal of capitalists changing the rules in their favor but a broad level of support for an open economy. The policies that create such consternation for blue-collar union workers have been beneficial for the growing number of office workers.

PRODUCTIVITY AND VALUE

To fully understand today's economy, we need to reconceptualize productivity, service work, and the role of technology. In the era of mass industrial production, goods were thought of as standardized, and productivity was defined narrowly as output-per-input. Since services were more difficult to mass produce, William Baumol hypothesized that there would be uneven growth between the two sectors.[18] Wages would be set in the overall labor market and services would suffer from a "cost disease" as the prices in the technologically more dynamic goods-producing sector would decline relative to prices in the service sector. According to the prevailing view at the time, high productivity in manufacturing would deindustrialize, reducing the number of good jobs, and low productivity in services would guarantee expansion of low-wage, low-skilled jobs.

As an example, to show that growth in services productivity is limited, Baumol noted that no matter how productive musicians are today, it takes as long to play a Mozart sonata now as it did in the eighteenth century. But this analogy is limited and fails to reflect the many ways that consumers can now enjoy music and other forms of entertainment. While going to a live concert at Lincoln Center is expensive, it is certainly more accessible than the private royal study at which Mozart held his concerts. Furthermore, modern stereo equipment with compact and laser discs can produce wonderful sound quality.

Has the price of entertainment gone down as much as the price of goods production? Probably not, but the differential is not that easy to determine and may not be large. In other words, there is no clear divide between goods and services production, and that divide is getting blurrier all the time. In entertainment, for example, there certainly are many physical goods in the form of equipment for which productivity has increased. Airline and other public transportation is considered a service, but a large proportion of the cost is connected to the fuel and depreciation of the plane. Similarly, there is more service content than ever before embedded in many goods. One study found that it took more secretaries than farmers to bring food to the American table.[19]

Not only do we have to reconceptualize what consumer goods are, we also need to rethink productivity to get a truer understanding of what inputs are necessary in today's economy. From a business point of view, profitability is determined by many factors other than simple productivity measures of output per unit of input. For example, many researchers have noted the importance of establishing a standard format in selling a new product. In home video, the original Beta technology was superior to VHS, but once the latter got a lead with better availability and inventory, even Sony did not have the marketing clout to overcome this original market disadvantage. Six years ago, there were approximately six router companies seeking to supply the growing server market that is the backbone of the Internet. Cisco Systems took an early lead and never looked back as many purchasing agents bought Cisco products under the time-honored dictum that you can never lose your job by buying from the leading provider. There are numerous other cases of what some economists call "path dependence" and what Robert Frank and Philip Cook call "winner take all."[20] The most productive path may not be the winning path.

Another example of how profitability and productivity do not neatly coincide concerns retailing. In today's market, the worst thing is for goods to remain on the shelves. They are not earning money, they are taking up precious space, and they will have to be sold at a deep discount as remainders. The whole just-in-time delivery of goods is based on the premise of small orders with the latest fashions and with the fewest mistakes. Some textile firms have switched from the bundle system to flexible teams in order to meet these requirements. From the narrow view of the textile firm, this is a less efficient method to produce the most garments in the least time. But in terms of the whole product cycle, it provides the most efficiency because the goods are sold more quickly off the shelf and with fewer returns because they meet customers' individual needs more readily.

The point of these examples is to highlight that modern production is much more fluid and requires much more coordination and promotion. Productivity is still important, of course, but in the new economy there also is economic value in variety, customized service, timely innovation, and entertainment value. Thus many things are changing to entice the consumer to purchase. Shopping malls were once thought of as innovations in shopping convenience. The newest malls today incorporate theme parks, hotels, and even zoos. Entertainment values have become commonplace in the quest to get the consumer's attention.[21]

The consequences of these changes are profound. As producing things has become easier and as clerical tasks and record handling have become computerized, the importance of strategic management and promotion has grown. The advertising industry has grown to nearly $200 billion a year as businesses try to convince consumers to buy their products. Management in retail and other establishments uses bar codes to keep better track of inventory and goods in transit. This information is "mined" to better understand consumer buying habits so that companies can tailor their pitches to ever-smaller groups of customers. The Internet is used by consumers to track the best deals on products, despite the number of blinking icons of advertising that seek to lure them from the quest.

In today's world, the upscale market is huge. Combining the large numbers and high wages of managers and professionals (the first four categories in the tables) results in a total that indicates these workers earn slightly more than 50 percent of all earnings. This still underestimates the buying power of the group because they are more likely to have outside property income. Various indicators such as the amount of money spent on health clubs and foreign travel show that high-earning workers are willing to pay for improved products and unique recreational experiences.

Even among low-cost producers, the share of administrative labor is up. Just-in-time production and better quality control (fewer defective products) require greater coordination. Wal-Mart has found that a crucial component of its high-volume–low-margin approach is managing inventory; goods that don't sell quickly have to be sold at deep discounts or remaindered. Therefore, its staff need to be able to quickly restock what is selling and to minimize loss on what is staying on the shelves. All this requires administrative labor.

It should also be noted that advances in transportation and communication have created an integrated world market. As a result, businesses have been under more competitive pressure, which has undercut their ability to earn market rents that can be shared with their workforce. The expanded scale of production has required more coordinating labor to manage far-flung suppliers and off-shore plants. While managers and high-level business professionals have seen their roles expand, this increased competition has undercut the bargaining position of less- and medium-skilled production workers.

Finally, more resources are devoted to managing our real and financial assets. In 1959, 4.5 percent of the workforce was involved in finance, insurance, real estate, and other personal business activities; by 1997, the employment share of this group had risen to 6.6 percent.

For all these reasons, the employment of high-level business managers has grown dramatically. New information technology was critical in meeting new competitive requirements. Information technology allowed higher tolerances for measuring and monitoring quality. Computers allowed variety and customization with a few keystrokes.

Flexible, team-based organizational formats complemented the new flexible technology. Information technology also enabled greater flexibility, higher performance, and more shared risk in complex production and service networks that displaced the top-down hierarchies of big business and big government. In the past, many firms thought that they could best manage production and profitability if they internalized all of their costs. Today, this approach—as exemplified by Ford's River Rouge plant—has been replaced by outsourcing and just-in-time production, with firms and suppliers developing close relations. Conversely, there previously had been little standardization in health care, education, and retail outlets. But high costs and other inefficiencies have forced more standardization and networking between firms and their suppliers in these industries. As these new networks of production and service delivery institutions have proliferated, more skilled workers (and consumers) are necessary to create and navigate in this new environment.

So the transition from primary (agriculture) to secondary (manufacturing) to tertiary (service) activities has been miscast. A better way to think of these stages of capitalist development might be from primary as subsistence production to secondary as mass production to tertiary as driven by complex consumer demand for nonstandard goods and services with performance standards more akin to service markets than the traditional market for material goods. In the tertiary stage, management, marketing, financial transactions, and other service functions add greater value in the increasingly complex production and service networks to deliver products high in quality, variety, entertainment value, customization, convenience, and continuous innovation.

CONCLUSIONS

We have seen that the shift to high-skilled services has initially led to increasing inequality and greater returns to college education. Have these trends plateaued? Are they going to reverse themselves? Or continue forward to high levels of inequality? Continued low unemployment in the mid-1990s has driven wages up at the bottom of the earnings scale and stabilized relative wages in general. This strong macroeconomic effect has been used by many economists to show that inequality is not connected to technological change, which is continuing to be adopted at high rates.

But growth is not likely to continue at this pace and is likely to be interrupted by periodic recessions. What will happen then?

In our view, unaided markets are unlikely to bring the supply and demand for skilled workers sufficiently back into balance to reestablish the more gentle income differences characteristic of the early postwar years. The differences between the nation's education haves and education have-nots are simply too great to rely on market forces to close them. The increase in the requisite cognitive skills is daunting. Fully 40 percent of Americans have skills below those with at least some college according to the National Adult Literacy Survey (NALS), the modal skill requirement in the new economy.[22]

The new problem-solving and interpersonal skill requirements have only upped the skill ante for good jobs. Moreover, the broader problem-solving and interpersonal skills necessary in the new service economy appear to be more culturally and class bound than the relatively narrow technical and vocational skills characteristic of the old industrial economy. One piece of evidence is that linguistic, racial, and class bias is showing up more in hiring for service jobs than we saw in the old manufacturing economy, where vocational and technical skills took precedence.[23]

This means that people without at least some postsecondary education will have difficulty getting jobs that train or are connected to the new networks of production and service delivery. The problems will be much worse for high school dropouts, who are likely to have extended periods detached from the labor market. The new welfare strategy, which limits duration and requires work, may be successful for some. But many do not have the skills to obtain jobs that pay more than the minimum wage.[24]

In the longer term, the preferred strategy for reducing earnings disparities is education. It is America's preferred "third way" between an expanded welfare state and runaway markets. It preserves the responsibility of individuals in determining their economic fate—a definite plus at a time when the policy dialogue has shifted from the language of "rights" to the language of "individual responsibility."

But education alone may also not be enough to reverse the high level of inequality we now have. As we have seen in the 1990s, a strong macroeconomic climate has many beneficial effects. And we should reconsider microeconomic sectorial policies that promote jobs and higher earnings for nonprofessional labor. For instance, now that we know that we can create good jobs in private services, we could consider creating more good service jobs to serve social needs. Today, our education and health-care systems are underperforming, and we are woefully underinvesting in critical social services, especially child care. By investing in critical social programs and services, however, we would promote the general welfare and create a whole new wave of high-wage, high-skilled jobs in white-collar service functions.

While expansion of publicly delivered child-care programs in the United States is unlikely, mixing private delivery with public tax incentives and regulation is a possible alternative. Tax-incentive programs could encourage more Americans to enter a private child-care market that would be governed by public quality standards and more rigorous professional certification.

The American economy has clearly enjoyed success in the second half of the 1990s—a surprise, perhaps, given its shift toward the services sector. It is using flexibility and scale to stay on a course of economic prosperity and growth. But flexibility and scale alone will not sustain us. Other nations are learning to be more flexible and are creating scale as well through partnerships such as the European Economic Union. Nations such as China and India that already have scale are beginning to accumulate human capital. Economic advantages are always temporary. In the final analysis, our economic and educational prospects depend on our investments in ourselves and in our children.

9

DISCRIMINATION IN THE LABOR MARKET

Patrick L. Mason

Predictive prophecy, especially of the short-term kind, is a notoriously risky business because it is subject to falsification. . . . It has been observed that the effect of disconfirmation is not, as we might imagine, the collapse of the belief system that gave rise to the prediction, at least not immediately, but rather explanations, rationalizations, reinterpretations of nonfulfillment, sometimes very ingenious, rescheduling of the predicted event . . . and a more intense campaign to persuade oneself, or the group, and possibly others, of the truth of the original prediction.
—Joseph Blenkinsopp, *A History of Prophecy in Israel*

1. INTRODUCTION

Like all other belief systems, economic theory is a mixture of faith and reason. Sometimes its predictions are inspired revelations regarding the production and distribution of wealth; sometimes its prophecies are little more than conservative political ideology masquerading as science. Much depends on how its laws are applied and how its predictions are interpreted. Economic theories and empirical studies of racial discrimination provide a particularly attractive venue for separating the elements of faith in orthodox economic theory from the observable reality of market outcomes.

Consider for example two pillars of the neoclassical tradition that will be the especial concerns of this chapter, the law of one price and the presumption that economic agents are rational actors. *The law of one price* states that identical goods and services will receive an identical price, as long as market competition is given free rein. In competitive labor markets, the law of one price means that workers with identical productive capacity will receive identical compensation. As *rational actors,* individuals (and firms) make use of all available economic information, engage in another unit of activity only when the additional expected benefits exceed the additional expected costs of the activity, and do not make systemic errors in economic prediction. When applied to the labor market, the rationality postulate suggests that workers will not accumulate costly attributes that do not provide a premium in the market. For example, many fewer workers would engage in on-the-job training if such training did not increase their market pay.

When applied to the issue of labor market discrimination, these two tenets of orthodoxy yield two rather extraordinary predictions. First, a commonly recognized prediction of the neoclassical theory of discrimination is that persistent racial (or gender or religious or any kind of noneconomic) discrimination is inconsistent with competitive markets. Nobel laureate Kenneth Arrow says that "if the logic of the competitive system is accepted, discrimination should . . . be undermined in the long run."[1] Nobel laureate Milton Friedman has also made a similar statement: "The preserves of discrimination against groups of particular color or religion is least in those areas where there is the greatest freedom of competition."[2] According to the orthodox perspective, discrimination may exist at any point in time. We may even observe regional or otherwise isolated instances of discrimination for or against a particular group. However, the fundamental orthodox prophecy is that the competitive forces of the market will swiftly eliminate systemic discrimination against a particular group. Hence it is argued that persistent racial discrimination will occur if and only if there are areas of social and economic life that are persistently shielded from competition.

When racial discrimination does not exist there are no economic benefits to racial identity. If the act of acquiring and maintaining racial identity is a costly enterprise with no economic benefits, rational individuals should cease to engage in racial differentiation.[3] Here then is the implicit prediction of the neoclassical theory of racial discrimination that to my knowledge has never been openly stated. Namely, in an economy characterized by competitive markets the intensity of racial identity will quickly decline and become insignificant. Competitive markets eliminate both racial discrimination and racial differentiation.

The new orthodoxy in macroeconomics also suggests that both predictions should come to fruition in "the long run." There is a consensus among macroeconomists that the economy will reach full employment at stable prices in the long run. This implies the law of one price will also have time to become fully operative. At full employment with stable prices, the assertion is that each worker who is willing and able to work is employed at exactly the number of hours that worker chooses at the wage that is determined solely by individual productive capability. Unfortunately, macroeconomists do not know how much calendar time must elapse before the economy is in the long run. Although many economists do not agree with "real business cycle" theorists who assert that the economy is always in long-run equilibrium, most macroeconomists would allow that a decade is more than sufficient time for competitive forces to assert themselves fully. If we apply the orthodox macroeconomic understanding of the long run to the orthodox theory of discrimination, all racial discrimination in the labor market as well as the racial identities themselves should be eliminated from the economy in less than a decade.

Regardless of whether one begins counting from 1865, 1945, 1965, or even from 1973, however, neither the withering away of racial discrimination in the labor market nor the withering away of racial identity in American society has been an empirical reality. After surveying a wide range of empirical studies, William A. Darity Jr. and Patrick L. Mason conclude that African-American men earn 15 percent less on average than white men due to labor market discrimination.[4] Douglass Massey and Nancy Denton establish that regardless of income level or region of the country African Americans live in heavily racially segregated neighborhoods.[5] From Cedric Herring and Charles Amissah, we learn that Native Americans, Asian Americans, Jews, West European Americans, and East European Americans are more likely than African Americans to object to having their children attend schools where up to half of the children are African Americans.[6] Asian Americans, West European Americans, Native Americans, and individuals professing no ethnic identity are much more likely than African Americans to favor laws banning interracial marriages. Each of these racial or ethnic groups, as well as Latinos, is less willing than African Americans to vote for an African-American presidential candidate.

Racial discrimination and racial identities have therefore not ceased to exist. Yet the belief system and specific theories that gave rise to these prophecies have not collapsed. The remainder of this chapter explores the explanations, rationalizations, and sometimes very ingenious reinterpretations of theory that have been used to explain why these events have not occurred. It also presents the theoretical and empirical weaknesses associated with the continuing campaign of empirical revisionism by some orthodox economists to persuade themselves, their profession, and the general public of the assertion that racial discrimination has disappeared or will soon do so.

Section 2 presents recent evidence of labor market inequality by race and by sex. Section 3 provides an understanding of what economists mean by labor market discrimination, so that we will have a common understanding of what it is that analysts are trying to explain. Section 4 takes a look at neoclassical or orthodox theories of discrimination. This is the dominant explanation of why discrimination exists and how it is affected by market competition. Section 5 examines the empirical evidence on persistent racial discrimination within the labor market. Because I conclude that orthodox theories of racial inequality are not in tune with the empirical evidence on racial discrimination, I provide a heterodox theory of discrimination in section 6. The penultimate section of this chapter briefly explores the emerging literature on the economics of racial identity formation. This section examines the relationship between the persistence of racial identity formation and wealth accumulation. The primary results of sections 6 and 7 are that the competitive process establishes incentives for persistent racial discrimination within the labor market and persistent reproduction of racial identities and racial conflict, respectively. I conclude with a discussion of this chapter's results and their implications for political action.

2. SOME RECENT LABOR MARKET OUTCOMES

The 1940s and the 1960s were periods of progress for African-American men. In 1940, the hourly wage ratio was 0.43—that is, African-American men earned 43 cents for every dollar earned by white men. By 1950, the wage ratio was 0.55. This ratio increased only by three percentage points during the 1950s, ending the decade at 0.58. During the twenty-year interval from 1960 to 1980 the wage ratio increased by 15 percentage points to 0.73. However, the bulk of this improvement occurred during 1965–74, the early years of the affirmative action era. This was a period of very tight labor markets, partially caused by the Vietnam War, and of significant federal spending on employment training and job creation.

There was a substantial decline in interracial inequality between the passage of the Civil Rights Act of 1965 and the deep recession of 1974. The primary cause of this improvement during 1965–74 was a relative increase in the return to education.[7] Thus the increase in the wage ratio was the result of substantial improvements in the quantity and quality of African-American education. But it also had to do, as we shall see, with greater demand for African-American labor as a result of declining labor market discrimination due to both government civil rights policy and tight labor markets.

Figure 9.1 (page 162) presents the average weekly wage by race and by sex from 1961 to 1996.[8] Regardless of race, recent wage outcomes for men have not been encouraging. For white men, weekly wages rose throughout the 1960s before peaking at $734 in 1972. From there the mean wage rate for white males ultimately declined to $698 in 1982. Although the late 1980s saw white male weekly wages reach the peak values of the early 1970s, by 1993 their weekly wages were $694. The final two years of data do show that white male weekly wages reached an all-time high of $763. Among African-American men weekly wage rates rose during the 1960s before encountering a plateau of $513 in 1972. During the late 1970s African-American male weekly wages moved upward slightly to $535, but the post-1978 period has been characterized by a long series of annual wage declines. For example, during 1978–84 their weekly wage dropped by $52 to $483. After experiencing a modest recovery during the mid-1980s, the weekly wage of African-American men declined from $536 to $495 during 1988–91. Weekly wages did rise during the 1990s but it was not until 1995 that African-American male wages had finally overtaken their 1978 peak.

There is a different pattern among women. Throughout the 1960s the weekly wage rose faster among African-American women than among white women. From 1972 to 1977, the wages of African-American women grew at a slower pace but continued to rise relative to those of white women. By 1977 there was racial parity at $361 in

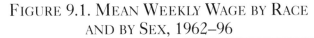

FIGURE 9.1. MEAN WEEKLY WAGE BY RACE
AND BY SEX, 1962–96

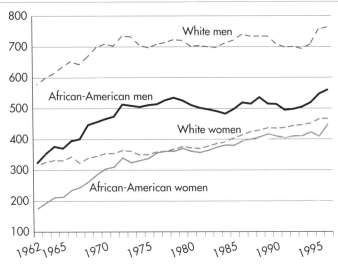

Source: U.S. Department of Commerce, Bureau of the Census, *Current Population Survey,*
Annual Demographic Files, March 1963–98.

women's weekly wages. Thereafter, the wages of white women grew faster but the wages of both races continued to rise. By 1996 white women were earning $467 per week while African-American women earned $448 per week.

There have been periods of sharp reductions in weekly hours of employment for both white and African-American men (see Figure 9.2). The decade from 1973 to 1983 saw white male weekly work decline from thirty-eight to thirty-five hours of employment. From 1983 to 1997 white male weekly hours of employment rose to thirty-nine. The recessions of the middle 1970s and the early 1980s had a much greater impact on the employment of African-American men. Moreover, African-American males' employment hours were also much more greatly damaged by the recession of the early 1990s than were those of their white counterparts. In 1973 African-American men averaged thirty-six hours per week of employment, an all-time high. By 1975 they averaged just twenty-nine hours per week. During the recovery of the late 1970s African-American male weekly hours of employment rose to thirty-four in 1978, before declining to thirty-one in 1983. Only during 1995–97 did African-American male employment begin to fluctuate around thirty-five hours per week, that is, the typical workweek of the

FIGURE 9.2. MEAN WEEKLY HOURS OF WORK
BY RACE AND BY SEX, 1968–97

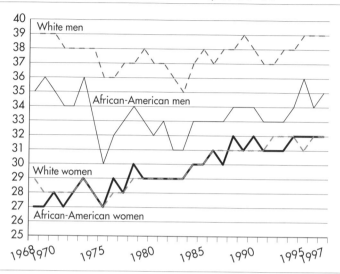

Source: U.S. Department of Commerce, Bureau of the Census, *Current Population Survey,* Annual Demographic Files, March 1963–98.

late 1960s. Notably, the peak years of African-American weekly hours of employment are equal to the better years of white male employment. Also, there seems to be a permanent gap (which rises during recessions) of at least four hours per week of employment between African-American and white men. Over the course of a year, then, white males can expect to enjoy 5.2 weeks more employment than African-American men, with this differential increasing during recessions.

Again, the picture is very different among women. Regardless of race, female weekly hours of employment rose continuously during the 1970s, 1980s, and 1990s. There are no appreciable differences by race. Hours of weekly employment for both groups of women rose from twenty-seven in 1975 to thirty-two in 1997.

Figure 9.3 (page 164) shows changes in the racial wage ratio for men and women. In 1965 African-American women earned 64 cents for every dollar earned by white women. By 1977 African-American women earned weekly wages equivalent to those of white women. Thereafter, the wage ratio declined to 88 cents on the dollar by 1995 before making a substantial rebound to 96 cents on the dollar in 1996. The male racial wage ratio shows an even more disappointing trend. Starting from 0.58 in 1965 the male ratio rose to 74 cents on

FIGURE 9.3. RATIO OF AFRICAN-AMERICAN WAGE
TO WHITE WAGE BY SEX, 1962–96

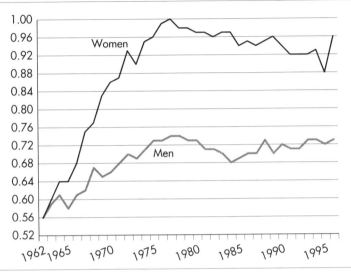

Source: U.S. Department of Commerce, Bureau of the Census, *Current Population Survey,*
Annual Demographic Files, March 1963–98.

the dollar in 1977. The male racial wage ratio declined for the next
seven years, bottoming out at 68 cents on the dollar in 1984. By 1996
African-American men earned 73 cents for every dollar earned by
white men—identical to the male wage ratio in 1975.

3. WHAT DO ECONOMISTS MEAN
BY DISCRIMINATION?

*When a person makes an explicit vow to The Lord con-
cerning the equivalent for a human being, the equivalent for
a male shall be fifty shekels of silver. . . . If the person is a
female, the equivalent is thirty shekels.*

—Leviticus 27:3–4

Racial economic inequality exists whenever there exist differential distributions of economic outcomes for individuals across racial groups.
Nevertheless, some racial economic inequality may not represent racial

discrimination in the labor market. There are at least four reasons for unequal economic outcomes. We may observe unequal economic outcomes because economically identical persons are engaged in income-producing activities with unequal noneconomic characteristics, such as the pleasantness of working conditions or the length of commuting time to work. Or unequal outcomes may occur because economically identical persons are treated differently within noncompetitive markets. We may observe inequality because individuals are unequal in terms of the income-producing capacities (assets) they bring to the market. These assets might include such factors as years of education, cognitive ability, class background, or years of experience. Finally, we may observe unequal economic outcomes because economically identical individuals are treated differently within competitive markets.

Suppose, for example, a sample of African Americans and a sample of whites are identical in terms of the attributes that are important in obtaining wages and salaries—the major form of income in the United States. In other words, the average level of education, training, experience, and other productive attributes are the same for both groups. However, the sample of African Americans has a higher fraction of persons who are employed at unpleasant work or work that is very dangerous. This is a case of economically identical persons engaged in income-producing activities with unequal noneconomic characteristics—unpleasant or dangerous working conditions. Ever since Adam Smith, economists have argued that competitive markets will yield differences in pay to compensate for the differences in such noneconomic characteristics. In this instance, the African-American workers should receive higher pay to compensate for their more undesirable jobs. So the total satisfaction of the jobs will be equal even though the financial compensation is not equal. Compensating wage differentials of this sort are not the focus of the economics of discrimination.

Economists of all stripes agree that differential treatment can occur when competitive forces are not in operation. Consider professional baseball before free agency. Players could move between teams only with the permission of their current team's owner. New teams could not enter the league without the collective permission of current owners. Because owners operated without competitive constraints, they could (and did) pay players differently than their productive contributions would warrant in a competitive marketplace. African-American players with the same competitive skills as whites were less likely to play in the major leagues and, if they were employed in the major leagues, they frequently received lower compensation. Since most areas of employment are subject to considerable labor mobility and competitive entry from other firms, especially over longer periods of time, the theoretical work on racial inequality has tried to explain racially differential outcomes when competitive conditions exist. Economists argue that discrimination exists when otherwise identical individuals receive differential treatment. The economics of discrimination then focuses on unequal compensation for economically identical groups that occurs for reasons other than compensating differentials.

Both individuals and groups arrive in the labor market with unequal income-generating capacity. If individuals with higher levels of education tend to require less supervision, make more imaginative decisions, and have a greater talent for problem solving, they will produce a greater amount of revenue during a given period of time than individuals with lower levels of education. Similarly, some individuals such as Michael Jordan or Michael Jackson arrive on the market with greater physical or artistic abilities than others. Persons with superior athletic ability will tend to win more sporting contests than those of lesser athletic ability, while persons with greater artistic ability may produce art of higher quality than persons with more limited capacities for artistic expression. Differences in skill, then, will produce inequality of income.

If income inequality between groups can be explained by differences in skill, then theories of racial inequality assert that no discrimination has taken place within the market. The absence of market discrimination in this instance, however, does not necessarily imply that the distribution of income that results from skill inequality is not a social problem. Moreover, the absence of market discrimination does not imply that no discrimination has taken place in the acquisition of skills prior to market entry. The education process, for instance, may be quite discriminatory. Also, the absence of wage discrimination does not imply the absence of employment, occupation, and training discrimination.

The bulk of theoretical and empirical research on the economics of discrimination has sought to determine whether and to what extent economically identical individuals receive differential treatment within competitive markets. Consider Figure 9.4. Here we have presented the residual African-American–white wage differential, by sex, for the years

FIGURE 9.4. RACIAL WAGE RESIDUAL, 1962–96

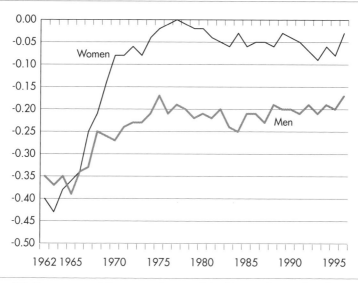

Source: U.S. Department of Commerce, Bureau of the Census, *Current Population Survey,* Annual Demographic Files, March 1963–98.

1967–92. The residual wage differential records the racial wage gap when we have adjusted for group differences in regional location, years of education, potential experience, region of origin, and marital status. After adjusting for racial differences in characteristics, we find that in 1996 African-American men and women earned 17 percent and 4 percent less, respectively, than their white counterparts.

The long-term pattern of the residual wage differential suggests that racial inequality is not declining, at least not since 1975. From the 1960s through the mid-1970s the male racial wage differential did decline. African-American males made 39 percent less in 1965 and 17 percent less in 1975. By 1984 the male residual had ballooned to 25 percent. After 1984 the male racial wage residual oscillated around 20 percent before declining to 17 percent in 1996.

Although there is less wage inequality among women, the long-term movement in female wage inequality is similar to that among men. In 1965 the female racial wage residual was 36 percent, but by 1977 racial parity was achieved. However, the female racial wage residual declined by nine percentage points over the next sixteen years, bottoming out at 9 percent in 1993. There was a recovery to 3 percent in 1996.

Despite the persistence of these residual racial wage differences, and indeed their expansion since the mid-1970s, many economists have come to believe that racial discrimination is no longer a major problem within the labor market. As we shall see, various economists have explained the residual wage difference in nondiscriminating ways. Their arguments, however, do not hold up.

4. Prophecies on the Existence and Abolition of Discrimination

Then I heard the voice of The Lord saying . . . make the mind of this people dull, and stop their ears, and shut their eyes, so that they may not look with their eyes, and listen with their ears, and comprehend with their minds, and turn and be healed.

—Isaiah, 6:8–9

A wage rate is, of course, a price. Economically identical workers who happen to differ by race or sex represent multiple providers of a homogeneous service to the market. As such, the existence of discrimination within competitive markets would mean that there are multiple prices for an otherwise homogeneous service. Such an empirical phenomenon does not rest easily within the boundaries of neoclassical economic theory. If the residual wage differential is a measure of labor market discrimination it implies that the labor market can have multiple wages for economically identical workers, an African-American male wage, an African-American female wage, a white male wage, and a white female wage.

As noted before, the so-called law of one price is among the most widely accepted notions of neoclassical economics. The law of one price says we cannot have multiple prices for a homogeneous good or service within competitive markets. The fundamental notion here is that competition creates uniformity—all goods and services that are alike are treated identically in the marketplace. If competitive conditions prevail throughout the economy, the law of one price implies that full employment will also exist. Indeed, the law of one price also assumes that economically identical individuals will have identical access to on-the-job training, identical occupational mobility and promotion, and identical chances of being fired or laid off.

PROPHECIES ON BIGOTRY

Racial and sexual discrimination in both the real world and in theoretical models are not the same things as racism and sexism. Indeed, most economic theories of racial and sexual discrimination are not based on an understanding of racism and sexism. As a rule, economic theories of discrimination do not attempt to provide an explanation of the socioeconomic construction of race or gender categories. Racial and gender identities are taken as given. That is to say, economists assume that noneconomic social, historical, or psychological factors are responsible for sorting individuals into racial categories. Orthodox economic theorists assume that the causal reasons for discrimination are either malevolent preferences (bigotry) or incorrect or insufficient information to judge justly (prejudice) the productive characteristics of workers. What I have labeled here as models of bigotry and prejudice focus on individual behavior and individual information and strictly avoid integrating power relationships between groups into the economic analysis of discrimination. But understanding racism necessarily requires a close examination of the distribution of economic and social power between African Americans and whites. In particular, an economic theory of discrimination that is based on racism must explain how phenotype and distinctive cultural practices factor into productive property or capital and persistent wage differentials.

Consider Nobel laureate Gary Becker's well-known "taste" or preference theory of discrimination as an economic examination of the interaction between competition and bigotry.[9] Becker asks a rather simple question: If there is a subset of individuals within society who regard economic association with other racially distinct individuals as psychologically undesirable, will these tastes for discrimination have a sustained impact on economic outcomes? The individuals with a preference for discrimination may be consumers, employers, or employees. Becker argues that although this form of bigotry produces segregation, such preferences will not produce sustained interracial differences in wages, employment, or occupational attainment when the general conditions for a competitive economy are met.

This cardinal conclusion of Becker's model flows directly from the law of one price, which maintains that the competitive forces of the market will undermine the economic impact of irrational preferences in the market. For Becker, bigotry is an irrational preference since it is exogenously given and can be maintained only at a prohibitive cost to the employer, employee, or consumer.

PROPHECIES ON PREJUDICE

Kenneth Arrow focused on the interconnections among discrimination, competition, and information.[10] Rather than assume malevolent preferences—that is to say, bigotry—Arrow explored the consequences of prejudice. Arrow asked, "what are the economic consequences of imperfect or incomplete information by employers regarding the future productivity of new hires?" In particular, suppose all employers are "white" while only some workers are "white" but others are "black," and employers have less accurate information about black workers than about white workers.

Arrow's informational asymmetry provides the basis for so-called statistical discrimination models. Suppose employers must hire both skilled and unskilled workers. Becoming a skilled worker requires both worker and firm investment in human capital. Employers invest human capital solely in qualified workers, where a worker is qualified who already has made a personal investment in human capital that is not observable without error. The worker's own investment does not refer to easily observable items such as education and experience, "but more subtle types [of human capital] the employer cannot observe directly: the habits of action and thought that favor good performance in skilled jobs, steadiness, punctuality, responsiveness, and initiative."[11]

Employers seek to earn an identical return on investment in black and white workers, but employers' prejudices lead them to believe wrongly that a smaller fraction of blacks are qualified than whites. In effect, "race" becomes a cheaply observable variable for identifying workers who are more or less likely to be qualified. Arrow showed that wage discrimination will exist against blacks. If for some reason employers are prevented from practicing wage discrimination, then their beliefs and profit-maximizing behavior will lead them to exclude blacks from the skilled labor group.

According to the statistical discrimination model, this discrimination must persist despite powerful long-run competitive dynamics. Given the entry and exit of firms over time, however, the discriminatory equilibrium will persist only if employers do not learn over time and a uniform distribution of prejudice exists across all firms. Arrow's model of prejudice is a short-run explanation of why discrimination may exist at a given point in time; however, it is not an adequate explanation of why discrimination persists over substantial periods of time. The law of one price may not hold in the short run, but it always rules in the long-run outcomes of neoclassical models of discrimination. Since Arrow's pioneering work, there have been a large number of theories of racial inequality that focus on information problems as the source of discrimination, but all information theories of racial inequality are merely specific models of prejudice. In the long run, none are consistent with the law of one price.

5. Cognitive Dissonance: Explanations, Rationalization, and Reinterpretations of Inaccurate Predictions

If you do not stand in faith, you shall not stand at all.
—Isaiah 7:9

Given the theoretical difficulties of explaining persistent discrimination, many empirical studies throughout the 1960s and 1970s sought simply to measure the extent of discrimination without providing a theory of its existence.[12] As noted, the law of one price implies that regardless of race, and after adjusting for compensating differentials and noncompetitive conditions, individual wage rates are determined by individual productive capacity (see Table 9.1, page 172). Of course, individual productive capacity is not directly measurable. Hence, empirical studies of the wage determination process employ a series of productivity-linked proxy variables, such as years of education, experience, employment tenure, and training. *It is further assumed that none of the productivity-linked characteristics are influenced by market discrimination.* If market discrimination has an impact on individual acquisition of a productivity-linked characteristic—for example, if there is racial discrimination in access to

TABLE 9.1. WAGE DETERMINATION PROCESS

Individual wage rate	◄─	Individual productive capacity
	+	compensating differentials
	+	noncompetitive characteristics
	+	race
Individual wage rate	◄─	Productivity-linked characteristics (education, experience, training, and so on)
	+	compensating differentials (region, location)
	+	noncompetitive characteristics (union)
	+	race

on-the-job training—it would be inappropriate to use that characteristic as an explanatory variable. Because racial identity is theoretically not a productivity-linked characteristic, the orthodox theory of discrimination argues that it will have no impact on individual wage rates. Yet a flood of economic studies have found a racial wage residual on the order of magnitude of those in Figure 9.4.[13]

How does one reconcile a persistent racial wage residual differential with a theoretical credo that says market discrimination cannot persist? What accounts for the post-1973 persistence of racial wage inequality, and for the increasing inequality seen in some years? Defenders of the orthodox faith resolve their cognitive dissonance by suggesting that so-called pre-market factors are primarily responsible for both the male and female racial residual wage differential. Pre-market factors are those attributes that affect skill accumulation prior to market entry. It is argued that the post-1973 increase in racial inequality may be explained by an increase in the rate of return to skill, but racial differences in skill accumulation are determined by racial differences in pre-market attributes. The canon of alleged pre-market factors includes racial differences in the quality of education, culture, genetic endowment, or household and community environment.[14] Similarly, a difference in actual versus potential experience is put forward as an explanation of black-white as well as male-female wage differences.[15] Some defenders of the orthodox faith also accept but do not attempt to corroborate that discrimination in pre-market activities may reduce the quality or quantity of productive attributes attained by African Americans and women.[16] The argument is that racial differences in these pre-market factors lead to relatively lower

cognitive skill accumulation among African Americans. It is therefore argued that the post-1973 change in the racial residual wage differential is not primarily a measure of labor market discrimination, it
is a measure of the impact of racial differences in pre-market factors.

The pre-market factors incantation preserves the law of one price.
It preserves the claim of equal pay in the labor market for equally
skilled persons, but allows that there is inequality in the pre-market
accumulation of productive attributes. Pre-market racial inequality
may persist because of racial differences in family values, genetic
endowment, schools, neighborhood culture and values, and individual
preferences and decisions regarding group association. Competition
among profit-seeking firms along with freely mobile workers ensures
equal pay for equally skilled workers within the market, but competitive forces are largely absent from the institutions and processes that
govern pre-market skill accumulation. Notably, as the pre-market factors explanation absolves institutions, persons, and processes within
the labor market of contributing to persistent racial inequality, it simultaneously says that racial wage inequality most likely exists because of
some form of deficiency among African Americans.

Consider Thomas Sowell's argument that the negative residual
wage differential results from African-American cultural values, such
as an alleged inability to engage in deferred gratification, rather than
market discrimination.[17] Sowell offers no empirical evidence to confirm his speculations. However, there is a wealth of data that strongly
contradicts his assertions. Jeremiah Cotton's analysis of non-Hispanic
white, non-Hispanic black, Hispanic white, and Hispanic black males,
drawn from the 1976 to 1984 *Current Population Survey*, finds a
pattern of earnings discrimination in favor of non-Hispanic whites.[18]
Cotton shows that 40 percent of the earnings differentials between
non-Hispanic white and Hispanic black and between non-Hispanic
white and non-Hispanic black can be attributed to differences in productive attributes such as education and experience and that 60 percent is due to the combination of minority disadvantage and white
advantage. Minority disadvantage is defined by below-average rates
of return to education, experience, and other individual attributes,
while white advantage represents above-average rates of return to
productive attributes. For non-Hispanic white and Hispanic white
earnings differentials, over 65 percent can be explained by differences in productive attributes with the remainder attributed to either
white advantage or minority disadvantage.

Many other empirical studies also contradict Sowell's assertions. Among Mexican Americans, Edward Telles and Edward Murguia found that "lighter" or European phenotype Mexican Americans earn more than "darker" or Native American phenotype Mexican Americans.[19] Among Latinos, Mason was able to show that white Latinos earn nearly 10 percent more than brown Latinos.[20] Brown Latinos earned less than white Latinos regardless of whether the sample includes all Latinos, only Mexican Americans, only native-born Latinos, only immigrant Latinos, or only non-Mexican Latinos. Darity, Guilkey, and Winfrey found that regardless of cultural heritage, there is a sizable wage penalty for African-American males.[21] That is to say, the group found that regardless of whether an African American is native-born, a Caribbean or African immigrant, or even if he has some European heritage, there is a wage penalty of about 15 percent relative to otherwise identical white males.

Finis Welch was an early proponent of the argument that relatively lower educational quality among African Americans is responsible for interracial wage differences.[22] Although the average level of education of all Americans has been on an upward trend for many decades, for nearly every decade since the end of slavery the African-American mean years of schooling has tended to show annual increases relative to white mean years of schooling.[23] Today, whites average only about 0.5 more years of schooling than African Americans. Also, during the 1970s and 1980s, as racial inequality was increasing, the educational achievement scores of African Americans were increasing relative to the achievement scores of whites.[24] Gerald Jaynes and Robin Williams write, "In sum, over the relatively short period from 1970 to 1980, the gap between average academic performance of white and black school children narrowed appreciably. The effects are visible for all levels of ability and for all types of communities. The data suggest that the largest impact was in rural areas."[25]

In short, although years of schooling and academic achievement (as measured by standardized test scores) among African Americans are lower than among whites, African-American growth in both years of education and educational quality outpaced white growth in these areas during the 1970s and 1980s. If the racial residual wage differential is only a measure of differences in educational quality, the residual should have declined throughout the 1970s and 1980s. Yet the residual stagnated after 1973 and began to expand after 1979–80.[26]

My own research directly challenges the notion that African-American household or community values are responsible for lower skill accumulation and hence racial inequality in the labor market. I find that although family values (or behaviors) matter, family values explain only a small proportion of the variation in wages, hours, or educational attainment within race-sex groups (see Table 9.2).[27] Class, as measured by the socioeconomic status of one's parents, grandparents, and neighborhood, tends to be nearly twice as important. Notably, interracial differences in class are directly related to past discrimination. I also found that interracial differences in family values explain little if any of the interracial differentials in wages, hours of employment, or educational attainment. Despite extraordinary controls for individual differences, family values, and family class status, I found that young African-American men received a 21 percent wage penalty relative to young white men, along with a 17 percent employment (320 hours) penalty. Relative to young white men, young African-American women receive a 33 percent wage penalty and a 48

TABLE 9.2. PERCENTAGE OF VARIATION EXPLAINED
BY VALUES AND CLASS, BY RACE AND SEX

	HOURLY WAGE	YEARS OF EDUCATION	ANNUAL HOURS OF WORK
African-American Men			
Values	2–5	5–9	2–4
Class	10–13	25–29	8–9
African-American Women			
Values	3–8	4–9	4–9
Class	7–12	20–26	7–12
White Men			
Values	1–3	6–22	3–3
Class	4–6	17–33	5–5
White Women			
Values	2–4	8–26	2–2
Class	4–6	15–33	5–5

Source: Patrick L. Mason, "Family Environment and Intergenerational Well-being: Some Preliminary Results," in William E. Spriggs, ed., *State of Black America* (Washington, D.C.: Urban League, 1999), pp. 45–90.

percent (882 hours) reduction in annual workhours. This is a clear indication that racial discrimination has reduced the demand for African-American workers. The lower demand for African Americans in the labor market occurred despite the fact that African Americans were able to transform a given amount of resources into greater educational attainment than otherwise identical young white adults.

The most sophisticated line of neoclassical research argues that the racial wage residual between whites and African Americans began to expand after 1979 when skill-biased technical change increased both intra- and interracial wage inequality.[28] The assertion is that technological progress—computerization, automation, and dramatic improvements in communications and transportation—produced an increase in the demand for cognitive skill among workers. Further, as the rate of return to cognitive ability has surged higher, wage inequality has increased among whites. As intraracial inequality among whites increases as a result of the rising skill premium, interracial inequality between whites and African Americans will also increase because African Americans are disproportionately located in the lower half of the skill distribution.[29]

Figure 9.5 presents changes in white male wage inequality for 1962–96. It does not show that interracial inequality follows the same pattern as white intraracial inequality. For example, white male inequality increased during 1966–73, but we know from Figure 9.4 that the size of the male racial wage differential was declining during this period. Similarly, as white male inequality was declining during 1973–80 the male residual wage difference grew by five percentage points between 1974 and 1980. Only during 1979–84 do we observe an increase in intraracial inequality among whites matched by stagnation in interracial inequality.

The argument that the 1970s and 1980s witnessed an increasing rate of return to skill does have some merit. Figure 9.6 shows that the male college graduate–high school wage premium was 35 percent in 1980 but 58 percent in 1996. For women, it shows that the college graduate–high school wage premium was 40 percent in 1978 but better than 61 percent for 1996. The least educated men, those with less than twelve years of education, earned 26 percent less than high school graduates in 1973 but 36 percent less in 1996. However, throughout the 1970s, 1980s, and 1990s the least educated women continued to earn about 30 percent less than women who graduated from high school. For both men and women with some education

FIGURE 9.5. WEEKLY WAGE INEQUALITY AMONG WHITE MALES, 1962–96

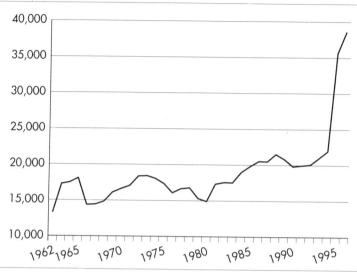

Source: U.S. Department of Commerce, Bureau of the Census, *Current Population Survey,* Annual Demographic Files, March 1963–98.

FIGURE 9.6. RATE OF RETURN TO EDUCATION, 1962–96

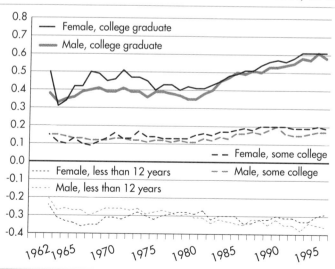

Source: U.S. Department of Commerce, Bureau of the Census, *Current Population Survey,* Annual Demographic Files, March 1963–98.

beyond high school, those described as having some college, the wage premium relative to high school graduates rose from 1979 to 1996.

Similarly, Figure 9.7 shows that the male rate of return to an additional year of experience rose during the late 1960s and early 1970s, but stagnated at about 2.3 percent during 1974–79. By 1985 the male rate of return to an additional year of experience had increased to 2.7 percent. However, for the next eleven years the rate of return to experience declined steadily, reaching 2.1 percent by 1996. The female rate of return to experience exhibited less dramatic and less consistent results, rising from 1.1 percent in 1969 to 1.4 percent in 1996.

In a more detailed study, I have found that an increase in the rate of return to cognitive ability (skill) has been a contributory factor to the post-1979 increase in male inequality among whites.[30] However, the rising skill premium occurred after African-American–white inequality began to expand in 1973. And the post-1979 increase in the rate of return to skill had no effect on the post-1979 growth in interracial inequality. Hence an increasing rate of return to skill may be a factor behind increasing intraracial wage

FIGURE 9.7. RATE OF RETURN TO EXPERIENCE, 1962–96

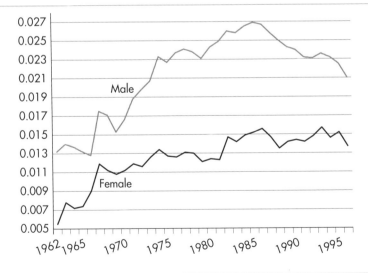

Source: U.S. Department of Commerce, Bureau of the Census, *Current Population Survey,* Annual Demographic Files, March 1963–98.

inequality—but it has only secondary importance for the rise in inter-racial wage inequality.

A similar result is found in the work of Mary Corcoran, and of John Bound and Laura Dresser.[31] Corcoran found that the African-American–white wage ratio remained stable during 1973–79, while Bound and Dresser demonstrated that the interracial wage differential began to deteriorate after 1973. Corcoran also reports that the inter-racial wage ratio for college graduates declined from 1.12 to 0.93 dur-ing 1973–91. That is, in 1973 young female African-American college graduates earned 12 percent more than their white counterparts (due primarily to greater actual labor market experience) but by 1991 they earned 7 percent less. The relative wage declines were even larger for African-American women with twelve or fewer years of education. So regardless of race the wages of young female high school graduates and dropouts fell during 1973–91—but the wages of African-American women fell faster. Also, regardless of race, the wages of college grad-uates rose during the 1980s, but the average wage of young white women increased faster. The largest wage declines during the 1980s for women with twelve or fewer years of education were in the Midwest, especially for African-American women.

Bound and Dresser show that in 1976 there was a 13 percent wage penalty for young African-American men relative to young white men. By 1985 this penalty had expanded to 28 percent. Over the same time period the white female-male wage penalty was cut in half, dropping from 33 percent to 16 percent. However, the African-American female—white male penalty oscillated around 30 percent. Bound and Dresser conclude that African Americans lost ground rel-ative to whites because of industrial shifts, especially in the Midwest. Deindustrialization, deunionization, and (for African-American women) a declining minimum wage had a disproportionate impact on African-American workers.

Finally, the notion that skill-biased technological change has led to an increasing demand for cognitive ability and thereby dramatically raised the wages of skilled workers relative to unskilled workers, with skilled workers replacing unskilled workers in many employment situ-ations, has not gone unchallenged.[32] Summarizing a large national and international literature, David Howell, Margaret Duncan, and Bennett Harrison uncover little direct evidence of a large-scale increase in tech-nological change that was capable of precipitating the sizable increase in wage inequality that occurred throughout the 1980s.[33] Most especially, they discredit the notion that computerization has been responsible for increasing wage inequality. They argue that computerization of the economy began in the mid-1980s—after wage inequality had already increased substantially. Howell and his colleagues conjecture that institutional and organizational changes may be primarily responsible for rising wage inequality. In particular, they argue that the combined impact of ideological changes by government, deregulation of industry and labor markets, deunionization, lower trade barriers, the reduced minimum wage, and communication and transportation changes that have increased the international mobility of capital have conspired to lower the wages of the most vulnerable workers.

After pointing to a number of empirical inconsistencies in the skill-biased technical change hypothesis, Dennis Snower also makes the case that an organizational revolution is responsible for increasing wage inequality.[34] According to Snower, more flexible human and physical capital, customization of products, vastly improved information technology (which reduces production snags), and greater decentralization of information and decisionmaking combined with more team-oriented production are dramatically reshaping the organization of work. Further, this workplace reorganization has increased the bargaining power and therefore wages of currently employed workers relative to potential replacement workers, as well as the work effort–wage relationship among workers. Thereby, the American economy has exhibited increasing inequality within and between education-experience groups.

6. Reconciling Theory and Data

The problem of the twentieth century is the problem of the color-line,—the relation of the darker to the lighter races of men in Asia and Africa, in America and the islands of the sea. It was a phase of this problem that caused the Civil War.
—William E. B. Dubois, *The Souls of Black Folk*

An alternative line of theoretical and empirical research suggests that what deterioration there has been in the racial wage differential reflects increasing labor market discrimination. A combination of factors is responsible for the increase in discrimination. First, there is the sub-stantial reversal of the federal government's commitment to antidis-crimination and affirmative action enforcement from 1981 onward.[35] Second, slack labor markets in the 1970s created greater incentives for employer and employee discrimination. There was greater com-petition for income among all workers, as well as reductions in the bar-gaining power and standard of living for many wage earners, especially production and nonsupervisory employees. As macroeconomic pres-sure and accompanying changes in the industrial structure pushed white males down the economic ladder, they began to dislodge African-American workers from lower-wage positions.[36] Third, the continuing decline of organized labor, especially in the private sector, contributed to both intra- and interracial wage inequality.

A focus on macroeconomic issues helps us to understand the slowdown initiated after 1973–75 and the deterioration in racial wage equality that occurred after 1979. According to the National Bureau of Economic Research, there was a sixteen-month recession from November 1973 to March 1975.[37] There was a six-month reces-sion from January 1980 to July 1980, with a one-year recovery from July 1980 to July 1981. However, the next recession also lasted six-teen months, July 1981 to November 1982. Prior to 1991 the average recession lasted just eleven months while the average boom lasted forty-three months. Excluding the 1973–75 and 1981–82 recessions, the two most severe postwar recessions, the average recession lasted just nine months.

The 1973–75 downturn saw the U.S. economy experience its first substantial period of stagflation as prices increased by a startling 8.95 percent in 1973–74 and 9.43 percent in 1974–75.[38] Prior to this reces-sion, the conventional wisdom among macroeconomists was that the economy could not experience a sustained period of rising unemploy-ment and inflation. Supposedly, a tradeoff existed between inflation and unemployment such that when one increased the other would decrease. The Federal Reserve System reacted to the stagflation of 1974–75 and the ensuing years of inflation by making a fundamental change in macroeconomic policy. The one-year "recovery" of 1980–81—the shortest recovery of the post–World War II era by half—was only a brief respite in a long period of stagnation from December 31, 1979 to December 31, 1982. Measuring output in 1992 dollars, the gross domestic product actually moved slightly downward from $4.63 trillion to $4.62 trillion during the three-year interval.[39]

Slack labor markets intensify job competition. Nontraditional theories of job competition have shown how racialized decisionmaking can lead to persistent racial discrimination within such a slack labor market. I have argued, along with authors such as William Darity and Rhonda Williams, that alternative approaches to competition—where competition is defined by a tendency toward equalization of rates of profit and where competition creates diversity of prices, products, management strategies, and compensation policies rather than homogeneity—are consistent with persistently unequal treatment because of race.[40] In short, the work of these articles applies a conception of the competitive process that abandons the law of one price. Culture in these models is not a mechanism for accumulating skill, it is a vehicle for collective action, especially action excluding "others" from economic opportunity. A labor market implication of this approach is that different pay across firms and industries for workers within the same occupation is the norm for competitive labor markets. In these models remuneration is a function of the characteristics of the individual and the job.[41]

A simple version of my own model suggests that the wage rate for the job is determined by the labor quality of the workforce, the competitive structure of the firm, and the bargaining power of workers. The competitive structure of the firm includes such factors as capital intensity, size of the firm, and the extent of fixed capital investment. The bargaining power of workers includes both the quality and the quantity of worker organization, where the quantity of worker organization represents the relative density of worker participation in collective activities (for example, the fraction of workers who are unionized) while the quality of worker organization represents the degree of effective cooperation among workers. So workers employed in jobs with high bargaining power, and those in large firms or firms with a large fixed capital investment, will earn more than identically skilled workers at jobs characterized by low bargaining power, or those in firms with low capital intensity or a low level of fixed capital investment. The competitive process then produces wage differentiation—not the wage homogeneity implied by the law of one price.

Inequality in hiring, remuneration, training, and promotion will tend to reduce worker solidarity. Some inequalities inhibit workers from focusing on the commonalities of their employment condition, for example, the struggle with management to increase the wages, hours, and working conditions of workers as a class rather than merely improving the circumstances of particularly favored individuals or a preferred group. Because inequality among a firm's workforce tends to reduce the quality of worker organization (and maybe even the quantity of worker organization), employers seek to obtain race-gender employment densities and wage differentials that will minimize worker solidarity. From the perspective of employers, the racial composition of the firm's workforce is simply an additional factor to be taken into account in the ongoing struggle between labor and capital over the distribution of income between wages and profit.

Workers, however, are not passive bystanders in determining the race-gender composition of the workforce. Racial and gender exclusion are also used by current job holders to make other-group workers less competitive for higher-paying positions. For example, access to persons embedded in positions of power and authority increases the probability of obtaining employment. A common "cultural identity," that is, a common racial identity, is one means of obtaining such access. In a nationally representative sample, Braddock and McPartland found that employers show preferential treatment for whites in targeting a potential pool of employees, hiring and entry, and promotion within the firm once hired.[42] Braddock and McPartland attribute this preferential treatment to segregated job networks, information bias, statistical discrimination, and closed internal labor markets.

Both managers and workers are recruited from racially segregated neighborhoods, from racially segregated families and non-market organizations, and from racially segregated market organizations (for example, professional associations). Such racially segregated environments will increase the competitive strength of those included in the organization even as they facilitate the exclusion of nonmembers. Racism and sexism connect labor supply and labor demand because managers bring to the decisionmaking process the values, norms, habits, and traditions of their family, their neighborhood, their political leadership, and their education system. All of these have been developed in racially segregated environments.

This job competition model, then, argues that persistent racial discrimination in the labor market is the result of a process involving two distinct conflicts: the conflict between labor and management and the conflict among different groups of workers. Racial discrimination in employment emerges as one element of the conflict between labor and management over the distribution of income and, thereby, the formation of inter- and intraindustry wage differentials. However, for a given distribution of wages, workers use race as a coalition-formation device and to exclude other-groups from the most desirable employment opportunities. During periods of unemployment this process is intensified.

7. Racial Property

Although the job competition model has sought to examine the nature of discriminatory treatment as the result of racism, rather than prejudice or bigotry, it takes racial categories as given. For the most part, both orthodox and heterodox economic theory have failed to examine the process of racial identity formation, that is, why racial categories are formed and how individuals are sorted into these categories. Racial categories are simply asserted, even though orthodox economists accept that racial affiliation has economic consequences and heterodox economists (among others) argue that racialized behavior connects and affects pre-market and market processes. Since no group of economists has publicly endorsed a biological theory of racial construction and it is also clear that race affects economic well-being, we might reasonably inquire into the economic aspects of racial identity formation.[43]

Typically, we think of racial identity as an individual characteristic that is not economically productive but that may have economic consequences.[44] Yet a greater or lesser ability to attract or appropriate income characterizes racial identities. Is it possible then that income-producing racial identities are selected as the outcome of individual and intergroup competition?

Legal theorist Cheryl Harris has suggested that white racial identity is a form of property.[45] Harris builds a well-documented historical-legal case that white racial identity carries with it expectations of privilege. These expectations of privilege are a form of property because African-American socioeconomic advancement can take place only if it does not violate the expectations associated with white identity. The Harris model then can explain why individuals (of appropriate skin color) self-identify as "white," and it even provides an economic rationale for why access to "whiteness" is not universal, that is, that universal access would dilute expected privileges. Interestingly, also, the Harris model can explain the phenomenon of "passing,"[46] that is, moving from a black to a white racial identity, among African Americans and why better than two-thirds of Latinos self-identify as "white."[47]

However, the Harris model of whiteness cannot explain why many individuals strongly identity themselves as "black" or as members of other nonwhite races. Indeed, if as Harris asserts "whiteness" is property—that is, expected privilege—then "blackness" is *non-property*, that is, it is a racial category that is socially disassociated with equality (and, of course, no expectation of racial privilege).

Darity, Mason, and Stewart have sought to develop an economic model that is capable of explaining both black and white racial identity formation.[48] After observing the enormous differences in wealth between African-American and white families, Darity and his colleagues argue that the racial wealth gap reflects the cumulative effects of both past and present racism. They suggest that the enormous wealth differences provide economic incentives that encourage the continual reproduction of racism in American society. In particular, the simultaneous reproduction of racism and wealth inequality results from the interaction of the personal identity and property aspects of racial identity formation. First, Darity and his colleagues argue that race is a form of individual and group property; simply put, it is a wealth-generating characteristic. Second, they write that race is also a form of personal identity, that is, a produced good whose demand is responsive to changes in the costliness of racial identity.

Race is a wealth-generating characteristic because participation in a racial coalition increases the wealth-generating capacity of individual attributes for own-group members while simultaneously reducing the wealth-generating capacity of individual attributes for other-group members. Race as a form of personal identity is related to both relative wealth differences and own- and other-group constraints on individual behavior. The personal identity and wealth effects encourage persistent reproduction of racial categories and racial conflict. Ultimately, short-run changes in the extent of discrimination fluctuate around the secular path of racial identity formation.

8. SUMMARY AND DISCUSSION

Orthodox economic theory is weighed down by the enormous burden of the law of one price; hence, most neoclassical economists have tried to explain the post-1973 increase in racial inequality while explicitly denying that racial discrimination within the labor market is a major cause of African-American–white inequality. This perspective has led to a large number of studies that attempt to locate sources of inferiority among African Americans. The most sophisticated neoclassical empirical work does not attribute inequality to genetic differences; instead, it combines the presumption that an inferior family and neighborhood background is the sole source of inequality between African Americans and whites with the presumption that skill-biased technical change has raised inequality within racial groups. By this view, the inferior family and neighborhood background of African Americans produced lower cognitive skill accumulation even as the rate of return to cognitive skill began to increase dramatically during the 1980s due to rapid technological change.

The job competition model does not adhere to the law of one price. Accordingly, in my view, it is able to explain why racial discrimination will persist over time, as well as why racial discrimination is likely to increase during periods of high unemployment such as the early 1970s. Firms often attempt to select racial workforce compositions that minimize the bargaining power of workers and thus increase profit and lower wages. In the struggle among workers for employment, racial identity often determines the extent of access to employment, especially for high-wage positions. Recent theoretical research has also begun to examine the economic foundation of the formation of racial identities. Since racial identity is both a form of property and an aspect of personal identity, this research has shown that the market provides material incentives for the persistent reproduction of both racial identities and racial conflict.

I close with a brief description of the implications of the research discussed in this chapter. First, neither intraracial nor interracial wage inequality is an inevitable social malady that we must tolerate as the price of an efficient allocation of resources and technological change. Intraracial inequality may be reduced by strengthening the bargaining power of workers.[49] Currently existing affirmative action and anti-discrimination laws would help reduce racial discrimination if they were vigorously enforced and appropriately funded. Second, since joblessness tends to exaggerate racial conflict, it is imperative to maintain a low-unemployment economy. Third, recent research on racial identity formation suggests that the creation of a more egalitarian wealth distribution might also eliminate or at least abridge the economic causes of racial conflict. Finally, to the extent that there is a racial gap in cognitive skills and that this gap is responsible for a substantive portion of the racial wage differential (say, at least 10–20 percent), then it would be desirable to have public assistance for those elements of the educational process that are most beneficial for raising the average level of cognitive ability and for closing the racial gap.

Regardless of the specific policies and political actions that are ultimately pursued, the most important contribution of this chapter is that it warns against assuming that the competitive forces of the market are sufficient for eliminating racial discrimination within the labor market. Quite the opposite is more likely to be true. Namely, competitive forces of the market can contribute to racial inequality, as well as to the reproduction of racial identities and racial conflict. This is not to say that so-called nonmarket institutions and processes—for example, family behavior, the education system, and neighborhood characteristics—should not be examined with an eye toward how they contribute to intraracial and interracial inequality. Rather, the hope is that we will remove the ideological blinders that trap popular and professional discussions of interracial and intraracial inequality into searching for behavioral flaws in individuals, families, and racial groups while avoiding serious discussions on how capitalist competition persistently contributes to the American dilemma.

10

ALTERNATIVE INDICATORS OF HEALTH AND THE QUALITY OF LIFE

Richard H. Steckel

Medical scientists have devised numerous measures of individual health, such as temperature, blood pressure, and pulse. Readings that fall outside the normal range suggest a need for additional inquiry or interventions to protect health, and doctors often perform a battery of tests before prescribing treatment for a sick patient.

In a like manner, social scientists have devised numerous measures of social performance that monitor a nation's standard of living or quality of life. Candidates for office and voters need to know whether economic and social conditions are improving or getting worse, and people in a position to influence policy require benchmarks of performance for evaluating policy outcomes.

Several measures developed by economists and demographers are well known and widely used. The former often employ monetary measures such as gross domestic product (GDP), defined as the market value of goods and services produced by a country in a given year. On the other hand, demographers prefer vital statistics, such as life expectancy at birth.

This chapter discusses health measures of the quality of life that are less familiar or less accessible to the general public than those just mentioned. The goal is to discern patterns in our nation's health that may go unnoticed, or at least be less apparent, using more familiar measures. The first group includes anthropometric measures, especially average stature, which reflect nutritional status during childhood. The second group is consumption of various foods and of substances such as alcohol, tobacco, and drugs, which are known to affect health.

While income and life expectancy have grown over the past three decades, the heights of Americans have stagnated. American heights are increasingly falling behind those of northern Europeans, and currently lag by approximately two inches.

The height pattern is puzzling in view of the substantial increase in expenditures on health care since 1970, which outpaced those of countries where people were growing taller. Languishing incomes and rising inequality might have been factors in the height stagnation for those who were growing as children during the 1980s and 1990s. It is unclear whether the trend can be explained by lifestyle choices that affect health and human growth. Smoking is down, consumption of fruits and vegetables is up, and alcohol consumption might have declined slightly in ways that improved health. But Americans are becoming more obese, and their dietary habits might be crowding more nutritious foods out of their diets; drug use has increased; and disability days rose significantly for children during the 1970s. The tallest nation on earth, the Netherlands, has a vigorous program of pre- and postnatal care that may be an important factor in its success relative to the United States.

Because some readers may be unfamiliar with these alternative approaches to monitoring social performance, a methodology section precedes discussion of results.

AVERAGE HEIGHT

There is a long tradition among biologists and nutritionists of using stature to assess health aspects of human welfare. The realization that environmental conditions influenced growth stimulated interest in the 1820s. The study of human growth for health reasons arose in France, where Villermé studied the stature of soldiers; in Belgium, where Quetelet measured children and formulated mathematical representations of the human growth curve; and in England, where Edwin Chadwick inquired into the health of factory children. Franz Boas identified salient relationships between the tempo of growth and height distributions, and in 1891 coordinated a national growth study, which he used to develop national standards for height and weight. A global explosion of growth studies occurred in the twentieth century.[1]

These studies establish that two periods of intense activity characterize the growth process following birth. Figure 10.1 shows that the increase in height, or velocity, is greatest during infancy, falls sharply, and then declines irregularly into the pre-adolescent years. During adolescence, velocity rises sharply to a peak that equals approximately one-half of the velocity during infancy, then declines rapidly and reaches zero at maturity. The adolescent growth spurt begins about two years earlier in girls than in boys and during their spurt girls temporarily overtake boys in average height. As adults, males are taller than females primarily because they have approximately two additional years of growth prior to adolescence.

Although genes are important determinants of individual height, studies of genetically similar and dissimilar populations under various environmental conditions suggest that differences in average height across most populations are largely attributable to environmental factors. In a review of studies covering populations in Europe, New Guinea, and Mexico, L. A. Malcolm concludes that

FIGURE 10.1. VELOCITY OF THE GROWTH PROCESS (BOYS)

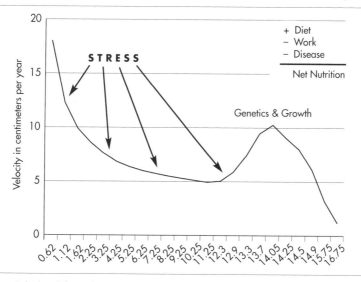

Source: Calculated from data in "NCHS Growth Curves for Children, Birth–Eighteen Years, United States," DHEW Publication PHS 78–1650 (Hyattsville, Md.: National Center for Health Statistics, 1977), p. 37.

differences in average height between populations are almost entirely the product of the environment.[2] Using data from well-nourished populations in several developed and developing countries, Reynaldo Martorell and Jean-Pierre Habicht report that children from Europe or of European descent, from Africa or of African descent, and from India or the Middle East have similar growth profiles.[3] Far-Eastern children or adults are an exception that may have a genetic basis. About two decades ago, well-off Japanese, for example, reached the 15th height percentile of the well-off in Britain. But large height gains have occurred in Japan in the past three decades, which suggest that the portion of the height differential that can be attributed to genetic influences is shrinking. Important for interpreting stature in the United States is the fact that Europeans and people of European descent and Africans and people of African descent who grow under good nutritional circumstances have nearly identical stature.

Height at a particular age reflects an individual's history of *net* nutrition, or diet minus claims on the diet made by work (or physical activity) and disease. Metabolic requirements for basic functions such as breathing and at-rest blood circulation also make claims on the diet. The synergy between malnutrition and illness may further reduce the nutrition left over for growth. Poorly nourished children are more susceptible to infection, which reduces the body's absorption of nutrients. The interaction implies that analyses of stature must recognize not only inputs to health such as diet and medical care but also work effort and related phenomena such as methods of labor organization. Similarly, it is important to realize that exposure to infectious disease may place claims on the diet.[4]

The sensitivity of growth to deprivation or biological stress depends upon the age at which it occurs. For a given degree of deprivation, the adverse effects may be proportional to the velocity of growth under optimal conditions. Thus young children and adolescents are particularly susceptible to environmental insults. The return of adequate nutrition following a relatively short period of deprivation may restore normal height through catch-up growth. But ingestion of toxic substances such as alcohol or tobacco *in utero* or in early childhood often creates permanent stunting regardless of subsequent nutritional conditions. If conditions are inadequate for catch-up, individuals may still approach normal adult height through an extension of the growing period by as long as several years.

Prolonged and severe deprivation results in stunting, or a reduction in adult size.

Because GDP per capita is the most widely used indicator of living standards, it is particularly useful to compare and contrast this measure with stature. Income is a potent determinant of stature that operates through diet, disease, and work intensity, but one must recognize that other factors such as personal hygiene, public health measures, and the disease environment affect illness, while work intensity is a function of technology, culture, and methods of labor organization. In addition, the relative price of food, cultural values such as the pattern of food distribution within the family, methods of preparation, and tastes and preferences for foods may also be relevant for net nutrition. Yet influential policymakers view higher incomes for the poor as an effective means of alleviating protein-energy malnutrition in developing countries. Extremely poor families may spend two-thirds or more of their income on food, but even a large share of their very low incomes purchases inadequate calories. Malnutrition associated with extreme poverty has a major impact on height, but (at the other end of the income spectrum) expenditures beyond those needed to satisfy calorie requirements purchase largely variety, palatability, and convenience.

Gains in stature associated with higher income are not limited to developing countries. Within industrialized countries, height rises with socioeconomic class. These differences in height are related to improvements in the diet, reductions in physical workloads, reduced exposure to pathogens (through sewage disposal, a cleaner water supply, and improved housing), and better health care. Expenditures on health services rise with income and there is a positive relationship between health services and health.

At the individual level, extreme poverty results in malnutrition, retarded growth, and stunting. Higher incomes enable the parents of growing children to purchase a better diet and the children's height increases correspondingly, but once income is sufficient to satisfy caloric requirements, individuals often consume foods that also satisfy many vitamin and mineral requirements. Height may continue to rise with income because a more complete diet or better housing and medical care are available. As income increases, consumption patterns change to realize a larger share of genetic potential, but environmental variables are powerless after individuals attain the maximum capacity for growth.[5] The limits to this process are clear from the fact that people growing up in very wealthy families do not turn into physical giants.

While the relationship between height and income is nonlinear at the individual level, the relationship at the aggregate level depends upon the distribution of income. Average height may differ for a given per capita income depending upon the fraction of people with insufficient income to purchase an adequate diet or to afford medical care. Because the gain in height at the individual level increases at a decreasing rate as income rises, one would expect average height at the aggregate level to increase with the degree of equality of the income distribution (assuming there are people who have not reached their genetic potential).

The relationship between average height and economic performance has been studied by linking data from mid- or late twentieth-century national height studies with estimates of per capita GDP. The height studies were conducted for national populations in the mid- and late twentieth century. The scatter diagram in Figure 10.2 confirms

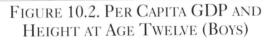

FIGURE 10.2. PER CAPITA GDP AND
HEIGHT AT AGE TWELVE (BOYS)

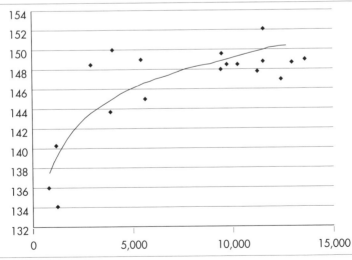

Source: Calculated from data in Phyllis B. Eveleth and James M. Tanner, *Worldwide Variation in Human Growth,* 2d ed. (Cambridge, England: Cambridge University Press, 1990); Robert Summers and Alan Heston, "The Penn World Table (Mark 5): An Expanded Set of International Comparisons, 1950–1988," *Quarterly Journal of Economics* 106, no. 2 (1991): 327–68.

the relationship between average height and per capita income discussed here.[6]

Scatter around the average relationship may be explained by variation across countries in the degree of income inequality, by differences in public health policies, by food prices, and by cultural factors that affect the distribution of resources within families. These conditions affect the number and the degree to which basic needs are being met within the population. Despite the large number of factors that may influence average height at a given level of per capita income, however, the simple correlations between a country's average height and the log of its per capita GDP are in the range of 0.82 to 0.88.[7]

Figure 10.3 shows the connection between average height and life expectancy at birth for the same countries as depicted in Figure 10.2. Unlike the height–per capita GDP relationship, which was clearly nonlinear, the pattern in Figure 10.3 is approximately linear. A one-year increase in life expectancy is associated with an increase in stature of about 0.56 centimeters (average for boys and girls).

FIGURE 10.3: LIFE EXPECTANCY AT BIRTH AND HEIGHT AT AGE TWELVE (BOYS)

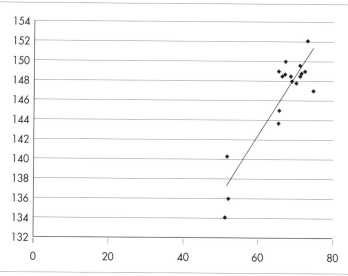

Source: Calculated from data in Phyllis B. Eveleth and James M. Tanner, *Worldwide Variation in Human Growth*, 2d ed. (Cambridge, England: Cambridge University Press, 1990); World Bank, *World Development Report* (various years).

FIGURE 10.4. AVERAGE HEIGHT OF AMERICAN-BORN WHITE MALES, 1710–1970

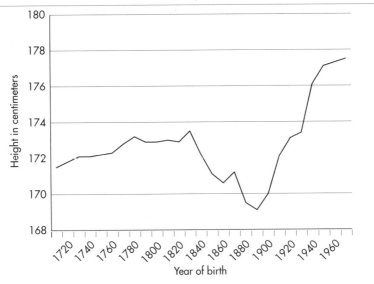

Source: Dora L. Costa and Richard H. Steckel, "Long-Term Trends in Health, Welfare, and Economic Growth in the United States," in Richard H. Steckel and Roderick Floud, eds., *Health and Welfare during Industrialization* (Chicago: University of Chicago Press, 1997), pp. 47–89.

HEIGHT TRENDS IN THE UNITED STATES

Figure 10.4 shows the time pattern in height of native-born American men, obtained in historical periods from military muster rolls, and for recent decades from the National Health Interview Surveys. This historical trend is notable for the tall stature during the colonial period, the mid-nineteenth century decline, and the surge in heights of the past century. Comparisons of average heights from military organizations in Europe show that Americans were taller by about four to six centimeters. Behind this achievement were a relatively good diet, little exposure to epidemic disease, and relative equality in the distribution of wealth. Americans could choose their foods from the best of European and Western Hemisphere plants and animals, and this dietary diversity combined with favorable weather meant that Americans never had to contend with harvest failures. Thus even the poor were reasonably well fed in colonial America.

Loss of stature began in the second quarter of the nineteenth century when the transportation revolution of canals, steamboats, and railways brought people into greater contact with diseases. The rise of public schools meant that children were newly exposed to major diseases such as whooping cough, diphtheria, and scarlet fever. Food prices also rose during the 1830s and growing inequality in the distribution of income or wealth accompanied industrialization. Business depressions, which were most hazardous for the health of those who were already poor, also emerged with industrialization. The Civil War of the 1860s and its troop movements further spread disease and disrupted food production and distribution. A large volume of immigration also brought new varieties of disease to the United States.

In this century, heights grew most rapidly for those born between 1910 and 1950, an era when public health and personal hygiene took vigorous hold, incomes rose rapidly, and there was reduced congestion in housing. The latter part of the era also witnessed a larger share of income or wealth going to the lower portion of the distribution, implying that the incomes of the less well-off were rising relatively rapidly. Note that most of the rise in heights occurred before modern antibiotics were available, which means that disease prevention rather than the ability to alter its course after onset was the cornerstone of improving health.

Between the middle of the century and the present, however, the average heights of American men have stagnated, increasing by only a small fraction of an inch over the past half century. Figure 10.4 refers to the native born, so recent increases in immigration cannot account for the stagnation. In the absence of other information, one might be tempted to suppose that environmental conditions for growth are so good that most Americans have simply reached their genetic potential for growth. But data on heights of military conscripts given in Figure 10.5 (page 198) show that this is not the case. Heights have continued to grow in Europe, which has the same genetic stock from which most Americans descend. By the 1970s America had fallen behind Norway, Sweden, the Netherlands, and Denmark, and was on a par with Germany. While American heights were essentially flat after the 1970s, heights continued to grow significantly in Europe. The Dutch are now the tallest, averaging six feet, about two inches more than American men.

Note that significant differences in health and the quality of life follow from these height patterns. The comparisons are not part of an odd contest that emphasizes height, nor is big per se assumed to be beautiful. Instead, we know that on average, stunted growth has functional implications for longevity, cognitive development, and

FIGURE 10.5. HEIGHTS OF MILITARY
CONSCRIPTS IN EUROPE

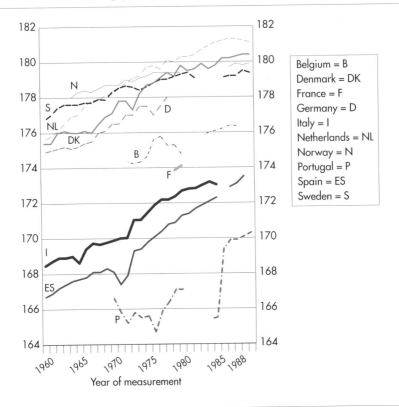

Belgium = B
Denmark = DK
France = F
Germany = D
Italy = I
Netherlands = NL
Norway = N
Portugal = P
Spain = ES
Sweden = S

Year of measurement

Source: See I. M. Schmidt, M. H. Jorgensen, and K. F. Michaelsen, "Height of Conscripts in Europe: Is Postneonatal Mortality a Predictor?" *Annals of Human Biology* 22 (1995): 57–67, and sources therein.

work capacity. Children who fail to grow adequately are often sick, suffer learning impairments, and have a lower quality of life. Growth failure in childhood has a long reach into adulthood because individuals whose growth has been stunted are at greater risk of death in each age group from heart disease, diabetes, and some types of cancer. Therefore it is important to know why Americans are falling behind.

A preliminary list of possible explanations can be compiled from factors thought to have affected American heights over the past two centuries: income, income inequality, diet, exposure to disease, and medical care. Although income growth in the past three decades has fallen to about one-half of benchmark historical standards, incomes have increased in real per capita terms by roughly 1 percent per year since the early 1970s. But economic growth also slowed in Europe over this time period. Thus it would be implausible to argue that an economic growth slowdown is responsible for the height stagnation in America.

A decline in resources devoted to health care is not to blame, either. Table 10.1 shows that the share of GDP spent on health in the United States rose from 7.1 percent in 1970 to about 13.5 percent in 1995. It was during the 1970s and 1980s that spending in the United States surged ahead of spending per person in northern European countries, where the population grew taller over the same time period.[8] In particular, the United States now spends nearly twice as much per capita on health care as the tallest country, the Netherlands.

Income stagnation combined with growing inequality would place the poor at greater risk than would income stagnation alone. Growing inequality in the 1980s and 1990s imposed a degree of economic stress on the poor. This argument has some merit but the timing, duration, and magnitude of inequality trends do not suggest that inequality is the major factor behind the height stagnation of those born after World War II. Inequality was perhaps at its lowest point of

TABLE 10.1. HEALTH CARE EXPENDITURES AS A PERCENTAGE OF GDP, BY COUNTRY

	DENMARK	NETHERLANDS	NORWAY	SWEDEN	UNITED STATES
1960	3.6	3.8	3.3	4.7	5.1
1965	4.8	4.3	3.9	5.5	5.7
1970	6.1	5.9	5	7.1	7.1
1975	6.5	7.5	6.7	7.9	8
1980	6.8	7.9	6.6	9.4	8.9
1985	6.3	7.9	6.4	8.9	10.2
1990	6.5	8	7.5	8.6	12.1
1994	6.6	8.8	7.3	7.7	13.5

Source: Data obtained from *Health, United States, 1996–1997 and Injury Chartbook*, National Center for Health Statistics, Table 117.

this century in the 1970s, declining from higher levels in the 1920s. This, combined with rapid economic growth of the 1950s and 1960s, should have propelled American heights rapidly upward if income growth and declining inequality were a potent combination, yet heights changed little during this era that was relatively good for the poor. Nevertheless, growing inequality of the past two decades could have been a factor in the height stagnation of recent birth cohorts.

If diets deteriorated over the past half-century, it was not due to rising food prices. Significant gains in agricultural productivity have given rise to increases in the supply of most foods, including grain, meat, poultry, eggs, and dairy products. Prices of these products have risen, but not as fast as those of consumer products in general. Thus food is relatively cheaper now than it was earlier in the century. Cheap food does not mean that families are making good dietary choices, however. While heights have been stagnating, Americans have been gaining weight, growing outward rather than upward. Most American children do not lack calories, but they may lack dietary balance that provides important nutrients such as calcium, zinc, iron, and iodine, which are important for growth. Carbohydrates and fats are crowding more nutritious foods out of the diet.

The germ theory of disease led to a revolution in public health and personal hygiene, all but eliminating most dreaded childhood diseases that impede growth. Has a reversal occurred, whereby children are now exposed to new, if undetected, pathogens? While this is conceivable, given the mobility of the world's population one would wonder why these same pathogens apparently have not infected Europe. Moreover, these pathogens must not be lethal, because mortality rates of children are lower than they were near the middle of the century.

Medical care is a likely suspect, or at least a suspect that deserves further scrutiny, for the stagnation in American heights. The tallest countries in Europe—the Scandinavian countries and the Netherlands—are known for their extensive health care systems. In the United States, on the other hand, coverage is often associated with employment, and the extent of coverage (specific procedures and deductibles) varies widely across employers. Perhaps 40 million Americans lack any coverage by health insurance, and many others may have coverage that is inadequate to achieve human capacities for growth. And for the rest, just having coverage does not mean that it is used, or used wisely. Ignorance or lack of knowledge about the importance of regular check-ups, diets, vaccinations, and so on likely plays a role as well.

We know that the most sensitive period for growth and development occurs in early childhood, when the velocity of growth is normally at its highest. Therefore, explanations for growth failure should target this crucial phase of development. In the past half-century the Dutch have created an extensive health care system and a culture of use that is vigorous in promoting pre- and postnatal checkups. Mothers regularly comply, keeping booklets that provide a history of examinations, and the system readily identifies instances of poor health and growth failure. America has extraordinary medical technology, but for various reasons the resources are unavailable to some (mainly because of lack of insurance), and when they are available, they are often not effectively used to achieve our potential for growth.

DIET AND SUBSTANCE USE

In recent decades, diet and substance use have increasingly been subjects of study about their effects on health.[9] A significant portion of the population, particularly well-educated professionals, absorbs the results of this research and has made changes in lifestyle in accordance with recommendations. It is a demanding process to not only read the outpouring of research but also to evaluate and act on suggestions. It is challenging for professionals to stay abreast of the field, and even diligent readers in the general public can be confused by the highly distilled versions of research that are often presented without perspective by the press.[10] For example, eggs were once portrayed as a villain that raised blood cholesterol, but recent press reports observe that they are high in protein, contain little saturated fat, and pose no significant health risk if consumed in moderation by people without high cholesterol levels.[11] Salt has been linked with hypertension, but now appears to be harmful only for those at risk for other reasons. No doubt some people concerned about their nutrition have simply thrown up their hands, retreating to dietary habits or to whatever is affordable and tastes good.

The apparent confusion in the field makes it more difficult to assess the responsiveness of the public. Some people are apathetic, but others trying their best may not change behavior simply because messages have not been consistent and powerful for long periods of time. Yet some recommendations have been consistently proclaimed, among them the benefits of eating fruits and vegetables and the harm of consuming large amounts of saturated fats.

There is good news on the consumption of fruits and vegetables.[12] Figure 10.6 shows per capita fruit consumption (fresh and processed) has risen irregularly from about 229 pounds in 1970 to nearly 281 pounds in 1995, a gain of more than 20 percent. Over the same time period fresh and processed vegetable consumption (Figure 10.7) also increased by approximately 20 percent, from 335 pounds to 405 pounds. Also at the same time, per capita consumption of red meat (Figure 10.8, page 204), which tends to be high in saturated fat, declined from 192 pounds to 163 pounds. This decline of 15 percent was replaced in the diet by a gain of more than 50 pounds per person in poultry, which is relatively low in saturated fat. Per capita consumption of total fat fluctuated but remained roughly unchanged at 155 pounds between 1970 and 1995.

The news is also good on smoking, which has been on the decline for the past two decades. Figure 10.9 (page 205) shows that about 40 percent of people aged eighteen and older smoked in 1970, but the share declined to about 26 percent in 1990 and has remained roughly constant since that time. The decline in smoking occurred across all age categories and ethnic groups.

Several studies suggest that alcohol consumption in small or moderate amounts may actually improve health, but public health officials are reluctant to recommend this substance because of its great potential for abuse and harm to health. It is therefore difficult to evaluate averages, which ignore the distribution of consumption across people and their consumption patterns over time (such as binge drinking). A short discussion of consumption patterns inevitably leaves many questions unanswered. It is known, however, that per capita consumption of distilled spirits has declined in the United States, falling from about 2.8 gallons per person per year in 1970 to about 1.7 gallons in 1995. At the same time, wine consumption rose from about 2 gallons per person per year in 1970, reached a peak of 3.3 gallons in 1986, and fell to 2.4 gallons in 1995. Beer consumption also peaked in 1986 (32.6 gallons per person per year), and by 1995 was up only 1.8 gallons from its level of 28.1 gallons in 1970. Because beer and wine contain less pure alcohol than distilled spirits, pure alcohol consumption has declined since 1970, as the beverage market saw greater consumption of coffee, tea, and bottled water.

The National Household Survey on Drug Abuse queries several aspects of drug use, including the number of initiates in each year

FIGURE 10.6. PER CAPITA FRUIT CONSUMPTION, 1970–95

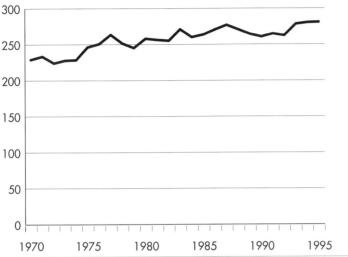

Note: Fruit consumption includes fresh and processed fruit.
Source: Data obtained from Judith Jones Putnam and Jane E. Allshouse, *Food Consumption, Prices, and Expenditures, 1970–95,* Statistical Bulletin No. 939, Food and Consumer Economics Division, Economic Research Service, U.S. Department of Agriculture, Table 15.

FIGURE 10.7. PER CAPITA VEGETABLE CONSUMPTION, 1970–95

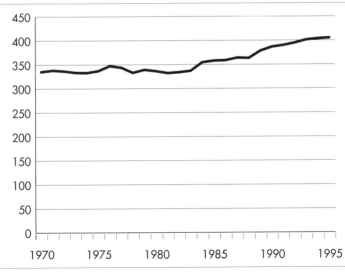

Source: Data obtained from Judith Jones Putnam and Jane E. Allshouse, *Food Consumption, Prices, and Expenditures, 1970–95,* Statistical Bulletin No. 939, Food and Consumer Economics Division, Economic Research Service, U.S. Department of Agriculture, Table 15.

FIGURE 10.8. PER CAPITA RED MEAT
CONSUMPTION, 1970–96

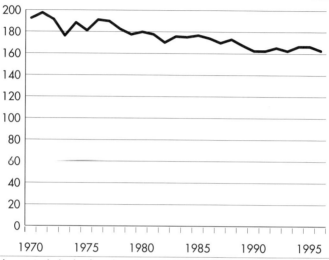

Note: Red meat includes beef, veal, pork, and lamb. Beef-carcass weight is the weight of the chilled hanging carcass that includes the kidney and attached internal fat, but not the head, feet, and unattached internal organs. Definitions of carcass weight for other red meats differ slightly. *Source:* Data obtained from Judith Jones Putnam and Jane E. Allshouse, *Food Consumption, Prices, and Expenditures, 1970–95,* Statistical Bulletin No. 939, Food and Consumer Economics Division, Economic Research Service, U.S. Department of Agriculture, Table 4.

for various types of drugs. The trends during the 1970s and 1980s and in the past few years are disturbing. The number of people who first tried cocaine increased from 77,000 in 1968 to 1,389,000 in 1982. It then fell to 480,000 in 1991 but has once again increased in recent years, reaching 675,000 in 1996. The first use of hallucinogens has also climbed dramatically, from slightly less than 100,000 in 1965 to over 1,000,000 in 1996. Most of the gains in this substance occurred in two waves—1967 to 1971 and from 1992 to 1996. Initiates to heroin declined from about 100,000 per year in 1970 to 32,000 per year in 1992, but the figure has since grown to 171,000 per year in 1996. Marijuana initiates climbed from 68,000 in 1962 to 3,185,000 in 1975, then fell to 1,376,000 in 1991; the figure has since increased to 2,540,000 in 1996. Overall, drug use grew rapidly in the 1970s and early 1980s, fell off during the mid- and late 1980s, but has surged again since the early 1990s.

*   *   *

FIGURE 10.9. PERCENT OF EIGHTEEN-YEAR-OLD AND OLDER POPULATION WHO ARE CURRENT SMOKERS, 1965–94

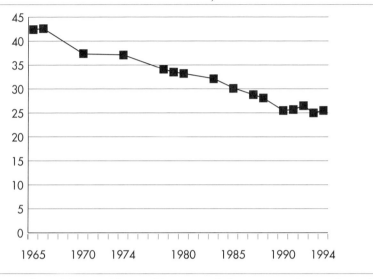

Source: Data obtained from *Health, United States,* annual editions, National Center for Health Statistics, Table 64.

Average height is a summary measure of health, reflecting numerous influences on growth and development. Two additional summary measures worth noting are disability days and the incidence of low birth weight. The latter summarizes health from conception to birth, and incorporates many influences on the health of the mother such as diet, disease, work effort, and ingestion of toxic substances. The incidence of low birth weight, which includes live births weighing less than 5.5 pounds, declined from about 8 percent of all live births in 1970 to a low of about 6.7 percent in the early 1980s, and has since risen to about 7.3 percent in 1995

The National Center for Health Statistics compiles various measures of disability for children, including school-loss days, bed-disability days, and restricted activity days. All climbed approximately 25 percent between the late 1960s and 1980, which is the era when American heights stagnated. In the early 1980s they abruptly fell to late 1960s levels, but then drifted upward to 1990, and thereafter two of the measures (bed-disability and school-loss days) fell to early 1980s levels.

Conclusions

Although monetary measures such as GDP per capita and wages have been the mainstay of analysis for economists, and demographers have drawn heavily on mortality rates or life expectancy, a variety of measures are required to complete the picture of social performance. This chapter draws attention to the value of anthropometric measures, especially average height, and to various lifestyle choices that affect health.

While the evidence at hand cannot answer the question of why American heights are falling behind those of northern Europeans, it is clear that a problem of child health exists and that we should invest more effort in discovering the answers. Possible causal suspects worthy of further study are growing income inequality, increasing drug use, inadequate pre- and postnatal care, and dietary imbalances.

Recent decades have witnessed a substantial growth in resources devoted to the health problems of older Americans. While not denying the importance of these efforts, this chapter calls attention to the health of America's children. Their quality of life depends on the answers, and after all, it is today's children who will be called upon to care for our aging population.

11

SOMETHING NEW IN THE 1990S?

LOOKING FOR EVIDENCE OF AN ECONOMIC TRANSFORMATION

Dean Baker

The economic picture in the fall of 1999 is overwhelmingly positive. We are experiencing the lowest unemployment rate in nearly thirty years. Inflation has virtually vanished as a concern. In the last four years economic growth has averaged nearly 4 percent and productivity growth has averaged over 2 percent. In the last year real wages have risen rapidly, close to 2 percent, and the gains have been widely shared, with those at the bottom of the income distribution benefiting most. And, as everyone knows, the government's budget projections show large surpluses into the indefinite future, and the stock market continues to reach new highs.

According to many economic analysts the economy has been fundamentally transformed in the 1990s. The government has moved from running large deficits to large surpluses, freeing up vast amounts of money. This newly freed money has in turn lowered interest rates and led to a surge in investment. Soaring investment has allowed the economy to rapidly assimilate information technologies. At the same time, the prudent monetary policies of the Federal Reserve Board have wrung inflation out of the economy. The net effect has been thirty-year lows in inflation and unemployment and a surge in productivity growth, setting the economy on a qualitatively higher growth path.

This chapter examines the economy's performance in the 1990s business cycle to determine the extent to which it shows evidence of entering a new economic era as opposed to simply continuing the trends of the prior two decades. It shows that, to a large extent, the strong economic performance of the last four years is simply offsetting extraordinarily weak economic growth earlier in the business cycle. Over the cycle as a whole, the economy's performance is only slightly better than its average over the prior two decades.

The chapter also examines the record of economic policy in the 1990s. It shows that the investment boom has been largely illusory. The main stimulus to the economy has been a stock market–driven consumption boom. This creates a very fragile path ahead, as the stock market could tumble from its inflated heights at any time. The risk of a large stock decline, along with the inevitable reversal of the nation's trade deficit, makes the economy's future prospects very uncertain.

The Basic Numbers

The best place to start an examination of the economy's current state is with a comparison with its past performance. The accepted way of making such comparisons is to consider the economy's performance over the length of a whole business cycle. The reason for making the comparison over a whole cycle is that the economy will typically grow most rapidly when it is coming out of a deep recession. For example, in 1984 the economy grew by 7 percent, the highest rate of the last forty years. The reason the economy grew so rapidly in 1984 was that it was recovering from the worst recession in the postwar period. The depth of the recession in 1981–83 left a large amount of slack that the economy could easily refill, once it began growing again. In the larger picture, the 7 percent growth rate in 1984 tells us much more about the depth of the earlier recession than the strength of the economy in 1984.

To avoid this sort of problem, economists usually compare the economy's performance from one business cycle peak to the next business cycle peak. This allows for the effects of an economic down-turn to be averaged over the whole length of a business cycle. It also ensures that we are looking at the economy's normal growth rate and not at an aberration due to unusual factors.

Table 11.1 presents some of the most important statistics about the economy in the current business cycle and each of the three preceding

TABLE 11.1. BUSINESS CYCLE PERFORMANCE

	ANNUAL AVERAGES					
	59–69	69–79	79–89	89–99	89–95	95–99
GDP growth	4.4	3.2	3.0	3.0	2.3	4.0
Job growth	2.8	2.5	1.8	1.5	1.4	1.8
Productivity growth	2.9	1.9	1.4	1.9	1.5	2.5
Growth in hourly compensation	2.7	1.7	0.6	1.1	0.5	2.1
Unemployment	4.8	6.2	7.1	5.7	6.4	4.7
Inflation	2.2	6.5	5.3	3.0	3.5	2.3
Interest rates (10-year bond)	4.7	7.5	10.6	6.8	7.2	6.1
Real Interest Rate	2.5	1.0	5.3	3.8	3.7	3.8

Source: Author's calculations (see Appendix 11.1, page 229).

cycles. The data for the current cycle goes through the first three quarters of 1999, since this is the most recent data available, although this will not be the peak of the current cycle unless 2000 turns out to be the beginning of a recession. It is worth pointing out that there was a severe recession in the middle of the 1970s, but for simplicity, the decade is treated as having a single business cycle.

As can be seen in the table, by most measures the 1990s do not appear to have been a particularly prosperous period. The 3 percent average rate of economic growth in the decade is the same as the 1980s growth rate, and slower than the growth rate of the two preceding decades. The 1990s growth rate is nearly one-third less than the 4.4 percent rate of the 1960s.

The drop-off in growth from the 1960s rate is attributable to slower job creation and also a continuation of the recent trend of slower productivity growth. The slower rate of job growth in the last decade can be attributed largely to demographic rather than economic factors. The huge baby boom cohort all entered the labor force by 1990; the cohorts that came of age in this decade were relatively small. The entry of women into the paid labor force was also largely completed by 1990. The percentage of women in the labor force increased by 8.2 percentage points from 1969 to 1979 and by another 6.5 percentage points from 1979 to 1989, when it reached 57.4 percent.

While women's labor force participation rates have increased somewhat further in the 1990s, hitting 60 percent in 1999, there is no
longer a large pool of adult women interested in entering the labor
force. These demographic changes can explain most of the slowdown
in the rate of job creation from the 1960s and 1970s to the 1990s.

While the economy should not be faulted for independent demographic trends, it is worth noting that the data on job growth contradict much recent reporting. Many commentators have described
the job performance of the United States in the 1990s in superlative
terms. And the rate of job growth certainly has been healthy, given the
underlying demographic factors. However, the fact remains that job
growth has actually been slower in the 1990s than in previous business cycles. The job performance of the economy has not been good
compared to its past record.

The record on productivity, the other major factor in economic
growth, has also not been particularly strong in the 1990s.
Productivity growth averaged close to 3 percent annually in the first
quarter century after World War II. In the middle of the 1970s, productivity growth slowed to just over 1 percent annually. The immediate factor bringing about this slowdown was the OPEC price
increases, which sent the price of oil skyrocketing first in 1974 and
then again in 1979. However, the economy has remained mired in a
pattern of slow productivity growth even as the price of oil first stabilized and then fell back to its earlier levels.

There is no generally accepted explanation for the productivity
slowdown, but the evidence from the 1990s is that the economy has
not escaped from its productivity problems. The 1.9 percent average
in the 1990s is considerably better than the 1.4 percent average for the
years from 1973 to 1989, but this growth rate does not come close to
the "golden age" growth rates that prevailed in the years prior to
1973. Moreover, changes in measurement are responsible for some of
this upturn.

It is worth noting that the last four years, 1996–99, have shown
unusually strong productivity growth for an economy approaching a
cyclical peak. This issue will be examined in more detail in the next
section, which discusses the timing of growth over this cycle. At this
point, it is worth noting only that the record on productivity growth
over these four years does not come close to meeting the standard of
proof that economists would typically require before accepting that
the economy has a new productivity trend.

The record of the economy on wage and compensation growth in this cycle has been mixed. Average hourly compensation has increased at just a 1.1 percent annual rate. This is better than the growth rate of real compensation in the 1980s, but considerably worse than in both the 1960s and the 1970s. Ordinarily, economists expect compensation growth to closely track productivity growth. The data in the table show a gap of 0.8 percentage points annually. This gap arises primarily as a result of a technical issue: the deflator that is used to measure real output (and therefore provides the basis for the productivity numbers) has risen less rapidly than the consumer price index that is used to measure real compensation. If the same deflator were applied to both output and hourly compensation, the data would show them rising at approximately the same rate in this cycle. This issue will be addressed further in the next section, at this point it is only worth noting that insofar as there has been any increase in productivity growth in this cycle, it has not led to large gains for workers.

This point can be seen even more clearly by looking at the trend in median, as opposed to average, wages. The median wage is the pay that a worker in the middle of the income distribution receives—half of all workers receive higher pay than the median worker and half receive less. If there is growing inequality, so that a higher portion of wage income goes to the best-paid workers, this will not be revealed by examining the average wage. On the other hand, the median wage shows what is happening to the wages of a typical worker.

The trend in median wages over this business cycle shows that typical workers have not been gaining much if at all over the course of the cycle. The median male worker actually experienced a 1.8 percent drop in real wages from 1989 to 1999. The median female worker experienced a 3.8 percent increase over this period, a gain that is more than eight percentage points below the growth rate of average compensation in the last decade. Taking men and women together, the median worker from the combined male and female distribution had a 2.2 percent increase in hourly wages from 1989 to 1999.[1]

These numbers suggest that the trend toward growing wage inequality, which began in the 1980s, has continued into the 1990s. The modest wage gains that workers as a whole have experienced in the last decade have disproportionately gone to those at the top end of the income distribution. More typical workers have experienced little or no real wage growth during the current cycle. As with productivity growth, the last four years present a somewhat better picture, with workers at all points along the income distribution experiencing significant wage gains. But it will take more than a few good years to make up the ground lost earlier in the decade.

By other measures, the economy's performance has been good but not extraordinary over the course of the cycle. The average rate of unemployment over this business cycle has been 5.7 percent. This is more than a full percentage point below the 7.1 percent average unemployment rate during the 1980s. It is a half percentage point below the 6.2 percent average of the 1970s but almost a full percentage point above the 4.8 percent average of the 1960s. The record on inflation looks better in comparison with previous cycles. The 3 percent average inflation rate for the cycle is more than two full percentage points below the 5.3 percent average of the 1980s. While it is still higher than the 2.2 percent average rate in the 1960s, inflation has fallen considerably over the course of this business cycle. It is also worth noting that interest rates have fallen sharply, with the nominal rate dropping by nearly four percentage points from its average in the 1980s. The fact that nominal interest rates have declined even more than the inflation rate means that the real interest rate has also declined. The 3.7 percent average real interest rate in this decade is 1.6 percentage points below the 1980s level, although it is still considerably higher than the real interest rates of the 1960s and 1970s.

PATTERNS OF GROWTH IN THE 1990S

In many ways the 1990s business cycle has reversed the typical pattern of growth for a business cycle. Usually the first years after a recession are years of strong employment, productivity, and GDP growth, as the economy quickly retakes the ground it lost in the recession. After the economy has regained its pre-recession levels of unemployment and capacity utilization, growth usually slows as the economy follows its underlying trend path of growth. In the 1990s, the first years after the recession were periods of relatively slow growth in employment, productivity, and GDP. It has been the later years, 1996 to 1999, where growth really picked up.

The average growth rate of GDP from the trough of the recession in 1991 through 1995 was 2.7 percent. By comparison economic growth averaged 4.4 percent from 1982 to 1986 and 4.8 percent from 1970 to 1973. This was very weak growth for an economy just coming out of a recession. The rate of job growth in the early and mid-1990s was somewhat more typical of the early phases of a business cycle expansion, with job growth averaging 2 percent from 1991 to 1995. In a single year, from 1993 to 1994, the economy added 3,450,000 jobs, an increase of 3.1 percent.

However, the implication of rapid job growth combined with slow GDP growth is low productivity growth. Productivity growth averaged 1.6 percent annually over the period from 1991 to 1995. This compares with a 2.7 percent average growth rate from 1982 to 1986, and a 3.4 percent average rate of productivity growth for the period from 1970 to 1973. In the short cycle that began in 1975, productivity grew at an annual rate of 2.1 percent in the period from 1975 to 1978, when another surge in oil prices sent the economy reeling. In short, productivity growth was extremely weak in the early phases of this business cycle, even compared with the other cycles after the beginning of the productivity slowdown.

Since 1995, economic growth has been quite solid by these measures. GDP growth averaged 4 percent over the four years from 1995 to 1999. Employment growth has averaged 1.8 percent over this period, and productivity growth has averaged 2.5 percent. We don't know exactly when this business cycle will end, so it is impossible to say whether we have actually hit the peak yet, but these growth numbers are quite impressive for a period that is clearly late in a business cycle. At the same time that the economy has been experiencing this rapid growth, the news on inflation has continued to be good, with the inflation rate actually declining through this period. The inflation rate as measured by the consumer price index had fallen to just 1.6 percent in 1998. (It has since risen slightly in the last year, but is still well under 3 percent.) Measured by the GDP price index, inflation was just 1 percent in 1998. The fall in the inflation rate occurred even as the unemployment rate was hovering at 4.5 percent, a full one and a half percentage points below the 6 percent level that most economists had previously believed would trigger accelerating inflation. At present the economy is enjoying low unemployment, low inflation, and healthy wage and productivity growth, on the whole a very bright picture.

But there have been other times since the onset of the productivity slowdown in 1973 when the economy has also experienced short periods of prosperity. For example, economic growth averaged 5.2 percent annually in the three years from 1975 to 1978, a period in which real hourly compensation rose at a 2.2 percent annual rate. In the three years from 1986 to 1989, growth averaged 3.4 percent, so the growth of the last four years is not extraordinary even compared to the recent past. It remains to be seen whether it will be maintained into the future.

THE ROLE OF MEASUREMENT

While the economy is clearly doing well at present, it is important to recognize that some of the good news has been due to changes in measurement. In recent years, the Bureau of Labor Statistics (BLS) has implemented a number of methodological changes to the consumer price index, most of which have the effect of lowering the measured rate of inflation. For example, the consumer price index (CPI) now assumes that if the price of Granny Smith apples rises rapidly, but the price of Macintosh apples falls, then consumers will switch from buying Granny Smith apples to Macintosh apples. Allowing for this type of substitution leads the CPI to report a lower rate of consumer inflation. According to the most recent *Economic Report of the President*, the cumulative effect of the changes made in the CPI prior to 1999 was to lower the measured rate of inflation by 0.44 percentage points.[2] This means that if inflation in 1998 (as measured by the early 1990s CPI) was 2.5 percent, the 1998 CPI would show an inflation rate of only 2.06 percent. The *Economic Report of the President* projects that further changes in the CPI, implemented in 1999 and 2000, will reduce the measured rate of inflation by an additional 0.24 percentage points. (For a fuller discussion of the debate over the CPI see Appendix 11.2, page 230.)

The changes in CPI also affect the measured rate of GDP growth, since the Bureau of Economic Analysis (BEA) takes much of its data for constructing GDP price indices from BLS. In GDP data, a logical implication of showing lower price inflation is that the growth of real output is greater. Therefore, the changes in the CPI implemented by BLS had the effect of increasing the measured rate of GDP growth. In addition, BEA has made some other changes to its price indices that have also had the effect of increasing the measured rate of GDP growth. The *Economic Report of the President* estimates that the changes made prior to 1999 have had the effect of raising the measured rate of GDP growth by 0.26 percentage points, with subsequent changes projected to add another 0.03 percentage points to GDP growth. The impact on the measured rate of productivity growth would be approximately the same.[3]

While the CPI is never revised, the BEA does go back and recalculate GDP using its current methodology. However, it has not fully incorporated the recent changes for years prior to 1978. This means that growth and productivity are being measured by different yardsticks in the periods before and after 1978. The methodology applied to years after 1978 has the effect of adding approximately 0.2 percentage points to the annual rate of GDP and productivity growth, compared with the earlier methodology. In other words, if GDP growth is reported as 2.5 percent using the current methodology, it would have been reported as 2.3 percent if we were still using the same techniques that were applied to measuring GDP in the 1960s and 1970s.

Many complex issues are raised by the measurement changes noted here and by others that have been debated in recent years; however, their significance for assessing the economy's recent performance is not really in dispute. The changes in measurement have made the economy's performance appear better than otherwise would have been the case. Instead of looking at a 4 percent GDP growth rate over the last four years, we would have had a growth rate of about 3.8 percent if the GDP measures of the 1960s and 1970s were still in place. Using the pre-1978 measures for productivity growth would have lowered the measured rate over the last four years to about 2.1 percent. Applying a consistent measure of productivity growth would have pushed the average for the cycle down to 1.7 percent, removing much of the improvement from the slow trend path in the years after 1973. A consistent measure of consumer inflation would still show an impressive decline in inflation over the course of the business cycle, but not quite as dramatic a drop as current numbers indicate.

THE EFFECT OF COMPUTERS ON PRODUCTIVITY GROWTH

There is an additional measurement issue that is worth discussing before turning to an analysis of economic policy in the 1990s. The extent to which computers increase workers' productivity has been a topic of considerable debate in recent years. This chapter has nothing to add to that debate. However, computers have added significantly to productivity growth in a way that has been less widely appreciated. The BEA's measure of quality has shown computers themselves improving at a rate of close to 40 percent annually over the last four years. This calculation is obtained by measuring the rate of increase of particular characteristics of computers, such as additional units of random access memory or hard drive storage space.

This means that if the economy produces the same dollar value of computers each year, the BEA's data would record a 40 percent increase in computer output. In other words, if the economy produced $100 billion in computers in both 1997 and 1998, BEA's measure of output would show that the value of computer output had risen by 40 percent from 1997 to 1998. Computer output is currently about 1 percent of GDP output. Therefore the BEA's method of measuring computer quality added approximately 0.4 percentage points to GDP growth in 1998. Without this adjustment for computer quality, the economy would have grown at a 3.9 percent rate from 1997 to 1998, rather than the 4.3 percent rate actually reported. The effect on growth in the two preceding years would have been approximately the same.

Since computers are produced in the business sector, the impact on measured productivity growth would have been even larger. Over the last four years, the impact of the measure of improved computer quality on productivity growth has averaged approximately 0.5 percentage points. Without the large improvements in computer quality shown by BEA's measurement technique, and without the new methodology for measuring GDP in years after 1978, productivity growth would have averaged just 1.8 percent annually over the last three years, not much higher than the long-term post-1973 trend.

While the impact of these measured quality improvements is striking, some qualifications are in order. First, BEA's measures of computer quality have been showing rapid improvements for a long time. However, until the last few years, the rate was typically between 15 percent and 20 percent. This is an extremely rapid rate of quality improvement, but well below the 35–45 percent rate of improvement reported in the last three years. (Presumably the rate of increase in computing power in successive generations of computers has gotten faster.) Furthermore, the rate of measured quality improvement in computers had somewhat less impact on GDP and productivity measures fifteen years ago, when computer output was a smaller share of GDP.

The second important qualification is that computers clearly are improving rapidly, therefore the BEA measure could be accurate. For economic purposes, the relevant question on quality improvements is not a technical one, it is not the RAM or speed that matters, but rather how much people value the computer. More than two-thirds of computers are sold for business purposes. The only relevant measure for computers as investment goods is the amount of revenue they generate. If this year's $2,000 desktop does not generate 40 percent more revenue than last year's $2,000 desktop, then its quality has not increased by 40 percent. For households, a 40 percent rate of quality improvement implies that a typical household would have been willing to pay $2,800 last year for the computer they can buy today for $2,000.

There is no point in trying to determine the rate of quality improvement in computers here, but it doesn't seem plausible that they are actually improving at the rate implied by official statistics.[4] It is worth speculating about what the economic data would show if the rate of improvement of computers was assumed to remain constant at 15–20 percent annually over the past twenty years. Table 11.2 shows the rates of GDP and productivity growth over the last four decades using this assumption. The current cycle is broken into two sections, its slow growth period from 1989 to 1995, and its rapid

TABLE 11.2. GDP AND PRODUCTIVITY: THREE VIEWS

| | ANNUAL AVERAGES | | | | |
	59–69	69–79	79–89	89–99	95–99
Published data					
GDP growth	4.4	3.2	3.0	3.0	4.0
Productivity growth	2.9	1.9	1.4	1.9	2.5
Consistent GDP measures					
GDP growth	4.4	3.2	2.8	2.8	3.8
Productivity growth	2.9	1.9	1.2	1.7	2.3
Consistent GDP measures and constant rate of computer quality improvement					
GDP growth	4.4	3.2	2.7	2.7	3.6
Productivity growth	2.9	1.9	1.2	1.6	2.1

Source: Author's calculations (see Appendix 11.1).

growth period from 1995 to 1999. (The construction of this table is explained in Appendix 11.1, page 229.) The first two rows show the data for GDP and productivity growth as currently reported with no adjustments. The second two rows show the rates of GDP growth and productivity growth assuming a consistent method of measurement throughout this period. (For simplicity, the method that was in place prior to 1978 is used.) The third set of two rows shows these growth rates assuming both a consistent method of measurement throughout this period and a constant 15–20 percent rate of quality improvement in computers.

As can be seen, applying a consistent method of measurement, by itself, eliminates a significant portion of the evidence of an upturn in productivity growth from its slow post-1973 trend, although the average rate of productivity growth for the cycle as a whole is still 0.5 percentage points above that of the 1980s. The last four years still show a relatively strong performance, but this is largely making up for the poor productivity growth earlier in the recovery. When a constant rate of computer quality improvement is assumed throughout this period, the data for the 1990s still looks better than the 1980s, but worse than the 1970s and much worse than the 1960s. The overall rate of GDP growth is 0.5 percentage points lower than in the 1970s, with the rate of productivity growth being 0.3 percentage points lower. Compared with the 1960s, applying these adjustments, the 1990s rate of GDP growth is 1.7 percentage points lower, while its rate of productivity growth is 1.4 percentage points lower. Even the last four years do not look particularly impressive under these assumptions. The rate of GDP growth would still be an impressive 3.6 percent, but the annual rate of productivity growth drops to 2 percent.

There is another measurement issue related to computers that is worth mentioning here. In the latest revisions to GDP, software was reclassified so that instead of being counted as an intermediate good, it is now counted as an investment good. This has the effect of raising the official measures of investment, GDP, and productivity growth. While this treatment of software is conceptually accurate, it does add another complication to the standard comparisons. Software depreciates very quickly. In fact, software depreciates so quickly that the addition to depreciation as a result of the change in classification was almost as large as the addition to gross investment.

If GDP is raised as a result of more depreciation, it is a gain of no real economic value. To see this point, imagine that we can use two different building materials, iron and steel, in constructing furniture. Suppose iron wears out relatively quickly, and is therefore classified as an intermediate good. Suppose steel lasts one day longer on average, which is sufficient to have it classified as investment. If furniture suppliers switch from iron to steel, it would be recorded as an increase in investment and GDP, but the actual gain to the economy would be virtually zero. The increase in investment would be almost fully offset by an increase in the amount of capital wearing out each year.

To a large extent, this is the impact of the reclassification of software. It has led to an increasing divergence between *net national product* (GDP minus depreciation) and GDP. A measure of productivity growth based on net national product would be approximately 0.1 percentage point lower over the last four years than the measure derived from GDP growth. Such a measure, along with the other adjustments discussed here, would put the annual rate of productivity growth between 1995 and 1999 at 2 percent, virtually the same as in the decade of the 1970s, although still far above the 1980s 1.2 percent rate.

In sum, a large part of the reported improvement in GDP growth and productivity in the 1990s cycle, and particularly in the last three years, is attributable to changes in measurement. Even ignoring any problems raised by BEA's measure of computer quality improvements, a significant portion of the evidence of a major upturn in productivity growth in the 1990s would be eliminated by applying consistent measures to the historical data. If the BEA's measure of the improvement in computer quality is leading to a substantial overstatement, then the productivity performance of the economy in the 1990s is not much above the slow post-1973 trend. In this case, even the last four years do not provide very compelling evidence of an upturn in productivity growth.

There is one final point that is worth making on measurement issues. Many commentators on the economy have argued that evidence of a productivity surge is being concealed by the inability of statistical agencies to accurately assess the value of the new technologies that are being produced. While there are clearly difficulties involved in trying to assess the value of new technologies, this problem did not first arise in the 1990s. New products and technologies have always played an important role in economic growth. For example, in the 1950s and 1960s, television, air travel, and the polio vaccine were all made widely available due to technological breakthroughs. An earlier generation witnessed the spread of home refrigerators, radios, telephones, and penicillin. The 1990s have seen vast improvements in computer and communication technology, as well as many significant medical breakthroughs. But there is no evidence that these technological developments are either more significant than the advances of preceding decades or less well captured in economic data than preceding technological advances. In fact, there is good reason to believe that changes in measurement procedures have improved the ability of statistical agencies to quantify the gains from these technologies, as compared with earlier technological advances. In the 1950s, 1960s, and even 1970s, there was relatively little attention paid to quality improvements in goods. During this period, new goods were often not included in price indices for more than a decade after their introduction. The claim that the new economy is being overlooked due to measurement problems is a story without any supporting evidence.

POLICY IN THE 1990S

If the overall economic picture looks somewhat different from the way it is often portrayed in the media, the evidence on the impact of economic policy is also somewhat at odds with the general perception. The most important policy decision in the 1990s was the Clinton administration's decision to make deficit reduction its top priority. Over the course of the decade it implemented a series of budget cuts and tax increases that were intended to reduce and eventually eliminate the budget deficit. The economic rationale for this policy is that lower budget deficits would lead to lower interest rates. Lower interest rates would in turn encourage investment. Higher levels of investment would lead to more rapid productivity growth, thereby making the nation wealthier. According to the conventional view, the Clinton administration's policy was a stunning success. The economic data suggest a somewhat different story.

Table 11.3 shows the share of GDP taken by each major component at the peak of the last business cycle in 1989 and in 1999. As can be seen, there is a large falloff in the share of GDP going to government expenditures. The government share declines by 2.4 percentage points, from 20 percent in 1989 to 17.6 percent in 1999. But only a small por-

TABLE 11.3. GDP DISTRIBUTION, 1989 AND 1999 (PERCENT)

| | SHARES OF GDP | | |
	1989	1999	NET CHANGE
Consumption	65.5	67.6	2.1
Government	20.0	17.6	−2.4
Housing	4.2	4.5	0.3
Investment	11.2	12.7	1.5
Net exports	−1.5	−2.7	−1.2
Investment plus net exports	9.7	10.0	0.3
Interest rates			
Interest rate (10-year bond)	8.49	6.1	
Inflation rate (CPI)	4.8	2.5	
Real interest rate	3.69	3.6	

Source: Author's calculations (see Appendix 11.1).

tion of the resources freed up by the diminished role of government went to the investment components of GDP. The share of GDP going to investment spending rose by 1.5 percentage points between these peaks, but this was largely offset by an increase in the trade deficit, as the negative balance on net exports rose by 1.2 percentage points. Net exports can be thought of as foreign investment, since they represent the portion of GDP that is being used to increase the nation's holdings of foreign assets. When the United States increases its net exports it is increasing the amount of money it is lending to other nations, which will be paid back in the future. In this case, the negative balance on net exports is showing the extent to which the United States is increasing its net debtor position internationally as a result of its trade deficit. The next line in Table 11.3, which sums the shares of GDP going to investment and net exports, can be thought of as showing the total share of GDP going to investment, both domestic and foreign. From 1989 to 1999 this measure increases by just 0.3 percentage points. This increase is too small to have any noticeable impact on productivity and accounts for just over a tenth of the resources freed up by the decline in the government share of GDP.

The bulk of the resources freed up by the drop in government spending went to consumption, not investment. The consumption share of GDP rose by 2.1 percentage points from 1989 to 1999. The data clearly show that this has been a consumption-led recovery, as consumption spending far outweighed the growth of other categories of GDP. Households have been borrowing and spending at unprecedented rates. The personal saving rate was just 2.1 percent in the third quarter of 1999. This compares to a saving rate of 7.5 percent in 1989, a time when economists were already loudly decrying the decline in savings. By the end of 1998, the ratio of consumer debt (nonmortgage) to disposable income stood at a record high of 24.2 percent. By comparison, the previous peak of the debt/income ratio— in 1990—was just 19.3 percent. In fact, these numbers understate the growth of consumer debt, since there has been a large increase in the number of new cars that are leased rather than sold. The leasing obligation is similar to debt in many ways, but does not appear as debt. At present, nearly one-third of all new cars are leased by consumers rather than purchased outright. If these lease commitments were added in, it would raise the debt/income ratio by close to two percentage points.

The surge in consumer spending and debt in this cycle is ironic because it has almost completely undermined the purpose of deficit reduction. Deficit reduction was supposed to increase national saving and investment by reducing the amount that the government borrowed. Instead, because of the rise in consumption expenditures, the reduced borrowing in the public sector was almost completely offset by increased borrowing by consumers. The portion of GDP left to support investment in 1999 was almost exactly the same as back in 1989. Measured by its stated goals, the policy of deficit reduction failed.

Ironically, deficit reduction may have played an important role in promoting the 1990s consumption surge, albeit through an indirect route. The main factor prompting consumer spending has been the soaring stock market. The stock market rose by nearly 225 percent in real terms from 1989 to the end of 1999. By comparison, real GDP increased by just over 34 percent during this period. If stock prices had just risen in step with real GDP, the market would be at just over 40 percent of its current level. The run-up in stock prices in excess of GDP growth has added more than $8 trillion in financial wealth over the last nine years. A conventional rule of thumb is that $1 of stock wealth increases consumption by 3 cents. This calculation would imply that the $8 trillion of excess stock market accumulation over the last nine years has increased annual consumption by $240 billion compared with a situation where the stock market had only kept pace with GDP. This additional consumption corresponds almost exactly to the 4.5 percentage point drop in the savings rate that the economy has experienced during this period.

Deficit reduction can be seen as partially responsible for this drop in saving. The low deficits were very popular on Wall Street and helped build the sort of optimism that fueled the boom in the stock market. The surging stock market then led individuals to consume more and save less. In fairness, there was more than just optimism fueling this boom. The Clinton administration's budget policies were symbolic of a larger pro-business agenda in areas such as trade, health and safety regulation, and environmental regulation. These policies, together with other factors, led to a large redistribution from labor to capital. The share of corporate output going to profit rose by more than two and a half percentage points between 1989 and 1998, from 14.9 to 17.5 percent. The profit rate reached its highest levels in the postwar period. The 1990s have definitely been a prosperous period for corporate America.

However, even the strong profit growth of the 1990s can't justify current stock valuations. The price/earnings ratio of the stock market is at a record high by almost any measure. For the S&P 500, the price/earnings ratio is now over 30:1. The only time in the past where the price/earnings ratio had gone above 20:1 was in 1961, when the economy was just coming out of a recession and on the verge of eight years of strong growth. By contrast, the Congressional Budget Office projects that real corporate profits are barely going to rise at all over the next ten years. As Alan Greenspan warned when the stock market was about 40 percent below its current level, "irrational exuberance" appears to be driving financial markets. This exuberance has created a huge bubble, which in turn has driven a consumption boom. But when the bubble bursts, it will not be a pretty picture.

THE DEATH OF THE NAIRU

There is another important aspect to economic policy in this decade that is worth noting. Prior to 1994, virtually all economists believed that the inflation rate would begin to accelerate if the unemployment rate fell below a certain level, known as the non-accelerating inflation rate of unemployment, or NAIRU. There were differences on where exactly the NAIRU was, but it was generally placed between 5.8 and 6.5 percent. Most economists felt that it was very important to keep the economy from falling below the NAIRU so as to keep inflation under control. For this reason, the NAIRU effectively placed a floor on the unemployment rate.

The economy first began to approach the NAIRU range in early 1994, as the unemployment rate fell close to 6 percent. At that point, the Federal Reserve Board took steps to try to prevent the unemployment rate from falling further. Specifically it began raising interest rates. In the twelve months from February 1994 to February 1995, the Federal Reserve Board raised the interest in the short-term money market by three percentage points, from 3 percent to 6 percent. Alan Greenspan was obviously quite serious about slowing the economy to keep the unemployment rate from falling.

This strategy didn't work. By the end of 1994, the unemployment rate had fallen to 5.4 percent, below almost everyone's estimate of the NAIRU. The unemployment rate stayed at roughly the same level through 1995 and 1996. Still inflation did not accelerate. In 1997, the unemployment rate fell even further, ending the year at 4.7 percent. It dropped even more in 1998, averaging just 4.5 percent for the year. Even though the unemployment rate was more than 1.5 percentage points below most previous estimates of the NAIRU, the inflation rate has remained well under control. In fact, by most measures it has been declining through this whole period.

To Alan Greenspan's credit, he and his colleagues at the Federal Reserve Board eventually gave up the fight against a nonexistent inflation problem. As the unemployment rate fell ever lower, and the predicted inflation did not materialize, the Federal Reserve Board gradually eased up on interest rates and allowed the economy to continue to grow. As a result, subsequent events have provided considerable grounds for questioning the NAIRU theory. Either the NAIRU never existed in the first place, or it is substantially below the range economists had previously estimated. Even with the unemployment rate falling to 4.3 percent in some months, there still has been no evidence of accelerating inflation in any significant sector of the economy.

The demise of the NAIRU is tremendously important. If the unemployment rate is allowed to fall to 4.5 percent, instead of the Federal Reserve Board's setting a floor at 6 percent, approximately 3 million more people will hold jobs. The gains from lower unemployment accrue disproportionately to the worst-off groups. As a rule of thumb, the unemployment rate for African Americans is usually close to twice the overall rate of unemployment. The unemployment rate for African-American teens is close to six times the overall unemployment rate. In 1993, when the overall unemployment rate was still 6.9 percent, the unemployment rate for African Americans was 13 percent. In January 1999, when the overall rate had fallen to 4.3 percent, the unemployment rate for African Americans was down to 7.8 percent. The unemployment rate for adult black men was down to 5.9 percent, slightly below the old measures of the NAIRU for the population as a whole. The unemployment rate for African-American teens in some months has fallen as low as 22 percent. This is still quite high, but it is far better than the 40 percent unemployment rates that this group was experiencing just six years ago.

Lower unemployment also means more output. "Okun's Law" is a rule of thumb that a one percentage point drop in the unemployment rate corresponds to a two percentage point increase in output. This means that an economy with a 4.5 percent unemployment rate is producing 3 percent more than an economy with a 6 percent unemployment rate. At present, this amounts to more than $250 billion in additional output. Since the unemployment rate first fell below 6 percent in 1994, the economy has produced more than $600 billion in additional output as a result of the fact that the unemployment rate was allowed to remain below the previously estimated levels of the NAIRU. This gain is at least ten times as large as economists would have hoped to derive from expanded trade or deficit reduction. In short, lower unemployment makes a huge difference to the economy as a whole, and an even larger difference to the nation's most disadvantaged people. We should all be thankful that the NAIRU seems to have been laid to rest.

HOW DEAD IS THE NAIRU?

Of course, the NAIRU isn't exactly completely dead just yet. There are still many economists who believe that the low inflation of the last few years has been an aberration. They argue that unusual factors have prevented inflation from rising the last few years, and that we cannot expect the economy to typically operate with an unemployment rate below 6 percent, or perhaps 5.5 percent, without accelerating inflation.

There clearly have been some unusual factors affecting inflation over the last three years. For example, energy prices have plummeted in the last two years, both lowering the overall inflation rate and causing significant increases in workers' purchasing power. Also, the price of imports from the developing world dropped sharply in 1998 in the wake of the currency devaluations that followed the financial panic in East Asia. In addition, the changes in measurement noted earlier changed the yardstick, so that a constant level of inflation would be reported as being about 0.3 percentage points lower by 1998. While these one-time factors can explain the drop in the inflation rate over the last three years, there still is no evidence that inflation would otherwise have been rising during this period.

Of course, there is one other dampening factor that has been less widely noted. The boom in the stock market has done more than just spur consumption. For many workers, a large portion of compensation comes in the form of stock options. This has been the case for some time with CEOs and other high-ranking executives, but increasingly workers further down the line are receiving a significant portion of their pay in stock options. This has been a particularly common practice in the software industry and in other high-tech areas. While workers are happy to accept options as part of their pay package when stock prices are soaring, options will appear less attractive in a flat or sinking market.

There is no easy way to determine the extent to which anticipated capital gains on stock options may have offset pressure on wages, since there is no reliable data on the value of these options. However, the potential impact of these options on relieving wage pressure could have been quite large. For example, if just 1 percent of the $8 trillion in excess stock gains noted earlier was given to workers through stock options in lieu of wage increases, this would have been equivalent to approximately 1.3 percent of total compensation. In other words, if workers had not received options in a booming stock market, they might have demanded an additional 1.3 percent in pay increases over the last three years. Wage increases of this magnitude might have provided a significant spur to inflation.

This linkage between wage growth and the stock market suggests another and perhaps more important potential problem once the stock market boom ends. Workers who have been receiving much of their compensation in stock options will again demand to be paid in straight salary. This will put upward pressure on prices just when the economy may be slumping into a recession, as declining consumption follows in the wake of a falling stock market. In other words, although the rising stock market may have boosted the economy both on the demand side (through its effect on consumption) and on the supply side (through its effect on dampening wage growth), a declining stock market can have exactly the opposite set of effects. The economy may look good right now, but it also looks precarious.

CONCLUSION

This chapter has argued that claims for a "new economy" cannot be supported by the data. The growth of the past few years is largely offsetting extraordinarily poor economic performance during the earlier part of the recovery. Furthermore, some of the recent growth is a statistical mirage, attributable to changes in measurement rather than increasing growth. When changes in measurement are taken into account, there is even less evidence that productivity growth in the 1990s has escaped the slow trend growth rate of the last quarter century.

This chapter has also pointed out that the deficit reduction policy of the 1990s has not had quite the desired effect. The main source of growth has been a consumption boom that has followed in the wake of a soaring stock market. The share of GDP going to investment is only slightly higher than at the peak of the last business cycle in 1989 when the country was running large budget deficits.

The one clear economic achievement of the past few years has been maintaining a low unemployment rate along with a declining or stable inflation rate. This has provided enormous benefits, particularly to the most disadvantaged groups in society. However, the bloated stock market hangs over this accomplishment, as well. A decline in the stock market may lead to additional inflationary pressures in the future, as workers seek to convert worthless stock options into real pay increases. The inevitable reversal of the huge trade deficit run-up in recent years poses a similar problem for the future of the economy.

In short, the current economic picture is very bright, but extremely precarious. As long as the stock market continues to rise, the economy should advance smoothly. But now that it has attained levels that are 50–70 percent above what would be dictated by historical measures, it is questionable how much longer the market can continue to advance. Once it stops rising, the good times are likely to end quickly. When the dust clears, we will be in a much better position to evaluate the new economy.

APPENDIX 11.1

The numbers that appear in Table 11.1 and the rows labeled "published data" in Table 11.2 are all based on data either from the Bureau of Labor Statistics or the National Income and Product Accounts (NIPA) produced by the Bureau of Economic Analysis. The real compensation numbers for the periods from 1959 to 1979 use the CPI-UX1 series for calculating inflation and thereby deriving real compensation from the published numbers on nominal compensation. The rows in Table 11.2 that are labeled "consistent GDP measures" have the measures of annual GDP and productivity growth in years after 1978 adjusted downward by 0.2 percentage points to reflect the amount that measurement changes in official data have raised GDP and productivity growth in the years after 1978, according to the estimates that appear on page 94 of the 1999 *Economic Report of the President*. The main factor in this difference is the application of geometric means to the GDP deflators for years after 1978.

The numbers that appear in Table 11.2 in the row labeled "consistent GDP measures and constant rate of computer quality improvement" were derived by first calculating the increase in GDP that was attributable to the reported decline in the price of computers. This was obtained by taking the difference between the GDP price index without computers and the GDP price index with computers, which has averaged approximately 0.45 percentage points over the last four years. This difference is approximately equal to the contribution of the recorded price decline in computers to GDP growth. It is assumed that the rate of quality improvement in computers in years prior to 1995 was approximately 45 percent of the measured rate of quality improvement in the years from 1995 to 1999. If the rate of quality improvement in computers has remained at its pre-1995 rate, it implies a reduction in the measured GDP and productivity growth of approximately 0.2 percentage points annually.

APPENDIX 11.2

THE COST-OF-LIVING DEBATE

Many economic commentators have argued that living standards have improved more in recent years than is indicated by economic statistics, because official data fail to fully account for the improved quality of goods and services or to appreciate the gains provided by new goods. By failing to accurately take account of these changes, it is argued that official data overstate the true rate of increase in the cost of living, and therefore understate the actual increase in wages and living standards.

The measure of inflation is central to determining how rapidly living standards are improving, since it provides the basis for determining the size of real gains in wages and income. For example, if wages increased by 4 percent on average, and the inflation rate was 3 percent, the increase in the real wage—the extent to which workers' purchasing power actually increased—would be 1 percent (4 percent minus 3 percent). However, if the measure of inflation turned out to have been overstated, so that the true rate of inflation was just 2 percent, then the true rate of real wage growth would be 2 percent (4 percent minus 2 percent).

The report of the Boskin Commission, a group of prominent economists appointed by the Senate Finance Committee to examine the accuracy of the CPI, is often cited as evidence to support this view. This report concluded that the CPI overstated the true rate of inflation by 1.1 percentage points annually. Others have used less careful research to make claims that people are far better off today than they were thirty years ago.[5]

These claims raise two issues. First, to what extent does the CPI overstate the true rate of inflation? Second, is the overstatement (if any) larger now than in prior decades? This second issue has generally been ignored in most public discussions of the topic, but it is actually the more important of the two. It would not be necessary to reassess the current strength of the economy, even if the CPI substantially overstated inflation, if the extent of the overstatement had been largely constant through time. For example, if the CPI overstates the rate of inflation by one percentage point each year, but has overstated inflation by a similar amount for the last half century, then the existence of this overstatement would not change the assessment of the

1990s compared to preceding decades. The overstatement would matter for purposes of historical comparison only if it could be shown that the overstatement has somehow gotten larger in recent years.

The Boskin Commission attributed the overstatement of inflation in the CPI to several factors, but the primary source was the index's treatment of new goods and quality improvements. The commission argued that the CPI was slow to include new goods such as cellular phones in its survey and therefore often missed the large price declines that these goods experience in the period after they are first placed on the market. In the case of quality improvements, the commission argued that there are many categories of goods such as electronics and medical care where the BLS methods of measuring quality improvements were inadequate. This causes price increases that are attributable to improvements in quality to be treated simply as inflation.

While there is some truth to both claims, the evidence is far more ambiguous than the commission implied in its report. New goods often were not included in the index for several years after their introduction into the market. But the importance of this for the typical consumer is rather questionable. The cellular phone was often cited in this debate, because its exclusion from the index (through an oversight) was an error of extraordinary magnitude. According to calculations from the BLS, its inclusion in the index would have lowered the annual rate of inflation by an average of 0.017 percentage points from 1985 to 1995. This is not altogether inconsequential, but given that this was an unusually prominent example of the exclusion of a new good, it suggests that any overstatement from the delay in including new goods in the sample is relatively small. It is also worth noting that BLS changed its procedures in 1998, so that most new goods should be included in the sample within a year of being placed on the market.

The second point about new goods can be made very well with the example of the cellular phone. Most households still do not own a cellular phone. For these people, the rapid decline in the price of cellular phones has had absolutely no impact on their cost of living. The people who experienced a significant decline in their cost of living as a result of the falling price of cellular phones were those who were willing to buy a cellular phone when it cost $1,000. Now these people may have to pay only $100 for a phone and therefore have saved themselves $900. For these people, the most wealthy in society, the failure to include the cellular phone in the CPI may have led to a substantial overstatement in their cost of living.

In other words, since the vast majority of consumers don't buy new goods when they first come on the market and are very expensive, the initial price decline of these goods has no impact on most people's cost of living. The price of goods affects the typical person's living standard only after it has fallen enough to have been incorporated into his or her consumption bundle. At that point, the good will almost certainly have been included in the CPI.

While the Boskin Commission did produce some evidence that the CPI was not adequately adjusting for quality improvements, on closer examination many of its claims turned out to be largely speculative, and in some cases based on a misreading of the data. For example, the commission's estimate of an understatement in the measured rate of quality improvement of foods and beverages (and therefore an overstatement of inflation) was derived from a subjective assessment of the improvement in foods and beverages over the prior twenty years. Its assessment of the understatement of the rate of quality improvement in housing turned out to be based on a misreading of data on the increase in the size of new homes.

It is also important to note that the Boskin Commission did not examine many cases where there is evidence that the quality of goods and services may have deteriorated or improved less than is indicated by the BLS measure of quality improvement. An example of the former is the spread of managed care. For many people, managed care is far inferior to the previous system of fee-for-service health care insurance. It often requires patients to spend a considerable amount of time going through paperwork and arguing with company representatives in order to get coverage for health care expenses. Any quality deterioration associated with the shift to managed care would not be picked up in the CPI.

Many observers in the debate fail to recognize that the BLS already included substantial adjustments in its measure of the rate of inflation. One area where these adjustments may have been excessive is in the case of new automobiles. The BLS based its assessment of the quality improvements in new lines of automobiles on the manufacturers' claims about the cost of changes in its cars. Since the manufacturers would rather have cost increases appear as quality improvements, they have an incentive to try to hide actual price increases by exaggerating the cost of quality improvements. Recent research suggests that BLS may have missed a significant quality deterioration in new cars. The greater complexity of new automobiles appears to have significantly increased the cost of auto repairs.

If BLS had adjusted correctly for quality, higher repair costs would be treated as a quality deterioration in exactly the same way as increased durability would count as a quality improvement.

In the area of quality measurement it is also important to note that BLS has made important changes in recent years. For example, it now uses the hedonic methodology recommended by the Boskin Commission to measure quality improvements in computers and televisions. There are few if any areas of the CPI where there is a clear case that the current BLS methodology leads it to understate the pace of quality improvement.

It is worth noting an important sense in which the CPI may understate the cost of living. The development and widespread adoption of new products imposes costs on people that are not picked up in the CPI. For example, someone who currently lacks Internet access is being excluded from a major form of communication. Such a person is actually made worse off by the development of the Internet, since information that would have been otherwise accessible in other forms may now be available only by going on-line. Therefore a person will have to encounter the expense of gaining access to the Web to be as well off as they were previously. The new cost of buying a computer and paying an Internet provider does not enter into the CPI.

It is common for such costs to arise as society develops. For example, at one time a phone would have been viewed as a luxury; now a person without access to a telephone is likely to have great difficulty communicating with friends and family. Similarly, many communities are oriented around car ownership, so that it is extremely difficult for someone to get to work or do shopping if they do not own a car. There are many other examples of situations where changes in society effectively make an item a necessity, so that someone becomes far worse off through time by virtue of not owning the new product. The CPI does not in any manner account for these additional costs. (It's not obvious how it could.) For this reason, the CPI may substantially understate increases in the cost of living.

OVERSTATEMENTS PAST AND PRESENT

Whatever may be the case about the accuracy of the CPI at present, there is absolutely no evidence that any overstatement is larger now than in the past. The concern about an overstatement of inflation in the CPI is long-standing. The Stigler Price Commission, which issued its report in 1961, made virtually all the same points as the Boskin Commission did in 1996. It pointed out the same problems with including new goods and measuring quality improvements as well as the other less important sources of inaccuracy in the CPI.

The BLS has been trying to respond to these criticisms over the years, and by almost any assessment, has improved its techniques enormously. While new goods may not get into the CPI for a year or two after going on the market now, in earlier times it was often decades before new goods were added to the index. Passenger air travel, home air conditioners, and clothes dryers all did not enter the CPI until 1964. By that point, all three items had been available to consumers for more than twenty years.

The methods of adjusting for quality also have improved enormously. Ironically, in assessing the CPI, the Boskin Commission relied largely on research that examined the CPI in the 1950s, 1960s, and 1970s—not the 1990s. This work found very large understatements of quality improvements, and therefore large overstatements of inflation during these decades. In the period since the 1950s, BLS has responded to its own research and that of outside academics and made many improvements in its measurement procedures. Given these improvements, it would be very hard to maintain that it is doing a worse job of measuring quality improvements in the 1990s than it did in preceding decades.

It is also important to recognize that the quality improvements and new products of prior decades had an enormous impact on people's lives; an impact at least as large as the technological breakthroughs of the last ten or fifteen years. For example, the development of the polio vaccine in the 1950s meant that parents need never worry that their children would fall victim to this crippling and often fatal disease. It is questionable whether all the medical advances of the last decade have had as much impact on people's lives as this single breakthrough. The same could be said of the discovery of penicillin in the 1930s.

In other areas, the breakthroughs of preceding decades were equally impressive. Radio allowed instantaneous mass communication of news and entertainment for the first time in the 1920s. Television had a similar impact in the 1950s. Air travel made it feasible to travel coast to coast in a single day. While all these innovations seem mundane today, that is only because they are all taken for granted by a population that has long become accustomed to them. However, at the time they were developed, these technologies were every bit as impressive and revolutionary as the personal computer or the Internet is at present. Only extreme myopia would allow us to view the present as a unique period of technological innovation.

CONCLUSION: MEASUREMENT ERROR ISN'T HIDING THE NEW ECONOMY

In short, there is no real case that there has been a surge in living standards in the 1990s that has been concealed by an overstated CPI. There are reasons for believing that the CPI overstates inflation, but the evidence for this view is more limited than is generally recognized. There are also reasons to believe that the CPI might understate the true increase in the cost-of-living index. The potential sources of understatement have not been examined with the same diligence as the possible sources of overstatement. For this reason, it is not possible at this point to even determine with certainty the net direction of bias in the index.

However, even if the CPI does presently overstate inflation, there is no evidence that this overstatement is larger than in the past. The BLS has improved its methodology considerably over the last fifty years. All the reasons that have been put forward to support the view that the CPI overstates inflation have also been present for fifty years. BLS has been attentive to these problems and made numerous improvements in the CPI to correct for them. As a result, there is no real basis for believing that any overstatement in the CPI is higher today than in preceding years. Measurement error is not hiding an economic boom.

12

THE UNITED STATES AND EUROPE

WHO'S REALLY AHEAD?

John Schmitt and Lawrence Mishel

Many people now argue that labor market rigidities are making Western Europe less competitive. But by key measures of economic strength, including GDP per capita and productivity, Europe is doing every bit as well as the United States in the 1990s.

Low unemployment in the United States—just 4.3 percent at present—has spawned triumphalism here and envy in much of Europe. According to the standard view, the United States can thank its "dynamism" and flexibility for its current good fortune. Europe, on the other hand, should blame its record unemployment rates on rigid labor market institutions (unions and high minimum wages, for example) and the burden of large welfare states. That the United States has considerably lower unemployment than Europe as a whole is both true and enviable. However, this statement, which is the primary basis for recent U.S. triumphalism, is a narrow and incomplete comparison. This chapter assesses some of the key claims made about the economic performance of the United States and the other advanced countries by presenting internationally comparable data on a broad range of economic indicators. We analyze both what the indicators tell us about the leading advanced economies' performance in the 1990s relative to earlier periods and what they tell us about performance of the "U.S. model" relative to economies with stronger labor-market institutions, including trade unions, minimum wages, and social benefits.

Specifically, we evaluate the economies of the Group of Seven (G7)— with some reference to other advanced industrialized democracies—in three areas: first, their ability to generate goods and services; second, their ability to create employment; and third, their ability to generate an equitable growth in earnings.

To summarize the main findings:

- In all the G7 economies—except Germany—growth in gross domestic product (GDP) per capita has been slower in the 1990s than it was in the 1970s and 1980s. Despite widespread praise of U.S. dynamism, per capita GDP growth in the United States in the 1990s through 1998 has been slower than that of Germany and the United Kingdom and only marginally better than rates in Japan, France, and Italy.

- In all the G7 economies except Germany and Italy, productivity growth has been slower in the 1990s than it was in the 1970s and 1980s. The United States and Canada have had the lowest productivity growth rates among the G7 economies in the 1980s and 1990s.

- High, sustained productivity growth has allowed many European economies to catch up to the higher productivity levels of the United States. Recent data from the Conference Board estimate that the economies of France, western Germany, the Netherlands, and Belgium are, on average, as productive as the U.S. economy.

- In all the G7 economies—including the United States—job creation rates are slower in the 1990s than they were in the 1970s and 1980s.

- In all the G7 economies except the United States, unemployment has been higher in the 1990s than in the 1970s and 1980s. The United States has achieved low unemployment rates in the late 1990s, but so have Austria, Denmark, Japan, the Netherlands, Norway, and Portugal.

- Real compensation growth has generally been slow throughout the 1990s. Earnings inequality increased sharply in the 1980s and 1990s in the United States and the United Kingdom, but changed little in the rest of the G7.

GENERATING GOODS AND SERVICES

The first set of indicators measures the capacity of each economy to generate goods and services for its population. Table 12.1 (see page 240) demonstrates that, among the G7 countries, the GDP growth rate during the 1990s (1989–98) has generally been lower than during the 1970s (1973–79) and the 1980s (1979–89). The one exception is Germany, which (with the United States) led the G7 countries in GDP growth in the 1990s with a 2.4 percent annual growth rate, up from a 1.8 percent annual growth rate in the 1980s. The remaining five G7 economies all have growth rates in the 1990s below 2.0 percent per year, with Italy (1.3 percent) growing at the slowest pace.

When population growth rates across countries differ widely, however, the growth rate in GDP may paint a misleading picture of the economy's capacity to provide goods and services for its population. Table 12.1, therefore, also reports annual growth rates for GDP per capita. Again, with the exception of Germany, growth rates across the G7 countries are all lower in the 1990s than in the 1970s or 1980s. Growth in GDP per capita is strongest in Germany (1.7 percent per year) and the United Kingdom (1.6 percent). Rapid population growth in the United States lowers the growth rate in GDP per capita there to 1.4 percent per year, not much above the rates in Japan (1.3 percent), France (1.2 percent), and Italy (1.1 percent). Canada's moderate GDP growth rate and fast population growth rate leave it with a 0.4 percent per year growth rate in GDP per capita in the 1990s.

The most important determinant of the growth of GDP per capita is the growth rate of productivity—the output of goods and services per hour worked in the economy. Productivity growth is a fundamental indicator of an economy's capacity to improve its efficiency. Estimates made by the Organization for Economic Cooperation and Development (OECD) of the annual average growth in labor productivity in the business sector for twenty OECD countries from 1960 through 1996 (Table 12.2, page 241) demonstrate that among the G7 countries, productivity growth rates were generally lower in the 1979–97 period than in two earlier periods (1960–73 and 1973–79). Five of the G7 economies had productivity growth rates of 2.0 percent or more per year during the period 1979–97: Japan (2.3 percent), Germany (2.2 percent), France (2.2 percent), Italy (2.0 percent), and the United Kingdom (2.0 percent). Over the same period, Canada

TABLE 12.1. REAL GROSS DOMESTIC PRODUCT, ANNUAL AVERAGE GROWTH RATES, 1973–98

	1973–79		1979–89		1989–98[a]	
	GDP	GDP PER CAPITA	GDP	GDP PER CAPITA	GDP	GDP PER CAPITA
G7						
United States	3.5	2.5	2.7	1.8	2.4	1.4
Japan	4.6	3.5	3.8	3.2	1.6	1.3
Germany	2.9	3.1	1.8	1.7	2.4	1.7
France	3.5	3.0	2.3	1.8	1.7	1.2
Italy	3.6	3.1	2.4	2.3	1.3	1.1
United Kingdom	2.4	2.4	2.4	2.2	1.9	1.6
Canada	4.9	3.7	3.1	1.9	1.7	0.4
Other Advanced OECD						
Australia	3.5	2.3	3.3	1.8	2.9	1.7
Austria	3.7	3.8	2.1	2.0	2.4	1.3
Belgium	3.2	3.0	1.9	1.8	1.9	1.5
Denmark	2.5	2.2	1.8	1.8	2.5	2.2
Finland	3.3	2.9	3.7	3.3	1.3	0.8
Ireland	4.9	3.4	3.1	2.7	6.9	6.6
Netherlands	3.1	2.4	1.9	1.3	2.8	2.1
New Zealand	1.7	0.8	2.3	1.8	2.1	0.9
Norway	4.8	4.3	2.6	2.2	3.5	3.0
Portugal	4.8	2.9	2.9	2.6	2.7	2.8
Spain	3.8	2.7	2.8	2.3	2.2	2.0
Sweden	2.0	1.7	2.0	1.8	1.1	0.4
Switzerland	1.1	1.3	2.1	1.6	0.7	−0.3

[a] Data for 1998 are OECD projections.

Source: Authors' analysis of Organisation for Economic Co-operation and Development (OECD) data, *Employment Outlook*, July 1996, June 1998, and December 1998.

TABLE 12.2. LABOR PRODUCTIVITY IN THE BUSINESS SECTOR, ANNUAL AVERAGE GROWTH RATES, 1960–97

	1960–73[a]	1973–79	1979–97[b]
United States	2.6	0.3	0.9
Japan	8.4	2.8	2.3
Germany[c]	4.5	3.1	2.2
France	5.3	2.9	2.2
Italy	6.4	2.8	2.0
United Kingdom	4.0	1.6	2.0
Canada	2.5	1.1	1.0
Australia	3.0	2.5	1.5
Austria	5.9	3.1	2.3
Belgium	5.2	2.7	1.9
Denmark	3.9	2.3	2.1
Finland	5.0	3.2	3.5
Ireland	4.8	4.3	4.1
Netherlands	4.8	2.6	1.5
New Zealand	2.1	−1.1	1.3
Norway	3.8	2.7	1.8
Portugal	7.5	0.5	2.4
Spain	5.9	2.8	2.7
Sweden	3.7	1.4	2.0
Switzerland	3.3	0.8	0.6

[a] Or earliest available year: 1961 for Australia and Ireland; 1962 for Japan and the United Kingdom; 1964 for Spain; 1965 for France and Sweden; 1966 for Canada and Norway; 1967 for New Zealand; 1969 for the Netherlands; and 1970 for Belgium.

[b] Or latest available year: 1993 for Portugal; 1994 for Norway; 1995 for Australia, Austria, New Zealand, and Switzerland; 1996 for Japan, Germany, France, Italy, the United Kingdom, Belgium, Denmark, Finland, Ireland, the Netherlands, Spain, and Sweden.

[c] First two columns refer to western Germany. The third column is calculated as the weighted average of West German productivity growth between 1979 and 1991 and total German productivity growth between 1991 and 1996.

Source: Authors' analysis of Organisation for Economic Co-operation and Development (OECD) data, *Employment Outlook,* July 1996, June 1998, and December 1998.

(1.0 percent) and the United States (0.9 percent) experienced the slowest productivity growth in the G7.

Some economists have argued that an acceleration in productivity growth in the United States late in the 1990s business cycle signals the emergence of a "new economy." In fact, productivity growth over the 1995–98 period was 2.1 percent annually, significantly better than the 1.2 percent productivity growth of the 1980s (these data, from the Bureau of Labor Statistics [BLS], differ from the OECD rates cited in Table 12.2). Incorporating this most recent productivity growth, however, does not alter the conclusion to be drawn from Table 12.2. Over the full decade of the 1990s, virtually all advanced countries have seen far better productivity growth than that of the United States. Whether the country can sustain the current productivity boost and keep pace with European productivity growth in the future remains an open question. However, we suspect that a significant part of the recent U.S. productivity surge is due to special circumstances that will not continue: a change in measurement, high demand growth at low unemployment, and a surge of computer investments.

The Conference Board productivity estimates in Table 12.3 are broadly consistent with the OECD data: a substantial slowdown in productivity growth rates in recent years, with Japan and the European G7 economies experiencing faster productivity growth rates than the United States and Canada did in the 1980s and 1990s. The Conference Board data also allow us to go beyond the growth in productivity to look at the actual level of output of goods and services across international economies. Historically, economists have argued that slower productivity growth in the United States was due to the country's lead in technological innovation: other economies had it relatively easy to catch up to the more technologically advanced United States. The most recent data from the Conference Board, however, suggest that the United States no longer has the world's most productive economy. Table 12.3 reports Conference Board estimates of real GDP per hour worked in 1960, 1973, 1987, and 1995, using the U.S. output level as the benchmark in each year. In 1960 and 1973, productivity levels in the other G7 countries were generally about two-thirds the level in the United States. The gap narrowed considerably between 1973 and 1987 and again between 1987 and 1995. By 1995, real output per hour worked in two G7 economies, France (102) and western Germany (101), had surpassed the level in the United States (100). Two other European economies, the Netherlands (98) and Belgium (97), were not far behind.

Other recent studies of international productivity levels provide independent confirmation that other advanced countries have reached U.S. productivity levels. BLS data for 1996, for example, show western German and Norwegian productivity levels about 7 percent

TABLE 12.3. REAL GROSS DOMESTIC PRODUCT PER HOUR WORKED, 1960–95

	As Percent of U.S. Level in Each Year				Average Annual Growth Rate		
	1960	1973	1987	1995	1960–73	1973–87	1987–95
G7							
United States	100	100	100	100	2.9	1.2	0.9
Japan	21	45	58	68	9.3	3.2	2.9
Germany[a]	52	69	84	101	5.2	2.7	3.3
France	54	73	96	102	5.3	3.3	1.7
Italy	40	64	78	90	6.7	2.7	2.8
United Kingdom	58	66	79	84	3.9	2.6	1.8
Canada	79	79	86	85	2.8	1.9	0.7
Other Advanced OECD							
Australia	73	70	77	76	2.5	1.9	0.8
Austria	44	64	79	83	5.9	2.9	1.5
Belgium	49	68	89	97	5.5	3.3	2.1
Denmark	48	63	68	74	5.0	1.8	2.0
Finland	37	55	64	74	6.1	2.4	2.8
Ireland	31	42	59	84	5.5	3.9	5.4
Netherlands	58	77	95	98	5.3	2.8	1.4
New Zealand	—	—	—	—	—	—	—
Norway	48	56	76	88	4.2	3.6	2.7
Portugal	22	37	40	38	7.2	1.8	0.5
Spain	23	44	57	70	8.1	3.1	3.7
Sweden	58	73	78	79	4.7	1.7	1.1
Switzerland	71	76	76	86	3.4	1.3	2.4
OECD (excluding the United States)	47	61	73	80	5.5	2.6	2.2

[a] Data refer to western Germany only.

Source: "Perspectives on a Global Economy: Understanding Differences in Economic Performance," report number 1187-97-RR (New York: Conference Board, Inc., Summer 1997).

above, and French productivity levels about equal to those of the United States. The same data suggest that Sweden and Japan trail the United States by substantial margins (by 17 percent and 29 percent, respectively). A study by Mary O'Mahony for the Institute for Public Policy Research in the United Kingdom also found higher productivity levels in France and western Germany than in the United States.

These studies naturally differ in their specific estimates of productivity in the various countries, but they all make the same important point: faster productivity growth in a number of major European countries has allowed those countries to catch up to the United States in actual productivity levels. This phenomenon clearly goes beyond other countries' benefiting from U.S. technological leadership—these other countries now have higher productivity levels in leading industries, if not the entire economy. Nor can the higher productivity in countries such as Germany be dismissed as a consequence of their higher unemployment (therefore, presumably, not having as many of their "less-skilled" workers employed). For instance, western Germany had an unemployment rate 1.8 percent higher than the United States in 1996 (using "standardized," comparable rates). If these extra unemployed were working, and were only 75 percent as productive as the average employed German, then western German productivity levels would be only marginally different, 6.3 percent rather than 6.8 percent higher than in the United States (using the BLS estimates of productivity).

Critics of European economies often argue that the "rigidities" in those economies have robbed them of the dynamism that is supposed to be evident in the United States. Data on the two most important measures of economic dynamism—growth in GDP per capita and productivity—however, give no support to this view. During the 1990s, Germany, Japan, and the United Kingdom have experienced per capita GDP growth on a par with that of the United States. In fact, per capita GDP growth in the United States in the 1990s has been only marginally better than that of France or Italy. With respect to productivity, all the G7 economies except Canada have outperformed the United States, usually by a substantial margin. While economists have historically downplayed faster productivity growth in Europe and Japan as evidence only that it is easier to follow than to lead, new data on international productivity levels suggest that many European economies have narrowed or eliminated the productivity gap with the United States. Whatever liabilities a developed welfare state, broad social protections, and strong unions may represent for a country, no evidence exists to suggest that these institutional arrangements lead to slower economic or productivity growth.

GENERATING EMPLOYMENT

The second set of indicators describes the ability of each economy to generate employment opportunities for its population. According to OECD data in Table 12.4 (see page 246), the United States led the G7 in job creation between 1989 and 1998, with an average annual job creation rate of 1.3 percent. Over the same period, Japan (0.7 percent) and Canada (1.0 percent) expanded employment at slower rates; France (0.1 percent) and the United Kingdom (0.0 percent) saw basically no change in employment; and Germany (–0.2 percent per year) and Italy (–0.4 percent) saw employment fall. Separate employment data from the BLS (not shown) show a similar pattern in the 1990s.

We can judge these job-creation rates along two dimensions: first, how the recent rates compare with the historical experience of each country; and second, how the rates in individual countries compare to others in the same time period. Although the United States has outperformed the rest of the G7 in the 1990s, its performance has been lackluster by its own historical standards. For instance, the OECD data (Table 12.4) show a deceleration in U.S. employment growth from 1.7 percent per year in 1979–89 to 1.3 percent in 1989–97. At the same time, the other G7 economies also experienced a deceleration in job growth in the 1990s relative to the 1980s, with the worst deceleration in Canada. Although the United States created jobs at a faster rate than the other G7 nations in the 1990s, three OECD countries outdid the United States over the period: Ireland (3.0 percent annual rate), the Netherlands (1.9 percent), and New Zealand (1.5 percent). Australia (1.1 percent) and Norway (1.0 percent) came close to the U.S. pace.

International comparisons of employment growth, like GDP growth, are sensitive to international differences in population (and, thereby, potential labor force) growth. Table 12.5 (see page 247), therefore, reports BLS estimates of the "employment-to-population rate"—the share of the working-age population in each country that

TABLE 12.4. EMPLOYMENT, ANNUAL
AVERAGE GROWTH RATES, 1979–98

	1979–89	1989–98[a]
G7		
United States	1.7	1.3
Japan	1.1	0.7
Germany	0.4	–0.2
France	0.2	0.1
Italy	0.2	–0.4
United Kingdom	0.6	0.0
Canada	2.0	1.0
Other Advanced OECD		
Australia	2.4	1.1
Austria	0.0	0.6
Belgium	0.0	0.2
Denmark	0.5	0.2
Finland	0.9	–1.2
Ireland	–0.5	3.0
Netherlands	0.7	1.9
New Zealand	0.1	1.5
Norway	0.8	1.0
Portugal	1.3	0.0
Spain	0.1	0.5
Sweden	0.6	–1.3
Switzerland	1.8	0.3

[a] Data for 1998 are OECD projections.

Source: Authors' analysis of Organisation for Economic Co-operation and Development (OECD) data, *Employment Outlook,* July 1996, June 1998, and December 1998.

has a job—in selected years from 1967 through 1998. In 1967, the employment rates for men in G7 countries were about 80 percent (the exception is Italy at 73.9 percent). Between 1967 and 1979, and again between 1979 and 1998, the share of men in employment fell in every G7 country, including the United States. This decrease reflects greater participation in postsecondary education and earlier retirement, as well as diminished employment opportunities for men.

TABLE 12.5. EMPLOYMENT RATES FOR CIVILIANS, 1967–98

	Employment Rate[a]					Change	
	1967	1973	1979	1989	1998	1979–89	1989–98
MEN							
G7							
United States	78.0	75.5	73.8	72.5	71.6	−1.3	−0.9
Japan	80.0	80.8	78.2	75.1	73.9	−3.1	−1.2
Germany[b]	78.2	75.3	69.8	65.9	59.3	−3.9	−6.6
France[c]	77.7	74.2	69.6	61.2	56.5	−8.4	−4.7
Italy	73.9	69.3	66.3	59.9	55.6	−6.4	−4.3
United Kingdom[c]	81.5	79.1	74.5	70.4	66.6	−4.1	−3.8
Canada	76.3	74.3	73.4	71.4	66.2	−2.0	−5.2
Other Advanced OECD							
Australia	83.8	81.8	75.3	71.9	67.8	−3.4	−4.1
Netherlands[c]	N/A	77.3	74.3	65.0	68.0	−9.3	3.0
Sweden	78.9	75.1	73.7	70.9	62.2	−2.8	−8.7
WOMEN							
G7							
United States	39.0	42.0	47.5	54.3	57.1	6.8	2.8
Japan	48.9	46.8	45.7	47.4	47.4	1.7	0.0
Germany[b]	38.0	39.1	38.4	39.7	39.2	1.3	−0.5
France[c]	37.2	39.2	40.5	41.2	40.9	0.7	−0.3
Italy	25.3	24.5	27.3	28.6	29.3	1.3	0.7
United Kingdom[c]	40.7	43.4	45.3	49.1	50.6	3.8	1.5
Canada	35.1	39.1	45.3	53.7	53.4	8.4	−0.3
Other Advanced OECD							
Australia	36.6	40.9	40.7	48.6	50.8	7.9	2.2
Netherlands[c]	N/A	27.3	29.2	37.4	47.1	8.2	9.7
Sweden	45.6	50.3	57.2	61.7	53.6	4.5	−8.1

[a] Total employment as a percentage of working-age population.
[b] Data for western Germany; data for 1998 refer to 1996.
[c] Data for 1998 refer to 1997.

Source: Authors' analysis of "Comparative Civilian Labor Force Statistics, Ten Countries, 1959–98," Bureau of Labor Statistics, April 1999, Table 5.

Between 1989 and 1998, the employment rates fell least in the United States (–0.9 percentage points) and Japan (–1.2). Declines were larger for western Germany (–6.6), Canada (–5.2), France (–4.7), Italy (–3.8), and the United Kingdom (–3.8).

The pattern of employment rates is different for women. First, in every country in every year, employment rates were lower for women than for men, generally reflecting women's nonmarket responsibilities. Second, rather than falling over the 1967–98 period, women's employment rates rose in all G7 countries. Between 1979 and 1998, women's employment rates increased most in the United States (9.6 percentage points), Canada (8.1), and the United Kingdom (5.3). Increases were smaller in Italy (2.0), Japan (1.7), Germany (0.8), and France (0.4). During the 1990s, however, the movement toward higher female employment rates generally decelerated and even turned negative in some cases. Women's employment rates grew in the United States (2.8 percentage points), the United Kingdom (1.5), and Italy (0.7); were unchanged in Japan (0.0); and fell in Canada (–0.3), France (–0.3), and Germany (–0.5).

The unemployment rate has been at the center of the current debate over economic policy. Table 12.6 shows the internationally standardized unemployment rates in 1979, 1989, and 1998. Between 1979 and 1998, unemployment rates increased in all G7 countries except the United States. Japan (with a 4.1 percent unemployment rate) and the United States (4.5 percent) had the lowest unemployment rates in the G7. The United Kingdom had an unemployment rate of 6.3 percent, while the rest of the G7 had substantially higher rates: Canada (8.3), Germany (9.4), France (11.7), and Italy (12.3). While the United States is widely considered to be the only OECD country that has resisted the general trend toward high unemployment (Japan is almost universally dismissed as a special case), several European economies have unemployment rates near or below 5 percent: Norway (3.3), the Netherlands (4.0), Austria (4.7), Portugal (4.9), and Denmark (5.1).

Some of the data in Table 12.6 demand careful attention. The unemployment data for Germany, in particular, are full of pitfalls. The unemployment rate that the German government typically reports is for unified Germany and is based on a definition of unemployment that is not consistent with the international definition reported in Table 12.6. In 1998, the official—but not internationally comparable—unemployment rate for unified Germany was 11.2

TABLE 12.6. STANDARDIZED UNEMPLOYMENT RATES

	1979	1989	1998
G7			
United States	5.8	5.3	4.5
Japan	2.1	2.3	4.1
Germany	—	—	9.4
Western Germany	2.7	5.6	7.5
France	5.3	9.3	11.7
Italy	5.8	10.0	12.3
United Kingdom	4.7	7.3	6.3
Canada	7.5	7.5	8.3
Other Advanced OECD			
Australia	6.1	6.2	8.0
Austria	—	—	4.7
Belgium	9.1	7.5	9.5
Denmark	—	7.4	5.1
Finland	6.5	3.3	11.4
Ireland	—	14.7	7.8
Netherlands	5.8	6.9	4.0
New Zealand	—	7.1	7.5
Norway	2.0	5.0	3.3
Portugal	—	4.9	4.9
Spain	7.7	17.2	18.8
Sweden	2.1	1.6	8.3
Switzerland	—	—	—

Sources: Authors' analysis of Organisation for Economic Co-operation and Development (OECD) data, *Employment Outlook,* December 1998; Annex Table 22 updated using OECD Web page; "Unemployment Rates in Nine Countries, Civilian Labor Force Basis Approximating U.S. Concepts, Seasonally Adjusted, 1975–98," Bureau of Labor Statistics, July 1999.

percent. This figure is above the 9.4 percent rate obtained when using the international standard; and well above the 7.5 percent rate obtained when the international definition is applied only to western Germany.

To sum up, job creation rates were slower in the 1990s than in the 1980s in all G7 countries. While the United States led the G7 in employment creation in the 1990s, U.S. performance—even including the strong results in 1998—has still been well below that of the 1970s and 1980s. Recent U.S. job growth has also been slower than in some other OECD countries, most notably the Netherlands. Job growth in the 1980s and 1990s has not been fast enough in any of the G7 countries, including the United States, to prevent a decline in the employment rates for men. At the same time, the United States, Canada, and the United Kingdom have had more success than other G7 economies in incorporating women into the labor market. The United States is the only G7 economy where unemployment was lower in 1998 than in 1979 or 1989, but Japan and five European economies enjoy unemployment rates near or below the U.S. rate in 1998. As a result, the employment and unemployment data do not fully support the view that European economies with strong labor market institutions such as trade unions, minimum wages, and social benefits must necessarily have low job creation and high unemployment rates.

EARNINGS GROWTH AND DISTRIBUTION

Finally, we examine the ability of each economy to generate equitable growth in labor income. Table 12.7 shows the annual real growth in compensation—that is, wage or salary plus benefits—per employee for twenty OECD countries from 1979 through 1998. Among the G7 countries, real compensation growth was generally slower in the 1989–98 period than it was in 1979–89 (only France managed to match 1980s growth rates in the 1990s). In the 1990s, real compensation grew fastest (between 1.0 percent and 1.3 percent per year) in the European G7 economies, followed by Canada (0.8) and Japan (0.5). Compensation growth was slowest in the United States (0.2), though better than it had been in the United States in the 1980s, when compensation fell 0.3 percent per year on average.

The estimates in Table 12.7 refer to annual compensation and have not been adjusted to control for changes in the average hours worked each year. Since annual hours have grown in the United States while they have fallen elsewhere, the data in Table 12.7 understate the degree to which real hourly compensation grew in other advanced countries relative to the United States.

TABLE 12.7. REAL COMPENSATION PER EMPLOYEE IN THE BUSINESS SECTOR, ANNUAL AVERAGE GROWTH RATES, 1979–98

	1979–89	1989–98
G7		
United States	−0.3	0.2
Japan	1.4	0.5
Germany	1.2	1.3
France	1.1	1.1
Italy	1.4	1.0
United Kingdom	2.1	1.0
Canada	0.5	0.8
Other Advanced OECD		
Australia	0.3	1.2
Austria	1.9	1.3
Belgium	0.9	1.5
Denmark	0.3	1.4
Finland	3.0	2.1
Ireland	1.6	2.0
Netherlands	0.0	0.4
New Zealand	0.1	−0.5
Norway	0.4	1.4
Portugal	0.1	3.3
Spain	0.1	1.8
Sweden	1.3	0.9
Switzerland	1.6	0.0

Source: Authors' analysis of Organisation for Economic Co-operation and Development (OECD) data, *Employment Outlook*, December 1998, Annex Tables 12 and 16.

Table 12.8 (see page 252) examines the growth of earnings inequality over the 1980s and 1990s among all workers (the data for men and women separately show similar trends), using data on full-time employees in all sectors of the economy. The table measures inequality as the ratio of earnings of high-wage workers (workers with earnings higher than those of 90 percent of the total workforce) to the earnings of low-wage workers (workers with earnings higher

TABLE 12.8. TRENDS IN OVERALL EARNINGS DISPERSION
RATIO OF NINETIETH- TO TENTH-PERCENTILE EARNINGS

	1979[a]	1989[b]	1995[c]
G7			
United States	—	—	4.39
Japan	3.01	3.16	3.02
Germany	2.69	2.46	2.32
France	3.24	3.28	3.28
Italy	2.94	2.16	2.80
United Kingdom	2.79	3.28	3.38
Canada	4.01	4.45	4.20
Other Advanced OECD			
Australia	2.74	2.87	2.92
Austria	3.45	3.51	3.66
Belgium	—	2.33	2.25
Denmark	2.14	2.18	—
Finland	2.46	2.57	2.38
Ireland	—	—	—
Netherlands	—	2.61	2.59
New Zealand	2.89	2.92	3.04
Norway	2.06	2.16	—
Portugal	—	3.49	4.05
Spain	—	—	—
Sweden	2.04	2.12	2.13
Switzerland	—	—	2.72

[a] Data for this year or for earliest available year. For Austria, Denmark, Finland, Norway, and Sweden, data refer to 1980; for Canada, data refer to 1981; for Germany, data refer to 1983; for New Zealand, data refer to 1984.
[b] For Canada and New Zealand, data refer to 1988; for Norway, data refer to 1987.
[c] Data for this year or for latest available year. For Belgium, Germany, Italy, Portugal, and Sweden, data refer to 1993; for Austria, Canada, Finland, France, Japan, New Zealand, and the Netherlands, data refer to 1994.

Source: Authors' analysis of Organisation for Economic Co-operation and Development (OECD) data, *Employment Outlook,* July 1996, Table 3.1, pp. 61–62.

than those of only 10 percent of the workforce). By this measure, in the early 1980s, Canada and the United States were the most unequal of the OECD countries. The ratio of earnings of the 90th-percentile worker to those of the 10th-percentile worker (the "90–10 ratio") was 4.01 in Canada and 3.65 in the United States, well above most of the rest of the economies in the table. Separate data for wage inequality for men and women (not shown in Table 12.8) demonstrate that inequality grew steadily in the United States throughout the 1980s and 1990s.[1] As a result, by the mid-1990s, the United States had surpassed Canada as the OECD country with the highest degree of earnings inequality among full-time workers.

The pattern of changes in inequality in the rest of the OECD economies was complex. In the 1980s, inequality grew in the United Kingdom (4.9 points per year), Canada (4.4), Japan (1.5), Australia (1.3), and Finland (1.2). It was relatively flat in Sweden (0.9), Austria (0.6), France (0.4), Denmark (0.4), and Norway (–0.7). And it fell sharply in Italy (–7.8) and Germany (–3.8). In the 1990s, inequality grew sharply in Italy (16.0) and Portugal (13.9) and less in New Zealand (5.3), Austria (2.9), Sweden (1.5), Belgium (1.4), and the United Kingdom (1.1, a significant deceleration from the 4.9 points of the 1980s). Over the same period, inequality changed relatively little in Switzerland (0.9), Australia (0.8), and the Netherlands (–0.3), and actually declined in Canada (–5.2), Finland (–3.7), Germany (–3.5), France (–3.2), and Japan (–2.4). In short, since the end of the 1970s, earnings inequality has grown substantially in the United States, the United Kingdom, and New Zealand, but has fluctuated within a much narrower band in most of the rest of the more regulated OECD economies.

In cross-country comparisons, economists have frequently linked the changing pattern of international inequality—the rise of earnings inequality in the United States (and the United Kingdom) and the relative stability of the earnings distribution elsewhere—to the pattern of rising unemployment in Europe. In this analysis, various forces such as technology and globalization have increased the relative demand for skilled (that is, highly educated) workers and lowered relative demand for unskilled workers. The "flexibility" of U.S. labor markets in allowing wages of the unskilled to fall, the argument goes, has allowed unemployment of unskilled workers to remain low in the United States. In contrast, in this view, European labor-market institutions such as strong collective bargaining systems, high minimum wages, and strong labor and social protections have prevented the wage structure from responding to external (primarily technological) forces, thereby inducing high unemployment for unskilled workers.

Table 12.9 (see page 254) assesses this claim about the causes of higher European unemployment—that Europe's labor-market institutions

Table 12.9. Unemployment Rates by Education, 1995

	Unemployment Rate		Ratio Low Ed/ High Ed	Difference Between Low Ed and High Ed
	Less Than Upper Secondary	Tertiary		
G7				
United States	10.0	2.7	3.7	7.3
Japan	—	—	—	—
Germany	13.3	4.9	2.7	8.4
France	14.0	6.5	2.2	7.5
Italy	33.6	9.6	3.5	24.0
United Kingdom	12.2	3.7	3.3	8.5
Canada	13.0	6.5	2.0	6.5
Other Advanced OECD				
Australia	8.5	4.0	2.1	4.5
Austria	5.7	2.0	2.9	3.7
Belgium	13.4	3.6	3.7	9.8
Denmark	14.6	4.6	3.2	10.0
Finland	21.6	7.6	2.8	14.0
Ireland	16.4	4.2	3.9	12.2
Netherlands	7.9	4.1	1.9	3.8
New Zealand	6.7	3.2	2.1	3.5
Norway	6.5	2.4	2.7	4.1
Portugal	6.2	3.2	1.9	3.0
Spain	20.6	14.5	1.4	6.1
Sweden	10.1	4.5	2.2	5.6
Switzerland	5.8	1.9	3.1	3.9

Source: Authors' analysis of Organisation for Economic Co-operation and Development (OECD) data, *Employment Outlook,* June 1998, Table D, pp. 203–5.

have priced less-skilled workers out of jobs. If this were the case, we would expect the unemployment rates of less-educated workers and better-educated workers to be relatively close to one another in the United States, where relatively weak unions, low minimum wages, and stingy benefits would have less of an effect on the employment prospects of less-educated workers (that is, wages can fall so as to promote more jobs for the less skilled). Conversely, we would expect the unemployment rates of less-educated and better-educated workers to be relatively further apart in Europe, where labor market institutions would, by conventional thinking, disproportionately hurt job creation for less-educated workers.

The data in Table 12.9 run completely counter to the conventional expectation. The unemployment rate for less-than-high-school-educated workers in the United States in 1995 (the latest year available) was 3.7 times higher than for college-educated workers—higher than the ratio of less-educated to better-educated unemployment in sixteen of the remaining eighteen countries in the table (Belgium at 3.9 and Ireland at 3.7 are the only exceptions). Thus it appears that Europe's strong labor-market institutions have not contributed to relatively higher unemployment rates among less-educated workers compared to the United States. If anything, the European institutions appear to be associated with substantially lower relative unemployment rates for less-educated workers.

CONCLUSIONS

Economists have grown reluctant to compare recent economic performance with that of the "golden age" from the end of World War II through the first oil shock in 1973. Even by the lower standards of the 1970s and the 1980s, however, all the G7 economies appear to be experiencing difficulties in the 1990s. In all the G7 countries, growth rates in GDP, GDP per capita (except Germany), productivity (except Germany and Italy), and employment (including the United States) are lower in the 1990s than they were in the 1980s. In all the G7 countries, employment rates for men were lower in 1998 than they were in 1979 or 1989, and overall unemployment rates, except in the United States, were higher. In most G7 countries, real compensation growth in the 1990s has been at or below its rate in the 1980s. While ongoing cyclical upswings in some G7 countries in the 1990s may yet improve overall performance for the decade, the gaps with the 1970s and 1980s are probably too large to close in what remains to be reported of this decade or these business cycles. By the same token, the performance of the United States, which is probably near the top of its current business cycle, is likely only to deteriorate.

The international data provide little support for the contention that U.S.-style labor-market reform will make European economies more dynamic. With the exception of Canada, the other G7 economies approximately match or exceed U.S. rates of per capita GDP growth in the 1990s. All (except Canada) already exceed U.S. productivity growth rates. Analyses from the Conference Board, the BLS, and other sources even suggest that by the mid-1990s several European economies had achieved productivity levels on a par with the United States.

Nor do the data hold out much hope that the "U.S. model" can spur job growth in European economies. U.S. labor-market institutions were unable to prevent a significant deceleration in the U.S. job-creation rate in the 1990s relative to the 1980s or in the 1980s relative to the 1970s. They were also unable to prevent a decline in the employment rates for men, despite absolute declines in real compensation in the 1980s and large increases in male earnings inequality. The European economy that has most emulated the United States in the past two decades, the United Kingdom, has not created a single job, on net, in the decade of the 1990s. Meanwhile, economies with much stronger labor-market institutions, such as Australia, Canada, and the Netherlands, have created jobs during the 1980s or 1990s at rates comparable to those of the United States. At the same time, U.S.-style labor-market reform does seem to be implicated in widening earnings inequality since the end of the 1970s, with large increases in both the United States and the United Kingdom.

III

GLOBALIZATION

13

RUSSIA, THE WEST, AND THE FAILURE OF THE FREE MARKET

Ngaire Woods

Only ten years ago the cold war had been won and many thought that political and economic stability could be brought to Russia through the free market. A decade later, the financial assistance and advice, the wild optimism and triumphalism have ended in failure. The Russian economy has shrunk, leaving a majority of Russians subsisting in a pre-market economy. World Bank data record a drop in Gross National Product from over US$600 million in 1990 to US$370 million in 1994.[1] In 1998 the IMF wrote of "eight years of deep output decline,"[2] and the U.S. Congress heard that along with a 40 percent drop in output since 1992, male life expectancy had dropped from 65.5 to 57.[3] Real incomes, even after a decade of decline, shrank by a further 9 percent in the first half of 1998 alone.[4] Today, the political system is perceived as corrupt and ineffectual. Western advice and solutions are now seen by many Russians as malevolent—a post–cold war attempt to weaken Russia. The West is perceived as a threat to Russia's interests and sovereignty. This became explicit in Russia's responses to the crisis in Kosovo. The free market, once billed as a cure-all to economic stagnation, seems to have produced much pain with little gain in either the political or the economic arena in Russia.

This chapter argues that the West's objectives in Russia were propelled by a mixture of strategic fears and cold war triumphalism. A combination of desperation to do something about Russia—a nuclear power posing a continuing strategic risk—and doctrinal belief

With thanks to Jeff Madrick for excellent comments on an earlier draft of this chapter.

about liberal capitalism led to a policy of trying to influence Russia's transformation primarily through the introduction of a more market-oriented economy. This approach has failed. Not only were there flaws in the economic prescriptions offered to Russia, but also—and perhaps more important—Western policymakers underestimated the task faced by the new Russian political elite, and failed to properly understand the political and historical conditions that would be necessary for Russia to begin to develop a democracy and a market economy. What we have learned—tragically—is that there are limits to market-oriented economic reform as an instrument of transformation.

The chapter is based on academic writings, official documents, newspaper reports (Russian, U.K., and U.S.), and interviews undertaken in Moscow during the presidential election of 1996, and subsequent interviews in Washington, D.C., and London.

1. The Victorious West and Russia at the End of the Cold War

When the cold war ended it was widely assumed in the West that a moral and ideological victory had been won. After a forty-five-year struggle, totalitarianism and the command economy could be extirpated from the former Soviet Union and its empire. This victory, however, posed serious challenges for an otherwise "triumphalist" West. Who would control the former USSR's nuclear arsenal? Could there be a stable political regime in Russia? How could the West ensure this? Gone was the old apparatus of control within the USSR and gone were the institutions and the balance of power that had provided external stability. The West was left with a set of economic incentives and levers to work with in its relationship with Russia. These included loans, aid, and assistance that could be extended both through bilateral channels and through multilateral institutions such as the International Monetary Fund (IMF), the World Bank, and the European Bank for Reconstruction and Development (EBRD).

It is worth underlining that the West's primary goal was to ensure political and strategic stability in Russia, given the country's remaining military and nuclear strength. Russia's economy per se does not represent a major part of the world economy, even if it holds out the possibility of being a large market in the future—in 1998, for example, the total value of Russia's imports was similar to that of Belgium or Switzerland.[5] Policymakers in the West hoped that economic reform would lead to a prosperous and stable Russia that in turn would be more democratic and more peaceful and cooperative in its international relations. There were few other options available for trying to influence Russia's transformation. Direct influence over politics in Russia would never have been acceptable. Active intervention to support democracy, such as the United States and United Nations undertook in Haiti, was out of the question—precisely for the geostrategic reasons that made stability in Russia an imperative.

The West had some reason to believe that economic diplomacy might work. Through the cold war economic means had been used to secure limited political objectives. Bilateral and multilateral assistance had been used to bolster the stability of Western-sympathizing regimes in countries as diverse as Indonesia, Turkey, the Philippines, and Zaire. However, democracy did not figure in Western objectives in any of these cases. Rather, throughout the cold war economic assistance was used as a lever to control a "client," with a blind eye being turned to its politics. The challenge at the end of the cold war was thus a different one: how to use economic levers to ensure both political and economic transformation—a democracy and a market economy in Russia.

The West did not initially seem particularly daunted by this task. A belief was widespread that all over Russia people were wanting and waiting to experience this transformation. The belief was expressed at the time by William Pfaff:

> The radiance of Western justice and success is the power that caused the East European nations and the Soviet Union to abandon what they were and attempt to become what we, the democracies, have made of ourselves. . . . It is a moment to seize.[6]

It was assumed that Western politics and economics were to Russians like a beacon shining in the distance. With appropriate incentives, their cooperation and development could be speedily secured.

In Russia, however, the reality was very different. The collapse of the Soviet Union had not been brought about through a mass revolt against the system. Change within Russia had occurred from the top down. First Mikhail Gorbachev, as general secretary of the Communist Party, launched reforms starting in 1985 under the labels of *perestroika* and *glasnost*. This set in motion a process that came dramatically to a head in August 1991 when a coup against the reformist project failed and paved the way for Boris Yeltsin, previously party leader in the Sverdlovsk region and then head of the Moscow party organization, to emerge as leader. It was Russia's leaders who were setting out to change the system.

Perhaps equally important, Russia was different from all other Central and Eastern European countries because it had been at the center of the Soviet Empire. While the West was sympathetic to ordinary Russians and arranged aid programs (see Gore's big initiative in the mid-1980s), Westerners often forgot that they were dealing with people who saw their own country as a superpower. During the cold war Soviet citizens had won record numbers of Olympic medals, they had led the world in space exploration, they had an empire of their own. For decades Russians had been brought up believing they were opposite but equal to the United States. To be told that they must now hold out a begging bowl to the West was unacceptable to most Russians—as was clearly and popularly expressed by General Alexander Lebed in his 1996 presidential election campaign.[7]

While the West focused on freeing Russia's markets in order to bolster democracy, the challenge facing Russian policymakers was much more complex. As George Breslauer writes, Russian policymakers had to take on three enormous challenges widely underestimated in the West.[8] They had to stabilize and reform the economy—that is, to break up state monopolies and demilitarize and restructure industry—in the face of supply-side depression, high inflation, corruption and organized crime, a radical new concentration of wealth into the hands of a few, theft of state property, and vast capital flight. They also had to build the state and political institutions, including basic constitutional, judicial, and legal systems, as well as political parties and other forms of associations. Finally, Russian policymakers had to rethink Russian national identity and Russia's place and role in the world.

The biggest challenge for both Russian policymakers and Western supporters lay in the fact that all three of these essential tasks were interrelated. Economic policies—or the failure thereof—could unleash social pressures and increasing crime while leaving the government with less capacity and less revenue to deal with it. This in turn could heighten pressures for a foreign policy that underlined and enhanced Russia's *grandeur* and national identity—whether it be saber-rattling in new areas or dealing with existing problems such as in Chechnya. The dependence of reform in any one area on the success of reforms in others was from the start the Achilles' heel of Russia's transformation—and, even more, of the Western aspirations of influence.

2. The Free Market as a Way to Reform Russia

Academics are divided about whether or not the free market could have stabilized both the economy and democracy in Russia. More generally, political scientists are divided as to whether democracy and economic reform can (or do) go hand in hand.[9] In regard to Russia many economists still maintain that a radical shift to a free market economy could have worked. The "free marketeers" (such as Anders Åslund, Jeffrey Sachs, and Andrei Illiaronov) argue that if reforms had been undertaken fast enough and radically enough, then they would have led to growth and consolidation of the new democratic regime. For this reason, the young reformers who came to power with Yeltsin at the end of 1991 should have received massive and immediate Western assistance so as to carry out radical reforms in 1992–93 while there was popular support. The halfheartedness of Western support at that time meant that the moment was lost, the reformers had to compromise, and as a result more gradualist reforms led to the evolution of state monopolistic capitalism.

The term *shock therapy* became popular as a description of what Russia needed. It describes the view that, as in electrotherapy, short sharp shocks could jolt the system out of its previous state and into a new, more positive one. The theory is both political and economic. It suggests that rapid liberalization of prices, removal of subsidies, cuts in government expenditures, and severe reductions in the money supply would rid the economy and the political system of state planning, state ownership, and bureaucracy. Shock tactics were necessary to keep political opposition from growing fast enough to prevent ongoing reform. As the former U.S. under secretary of the treasury for international affairs described this view, "Reform is like a bicycle. The faster you pedal, the easier it is to stay up. . . . Russia cannot escape the need for bold economic reform."[10] Once rid of these shackles, the Russian economy could grow. Furthermore, positive social and political pressures would be unleashed that would ensure wider and deeper reforms, not just economic but also to the political system, reinforcing democracy.

The theory of shock therapy was simple and many found it intuitively attractive. However, there was little evidence to back it. Prior to the 1990s, some countries had tried liberalization and privatization—although none had tried "shock therapy." In countries such as Chile, Thailand, Turkey, Korea, and Taiwan, policy liberalization had undoubtedly produced some economic benefits. Unfortunately, in all of these cases the successful policy changes had occurred under non-democratic regimes—leading some to argue that economic reform is more successfully undertaken by authoritarian regimes. Those arguing for radical reform in Russia prefer to cite the successes of the Czech Republic and other Central and Eastern European countries, using these same examples to defend themselves from the criticism that shock therapy can produce political instability and greater inequality and corruption.[11]

The evidence that shock therapy would benefit Russia, however, is not clear. In none of the aforementioned countries was shock therapy sustained. Poland undertook the most radical package of policies over 1990–91. However, the government soon ran into political and economic difficulties that led to the resignation of the architect of that country's shock therapy experiment.[12] By the end of 1991, the fixed exchange rate had been abandoned, the excess wage tax rules were relaxed, inflation remained high, and industrial output had fallen by 37 percent. Politically, shock therapy created widespread hostility that was reflected in the October 1991 elections. The coalition government that was elected opposed a continuation of the radical reforms. Those who argue that shock therapy was successful in Poland point chiefly to the fact that it paved the way for a slower and more constructive development of the economy. Crucially, in Poland, shock therapy did not result in a centralization of political power and the creation of vested interests that would distort the results of subsequent political and economic liberalization. This was largely due to the presence of legal, social, and economic preconditions that economists would later recognize as necessary for reform to work. A core problem for Russia was that these conditions were absent.

Poland, as Anders Åslund has written, was one of several Central and Eastern European countries that "benefited from fewer economic distortions, more economic and legal norms, a better-functioning state, and a stronger civil society than existed in the former Soviet Union."[13] Crucially in Poland (and some other countries), democracy, capitalism, and other necessary institutions had been experienced prior to the Second World War and were still in the memory of part of the population in the early 1990s. In Poland even under communism 80 percent of farms were not collectivized and some 10–15 percent of the society was operating on a private basis. Russia had no such history. Equally important, in Central and Eastern European countries the end of the cold war meant the end of foreign (Soviet) dominance. There was a genuine, nationalistic, popular desire to be rid of Soviet control and to embrace a new system. In Russia, as mentioned earlier, reform had been top-down from the outset and the Communist Party remained popular, presenting a serious challenge to Yeltsin in the presidential elections of 1996.

The argument being made here is that even if a jolt of rapid liberalization and privatization could bring about significant economic and political benefits, in Russia these were unlikely to emerge. In Russia crucial political, legal, and social institutions and constraints were lacking.[14] Shock therapy did not jolt the economy out of stagnation and inflation. Rather, to the extent that economic reform was undertaken in the absence of necessary institutional conditions, it created some seriously detrimental economic and political effects.

3. THE POLITICS OF MARKET REFORM IN RUSSIA

Russia began an ambitious program of economic reform in January 1992, after the Congress of People's Deputies, the Russian parliament, granted Boris Yeltsin broad powers to rule by decree for one year. A group of young reformers headed by Yegor Gaidar removed most controls over consumer and producer prices, freed internal trade, and floated the ruble. This was Russia's first major step toward a free market economy, and the young reformers expected assistance from the West that had been promised amid fears of a "fall toward fascism or anarchy" in Russia.[15] Some aid was forthcoming, but it was nowhere near the degree that many advisers were proposing at the time.[16]

The immediate effects of these first reforms were a plunge in the value of the currency and a dramatic rise in inflation that the reformers sought to stabilize through a drastic cut in the budget deficit. Over 1992–93, Russia's GDP fell 29 percent, industrial production dropped 31.3 percent, export volume fell by 25 percent, and imports fell by 21 percent in spite of an increase of 37 percent in grain imports over 1991 levels.[17] Politically, opposition to the reforms emerged almost instantly with nationalist critics calling on the government not to accept outside assistance or advice.[18] Less obvious but more influential was the pressure Yeltsin came under to appoint into government representatives of industrial lobbies such as Viktor Chernomyrdin and Georgii Kizha, who became a powerful lobby alongside the parliament for subsidies, credits, and advantages to be provided to industry. Once Viktor Gerashchenko was appointed chairman of the Central Bank of Russia, an explosion of credits to industry marked the beginnings of a transformation not to the idealized "free market" but to a rent-seeking economy in which particular industrialists and other specially privileged groups could dramatically improve their own position and resources at the expense of all others.

Discontent with the first stage of reform grew quickly within the parliament, and the year 1993 was marked by constant and open wrangling for power between Yeltsin and the Congress of People's Deputies. Dramatically, on September 21, 1993, the president declared (at first a metaphoric) war on the parliament, by issuing a decree dissolving the Supreme Soviet and calling for new legislative elections on December 12, 1993. Supporters of the parliament, however, refused to leave the White House—the building where the Russian parliament meets—and eventually stormed the Moscow mayor's office and the Ostankino radio tower. In response, Yeltsin ordered tanks to fire on the building, killing over a hundred people and forcing the few hundred deputies and their supporters inside to surrender. Yeltsin's advisers then produced a revised constitution that vastly increased the president's already considerable powers. In the words of one analyst, "Yeltsin had opened the door for an even more ruthless and cynical round of politics in Moscow. . . . [and] created the basis for an authoritarian regime with little counterbalance to presidential power."[19]

The new government formed in January 1994 was headed by industrialist Viktor Chernomyrdin. Significantly for the politics of economic reform, the new regime entrenched a "court politics" whereby reformers would take their place behind industrialists, bankers, and the like in the circles around the powerful president. The industrialists would embrace free market reforms for as long as it helped them to consolidate their own personal wealth and power.

Meanwhile, the West—still enthusiastically endorsing the free market—applauded any move to build "capitalism" in Russia. Sadly, policymakers overlooked the fact that "depoliticizing the economy," "activating markets," and "instituting private ownership of the means of production" (a definition of building capitalism)[20] was building a rotten, corrupt, and antidemocratic system in Russia where liberalization and privatization provided the means by which state managers, officials, and commodity traders would appropriate a large slice of the country's GDP to themselves.[21] Their wealth subsequently enabled them to enjoy enormous influence over the president and government of Russia. The process worked in several ways.

The liberalization of exports and export prices led to the sale of oil, gas, and metals by state enterprise managers and commodity traders so as to generate vast personal profits. Through 1991 and 1992, while the price of raw materials was still fixed within Russia, these prices were as little as 1 percent of the world market price. Those with access to these commodities could thus buy them for ridiculously low sums and sell them abroad at the world market prices, diverting an estimated 30 percent of Russia's GDP into their own pockets.[22] Similarly, the opening up to world markets was accompanied by import subsidies that resulted in commodity traders in Moscow benefiting massively from subsidies amounting to 15 percent of GDP—which had been introduced in order to allow items such as essential foods to be imported at only 1 percent of the official exchange rate.[23] By mid-1992 a further diversion of resources into the hands of privileged industrialists occurred as the Central Bank created credits (of up to 33 percent of GDP) and directed them with hugely subsidized interest rates toward the agrarian and energy sectors and enterprises in the northern regions of Russia.

By the time these various subsidies were abolished (in 1995), the profits made from them had been consolidated and had empowered the recipients to gain control over major parts of the economy. This was accentuated by the process of privatization that further amassed power and wealth in the hands of a few. Some seventeen thousand large and medium-sized enterprises had gone through voucher privatization by the spring of 1996. Initially only about 8 percent of ownership went to the managers of these enterprises, but this rose quickly to 18 percent and subsequently continued to rise. More important, large numbers of shares ended up in the hands of the new financial-industrial groups who owned the banks that had organized auction-privatizations. This led to the so-called shares-for-loans scandal of November–December 1995, when it was revealed that auctions had been rigged in order to facilitate the banks' gaining control of most of the valuable raw-material companies for a pittance.

Yet more seriously, the financial-industrial groups—later called *oligarchs*—who so benefited from these liberalization and privatization measures came to exercise enormous political power, which they would eventually use to block any further reforms. However, at first they used their power to demand tax exemptions, or more simply to avoid all tax obligations. Gazprom, for example (whose state manager had been Viktor Chernomyrdin), has notoriously avoided taxes. In 1998 the World Bank calculated that had it been required to pay all of its tax obligations in 1995 this would have boosted revenue by 2–3 percent of GDP, equivalent to about one-third of the federal deficit. Instead, Gazprom has continued to hold billions of rubles in a tax-free "stabilization fund" for investment.[24]

The proponents of a free market in Russia argue that all of these rent-seeking activities were the result of inadequate liberalization. If the free market had been embraced more thoroughly from the outset, the rent-seeking would have been avoided. In other words, if the government had eschewed all domestic protections and subsidies, then the operation of markets—be it for raw materials, essential foodstuffs, or credits—would have resulted in a more equitable sharing of profits. The assumptions underpinning this view are, to say the least, heroic.

In the first place, the shock therapy argument conveniently overlooks the extent to which many of the sectors in which rent-seeking grew would never have operated as free markets, because their structure was monopolistic or at best oligopolistic, as in the raw materials sectors. Hence the issue of control and regulation was always one that had to be dealt with politically—as, indeed, Western countries found when they privatized large state enterprises in the 1980s.[25] Furthermore, as the experience of industrialized economies shows, one cannot simply "assume away" the existence of vested interests and rent-seekers who do not seek to compete in open and free markets but rather to create and protect their own privileged position. They thrive even in the most free market economies such as the United States, be it in the financial sector or in the agricultural sector. In Russia no amount of shock therapy could have overcome that problem.

Finally, it is too easy to overlook the reasons why price, import, and credit subsidies were introduced. They were introduced because the liberalization of exports and imports was undertaken so fast that a buffer was needed to prevent the disastrous shortages and suffering that would ensue. The argument here is not that subsidies worked but that economists who argue that reform would have worked if all subsidies had been abolished are making a theoretical case that suffers from little empirical proof and a happy disregard for what was politically feasible at the time.

In opposition to the free market argument is a political one that focuses on the degree to which stabilization, liberalization, and privatization created new opportunities for amassing resources and power in the absence of institutions of restraint and supervision. In this view, the rent-seeking activities occurred as market-opening measures were exploited. Stabilization policies that maintained the value of the ruble and aimed at controlling inflation inevitably provided opportunities for profiteering, as did the opening up of the capital account, which permitted wealth to flow out of the country to "safe havens" abroad. These measures greatly enhanced the wealth, and subsequently the political power, of a very small and highly concentrated group controlling the financial sector. This is not to argue that the measures were in themselves wrong. Rather, it is to highlight that the absence of institutional constraints and supervision made market-opening measures harmful—not just economically, but more especially politically since they created powerful vested interests that would make subsequent institutional reform virtually impossible.

The argument is reinforced by the conflicts that have subsequently arisen in the West's negotiations over reform and assistance with the Russian government. In the second half of the 1990s, the evidence of rent-seeking and corruption in the Russian economy became impossible to ignore. Furthermore, the market-oriented reforms had not resulted in growth in the Russian economy—after the IMF analysis of eight years of "deep output decline," the Russian economy continued to contract through 1998 and 1999.[26] Finally, the collapse of economic policy and the financial crisis of August 1998, following on from the East Asian crisis of 1997, illuminated the inadequacies of the government and the uses and abuses of Western assistance. In the words of the EBRD's *Transition Report 1998* (emphasis added):

> In a number of other countries, in particular Russia, the contagious effects of East Asia's crisis were readily propagated in an environment where reforms were unsound and incomplete. Problematic corporate governance, slow restructuring and weak financial systems imposed a serious handicap on the transition process, constraining growth prospects and exacerbating instability. In many cases, these defects in reform reflected weaknesses in the state itself. *In Russia, the government failed to overcome strong and manipulative vested interests, both from the old structures and the new oligarchs, in its attempt to pursue reform.* The recognition of these political bottlenecks led to a collapse in the confidence of financial investors and to crisis. The Russian experience further underscores that institutional reform is essential if the potential gains from privatisation and liberalisation are to be realised in terms of growth and stability.[27]

The system that has emerged in Russia, as expressed in uncharacteristically outspoken terms by the (then) managing director of the IMF in 1998, is "crony capitalism."[28] In other words, "the exceedingly close relationship between the government and a number of large enterprises, which allows many to benefit from explicit or implicit tax exemptions, to exploit flaws in the tax system to avoid paying taxes—and even to engage in tax evasion."[29] The issue of tax evasion goes to the heart of the government's capacity to govern, regulate, and to provide for law and order. If the Russian government cannot raise revenue, then it is difficult to see how it might create and maintain the legal and social infrastructure that is now widely accepted as necessary for economic and political progress. Yet as mentioned earlier, the likes of Gazprom manage to avoid almost all tax obligations. The more general result is that by 1998, federal government revenue had declined from 15.6 percent of GDP in 1992 to 10.2 percent of GDP in 1998, even as GDP itself fell.[30]

These results reflect the disease at the heart of the oligarchal-court system mentioned at the outset of this chapter. Once the tide of reform and assistance turned toward bringing the industrial-financial conglomerates within the rule of law (and within the taxable economy), so these oligarchs moved against reform.[31] In March 1998 a new government of reformers, led by Sergei Kiriyenko, tried to introduce measures that would improve tax collection. These included a Temporary Extraordinary Commission on Strengthening Tax and Budget Discipline, which was empowered to seize and sell off the assets of tax debtors. Such actions, and IMF support for them, provoked a furious response from the oligarchs. Boris Berezovsky, head of the LogoVAZ group and one of those most threatened, had close ties to Yeltsin's family. The newspaper *Nezavisimaya Gazeta* that he owned printed excerpts of letters from the IMF and World Bank to Prime Minister Viktor Chernomyrdin under the headline "Why Does Russia Need a Government of Its Own?"[32] Less than two weeks later the powerful mayor of Moscow, Yuri Luzhkov, weighed in on the same theme of national dependence on the IMF, describing it as a "national disgrace."[33] The oligarchs had exhausted the use of free market reform and were now intent on preserving their protected position. They were subsequently assisted by a series of governments—each one being dismissed by Yeltsin if it ventured too far in efforts to control or to tax Russia's oligarchs.

4. LESSONS FOR THE WEST

The West has sought to assist Russia in a transformation to a stable, free market democracy so as to deal with the host of threats that Russia posed when the cold war ended. Regional instability and insecurity, environmental degradation, and nuclear accidents or proliferation were all risks of which the West was aware and problems in each of these areas have continued to simmer over the past decade. The more specific project of consolidating economic growth and a strong democracy in Russia seems to have failed. Russia today is not economically stronger nor is democracy flourishing. At the time of writing, a new president—Vladimir Putin—was continuing attacks on both rebels and civilians in Chechnya in spite of Western disapproval and condemnation. Alongside the war in Chechnya, Russian society was being remilitarized with new decrees reintroducing military training in schools and mandatory training for reservists, as well as an overall tightening of conscription rules and a visible increase in the

role of senior military figures and President Putin's former KGB colleagues in government. It remains to be seen whether President Putin
will challenge the power of the oligarchs: they helped him to power,
but optimists argue that his alternative power bases in the KGB and
in the military may make some action possible. There are several
reflections that might be made about the political and economic
aspects of Russia's transition and the West's attempts to influence it.

In the first place, there has been confusion in Western strategy as
to who or what to support in the effort to influence politics and the
Russian economy. The IMF has consistently argued that it has supported policies and not people.[34] Yet this is misleading—the Fund has
at times, under fierce pressure by Western governments, given support to particular individuals to prevent anti-Western forces from coming to the fore. For example, the large loan that supported Yeltsin
immediately prior to the 1996 presidential election—when Western
fears were that the Communist candidate Zyuganov might win the
election—was hardly apolitical. Yet donors shy away from recognizing
this because of its obvious dangers. Indeed, recall that supporting
Yeltsin left the West little alternative in 1993 but to continue to support
him even as he laid siege to the parliament building and introduced a
new authoritarian constitution that stripped the parliament of its powers over appointments, legislation, and even over its own existence.
Here the policy of support for Yeltsin (because of his reformist credentials) undermined the democracy the West was trying to endorse.

The alternative approach has been to support policies rather than
people: in other words, to make assistance conditional on particular
policies being followed (whomever by), rather than assisting particular
policymakers. However, policy support has led to problems of its
own. It requires setting particular targets and making the release of
loans dependent upon them, yet it is not clear that this has worked.[35]
Moreover, such targets have in some cases distorted both policies and
policy goals—encouraging the Russian government to prioritize bal-
ancing the budget instead of, say, strengthening the rule of law, and
encouraging it to balance the budget by cutting expenditure rather
than by raising revenue through taxing the likes of Gazprom.

Further complicating the West's approach has been an emphasis
on creating and fostering a private sector in Russia—often attempting
this through the Western private sector. Hence, privatization assistance was contracted to consulting firms and in particular the
accounting firms who received contracts from the World Bank, the

EBRD, USAID, the EU, and the British-Know-How-Fund. On the other side of the equation, in Russia a new class of gatekeepers of Western aid sprang up as a small clique of new businessmen and others quickly realized that they could create foundations, use the politically correct language not just of the market but also of civil society, and win virtually all contracts being offered by the West.[36] The problem with this approach has been that on both sides of the equation it circumvented government rather than working to modernize or to strengthen it. Yet it is precisely the latter goal that is now widely recognized as vital to the success of reform in Russia.

All in all the West's rather confused approach has worked to strengthen the power of private vested interests in Russia just at a point when for both economic growth and democracy a stronger government has been necessary.

A second reflection on the West and Russia concerns the aims and the timetable of assistance. Curiously the forecast of success has become shorter and shorter even as real success seems to have become less and less attainable. As each year of so-called reform has ended with the Russian economy producing less output and no growth, policymakers and advisers have nevertheless argued that success is just around the corner—this is reflected in book titles such as *The Coming Boom in Russia*, or yet more confidently, *The Success of Russian Economic Reforms* and *How Russia Became a Market Economy*. For any student of Russian history, such confidence is astonishing. It also seems to reveal an unconscious assumption that Russia's transformation has been a matter of liberating "capitalist forces" from their communist straitjacket. In reality, Russia has never proceeded very far along a pathway to a modern capitalist economy.

It is worth recalling that in 1914, three-quarters of Russia's workforce was still employed on the land, reflecting an agrarian economy largely based on primitive farming techniques. Due to a lack of investment and a high rate of population increase, Russia entered the twentieth century with a falling standard of living for some sections of its peasant population. Looking further back, to the end of the eighteenth century, it seemed for a while as though the country might modernize under the reforms of Peter the Great. Its failure to capitalize on that early start has been attributed to serfdom, inadequate capital formation, late development of capital transactions, and a lack of initiative displayed by government and by private enterprise.[37] Throughout the nineteenth and early twentieth century Russia also suffered from currency fluctuations, a very primitive system of taxation, a perennial deficit in state revenue, and mass poverty.[38] Many of these problems surface as present-day diagnoses for Russia's economic failure. This is not to argue that Russian economic failure is predetermined by history, but rather to underline that the free market has never played a major role in the Russian economy and hence that to reform and modernize Russia's economy *by using the free market* was always an enormously ambitious project.

This takes us to the question of whether or not there were (or indeed are) alternatives for Russia. Many academics and scholars have outlined alternative approaches and these are worth attention. Joseph Stiglitz, when he was chief economist of the World Bank, argued in the late 1990s for a different kind of transition. He argued that economic restructuring through decentralization would avoid many of the worst economic, social, and political effects brought about through free market reforms. Social and organizational capital needed to be protected, as did stakeholders of a much wider variety than the free market reformers defined. Instead, privatization maintained the centralized power and perquisites of major economic enterprises in Russia and simply transferred ownership into the hands of an elite who failed to resist the urge to "grab everything they could for themselves" once "the institutional blitzkrieg" of free market reforms had "destroyed without replacing the old social norms—removing the last restraints against society-threatening levels of corruption."[39] It was not just rent-seeking that distorted Russia's economic transformation, it was the failure to include most Russians in the process, and the failure to recognize and build on existing social and organizational norms.

Reform by decentralization, by contrast, could have encouraged entrepreneurial change not only by including workers, local communities, suppliers, and customers, but also by offering these stakeholders a new set of incentives and accountability. A further advantage of decentralization is that it would have made greater experimentation with new approaches possible. New and complex situations, Stiglitz reminds us, call for experiments, not one but many experiments. The great error made by the free market reformers was to assume that they had "the solution" and needed to eliminate root-and-branch the old system so as to apply it across the board.

Some broadly similar critiques of shock therapy underpinned an open letter to the Russian president published in *Nezavisimaya*

Gazeta in July 1996. In that letter, a group of prominent Russian and Nobel Prize–winning economists argued that Russia needed a more gradual and growth-oriented approach to reform.[40] They presented the president with a five-point agenda for economic policy, which called for the government (1) to play a more important role in the economy, especially in creating infrastructure and institutions such as law and taxation; (2) to reverse the criminalization of the Russian economy; (3) to foster and channel investment away from the speculative and nonproductive luxury sectors of the economy and into productive capital formation, and to ensure that the rents from mineral wealth are converted into government revenues and public investments; (4) to create a new social contract and a social safety net for the Russian people; and (5) to understand that if there is a "secret" of a market economy it is not private ownership per se but rather competition, especially in light of the fact that privatization and liberalization have not altered the excessive size, extreme vertical integration, obsolete technology, lack of initiative, and incompetent management of Russia's enterprises. This agenda for reform included many points now widely recognized as necessary for any improvement in the Russian economy.

The 1990s began with a grand vision of what Russia might become and how the West might assist that transformation. Nine years later, that vision is much tarnished—and so is the optimism that accompanied it. The alternative approaches to a free market way of assisting Russia in its economic and political evolution tend to have been more modest in their aspirations, and more microeconomic and hands-on in their approach. Looking back over the experience of nine years it would seem that there is wisdom in the more modest approaches. Importantly, their authors perceive the need for change to proceed in ways that strengthen Russia's economy, society, political system, and foreign relations at one and the same time.

At the beginning of the new century, there is widespread agreement in Washington that Russia needs to reform its state apparatus so as to strengthen the rule of law and the transparency and effectiveness of the institutions of government. The challenge for Western policymakers is to avoid the temptation to find a simple and short-term way of trying to achieve this. The policy of working through and with the private sector must be reviewed. Future policies must recognize instead that what remains of Russia's society—its workers, consumers, suppliers, and communities—must be involved in the planning and implementation of any future programs if Russia is to be transformed. The free market has many virtues, but it has failed as an instrument of transition in Russia.

14

THE CASE FOR INTERNATIONAL CAPITAL CONTROLS

James Crotty

1. INTRODUCTION

A central lesson drawn by policymakers of the day from the experience of the decades between the World Wars was that the economic
and political fate of the world could not be safely entrusted to unregulated, free market national and global economic systems. History
warned that this was a path to economic instability, global depression,
and political chaos. In the aftermath of World War II, key aspects of
national economies, even those in which markets played a powerful
role, would be placed under the ultimate control of governments,
while international economic relations would be consciously managed by the International Monetary Fund (IMF) and World Bank.
Trade was expected to rise in importance, but it was thought at the
time that the degree of global financial integration would remain
modest, with cross-border money flows under tight government control. The global prosperity that characterized the quarter century following the war—the "Golden Age" of modern capitalism—reinforced
belief in the wisdom of social regulation of economic affairs.

The economic instability that erupted in the 1970s has led us
back to the future. The troubles of that decade created a powerful
movement to roll back the economic regulatory power of the state,
replacing conscious societal control with the "invisible hand" of
unregulated markets—just as in the prewar period. Though governments still play a large role in most economies, they have ceded much
of their economic power to global markets. Neoliberal enthusiasts

promised that this new laissez-faire era would dramatically improve economic performance in both developed and developing countries. Unfortunately, these promises have not been kept. In the neoliberal era, global growth has slowed, unemployment has risen, financial crises are common, and inequality has increased almost everywhere. The recent Asian crisis is just the latest signal that the basic structures of the new global marketplace are dangerous to the economic interests of the majority of the world's people.

Section 2 describes the rise and fall of state-led development in the Golden Age, and its replacement by neoliberal institutions and policies. Section 3 then presents evidence showing that, on average, global economic performance has deteriorated in the past two decades. Section 4 offers suggestions on how to move from our current dangerous trajectory toward a global economic system that can better meet human needs. Government controls over the cross-border movement of capital are supported as a limited but essential tool to help restore the political and economic conditions required for improved global economic performance.

2. FROM THE GOLDEN AGE TO THE NEOLIBERAL ERA

As Western nations faced the transition from war to peace in the late 1940s, powerful political forces developed in support of a "Great Transformation" from control of economic life through the blind forces of free markets to social or state responsibility for economic performance. In the West, returning soldiers and an invigorated labor movement demanded that governments guarantee full employment and rising wages. Even business became a reluctant supporter of the new economic transformation because it feared the political and social consequences that would follow if a return to the prewar system led once again to depression. Meanwhile, experience with running wartime planned economies and new developments in the theory of government economic policy associated with the Keynesian "revolution" provided the guidelines government officials required to create and operate a state-regulated peacetime economic system. A general political consensus thus developed committing Western governments to the promotion of high employment and strong growth, and the use of tax and spending policy to contain inequality and poverty and provide essential social services to all citizens, no matter what their income.

Government power to regulate national economic activity depended crucially on the modest extent of global economic integration and on control of cross-border economic activity. Cross-border mobility gives industrial and financial capital the power to frustrate government policy. When money is free to flee the country in search of higher returns if the government tries to lower interest rates in pursuit of growth, low interest rates may be impossible to sustain. If inflation picks up at full employment, capital flight can boost interest rates, triggering a recession. When businesses can produce and invest abroad as easily as at home, any government policy not perceived to be business-friendly may induce the export of jobs and productive capital, frustrating the achievement of policy goals.

For much of the Golden Age, however, governments did not have to confront this problem. Outside the United States, all governments tightly regulated the movement of money across their borders. This allowed them to keep average interest rates low, which helped sustain strong growth in investment and income. Moreover, trade was a relatively small percentage of GDP and was subject to government control; even the largest corporations produced and sold almost all their goods at home. When governments used tax cuts and higher spending in pursuit of growth, their efforts were not undercut by an excessive rise in imports.

Limited global economic integration and government control of cross-border economic transactions also gave governments an important degree of political autonomy from the business sector. With substantial capital mobility and global integration, governments know that business and financial interests can prevent the achievement of policy objectives they oppose. They therefore tend to avoid initiating policies offensive to business. Integration per se is not the problem; lack of state control over international transactions is. But given free mobility, capital's power to frustrate state policy is proportional to the extent of global integration. By keeping financial and industrial capital at home—eliminating their "run-away option"—regulation of capital flows and trade in the Golden Age gave governments the ability to choose and the power to achieve policy objectives that did not have business backing, such as sustained full employment, regulation of business activity, strong unions, a large social safety net, or reduced inequality.

The Bretton Woods international financial system, created by the United States in concert with Britain at war's end, was designed to reinforce the ability of governments to regulate their national economies in pursuit of growth and full employment. The top negotiators for the United States and Britain—Harry Dexter White and John Maynard Keynes, respectively—supported the expansion of trade. But they believed that the growth of trade could not be sustained in the long run if money was allowed to freely cross national borders, creating unstable exchange rates in the process. As national economies became more trade dependent, exchange rate volatility would create ever-increasing real sector instability. To prevent this, the Bretton Woods system was based on fixed exchange rates, which can be maintained only if governments limit cross-border money flows. Moreover, Keynes and White knew that governments would not be able to achieve sustained full employment if financial capital was free to cross borders in search of higher interest rates or lower inflation. To make the maintenance of both full employment and exchange rate stability possible, the Bretton Woods Agreement authorized governments to regulate all cross-border financial transactions other than those needed to finance trade. "I share the view," Keynes wrote in the early 1940s, "that central control of capital movements, both outward and inward, should be a permanent feature of the post-war system."[1]

The general trend in the developing world was also toward state-led development, based on industrial policy (through which the state directs resources toward sectors of the economy seen as crucial to the development process), manipulation of interest rates, taxes, and government spending in pursuit of high growth, and government regulation of trade and cross-border flows of real and financial capital. This was obviously the case in Asia, where the spectacularly successful "East Asian Model" relied heavily on state economic intervention, but it was true as well of much of Latin America. Some of these governments were authoritarian, some were corrupt, and some did a poor job of economic management; state power to regulate economic affairs is clearly no guarantee of successful economic performance. However, on average, good growth rates were widely achieved. In the words of Harvard economist Dani Rodrik: "The postwar period up until 1973 was the golden age for economic growth. Scores of developing countries experienced rates of economic expansion that were virtually unprecedented in the history of the world economy."[2]

In the late 1960s, rising competition between nations, moderate inflation, international payments imbalances, and declining profitability began to weaken Golden Age institutions and policies. The breakdown of the Bretton Woods fixed exchange rate system and the burst of inflation triggered by the first OPEC oil price tripling in the early 1970s caused further damage. The second OPEC price hike in 1979–80 accelerated inflation yet again, creating exchange rate instability and financial market chaos.

The 1970s proved to be a disastrous decade for U.S. business and financial interests, leading to a demand for a drastic change in economic arrangements, one that would shift the burdens of slower growth and instability to working people and those forced to rely on the social welfare system. In response, the United States under President Reagan and Federal Reserve chairman Volcker, and the United Kingdom under Prime Minister Thatcher, launched yet another Great Transformation—from the state-managed Golden Age institutions toward a market-controlled system often referred to as the global Neoliberal Regime (or NLR). Other advanced industrial nations followed the United States and United Kingdom down the Neoliberal path, though their business leaders did not possess the political power needed to move as quickly and decisively as the Anglo-Americans.[3]

The NLR had two key dimensions. On the domestic front, nations were pressed to deregulate business, liberalize or decontrol financial markets, privatize public businesses, shrink the social safety net, remove or weaken the laws protecting labor unions and employment security, and privilege "savers and investors"—rich households and large corporations. And the focus of government interest rate and budget policy was shifted from promoting growth and employment to minimizing inflation. The Neoliberal revolution also called for the removal of government control over all cross-border economic activity—trade, direct foreign investment, and financial flows—in the context of an increasingly integrated global market system.

Neoliberal policies were, to a considerable extent, imposed on the developing nations of the world by external agents—the United States and other G7 nations, the IMF and World Bank, and multinational corporations and banks—though domestic businessmen were often allies in this project. The Third World debt crisis of the early to middle 1980s gave these agents considerable leverage. Given the large foreign debt buildup that took place in the developing world in the

1970s, the high interest rates and rising oil import bills of the early 1980s—along with the collapse of export markets brought on by the global recession of the period—pushed many developing nations to the verge of default. The First World response was to force a policy package on the debtor nations that came to be known as the "Washington Consensus." In return for loans needed to keep up interest payments, indebted countries had to implement "austerity" or recession-inducing interest rate and budget policies so they could earn trade surpluses. By lowering domestic production and income, recessions reduced imports. By raising unemployment and creating excess capacity, recessions lowered wages and the price of intermediate goods, making exports cheaper. The long recession in much of the Third World in the 1980s did succeed in creating the trade surpluses needed to pay interest on foreign debt, but only at the cost of widespread economic deprivation. In Latin America, people still refer to the 1980s as the "lost decade."

Debtor nations were also forced into "structural adjustment." Government control over trade, capital flows, and the rate of growth was substantially weakened, as was the ability to apply industrial policy. These changes eliminated the key policy tools that developing country governments had used to regulate their national economies in the Golden Age. By the end of the 1980s, the only important area of resistance to Neoliberal institutions and policies was East and Southeast Asia.

3. Neoliberalism: Promise and Performance

Can an integrated, largely unregulated global market system produce long-term stability and prosperity for the majority of people in the advanced and developing countries of the world? This is the central question raised by the Great Transformation to global Neoliberalism.

Proponents of Neoliberalism argued that once the distortions created by government interference were removed from global markets and the benefits of the new information-based technical revolution were free to flow everywhere, high growth, accelerated productivity gains, and declining unemployment would follow. Financial liberalization would lead to lower interest rates and higher global investment.

Unconstrained by capital controls, credit and technology would move from the capital- and knowledge-rich advanced nations to the opportunity-rich poorer ones. Proponents argued not only that maintenance of the status quo could bring only continued instability, but also that Neoliberalism was the only economic and political alternative to current economic structures and practices. The latter proposition came to be known by the acronym TINA—There Is No Alternative (to Neoliberalism).

Opponents of Neoliberalism argued that unregulated market systems, like that of the United States in the prewar years, suffer from cyclical instability, the maldistribution of income and wealth, and, on occasion, depression. Unregulated global financial markets are especially unstable, generating irregular patterns of bubbles, panics, and crashes. Globalization, financial liberalization, the rollback of the welfare state, and the rejection of activist government policy to regulate growth were therefore seen as a recipe for sluggish and unstable economic growth, rising inequality, and perhaps, at some point, another global depression. Opponents agreed with Neoliberals that the status quo was unviable, but insisted that any program of institutional and policy reform would have to contain an effective regulatory role for the state in order to be successful.

The Neoliberal revolution is now two decades old. On the basis of economic performance to date, it is hard to make a convincing case that Neoliberal policies have generated the results their supporters predicted for them.

Financial capital has indeed become extraordinarily mobile, as the Neoliberals intended. In 1977, in the midst of petrodollar recycling, about $18 billion of currency trades took place daily; in 1983 the figure was $83 billion. In 1989, it was $590 billion. By 1998, $1.5 trillion moved across borders every day. Not surprisingly, such hyperactive trading has been accompanied by increased instability in exchange rates. John Eatwell reported that, on average, "the monthly volatility of G7 exchange rates has tripled, with far larger increases in volatility being experienced by [developing] countries."[4]

But has such freedom of capital flows brought lower real (or inflation-adjusted) interest rates as promised? On the contrary, the Neoliberal era has been accompanied by the highest real interest rates of modern times. For the G7 nations, real long-term interest rates averaged about 2.6 percent from 1959 through 1970, 0.4 percent from 1971 through 1982, but jumped to 4.9 percent in the 1983–94 period.[5] High interest rates are one reason why inequality has risen in recent decades; ever larger shares of national income are being transferred from workers and other income claimants to owners of financial assets, who are the richest group in society. With interest rate and exchange volatility risk so high, it is not surprising that most studies report a slowdown in capital investment in the Neoliberal era.

Most important, economic growth has slowed significantly. The most widely cited data on global growth rates was compiled in 1995 by Angus Maddison for the Organization for Economic Cooperation. He reports that while annual real GDP growth in the world economy averaged 4.9 percent in the Golden Age years from 1950 to 1973, it slowed to 3 percent in 1973–92. Western European growth rates fell from 4.7 percent in the former period to 2.2 percent in the latter. Latin America's growth averaged 5.3 percent from 1950 to 1973, but only 2.8 percent from 1973 through 1992. Africa grew at a 4.4 percent pace in the first period, but at a 2.8 percent rate in the second one. Asia, the last bastion of state-led development, was also the only major area not to experience a significant post–Golden Age slowdown, maintaining growth between 5 percent and 6 percent for the entire era.[6]

We get the same results if we focus on the 1990s. World GDP growth averaged but 2.4 percent from 1990 through 1998, the slowest growth of the postwar era. Developed nations had an average GDP growth rate of only 2.0 percent from 1990 through 1998. In Latin America growth averaged 3.4 percent from 1990 through 1998, better than in the "lost decade" of the 1980s but much lower than in the Golden Age. Desperate Africa showed GDP growth of only 1.8 percent a year from 1990 through 1998. However, the state-led economies of Asia grew by 6.4 percent from 1990 through 1997, prior to the outbreak of financial crisis in that region.[7] Other crucial performance indicators, such as average unemployment and productivity growth rates, show the same pattern.

It has been argued that at least the United States, as the master of the new information technologies and the pioneer of corporate restructuring, has prospered in the current era. But the concept of U.S. exceptionalism is not supported by the data. U.S. GDP growth averaged 4.2 percent a year from 1959 through 1973, but only 3.0 percent in the Neoliberal years from 1979 through 1998. From 1989 through 1998, GDP growth averaged just 2.9 percent per year. And the average U.S. unemployment rate, which was 4.8 percent from

1950 through 1973, rose to 6.6 percent in 1980 through 1998.[8] The United States has also run the largest trade deficits in the world in the past twenty years. The current account deficit in 1999 was $340 billion—a record 3.7 percent of GDP.

Economic performance in the United States has improved significantly in the past four years. Real GDP growth averaged 4.1 percent from 1996 through 1999. Unemployment has been below 5 percent for three years, yet inflation remains subdued. Even real wages and median real family income, in decline or stagnant, respectively, for so long, have been rising for the last three years. In addition, recent revisions to government data significantly increased estimates of productivity growth in the 1990s—from 1.4 percent to 2.0 percent a year. Though this is one-third higher than previous estimates, it is still about one-third lower than the 2.9 percent annual growth achieved in the Golden Age. Moreover, Robert Gordon of Northwestern University, one of the country's leading productivity experts, cautions that the recent increase in productivity is highly concentrated in the computer and software industries, with little structural improvement in productivity performance in other areas of the economy.

It might be premature to conclude, based on the record of the past few years, that the United States has entered a "New Era" whose economic achievements will equal or exceed those of the Golden Age. The current expansion has been driven by a number of unsustainable forces—household purchases fueled by an increasingly overvalued stock market, heavily debt-financed consumption and investment spending, and financial markets fed by huge inflows of foreign funds. When the stock market suffers its long anticipated "correction," and the limits of debt-financed consumption and investment have been reached, a sharp downturn can be expected to ensue, exacerbated by the huge trade deficit. At this point, one would guess, arguments in support of the "New Era" thesis will be harder to find.

If we look below national economic performance and examine the situation confronting ordinary American workers and their families, things look even worse. Following an era of impressive growth from the war's end through 1973, the median real wage of all full-time workers fell by 5.5 percent between 1979 and 1997, while the male median wage declined by 15 percent in the same period. The drop in male wages affected all but the highest-paid workers. The real wage of male college graduates was lower in 1997 than in 1973. Median real family income rose by 2.9 percent a year from 1947 through 1973, but by just 0.2 percent per year from 1979 through 1997.[9] Even that small gain was achieved only by a substantial increase in hours worked per family each year. Since both wage and family income inequality rose substantially, and the poverty rate rose moderately over the past two decades, it seems reasonable to conclude that the Neoliberal era has not been kind to the majority of Americans.

In 1997 the United Nations Conference on Trade and Development evaluated global economic performance in the Neoliberal era. Their report drew the following conclusions:

◆   Taken as a whole, the world economy is growing too slowly to generate sufficient employment with adequate pay or to alleviate poverty;

◆   This has accentuated longstanding tendencies for divergence between developed and developing companies;

◆   Finance has gained the upper hand over industry, and rentiers over [business] investors;

◆   Capital has gained in comparison with labor, and profit shares have risen in developed and developing countries alike;

◆   Growing wage inequality between skilled and unskilled labor is becoming a global problem;

◆   The hollowing out of the middle class has become a prominent feature of income distribution in many countries;

◆   There is almost everywhere increased job and income insecurity.[10]

Of course, there were forces other than Neoliberalism at work in this era, adversely affecting economic performance—the two cataclysmic oil price shocks with their inflationary consequences, for example. And it is also the case that serious tensions and contradictions emerged within the Golden Age: although Neoliberalism was certainly not inevitable, some important institutional change was necessary to restore growth and stability. Finally, even in a best-case scenario, it would take time for the benefits expected from Neoliberal reforms to develop. Nevertheless, the experience of the past twenty years seems inconsistent with the hopes and predictions of supporters of Neoliberalism. It is simply not true, as is often argued, that while subgroups like the unskilled and uneducated have suffered, liberalization has been good on average, or for most people, or for most countries. Economic performance has deteriorated—on average and for majorities—virtually everywhere but in pre-crisis Asia.

4. What Is to Be Done? The Contribution of Capital Controls to the Restoration of Global Prosperity[11]

The evidence presented in the preceding section indicates that there are many serious economic problems in today's global economy; the search for institutional and policy solutions for all these problems is a daunting challenge indeed. Here we focus on but one key question: what must be done to reverse the global growth slowdown?

The weakening of state regulation of cross-border capital mobility in recent decades, and the subsequent leap in the magnitude and speed of capital movement across national boundaries, have led to a reluctance by governments around the world to adopt expansionary policies and to a decline in the effectiveness of those expansionary policies that have been adopted. Central banks are now obsessed with pleasing fickle global financial investors, who fear inflation but are comforted by low growth and high unemployment because they hold inflation down. Financial investors have also pressured governments to reduce spending and eliminate demand-sustaining budget deficits so as to eliminate inflation. In Europe, the demand to reduce deficits now has the force of law. Should governments fail to raise interest rates or eliminate budget deficits, global investors punish them through capital flight, which itself raises interest rates and creates exchange rate crises. Thus the reimposition of capital controls by both developed and developing economies, though certainly not a panacea for all the problems of the era, would help remove serious political and economic impediments to the restoration of effective expansionary government credit and budget policies.

Widespread liberalization of domestic financial markets and cross-border capital flows has slowed developing country growth in two important ways.[12] First, liberalization has created serious, recurrent, speculative boom-bust financial cycles that have constrained average growth rates.

Second, by weakening or eliminating capital controls and state regulation of credit allocation, financial liberalization has made it difficult to adopt and impossible to maintain the state-led development models that were in large part responsible for the high Third World growth rates experienced in the Golden Age and the decades-long East Asian "miracle." The most effective of these models relied on capital controls to perform some or all of the following tasks: help stabilize financial markets and limit speculation, facilitate government control of interest rates, reinforce state control over the allocation of credit flows (which is required for effective industrial policy), prevent the disruption of sustained economic expansion by capital flight, and help the government maintain some political autonomy from business interests by eliminating the run-away option and keeping firms dependent on the state for adequate finance.[13]

Turning first to the issue of financial instability, it is clear that financial liberalization has dramatically increased turbulence in global financial markets. The Neoliberal era has been characterized by the continuous outbreak of financial crises. "Financial crises seem now to happen with almost monotonous regularity," the *Economist* recently observed.[14] And every serious developing country financial crisis of the past two decades was preceded by financial liberalization. A recent United Nations report states that "financial deregulation and capital account liberalization appear to be the best predictors of crisis in developing countries."[15] Moreover, it is now widely acknowledged that liberalization of domestic financial markets and cross-border capital flows was a key cause of the recent Asian crisis.[16]

According to Joseph Stiglitz, the World Bank's chief economist, "it is unlikely that the [Asian] crisis could have occurred without the *liberalization of capital accounts*."[17] Problems began with the acceleration of Asian financial liberalization in the 1990s. Foreign investors were anxious to get the opportunity to profit from the "miracle" economies of Asia that such liberalization offered. When Asian markets opened to them, they poured money in. In 1996 alone, there was a net inflow of $93 billion in private foreign capital into the five countries most affected by the crisis. Most of the capital was short-term, and most of the short-term capital was bank loans, not portfolio investment. Korea alone doubled its foreign debt from $60 billion in 1994 to $120 billion in 1996; two-thirds of this debt was short-term.

Much of the foreign money was used, either directly or via intermediation through local financial institutions, to help fuel speculative investment booms. Between 1986–90 and 1991–95, investment as a percentage of GDP rose from less than 32 percent to almost 38 percent in Korea, from 23 percent to 39 percent in Malaysia, and from 33 percent to over 41 percent in Thailand.[18] In Thailand, residential and commercial real estate were the primary targets of speculation, though stocks were also important. Loans from domestic and foreign financial institutions to Thai property developers almost tripled between 1993 and mid-1996, eventually creating a rising excess supply of housing and office space that triggered a price collapse in 1996. Foreign capital inflows also helped push Thai stock prices up by 150 percent between 1991 and 1994, then helped sustain them at an inflated level until the market burst in 1996. In Korea, short-term foreign capital flowed primarily into capacity expansion in basic industry. The problem here was that much of this capital was invested in industries such as autos and semiconductors in which Korea already produced far more than it could consume domestically—two-thirds of auto production was targeted for export—and export prospects were poor because of large global excess capacity. For example, oversupply drove the price of semiconductors, Korea's major export earner, down by almost 80 percent in 1996.[19]

We should not be surprised that a good deal of the capital flowing into Asia turned out to be invested imprudently. At any point in time, there is a limit to the number of investment projects, private and public, that offer an attractive rate of return; economists refer to this as the "law of diminishing returns." Domestic saving in East Asia, at 30–40 percent of GDP, was large enough to finance almost all profitable projects. There might have been unusually large public infrastructure projects and key foreign technologies that required foreign financing (which should have been done on a long-term basis), but with this important exception, the additional Asian investment projects funded with foreign money were likely to be only marginally profitable. As Furman and Stiglitz noted, "In the case of East Asia, where the saving rate was very high, the benefit to the extra capital accumulation that followed liberalization may have been relatively low."[20]

In sum, local firms and banks had used short-term foreign loans to finance long-term, risky domestic investment. This meant that any number of not unlikely events could trigger a repayment crisis—a rise in foreign or domestic interest rates, a fall in the exchange rate (which would make repayment through domestic earnings harder), a rise in the exchange rate (which would lower the export earnings of domestic firms), an increase in the trade deficit, the end of an asset bubble, or a fall in domestic profit rates. Overreliance on short-term domestic loans to finance long-term investment is unwise; overreliance on short-term foreign loans to do so is grossly irresponsible.

By 1996 it was becoming clear to informed observers that the speculative real estate and stock market booms in Thailand were ending, as all such booms must. Domestic and foreign investors began to shift money out of the country, which caused a collapse of domestic asset prices, and put downward pressure on the bhat. The government had maintained a fixed bhat–dollar exchange rate for many years to attract foreign investors by eliminating fear of exchange rate loss. They continued to defend the bhat in 1997, but the rising swell of money leaving the country forced them to let it float in July. It proceeded to sink like a stone. Panic eventually spread to other markets in the area. The huge capital inflow of 1996 was followed by a net capital outflow of $12 billion in 1997. This one-year turnaround of $105 billion was about 11 percent of the pre-crisis GDP of the five affected countries.

No financial system in the world, no matter how modern or well regulated, could have withstood such drastic capital flow volatility without experiencing economic trauma. In the United States, for example, a proportionate year-to-year capital flow swing would be almost a trillion dollars, enough to create financial chaos. Foreign banks pulled $36 billion out of the area in 1997. Since the loans had financed long-term investments, repayment of principal out of profits was not possible, while the forced sale of assets purchased with the loans only worsened the collapse in their prices. Naturally, Asian currencies plunged, interest rates spiked, domestic banks either became insolvent or stopped making loans out of fear of insolvency, large numbers of local firms went bankrupt, and the whole area sank into recession.

Korea, Thailand, and Indonesia were forced to sign agreements with the IMF to avoid debt default. Governments were ordered to raise interest rates dramatically and to run budget surpluses in order to induce recessions, thereby generating the trade surpluses needed to pay back the debt. The IMF even demanded the removal of all remaining controls over short-term capital flows, in spite of the fact that most observers believed that the relaxation of previously tight controls helped cause the crisis in the first place. Most important, the U.S.-dominated IMF took advantage of the weak bargaining position the crisis had put these countries in by making its loans contingent on a commitment to adopt lasting Neoliberal reforms.

Thus, by contributing to the outbreak of severe financial crisis, the irresponsible deregulation of domestic financial markets and the weakening of controls over international capital flows across Asia helped bring the fastest-growth area on earth to its knees. Comparing 1998 to 1996, Korea's economy shrank by 5.8 percent after growing at a 7.1 percent rate; Indonesia's GDP fell by 13.1 percent after rising by 8 percent; Thailand's economy suffered a 7.6 percent contraction compared with 5.5 percent growth; Malaysian GDP fell by 6.7 percent as opposed to an 8.6 percent growth; and the Philippines' economy dropped 0.5 percent after growing by 5.7 percent. The shift from high growth to stagnation in Asia lowered global growth to about 2 percent a year in 1998 and 1999.

In my view, however, the greatest threat to developing country growth prospects in the longer run in the current era may come not from the effects of recurrent short-term financial instability per se, but rather from the pervasive pressure in this period to weaken or eliminate state-led development models. As noted, not all efforts at state-led development have been successful, but all successful development models have relied on substantial state economic regulation. It is hard to think of a single example of high growth sustained over a long period in a developing country, in either the prewar or postwar era, in which the government did not consistently violate key tenets of Neoliberalism and deliberately interfere in important ways with market processes.

Until the crisis, Asia was living proof that TINA was an ideological slogan rather than a scientific law. Though the precise economic role played by the government varied from country to country, for three to four decades most of Asia relied heavily on state economic intervention, including the widespread use of capital controls, to maintain the highest growth rate in the world. Though East and Southeast Asia account for only about 25 percent of global production, they generated about half of global growth from 1990 through

1996. If the current IMF-driven liberalization of Asia results in the replacement of East Asian development models with Neoliberal structures (an outcome that, though uncertain, is the stated intention of the liberalizers), it will probably signal the end of above-average growth rates in the area, and thus a permanent decline in global growth rates as well. If the Neoliberal growth model were to become the only permissible development vehicle, economic prospects for the majority of the world's population would be very dim indeed.

But the damage done by free capital mobility is not limited to less developed nations. Unregulated capital movement also prevents developed country governments from consistently creating enough growth to generate rising wages and low unemployment. Fast growth and sustained low unemployment may be accompanied by rising inflation, a deterioration of the trade balance, and a falling exchange rate. Inflation and falling exchange rates in turn induce financial capital flight because they erode the return on domestic, relative to overseas, investment. Meanwhile, the wage increases that often accompany low unemployment may motivate industrialists to shift production abroad. In the absence of capital controls, the mere anticipation that these events will follow the implementation of expansionary policy can trigger a rapid money capital outflow, which itself will kick interest rates up, put downward pressure on stock and bond prices, depress the exchange rate, and increase inflation. With capital now able to flee en masse at the first premonition of trouble, problems that expansionary policy might have generated only slowly and in concert with its benefits in previous decades are now magnified by capital mobility and appear before the benefits of the policy have a chance to develop. Capital mobility thus destroys the economic viability of expansionary government policy even in developed countries because it simultaneously raises its costs and lowers its expected benefits.

Most economists do not doubt that capital flows can be controlled if the government is determined to control them. Debate concerns the costs and benefits of controls. Neoliberal economists assume that unregulated markets operate with impressive efficiency. Since controls interfere with market processes, it is assumed that they must have serious costs, yet because the efficiency of markets is taken for granted, the potential benefits of controls are seen as modest at best. Supporters of capital controls agree that they can have costs, especially if poorly implemented. Controls can be used to protect domestic monopolies, reduce the efficiency of the price mechanism, and create incentives for corruption, as well as to facilitate egalitarian growth. History contains many examples of the misuse of controls. But it also reminds us that in the Golden Age and even beyond, almost all advanced countries used controls on both inward and outward capital flows to help generate sustained high growth. So did most developing nations. The creation of the economic "miracles" in Japan, Korea, Singapore, Taiwan, and later China would have been impossible without strict regulation of capital movement.

Thus the historical record demonstrates that although controls are often imperfect, they are also feasible, and have been integral components of almost every economic success story of the postwar period. Any reasonable estimate of the possible efficiency loss associated with the use of capital controls pales in comparison with the cost of the slow growth, financial instability, and high unemployment that financial liberalization has helped generate in the Neoliberal era.

The financial panic that raced across the globe following the Asian crisis has put the debate on capital controls back on the political agenda. And the fact that those Asian countries that maintained strong capital controls, such as Taiwan, China, India, and Vietnam, did not suffer the direct effects of the crisis, has strengthened the position of those who support controls. The *Financial Times* ran an article titled "Japan: Government Ponders Capital Controls."[21] The *Wall Street Journal* reported that German chancellor-elect Gerhard Schroeder "gave his strongest endorsement yet of placing greater controls on international capital flows and restructuring the global financial system"; it noted that the French government shared his view.[22] *Business Week* expressed concern over "the anarchy of markets that globalization has unleashed," adding that "the idea of limited capital controls is picking up support from top economists as well." It quotes the World Bank's Joseph Stiglitz as arguing "that it's time to consider some form of taxes, regulations, or restraints on international capital flows."[23] The *New York Times* observed that there is "a growing number of economists calling for new steps to control these capital flows or at least soften their impact." The article points out that "it is the holdouts with respect to capital controls, like China and India, that have weathered the crisis much better than the others, because they were not vulnerable to a sudden exodus of capital."[24] Respected *Financial Times* columnist Martin Wolf argued that "it is impossible to pretend that the traditional case for capital market liberalization remains unscathed. . . . After the crisis, the question can no longer be whether these flows should be regulated in some way. It can only be how."[25]

Finally, the Asian crisis led influential Harvard economist Jeffrey Sachs to conclude that governments must control short-term capital flows, limiting inflows to the amount needed to finance trade, while prohibiting their use in financing long-term investment. "One could approach such limits through taxation . . . or through outright supervisory limits," he argued, adding that the thesis that "short-term flows essentially cannot be controlled is not convincing."[26]

Policies to control cross-border capital movements could be implemented at the international or domestic level, or both. A system of international controls on capital flight could be negotiated that required countries to return capital that entered their markets in violation of the laws of the nation of origin. Both Keynes and White supported such international cooperation, which would be especially helpful to the efforts of smaller, poorer countries to enforce their controls. International cooperation in monitoring and controlling the movement of funds is already occurring, as countries look for more effective ways to restrict the laundering of drug money and minimize the extent of tax evasion by their multinational corporations.

The Tobin Tax—a small percentage tax on all foreign exchange transactions—is another globally coordinated measure that has received wide support among academics and some international organizations.[27] It is designed to discourage excessive short-term speculation—80 percent of all currency transactions are reversed within one week—without impeding longer-term capital flows. Tobin points out that such a tax would have to be levied globally, or at least in all major financial centers, otherwise foreign exchange transactions would simply move to an untaxed locale. Of course, if the United States and Britain simply announced that no country that failed to enforce the Tobin Tax would be allowed to use Anglo-American financial markets, the rest of the world would immediately agree to enforce it.

However, there are serious limitations to the Tobin Tax as a mechanism for dealing with very large speculative flows of short-term capital such as those associated with the recent Asian crisis. Effective controls on large speculative flows are most likely to be implemented at the national or regional level, where they are more feasible politically. Progressive cross-border labor and citizen alliances are developing, but are not yet at the point where they can have a serious impact on global economic policy. As Manfred Bienefeld explained: "The focus on nation states derives primarily from a pragmatism born of a total inability to conceive, let alone construct, a meaningful political process at the global level."[28]

A paper I published with Gerald Epstein,[29] and the United Nations *Trade and Development Report 1998,* are two of many available sources that discuss in detail the great variety of capital controls that have been used successfully by a large number of nations in the post-war period. There have been a dazzling array of quantitative or size restrictions on the flow of capital used by different countries at different times. For example, in 1975, 17 industrial countries and 85 developing countries had some types of quantitative restrictions on international capital transactions on the books. By 1990, 11 industrial countries and 109 developing countries still had legislation that enabled their use. Other powerful and widely used forms of control over financial capital include restrictions on bank lending to nonresidents, dual exchange rates to reduce the impact of capital movements on the costs of imports and exports, and strict rules on importing and exporting foreign currencies.

However, I would argue that the easiest and most efficient way to reduce destructive capital mobility is to use a well-developed, politically accepted institution that all industrial countries rely on—the tax system. The great advantage of using the tax system is that it involves no new bureaucracy and, at least in the advanced countries, is reasonably cost-effective. Consider first the imposition of a tax on the sale of financial assets, which could be limited to the sale of assets held for less than some target length of time if desired. Such a tax is sometimes referred to as a "Keynes Tax" because in *The General Theory* Keynes argued for the "the introduction of a substantial government transfer tax on all transactions" in the stock market so as to minimize speculative trading.[30] The Keynes Tax is a natural complement to the Tobin Tax because before a large sum of money can flee a country, it must first be accumulated by a speculator through the sale of domestic assets or by borrowing. Taxing the sale of the asset and taxing the foreign exchange transaction should have the same qualitative effect on the profitability of flight. Most important, a Keynes Tax can be applied unilaterally.

Similar results could be obtained through changes in the provisions of the capital gains tax: penalty rates (relative to ordinary income) applied to the sale of assets held for less than some target period could be very effective. Tax systems have also been used to change the relative returns on foreign versus domestic financial assets. Institutions such as pension funds and insurance companies hold large and rapidly rising shares of advanced country domestic financial wealth, and they are trading securities across national borders at an increasing rate. By taxing the gains from cross-border investments at a penalty rate and by discriminating against the deductibility of cross-border losses, governments could substantially reduce the propensity of money to move into and out of the country.

A major advantage of using the tax system to regulate capital movement is that it is easy to change the rate of taxation from time to time; the government can thus encourage, as well as discourage, capital flows when it seems advisable to do so. Chile has used a taxlike mechanism to successfully regulate short-term capital flows. Chileans who take out foreign loans with a maturity of less than one year must deposit a percentage of the loan in a non–interest-bearing account at the Central Bank. By varying that percentage, the government has exercised substantial control over the volume of short-term foreign borrowing.

Enforcing international capital controls need be no harder (and no easier) than imposing taxes. Taxes, like capital controls, are, to some degree, evaded. It costs money and takes effort to collect taxes, as it does to control capital mobility. But where there is a will to collect taxes, they are collected. Changes in the tax law would simply extend this mechanism to the regulation of international capital mobility.

It is often argued that any attempt to implement capital controls is self-defeating because capital will flee the country as soon as the enforcement legislation is given serious political attention, before the controls can be implemented. There is some validity to this argument, but it applies as well to any serious policy proposal (such as low interest rates, higher taxes on the rich, or tighter financial market regulation) perceived to be against the interests of the wealthy.

Careful consideration suggests that this impediment to the effective use of controls is manageable. If capital controls are part of a sensible general plan to raise the rate of economic growth and reduce economic uncertainty over the longer run, some holders of longer-term real and financial assets might not see flight as their most profitable option. Keep in mind that fast-growth East Asian countries had no trouble raising foreign capital even when their capital controls were extremely tight. More important, the sequence in which various controls are introduced can limit the severity of capital flight. Suppose relatively moderate Keynes and Tobin taxes are introduced first. If more powerful controls are contemplated thereafter, they can be preceded by a substantial rise in the magnitude of these taxes—the cost of flight can be raised just as the incentive to flee goes up. In the same vein, taxes on some transactions involved in the flight of capital can be applied retroactively, again limiting the gain from flight. And it is possible to enact standby controls in conditions where there is no immediate plan for their implementation. At some future time when more comprehensive controls are needed, the standby controls can be used without prior notice to prevent anticipatory capital flight.

According to a recent study of financial crises by the United Nations Conference on Trade and Development:

> Use of capital controls has been a pervasive feature of the last few decades. In early postwar years capital controls for macroeconomic reasons were generally imposed on outflows as part of policies for dealing with balance-of-payments difficulties and for avoiding, or reducing, the size of devaluations. Moreover, there was widespread use by both developed and developing countries of controls on capital inflows for . . . longer-term development or structural reasons. . . . With the return to freer capital movements from the 1960s onward, large capital flows caused problems for the governments of certain industrial countries such as Germany, the Netherlands and Switzerland, which responded with various controls. . . . More recently, a number of developing countries experiencing similar macroeconomic problems as a result of large capital inflows have resorted to capital controls as part of their policy response.

The continued outbreak of "financial crises and the frequent recourse by countries to controls to contain the effects of swings in capital flows," the study concludes, strongly point to the need for governments to continue to regulate capital mobility.[31] It is clear that there are no serious technical or economic—as opposed to political—impediments to the use of capital controls.

5. Conclusion

The second Great Transformation to global Neoliberalism is two decades old. Enough evidence has now accumulated to make a strong case that relatively unregulated, globally integrated markets still generate slow growth, high unemployment, financial instability, and rising inequality, just as they did in the decades before the Golden Age. If economic performance is to improve significantly, governments will have to once again take greater responsibility for, and exercise greater authority over, economic processes and outcomes.

Two immediate challenges are posed by the issues considered in the preceding section. The first is political. The economic interests of the majority must replace the demands of business and finance as the main concern of government policy. The second is economic. Conditions must be created that make expansionary macroeconomic policy more effective. Both tasks would be facilitated by the widespread reimposition of capital controls. That controls are feasible is not in dispute even on the right: as the *Economist* put it, those "who demand that the trend of global integration be halted and reversed, are frightening precisely because, given the will, governments could do it."[32]

Capital controls can help with the political challenge by regulating and reducing capital mobility, thereby eliminating one of the main channels through which business and financial interests dominate the political process. Removing their run-away option would make progressive economic policies of all kinds far more likely to be taken seriously. As Dani Rodrik put it, under current conditions, "it is global markets that dictate policy, not domestic priorities";[33] controls can help reverse this political imbalance. Controls would also help meet the economic challenge because they make expansionary macroeconomic policy more effective by substantially reducing its costs and raising its benefits. Capital controls are thus an important weapon in the fight to construct national and global economic systems that serve the interests of the majority, not just of the privileged and powerful.

15

VISION AND FACT

A CRITICAL ESSAY ON THE GROWTH LITERATURE

Jan Fagerberg

INTRODUCTION

Many people think about growth theory as complicated mathematics. Others identify it with complex statistics. And it is true; growth theory is about both of these things. But first and foremost, I will argue, growth theory is about *vision*. It is concerned with questions such as these: Where are we heading, and why? What are the options we have to influence the direction? Which actions are needed to arrive at the preferred state? Thus growth theory is by its very nature deeply political.[1]

To provide answers to such questions, growth theory has to be based on a clear understanding of what the drivers of growth are. It is only natural that as capitalism has progressed and changed, so have the perceptions in the economic profession about what drives growth. From the Industrial Revolution onward, the main driver of growth was considered to be *mechanization*, that is, the substitution of machinery for human labor. This led in many quarters to a focus on how sufficient funds for investment in further mechanization could be generated, the division of total income into wages and profits, and the transmission of these sources of income into consumption and saving and investment. The prominent role that some economists attach to income policies is often based on this perspective. However, more recently, growth theorists have come to recognize the increasing role of knowledge, or the "human factor," in growth, and this has led to an accelerating focus among growth theorists and practitioners on understanding the institutions and organizations in capitalism that produce and transmit knowledge, including the role that public policy may play. This chapter traces these changes in our understanding of growth and the sources of these changes as emphasis has shifted from a focus on the availability of financial capital to the quality of human capital.

RETROSPECT

The political nature of growth theory became abundantly clear as soon as the theory began to take shape two centuries ago, when writers such as Adam Smith and David Ricardo tried to convince people that stagnant growth and generally poor living conditions were not at all necessary, if only institutions and policies were geared toward allowing the capitalist machine to work at full speed. They argued forcefully that changes in institutions and policies, although detrimental to the narrow interests of some stakeholders in the existing system, would be enormously beneficial to society as a whole. This "free market" optimism has been a central ingredient in many economists' basic beliefs ever since.

Not all writers on growth were equally cheerful about the long-run outcome of free market capitalism, however. For instance, writers such as Thomas Malthus and Karl Marx both held that an unregulated capitalist market system was doomed to stagnation, crises, and possibly collapse, though for different reasons. Although mainstream (orthodox) economists generally rejected such ideas as faulty, economic developments in the first part of this century actually seemed to confirm the crisis-ridden character of capitalism. The view that capitalist growth if left to itself was not sustainable gained credibility as the crisis deepened and unemployment soared during the Great Depression of the 1930s. The central advocate of this view in the 1930s was of course John Maynard Keynes, who emphasized the importance of demand and the essential role of the government in managing the economy. His analysis—which was largely confined to the short run—was extended to the long run by Evsey Domar and Roy Harrod, among others, in the so-called post-Keynesian growth theory.[2] These theories showed that long-run growth with full employment was indeed possible but depended on extensive intervention by the government (especially with respect to income distribution). By the end of the Second World War the Keynesian view of the need for an active government had become widely shared among policymakers and stakeholders in the Western world.

THE RETURN OF ORTHODOXY

The Keynesian dominance of growth theory did not last long. There were several reasons for this. First, the conclusions of the Keynesian and post-Keynesian theories were in conflict with what most economists had been teaching since the days of Adam Smith, that is, that capitalism is a self-regulating system that performs best when interference in markets is at a minimum. For many economists, acceptance of this belief was (and in many quarters still is) the most important criterion for being a member of the profession. Second, the times were changing. The 1930s had produced depression and unemployment. Now, in the 1950s, the economies of the West were running at full speed. Rather than economic misery, the real threat to Western societies was generally conceived by many observers, not just most economists, to be the expansion of the state-led systems in Eastern Europe and Asia (the Soviet Union in particular). An economic theory that advocated extensive state intervention in the economy must have looked odd from such a perspective.

Whatever the reason, several orthodox economists started to search for a new growth theory. The so-called neoclassical growth theory developed by the Nobel laureate Robert Solow and others in the 1950s proposed that long-run growth with full employment was indeed possible as long as market forces were allowed to operate freely. However, the assumptions behind this conclusion were severe. The theory rested on the idea of "perfect competition," and on an economy with many competing firms, each of them too small to have a real impact on the market. In this idealized economy, economies of scale were ruled out by assumption, since this was believed to imply that large firms would have lower unit costs than smaller firms do and, hence, would be able to drive the latter out of the market. Thus constant returns to scale were imposed—a 1 percent increase in all inputs yields exactly 1 percent growth in output. Technology was regarded as an exogenous force, a "public good," readily available to everyone free of charge. By *exogenous*, economists meant that advances in technology were created outside the economic system that they were describing. The required assumption was that business exploited these technological advances but was not truly responsible for creating them. Investments by firms in the creation of new technology were thus also ruled out as a criterion of growth, since such investment would carry no particular financial reward for the firm that undertook it.

In such an economy, the only way for a firm or country to increase its productivity relative to its competitors would be to increase the amount of capital per worker, which is to say, to mechanize. But neoclassical economists also assumed that the rewards of such substitution of capital for labor gradually diminish as the amount of capital per worker increases. For a given level of technology, it was presumed that there exists a limit beyond which accumulation of capital per worker will not be profitable. When an economy has reached this limit, the amount of capital per worker has reached its "steady state" (equilibrium), and labor productivity will be constant (unless technology advances exogenously). Or, to put it differently, from this perspective the only source of long-run productivity growth is exogenous technological advance—that is, through discovery and invention that is purported to be separate from the natural workings of the economy.

As long as we accept these assumptions, this neoclassical theory leads to an important prediction when applied to the global economy. Countries that differ in terms of initial productivity levels will converge toward the same level of productivity and the same rate of productivity growth. If countries differ also in other influential respects, such as the growth of population or the propensity to save, convergence toward the same rate of growth of productivity will still be achieved, but long-run productivity levels will differ. In the literature, the latter is often called "conditional convergence."

Hence, the neoclassical growth theory developed by Robert Solow and others in the 1950s implied a liberal and optimistic view for global economic development. As long as market forces were allowed to operate freely, and other factors did not differ too much, everyone would be equally well off in the long run.

GROWTH ACCOUNTING

Although highly abstract and based on very strong assumptions, the neoclassical theory of growth was heartily welcomed by empirical growth analysts at the time, who felt that it might give theoretical backing to their attempts to calculate the contribution of increased use of labor and capital to the growth of GDP and productivity. This was so because, according to the theory, the price of any factor in production will reflect the contribution to GDP from using one more unit of it to produce goods and services (marginalism). Hence, following this, one could simply use the observed prices of labor and of capital (wages and profits) to calculate the contribution from increased use of labor and capital to growth of GDP. This practice came to be known as "growth accounting."[3] In the 1950s it was applied to historical data in the United States by Moses Abramovitz and others and in the 1960s and later to selected OECD countries by Edward Denison. Over the years this methodology has also been applied to many individual countries.

In the absence of exogenous technological progress, the contributions from growth of labor and capital should theoretically add up to the total growth in the economy. In practice, the first exercises carried out in this area showed that only a small part of actual growth could be attributed to growth of labor and capital. If there is more growth than what can be accounted for by increased use of labor and higher capital expenditures, the theory suggests that this is the contribution from exogenous technological progress and perhaps some other unknown factors. In fact, when the empiricists gathered their data and did their analyses, up to 80 percent of annual rates of growth remained unexplained by inputs of labor and capital.

That the lion's share of actual growth had to be explained by exogenous technological progress and other unidentified sources was something that left many economists skeptical. Various remedies were considered to improve on this rather odd and even embarrassing result. The first was to adjust the factors themselves by taking into account the changes in quality and composition of both capital and labor. For instance, newer vintages of capital, embodying the most recent technologies, were assumed to be more efficient than previous ones. However, though useful for accounting purposes, this did not really provide an explanation of why new vintages of capital were more productive than previous ones. Hence, to some extent this

practice boiled down to no more than building the unexplained part
of actual growth (exogenous technological progress and so forth)
into the factors themselves. As for labor, its quality was assumed to
increase with higher educational levels, the economic effect of which
was normally calculated by observing the wage gaps between workers with different educational attainments.

A second general approach was to attempt to take into account
entirely different factors that might directly affect growth, such as
economies of scale, investments in R&D, structural change, and differences in the scope for imitation of best-practice technology. When the
contribution to growth from these factors was added, a much larger
part of actual growth was explained. There is one problem, however.
The apparent influence of some of these additional factors actually
contradicts the assumptions of the theory on which the analysis was
based. For instance, as shown earlier, the theory explicitly assumes no
economies of scale and does not really allow for R&D in firms. But if
such additional factors as economies of scale and R&D are indeed
important drivers of economic growth, and the available evidence suggests that they are, what you may need is a new theory. In other words,
to make growth accounting work, so many new factors had to be taken
into account that the underlying theory itself was called into question.

In fact, Richard Nelson pointed out the limitations of growth
accounting long ago.[4] He argued that growth accounting is not a
tested theory of growth. Rather, he argued, it is merely a description
of a growth process that is based on certain assumptions, the validity
of which have generally not been proven or even tested. It is important to keep these inadequacies in mind when assessing applications
of this methodology. Consider, for instance, Alwyn Young's recent
work on the East Asian countries, which was widely cited in the
media.[5] Using growth accounting, he claims that accumulation of
capital and labor account almost entirely for why these economies
grew so rapidly. In other words, there was little technological progress
in these countries, implying that whatever they did to speed up technological change, it cannot have been of much importance. However,
such claims rest on a number of assumptions that do not necessarily
hold in these countries. Were there no large firms with market power?
Were there no economies of scale? Was technology available to everyone free of charge? Without affirmative and unambiguous answers to
such questions, such growth accounting exercises cannot be used to
draw simple conclusions about what drives growth. As Robert Lucas

pointed out in reference to Young's findings, just observing the fact that input and output growth tend to go hand in hand explains nothing.[6] It merely shows that labor and capital inputs rise as GDP grows, but it does not necessarily assign causality. Arguably, any theory of growth would be consistent with observations of this sort.

With hindsight, the empiricists' attempt to base their work on the neoclassical theory of economic growth was less successful than initially conceived. Perhaps what the empiricists failed to recognize was that the theory was not at all geared toward the real world, but toward a largely artificial world of so-called perfect competition, in which many of the growth-enhancing factors in the real economy had been eliminated by assumption. For the theoreticians this did the trick, since in this way they were able to demonstrate that full employment was consistent with a market-oriented system of regulation. They did so at a high cost, however, because in contrast to the already existing post-Keynesian models of economic growth, the neoclassical model was unable to explain how the economy generates long-run growth in GDP per capita. In fact, the only type of growth that the model could truly explain was transitional in character (on the path toward long-run equilibrium) and the result of the substitution of capital for labor (that is, mechanization). In the long run, this type of growth was bound to cease as returns diminished. Once equilibrium was reached, there was no more growth to be had, except by exogenous technological advance. Such growth was simply "manna from heaven" to economists, over which there could be little control.

ALTERNATIVE PERSPECTIVES

I have used much space to explain how modern (neoclassical) growth theory and its empirical applications developed from the 1950s onward. The reason I did so is that it dominated the economic thinking about growth for a long time. Indeed this perspective is still highly influential, although there is growing controversy about it in the profession. This is not to say that the neoclassical views were the only ideas about growth around at the time. For instance, alternatives to the neoclassical interpretations of events had for a long time been advocated by a diverse group of historically oriented economists and economically oriented historians. For lack of a better word, I will classify these economists and historians as *evolutionaries*.[7]

I have chosen this word to signal the importance that these people attached to the study of economic evolution of actual, real-world economies. In particular, they were concerned with the relationship between technological advances and the workings of the economy. Technology to these analysts did not simply arise freely as "manna from heaven," but was the direct consequence of the interaction between business, institutions, and ideas. Rather than exogenous, it was—at least to some extent—considered *endogenous*.

The central contributor here was the Austrian-American economist Joseph Schumpeter.[8] In contrast to the traditional emphasis in economics on capital accumulation, Schumpeter focused on innovation in firms. To him, it was the driving force behind economic growth.[9] Essentially, he saw innovation as "new combinations" of existing pieces of knowledge, whether drawn from science, engineering, market research, organizational experience, or other sources, but always with a view toward commercial application. His concept of innovation is broad and goes beyond the mere invention of a new product or process. Innovative firms are assumed to benefit economically due to the temporary monopoly they get from the innovations they make. If you make a new successful product, you will profit until others learn to imitate and compete with it in the market. Eventually the knowledge embodied in innovations will diffuse to other firms and industries, and this will fuel further growth.

While Schumpeter particularly focused on deliberate and direct innovation strategies by firms, other writers in this tradition, such as Nicholas Kaldor,[10] Bengt Åke Lundvall,[11] and Nathan Rosenberg,[12] emphasized the importance of learning within firms and on plant floors as the source of technological progress and economic growth. Such learning occurs because people in their daily life, particularly at work, experience problems and—upon reflection—come up with new and improved solutions that increase productivity. These may originate in production, through investments and the subsequent application of new machinery, as the result of interaction with customers or suppliers, or through organized links with other firms or organizations. Learning may also give rise to organized R&D of the type emphasized by Schumpeter, to some extent blurring the traditional distinction between innovation and diffusion of technology. Hence, in this literature, learning is increasingly analyzed as an interactive process, with feedback to and from organized R&D whether in the private or public sector. This has recently led researchers in this area to view a country's innovation and learning performance as an entire system, focusing not only on the individual institutions and organizations that take part in innovation and learning but also on their mutual interaction. The concept "national system of innovation," used in several recent studies, reflects this perspective.[13]

The economic historian Alexander Gerschenkron pioneered the study of the international aspects of this process of innovation and learning. Some countries are at the technological frontier, he pointed out, while others lag behind. Although the technological gap between a frontier country and a laggard represents "a great promise" for the latter to catch up, there are also various problems that may prevent backward countries from reaping the potential benefits. Gerschenkron suggested that if one country succeeds in embarking on an innovation-driven growth path, others might find it increasingly difficult to catch up, and that they would have to compensate for this by developing new institutions, organizations, and policies that support industry. His favorite example was Germany's attempt to catch up with Britain a century ago. When Britain industrialized, technology was relatively labor intensive and small-scale. But in the course of time technology became much more capital and scale intensive, so when Germany entered the scene, the conditions for entry had changed considerably. Germany had to develop new institutional instruments for overcoming these obstacles, above all in the financial sector, "instruments for which there was little or no counterpart in an established industrial country."[14] He held these experiences to be valid also for other technologically lagging countries.

Moses Abramovitz,[15] arguing along similar lines, used the concepts "technological congruence" and "social capability" to characterize the situation that lagging countries face. The first concept refers to the degree to which leader and follower country characteristics are congruent in areas such as market size, the availability of labor, natural resources, and so forth. The second points to the various efforts and capabilities that backward countries have to develop in order to catch up, such as improving education, infrastructure, and technological capabilities (such as R&D facilities) in general. He explains the successful catch-up of Western Europe vis à vis the United States in the post–World War II period as the result of both increasing technological congruence and improved social capabilities. As an example of the former, he mentions how European economic integration led to the creation of larger and more homogenous markets in Europe, facilitating the transfer of scale-intensive technologies initially developed for U.S. conditions. Regarding the latter, he points among other things to such factors as the general increases in educational levels and the rise in the share of resources devoted to public and private sector R&D. In a similar vein, the failure of many so-called developing countries to exploit the same opportunities is commonly explained with reference to lack of technological congruence and missing social capabilities, such as inadequate education.

In some respects, these alternatives to neoclassical growth theory paint a much bleaker picture of the prospects for catch-up. Catch-up is not something that can be expected to occur only by allowing market forces to unfold; it requires a lot of effort and institution building on the part of the backward country. One main reason for this is that technology is viewed differently than in the standard neoclassical approach. Rather than something that exists in the public domain and can be exploited by anybody everywhere free of charge (the public good assumption), technological competence, whether created through learning or organized R&D, is commonly seen as deeply rooted in the specific capabilities of private firms and their networks and environments, including in many cases parts of the public sector.

THE CONVERGENCE CONTROVERSY

For a long time, empirical work on economic growth was dominated by measurement (attempts to measure productivity in different countries, sectors, and industries) and growth-accounting exercises. However, as the empirical research agenda shifted from description toward the understanding and explanation of differences in growth rates between countries, researchers started to supplement this descriptive work with econometric techniques (such as multivariate regression) using cross-country datasets with the purpose of distinguishing between the potential for catch-up and the various factors that determine to what extent this potential is actually exploited.[16] The potential for catch-up was normally measured by the gap in productivity (or GDP per capita) between the country in question and the economically leading country of the sample (normally the United States). Other cross-country variables that were taken into account included differences across countries in rates of investment, educational attainment, R&D and innovation performance, openness to trade and competition, and size of government.

Initially, most studies were confined to the developed market economies for which data were most easily forthcoming (the OECD countries). It was shown that among these countries, a process of catching up had taken place from the 1950s onward, that is, that the initially poorest countries in the area had grown much faster per capita than the economically leading country, the United States. Moreover, the differences in GDP per capita had steadily been reduced between the OECD countries, suggesting a tendency toward convergence to a common level of GDP per capita for the area as a whole. It was also shown that these tendencies toward catch-up and convergence were much stronger when other conditioning variables were taken into account, indicating that the potential for catch-up and convergence was larger than what was actually realized. Many variables were found to contribute to this process, including—notably—investment, education, and R&D and innovation performance.[17]

Although several of these studies were inspired by evolutionary views on technology and catch-up, the results could also be interpreted as supportive of the basic neoclassical growth theory, since convergence to a common level of productivity was indeed found to take place. However, this evidence turned out to be more controversial than initially conceived. For instance, Bradford De Long pointed out in 1988 that the sample of OECD countries might be biased, since it consisted mainly of the countries in the global economy that had done reasonably well after the end of World War II.[18] He also presented some preliminary evidence suggesting that a similar tendency toward convergence could not be established for a more balanced sample. This suggested that larger samples than just the countries of the OECD area were required. This was made possible by the construction of new and larger datasets that were made available toward the end of the 1980s.[19]

Inspired by the work by Abramovitz and others on technology gaps and growth, William Baumol and co-authors applied regression models of the type just discussed to cross-country samples including up to a hundred countries or more.[20] The conclusion of this work was that although a tendency toward convergence could perhaps be established for the OECD countries in the postwar period, and may be extending to some other countries as well, it does not hold for the world as a whole. In fact, many poor countries fail more or less completely to exploit the potential for catch-up, something that obviously does not conform to the predictions of the traditional neoclassical theory. But the new evidence confirmed the finding of a considerable potential for catch-up by poorer countries, which, however, is not fully exploited due to lack of "social capability" and other factors.

Hence the evidence pointed toward a quite complex picture, with groups of countries with certain common characteristics performing differently in terms of rates of growth and convergence. One interpretation of this evidence was that there existed a multitude of different "convergence clubs."[21] For instance, the member countries of the OECD are often pointed to as an example of such a club, as in the opposite sense are the countries in Africa. How should this be explained? Would it be possible to explain this diversity within a common theoretical framework, though necessarily more complex than the neoclassical one that had dominated up to this point? This was the challenge confronting growth theorists toward the end of the 1980s.

THE NEW ORTHODOX THEORY

Some neoclassical economists recognized the problems of traditional growth theory and its empirical applications in explaining the observed patterns of long-run growth in the world economy, as well as the emergence of other, competing approaches. This led eventually to a search among neoclassical theorists for new models of growth. What they wanted was a formal model that continued to be based on the orthodox vision of the economy as a set of rational agents determined to maximize their economic utility (and endowed with perfect information and foresight). But they wanted a model that yielded predictions empirically consistent with what was actually observed.

The central contributor here has been Paul Romer. There were in particular two aspects of the old neoclassical theory of economic growth on which he wanted to improve. First, he wanted a theory (or "model") that could explain long-run growth without having to rely on the assumption that technological progress was essentially exogenous. Hence, he wished to endogenize technological progress. For this reason the theories that he helped to create are sometimes called "endogenous growth theories." These theories are also sometimes dubbed "new growth" theories, which is, of course, not very informative and—as time goes by—not very accurate either. Much of this thinking was anticipated by earlier growth economists, if in less formally mathematical ways.

Second, Romer wanted his model to yield predictions that were consistent with the diversity of growth patterns that empirical research had found to exist. In particular, he wanted to be able to explain why the poor countries did not catch up with the rich ones, but continued to stay poor (at least in relative terms).

In so doing, he encountered the problem that we have already discussed at some length, namely that within the usual neoclassical framework (and abstracting from exogenous technological progress) there is no incentive to further accumulation of capital per worker and, hence, no productivity growth in the long run. This result follows from two basic theoretical assumptions, so-called decreasing returns to capital-labor substitution and constant returns to scale. The first postulates that the profitability of new investments will decline as capital grows large relative to labor, the second that the growth of the economy will be independent of its size. However, if you dispense with the latter and instead allow for increasing returns to scale (as had been previously suggested by Nicholas Kaldor, among others, back in the 1950s), the long-run outlook for the economy may be quite different. In this case, the returns to further investments may continue to stay high, because the negative impact on profitability and growth by continuing accumulation of capital per worker may be counteracted by the positive scale-effect (which implies that all factors become more productive as the economy grows larger). The reason why orthodox theorists avoided this option for so long was probably that it was believed to be in conflict with their vision of a self-regulating market, since under such conditions, large firms would be more efficient than smaller ones.[22] In the long run, this might lead to some kind of monopoly. In such a situation, neoclassical theory would actually justify extensive intervention in the economy by the government, in contrast to what economists generally held to be the preferred public policy stance.

However, Romer showed that there was an easy way out of this, and that was to assume increasing returns to scale at the level of the country or industry rather than at the firm. The idea behind this assumption was a simple one—suggested by among others Kenneth Arrow and Kaldor two decades earlier—that the use of new forms of capital equipment leads to learning that may improve new generations of machinery. The beneficiaries of this learning will be the users of the new generations of capital equipment. The firm in which such learning occurs will also benefit, but not more than other users of the new equipment. Hence, the learning process will leave the relative competitive position of firms unchanged, and will—therefore—not induce changes in their behavior vis à vis each other. Firms continue to operate as if they were living within a world characterized by "perfect competition."[23]

At the aggregate level, however, the consequences are different from those of the traditional Solow model. As pointed out, all firms in a country are assumed to benefit collectively from the learning that goes on, in the form of new and more productive machinery. The ever-increasing productivity of new generations of capital, caused by learning, checks the tendency toward decreasing returns to capital accumulation that would otherwise have led productivity growth to slow down and eventually—in the absence of exogenous technological progress—to cease altogether.

Hence, because of learning, capitalists will continue to find it profitable to invest in new machines. As a consequence growth can be sustained into the long run, according to this model, even after equilibrium has been reached. This also implies that the forces in the traditional Solow model that were assumed to lead to convergence between rich and poor countries are no longer operative, because there is no longer an inherent tendency for capital accumulation to slow down as the amount of capital per worker increases. Hence, rich countries may grow as fast as the poor ones, consistent with the apparent lack of convergence in the global economy.

To some extent this model attained its objectives. But it had a major disadvantage. It did not allow for technological progress to be caused by organized R&D within firms. Obviously, in a world where a firm cannot accrue unique benefits to itself by investing in R&D, there will be no investment in R&D. To allow for technological progress to be caused by R&D, firms investing in R&D must—at least on average—receive an adequate return on these investments, as empirical research indeed suggests that they do.[24]

But what is the economic mechanism generating such returns? The great bulk of R&D investments are typically made early in the life of a product, often before it enters the market, and—in the case of success—paid back over the product's lifetime by keeping prices well above production cost. This implies, however, that the innovating firms have sufficient market power to keep prices at that level, in contrast to what is assumed to be the case in "perfect competition," where no firms have pricing power. Joseph Schumpeter, to repeat, had explained this as the result of the temporary monopoly that innovating firms get on the innovations they make, which might be related to legal forms of protection (patents and copyrights), but also—and perhaps more commonly—to the fact that imitation in many cases is difficult, time-consuming, and costly.

Based partly on these ideas, Paul Romer suggested an alternative theory in which both economies of scale and imperfect competition are assumed.[25] In contrast to the previous model, in which technological progress was considered as an unintended side effect of normal economic activity (a "positive externality"), the alternative approach proposes that innovation is the outcome of efforts by firms that do have sufficient market power to prevent the immediate and costless diffusion of their innovations to other firms and countries.

Romer's point, however, is that these R&D-based innovations have benefits beyond the individual firm. Every innovation, he argues, has two aspects. The first is specific and relates to a new product or process that may be protected by patents, trademarks, secrecy, or other means. The other aspect is general, not secret, and contributes to the advance of scientific and technological knowledge in society as a whole. This second aspect improves the capability to produce new innovations in the future. It is this continuous improvement in our capability to innovate that in this framework prevents decreasing returns on investments in R&D or other innovative activities.

Hence, in this second approach, long-run economic growth is explained through the interplay of imperfect competition, which enables companies to make profits from their R&D investment, and spillovers from these R&D investments to the general level of knowledge in society—and hence to our capability to produce innovations in the future. The main difference between this framework and Romer's previous one is that in this case it is the resources devoted to R&D—and the factors that influence the allocation of resources to this purpose—that determine economic growth, not capital accumulation in the traditional sense.

These new theories have interesting implications for policy. In the old neoclassical framework, where productivity growth in the long run depended only on exogenous technological progress, policy by definition could not have a long-run impact. In these new models this is no longer so. Policies that influence the propensities to invest in physical capital (the first type of model) or R&D and innovation (the second one) may raise growth permanently. Hence, as pointed out by Robert Lucas, from this perspective it is quite easy to conceive situations in which intervention by the government in the economy might have a significant, positive effect for the long-run performance of an economy.[26] However, it is difficult within such a framework to draw very firm conclusions on the use of specific policy instruments, since the appropriateness of these will depend on the characteristics of the country in question. These characteristics include country size, industrial structure, the skills of the labor force, and the country's relations with the global economy.[27]

One of the more controversial predictions from theories assuming economies of scale is that large countries, simply because of their size, tend to have faster technological progress and growth than other countries. Another is that as the economy grows larger, the rate of growth should be expected to increase. These "scale effects" imply that there are large potential benefits from economic integration (or "openness"). Moreover, if there is one economic activity characterized by economies of scale in the form of extensive spillovers between firms (say, R&D-intensive industry), and another that is not (say, traditional industry), the theory suggests that large countries tend to specialize in the former and small countries in the latter. If true, this implies that countries of different sizes may find themselves in quite different situations and would thus be inclined to choose quite different policy responses.

THE EVIDENCE

These theoretical advances led to a surge of empirical investigation. As the new theory differs from the old one in important respects, one might perhaps have expected that a new type of empirical work would have developed, focusing on new issues, using new data, and applying new methods. This, however, has generally not been the case, or at least not until very recently. An exception to this trend is the attempt by Charles Jones to test for the existence of "scale effects" on growth, especially that growth should be expected to increase through time as the economy becomes wealthier (and the investments in physical capital and/or R&D grow larger).[28] He finds little evidence of such "scale effects," raising doubts about the validity of formal models of this type and some of the predictions they give rise to.

What most applied researchers in this area have done is to follow the tradition of applying regression models to cross-country datasets. Ross Levine and David Renelt have summarized much of this work. What they did was to test the various factors that have been emphasized in the empirical literature in a systematic way in order to establish how robust the findings are.[29] The principal finding of Levine and Renelt was that the most robust relationship is between growth and investment. Some empirical support was also found that suggested there was a degree of catch-up on the part of lagging countries and also that educational effort influenced growth. All other explanatory variables were found to be fragile, including a large number of policy variables, openness to trade or competition from abroad, and political factors (such as democracy and political stability).[30]

But I will argue that there is not very much to learn from this new generation of empirical research. That investment is correlated with growth should come as no surprise. Indeed, this is something that would be consistent with most theories in this area, including those that consider investment as endogenous to the growth process, as some available evidence on time series data seems to suggest.[31] In other words, growth itself induces investment. The study by Levine and Renelt also fails to include R&D and innovation, and thus throws little light on the mechanisms highlighted by the most recent generation of growth theories.

Where the results from the empirical literature are useful is that they urge us to use some caution when assessing the impact of policy on growth. This lesson is especially relevant for those who believe that a so-called correct set of macroeconomic policies in combination with trade liberalization and deregulation are enough to foster development and growth. The World Bank, for example, makes such an argument.[32] In fact, as pointed out earlier, there is very little scholarly support for such an interpretation of events. On the contrary, it is clear that the governments in the most successful "catching-up" countries in the post–World War II period have all intervened extensively in the markets through various types of proactive policies.[33] Although the chosen policies may have differed from one country to another, they have by and large performed the same function. They generally increased the share of national resources devoted to growth and steered these resources to the technologically most progressive parts of the economy. This is a recipe for high growth that would be consistent with several versions in the most recent generation of growth theory.

Another relevant strand of research attempts to measure private and social returns on R&D and innovation. This type of work has been undertaken for a long time, independently of the developments in growth theory, but has attracted a growing interest due to the recent changes in formal theorizing. Generally, these empirical exercises tend to find high private returns on investments in R&D, about twice as high as for other types of investment.[34] This, of course, runs counter to traditional neoclassical perspectives on investment, according to which returns on different types of investments should be equalized. Hence one of the central issues in this area, which we will not venture into here, has been how these high private returns can be explained. High as these private returns may be, social returns are commonly found to be even higher, indicating important positive spillovers from R&D, especially when conducted in private firms. These findings suggest that from a social point of view, substantial underinvestment in (private sector) R&D is taking place, and that is an area where governmental intervention might be justified.

Recently, there have been some attempts to address these issues from a perspective that draws more explicitly on the advances in the growth literature. Central questions are: (a) to what extent the diffusion of new technology from one firm to the next is influenced by geographical, institutional, and cultural boundaries; (b) whether country size matters for the degree of success in innovation (as suggested by some recent theorizing); and (c) what the most efficient carriers of technology diffusion are. In fact, new technology may diffuse in many different ways—embodied in goods or services that make use of new technology, through foreign direct investments by multinational firms, or by imitative activities by domestic firms. There is some theoretical backing for all of these but there has until recently been little if any evidence on their relative importance.

Although research in this area is still in an early stage, the available evidence seems to indicate that diffusion of technology (knowledge spillover) is hampered by distance and is generally easier and quicker within than across country borders.[35] There is also some statistical evidence suggesting that returns to R&D investment may be higher in large countries, consistent with what the new growth theories predict.[36] On the last question—which carrier of technology is the most efficient—there is especially little evidence. For instance, some recent research suggests that R&D embodied in imports of goods and services is a very efficient way of transmitting new technology.[37] However, others, using essentially the same type of indicator, fail to reproduce these results.[38]

The picture that emerges is that innovation and diffusion of technology play an essential part in economic growth. Furthermore, the available evidence indicates that, from a social point of view, there is considerable underinvestment in innovation. This means that if firms could be induced to undertake more R&D, growth and welfare would be higher. Contrary to the assumption in exogenous technology models, the diffusion of technology is a difficult and costly process that requires a lot of effort. Moreover, the research shows that "national factors" still have an important role to play for diffusion processes. In fact, several recent studies indicate that there exist persistent differences across countries in their capacity to absorb new technology and that this can only partly be explained by differences in market size, investment in education, and other easily measurable factors.[39] This points to the potential importance of factors such as culture, language, and institutions. These are not easy to quantify, but nevertheless deserve serious attention.

CONCLUSION

What the various perspectives on growth discussed in this chapter have in common are two basic elements: *a view on what drives growth* and *what form of regulatory mechanisms may be necessary to stimulate further growth.*

Concerning the factors that drive growth, the dominant view has over the years largely identified the accumulation of capital as primary. This was the view of the classical political economists, including Karl Marx, post-Keynesian growth theorists such as Sir Roy Harrod or Evsey Domar, or Nicholas Kaldor for that matter, and—at least until very recently—all neoclassical theorists, including Robert Solow and Kenneth Arrow. From a historical point of view, it is not difficult to understand why this view emerged as the dominant one. Clearly, during the so-called Industrial Revolution and the period that followed, the capital accumulation involved with mechanization was a vital ingredient.

It is perhaps less evident why this view should have dominated economists' perceptions of the world for so long. In my view, the great achievement of Joseph Schumpeter (although he was not without forerunners) was to break with this one-sided view and bring to the economists' attention a totally different argument about what drives growth, focusing on qualitative (that is, innovation) rather than quantitative change. With hindsight, it was probably no coincidence that Schumpeter's own professional career ran parallel with the rise of science-based industry, organized corporate R&D, and the development of various types of institutions and organizations relating to this process. It testifies to his qualities as an analyst of contemporary developments that he was able to grasp the full impact of these tendencies at such an early stage. In fact, it took a long time for science-based industry and organized R&D to acquire the prominence it has today. Although pioneered in Germany at the turn of the century, it was only during the Second World War and the cold war that followed that these developments took off, and then primarily in the United States.

While most writers on growth initially shared a common perception of what drove growth, this was not the case for state regulation. Since the beginning, discussions of regulation have been dominated by adherents of two diametrically opposite positions— laissez-faire capitalism and state planning (or very extensive intervention). Among the classical political economists, who all saw the economy from the mechanization perspective, some, such as Adam Smith and David Ricardo, were liberal free marketers, while Karl Marx believed that laissez-faire was doomed to collapse, and had to be replaced by state planning. In the first half of this century, the view that a capitalist order ruled by free markets was basically unstable gained prominence as the crisis of the interwar period deepened, and led to the formulation of (the so-called post-Keynesian) growth theories advocating extensive state intervention in the economy. However, under the impact of the postwar boom and the cold war that followed, the nineteenth-century liberal view again got the upper hand, as reflected in the neoclassical model of economic growth developed by Robert Solow and others.

In my view, the main problem with the traditional neoclassical growth theory was that it was based on an outdated understanding of what drives growth and how the capitalist system, including its institutions, works. It simply did not have any useful advice for policy-makers who were concerned about the real workings of the economy. This is the reason why the works of Joseph Schumpeter and other economists with insights into how innovation and learning are shaped by—and shape—the economy started to gain prominence again from the 1960s onward, mainly through the writings of applied economists such as Christopher Freeman.[40] Although Schumpeter himself was a devoted free market liberal, much of the work that based itself on his ideas came to focus on limitations to the working of markets, particularly with respect to innovation and diffusion of technology, and what the government—in countries at different levels of development—might do to improve the economy in this respect.

What has happened in the area of theorizing in the last decade is that this agenda has been taken over by formal theorists. This has led to the creation of more complex models, incorporating technology and innovation, that arguably explain growth in a better way than before. These models are also more open in the sense that many different outcomes are possible, depending on what the key assumptions are. They also allow for more room for public policy. These new theories have, in turn, led to a new agenda for empirical research that is both more meaningful and more interesting than what we had before. However, the most important contribution that empirical work can make to theoretical work is not to test for the "truth" of these formal relationships but to improve the assumptions that theoreticians make use of.

While formal modeling in this area has greatly improved, other basic neoclassical features have been retained, including the idea of a "representative agent" that neoclassical theorists use when they construct their models. This implies that all agents (buyers and sellers) in the economy are treated as identical. In addition they are assumed to be "rational," to maximize their self-interest, and to be endowed with "perfect information." This necessarily runs counter to one of the most basic arguments of evolutionary reasoning—that economic agents are heterogeneous, and that it is this very difference that creates diversity and drives innovation. This is an area where more empirical work is needed, and one that potentially could be of great importance for formal theorizing.

However, to be able to respond to this challenge, empirical researchers have to go beyond approaches that essentially consist of filtering out heterogeneity. Arguably, to get a firm grasp on heterogeneity, one will need more case-oriented research of the type undertaken in many other disciplines, and frequently used by many of the grand economic masters of the past, including Adam Smith, Karl Marx, Alfred Marshall, and Joseph Schumpeter.[41]

NOTES

CHAPTER 3

1. Robert Kuttner, *Everything for Sale: The Virtues and Limits of Markets* (New York: Knopf, 1997).

2. Paula England and Nancy Folbre, "The Cost of Caring," *Annals of the American Academy of Political and Social Science* 561 (January 1999): 39–51; Nancy Folbre and Thomas Weisskopf, "Did Father Know Best? Families, Markets, and the Supply of Caring Labor," in Avner Ben-Ner and Louis Putterman, eds., *Economics, Values, and Organization* (Cambridge: Cambridge University Press, 1998); Nancy Folbre, "Care and the Global Economy," in "Globalization with a Human Face," *Human Development Report*, vol. 1 (New York: United Nations, 1999), pp. 57–84.

3. Thomas Princen, "The Shading and Distancing of Commerce: When Internalization Is Not Enough," *Ecological Economics* 20, no. 3 (1997): 235–53.

4. Amartya K. Sen, "Capability and Well-Being," in Martha Nussbaum and Amartya Sen, eds., *The Quality of Life* (Oxford: Clarendon Press, 1993), pp. 30–53; Amartya K. Sen, "Human Capital and Human Capability," in *World Development* 25, no. 12 (December 1997): 1959–61.

5. Paula England and Nancy Folbre, "Reconceptualizing Human Capital," in Werner Raub and Jeroen Weesie, eds., *The Management of Durable Relations* (Amsterdam: Thela Thesis Publishers, 1999); Daniel Goleman, *Emotional Intelligence* (New York: Bantam, 1995).

6. James Coleman, "Social Capital in the Creation of Human Capital," *American Journal of Sociology* 94 supplement (1988): S95–S120; Robert Putnam, "The Prosperous Community—Social Capital and Public Life," *American Prospect* 4, no. 13 (Spring 1993): 35–42; F. Fukuyama, *Trust: The Social Values and the Creation of Prosperity* (New York: Free Press, 1995). This point can also be framed in terms of the evolution of strong reciprocity; see Samuel Bowles and Herbert Gintis, "The Evolution of Strong Reciprocity," Santa Fe Institute Working Paper #98-08-073E, 1998; and Samuel Bowles and Herbert Gintis, "The Moral Economy of Community:

Structured Populations and the Evolution of Prosocial Norms," *Evolution and Human Behavior* 19, no. 1 (January 1998): 3–25.
7. Folbre, "Care and the Global Economy."
8. Kari Waerness, "On the Rationality of Caring," in A. S. Sassoon, ed., *Women and the State* (London: Hutchinson, 1987), pp. 207–34.
9. Emily K. Abel and Margaret K. Nelson, "Circles of Care: An Introductory Essay," in Emily K. Abel and Margaret K. Nelson, eds., *Circles of Care: Work and Identity in Women's Lives* (New York: State University of New York Press, 1990), p. 4.
10. Nel Noddings, *Caring: A Feminine Approach to Ethics and Moral Education* (Berkeley: University of California Press, 1984).
11. Arlie Hochschild, *The Managed Heart: Commercialization of Human Feeling* (Berkeley: University of California Press, 1983).
12. Amitai Etzioni, *The Moral Dimension* (New York: Free Press, 1988).
13. Lee Badgett and Nancy Folbre, "Assigning Care: Gender and Social Norms," *International Labour Review* 138, no. 3 (1999): 311–26.
14. Nancy Folbre, *Who Pays for the Kids? Gender and the Structures of Constraint* (New York: Routledge, 1994).
15. Deborah Ward, "The Kin Care Trap: The Unpaid Labor of Long Term Care," *Socialist Review* 23, no. 2 (1993): 103.
16. Folbre and Weisskopf, "Did Father Know Best?"
17. Francine Deutsch, *Halving It All: How Equally Shared Parenting Works* (Cambridge, Mass.: Harvard University Press, 1999); Rhona Mahoney, *Kidding Ourselves: Breadwinning, Babies, and Bargaining Power* (New York: Basic Books, 1995).
18. Folbre and Weisskopf, "Did Father Know Best?"
19. Bruno Frey, *Not Just for the Money: An Economic Theory of Personal Motivation* (Cheltenham, England: Elgar, 1997); Samuel Bowles, "The Production Process in a Competitive Economy," *American Economic Review* 77, no. 1 (March 1985): 16–36; George Akerlof, "Labor Contracts as Partial Gift Exchange," *Quarterly Journal of Economics* 97, no. 4 (1982): 543–70.
20. Robert J. Sampson, Stephen W. Raudenbush, and Felton Earls, "Neighborhoods and Violent Crime: A Multilevel Study of Collective Efficacy," *Science* 16 (January 1997).
21. Paula England and Nancy Folbre, "The Cost of Caring," *Annals of the American Academy of Political and Social Science*, 561 (January 1999): 39–51.
22. Jane Waldfogel, "The Effect of Children on Women's Wages," *American Sociological Review* 62, no. 2 (1997): 209–17.
23. Paula England, Karen Christopher, and Lori L. Reid, "How Do Intersections of Race/Ethnicity and Gender Affect Pay Among Young Cohorts of African Americans, European Americans, and Latino/as?" in Irene Browne, ed., *Race, Gender, and Economic Inequality: African American and Latina Women in the Labor Market* (New York: Russell Sage Foundation, 1999).

24. See Beth Birnbaum, "Send Your Child to the Village," *In These Times* (June 27, 1999): 30.

25. Nancy Folbre, "The Unproductive Housewife: Her Evolution in Nineteenth Century Economic Thought," *Signs: Journal of Women in Culture and Society* 16, no. 3 (1991): 463–84.

26. William Baumol, "Macroeconomics of Unbalanced Growth: The Anatomy of Urban Crisis," *American Economic Review* 57, no. 3 (1967): 415–26.

27. Susan Donath, "What's Feminist About Feminist Economics," Key Centre for Women's Health in Society, University of Melbourne, Australia, 1998.

28. Barnet Wagman and Nancy Folbre, "Household Services and Economic Growth in the U.S., 1870–1930," *Feminist Economics* 2, no. 1 (Spring 1996): 50.

29. Robert Eisner, *The Total Incomes System of Accounts* (Chicago: University of Chicago Press, 1989); Duncan Ironmonger, "Counting Outputs, Capital Inputs, and Caring Labor: Estimating Gross Household Product," *Feminist Economics* 2, no. 3 (Fall 1996): 3.

30. Wagman and Folbre, "Household Services and Economic Growth in the U.S."

31. Herman E. Daly, *Beyond Growth: The Economics of Sustainable Development* (Boston: Beacon Press, 1996). For quantitative estimates, see the Redefining Progress Web site at http://www.rprogress.org.

32. Marjorie Devault and Catherine Stimpson, *Feeding the Family: The Social Organization of Caring as Gendered Work* (Chicago: University of Chicago Press, 1994).

33. John Robinson and Geoffry Godbey, *Time for Life: The Surprising Ways Americans Use Their Time* (University Park: Pennsylvania State University Press, 1997), p. 107; W. Keith Bryant and Cathleen D. Zick, "Are We Investing Less in the Next Generation? Historical Trends in Time Spent Caring for Children," *Journal of Family and Economic Issues* 17, no. 3 (1996): 385–92; Michael Bittman and Jocelyn Pixley, *The Double Life of the Family: Myth, Hope, and Experience* (Sydney: Allen and Unwin, 1997), p. 94.

34. W. Keith Bryant and Cathleen D. Zick, "An Examination of Parent-Child Shared Time," *Journal of Marriage and the Family* 58 (1996): 227–37.

35. Francine D. Blau, "Trends in the Well-being of American Women, 1970–1995," *Journal of Economic Literature* 36, no. 1 (March 1998): 112–65.

36. Trond Petersen and Laurie A. Morgan, "Separate and Unequal: Occupation-Establishment Sex Segregation and the Gender Wage Gap," *American Journal of Sociology* 101, no. 2 (September 1995): 329–65.

37. Hochschild, *The Managed Heart.*

38. Richard Anker, *Gender and Jobs: Sex Segregation of Occupations in the World* (Geneva: International Labour Office, 1998), p. 163.

39. Susan Christopherson, "Childcare and Elderly Care: What Occupational Opportunities for Women?" in *Labor Market and Social Policy Occasional*

Papers 27 (Paris: Organisation for Economic Co-operation and Development, 1997).

40. J. Davidson Alexander, "Gendered Job Trails and Women's Occupations," Ph.D. dissertation, Department of Economics, University of Massachusetts at Amherst, 1987; Rosabeth Moss Kanter, *Men and Women of the Corporation* (New York: Basic Books 1993).

41. James P. Spradly and Brenda J. Mann, *Cocktail Waitress: Women's Work in a Man's World* (New York: McGraw Hill, 1975).

42. Hochschild, *The Managed Heart.*

43. Jennifer L. Pierce, *Gender Trials* (Berkeley: University of California Press, 1995).

44. Julie Nelson, "Of Markets and Martyrs: Is it OK to Pay Well for Care?" *Feminist Economics* 5, no. 3 (Fall 1999): 43–59.

45. Karl Polanyi, *The Great Transformation* (Boston: Beacon Press, 1957).

46. Clare Ungerson, "Social Politics and the Commodification of Care," *Social Politics* (Fall 1997): 377.

47. Figure for 1959 from Robert E. Yuskavage, "Improved Estimates of Gross Product by Industry, 1959–94," *Survey of Current Business* (August 1996): Table 11. Figure for 1997 from Bureau of Economic Analysis National Accounts Data, "Gross Domestic Product by Industry in Current Dollars as a Percentage of Gross Domestic Product, 1992–1997," http://www.bea.doc.gov/bea/dn2/gposhr.htm.

48. Suzanne Gordon, "Healing in a Hurry: Hospitals in the Managed-Care Age," *Nation* 268 (March 1, 1999): 11.

49. Judith J. Hibbard, "Can Medicare Beneficiaries Make Informed Choices?" *Health Affairs* (November/December 1998): 181–93.

50. Sheryl Gay Stolberg, "Report Says Profit-Making Health Plans Damage Care," *New York Times,* July 14, 1999.

51. Gordon, "Healing in a Hurry."

52. Neil Weinberg, "Blood Money," *Forbes,* March 22, 1999, p. 123.

53. Alison Mitchell, "Senate G.O.P. Again Prevails on Health Care Bill," *New York Times,* July 15, 1999.

54. Peter T. Kilborn, "Nurses Put on Fast Forward in Rush for Cost Efficiency," *New York Times,* April 9, 1998, p. A1.

55. Suzanne Gordon, *Life Support: Three Nurses on the Front Lines* (New York: Little, Brown, 1998), p. 255.

56. Deborah Stone, "Care and Trembling," *American Prospect* 10, no. 43 (March–April 1999): 62.

57. Suzanne Helburn, ed., *Cost, Quality, and Child Outcomes in Child Care Centers,* technical report (Denver: University of Colorado Press, 1995).

58. Marcy Whitebook, *NAEYC Accreditation and Assessment* (Washington, D.C.: National Center for the Early Childhood Work Force, 1997).

59. Helburn, *Cost, Quality, and Child Outcomes in Child Care Centers.*

60. Susan C. Eaton, "Beyond 'Unloving Care': Promoting Innovation in Elder Care Through Public Policy," Radcliffe Public Policy Institute, Changing Work in America Series, Cambridge, Mass., 1996.
61. Editorial, *New York Times*, April 26, 1999.
62. Eaton, "Beyond 'Unloving Care,'" p. 7.

CHAPTER 4

1. Federal Highway Administration, U.S. Department of Transportation, *Summary of Travel Trends, 1995 Nationwide Personal Transportation Survey* (draft prepared by Patricia S. Hu, Center for Transportation Analysis, Oak Ridge National Laboratory, and Jennifer R. Young, Systems Development Institute, University of Tennessee, January 8, 1999), p. 12.
2. This is based on the assumption that the length of the average intercity auto trip is less than two hundred miles, a very safe assumption. Other data for the calculation are to be found in Rosalyn Wilson, *Transportation in America 1998* (Washington, D.C.: Eno Transportation Foundation, 1998), pp. 47–48.
3. There are a lot of measures for the size of the road network. Miles of paved road is convenient here because it is easy to understand, and the historical data are readily available and consistent over time. Its drawback is that it does not allow for increases in the number of lanes.
4. Federal Highway Administration, U.S. Department of Transportation, *Highway Statistics 1997*, November 1998, p. V-68.
5. Transportation Research Board, National Research Council, *Highway Capacity Manual*, Special Report 209, 3rd ed., 1994, pp. 2-10, 2-29. The 1994 *Highway Capacity Manual* provides the data on vehicle flows in the early 1990s. For flows in the mid-1980s, data are from James Getzewich, interview with author, August 3, 1999.
6. Federal Highway Administration, U.S. Department of Transportation, *Highway Statistics Summary to 1995*, July 1997, pp. V-26, V-28.
7. Alan Pisarski, *Commuting in America II: The Second National Report on Commuting Patterns and Trends* (Washington, D.C.: Eno Transportation Foundation, 1996), pp. 73–74.
8. Pisarski, *Commuting in America II*, pp. 89–90.
9. Pisarski, *Commuting in America II*, p. 79 for job concentration, p. 92 for travel times.
10. Federal Highway Administration, U.S. Department of Transportation, *Summary of Travel Trends, 1995 Nationwide Personal Transportation Survey*, p. 13.
11. Jose Gomez-Ibanez, "Estimating Whether Transport Users Pay Their Way: The State of the Art," in David L. Greene, Donald W. Jones, and Mark

A. Delucchi, eds., *The Full Costs and Benefits of Transportation* (Berlin: Springer-Verlag, 1997).

12. Mark A. Delucchi and others, *The Annualized Social Cost of Motor-Vehicle Use in the United States, Based on 1990–1991 Data,* a series of twenty reports (Davis: Institute of Transportation Studies, University of California, Davis, 1996 and 1997).

13. Mark A. Delucchi, "The Annualized Social Cost of Motor-Vehicle Use in the U.S., 1990–1991: Summary of Theory, Data, Methods, and Results," report 1 in Delucchi and others, *The Annualized Social Cost of Motor-Vehicle Use in the United States,* p. 10.

14. M. Ishaq Nadiri and Theofanis P. Mamuneas, *Contribution of Highway Capital to Industry and National Productivity Growth,* Office of Policy Development, Federal Highway Administration, U.S. Department of Transportation, Washington, D.C., September 1996.

15. Kazem Attaran, chief economist, California Department of Transportation, telephone conversation with author, September 28, 1999.

16. Ross Crichton, Office of Legislation and Strategic Planning, Federal Highway Administration, telephone conversation with author, September 28, 1999.

17. Note for statisticians: I'm using the term loosely.

18. David A. Aschauer, "Is Public Expenditure Productive?" *Journal of Monetary Economics* 23, no. 2 (1989): 177.

19. Nadiri and Mamuneas, *Contribution of Highway Capital to Industry and National Productivity Growth,* p. 8.

20. Alicia H. Munnell, "Why Has Productivity Growth Declined? Productivity and Public Investment," *New England Economic Review* (January/February 1990): 3–22.

21. The reviews of this literature are written by economists for economists and can be rough going for a nonspecialist reader. Nadiri's review, in Chapter II of the report cited in Note 14, is useful but requires some grasp of the elements of statistics and economics. The discussion in the following paragraphs is based on Nadiri's review.

22. Alicia H. Munnell and Leah M. Cook, "How Does Public Infrastructure Affect Regional Economic Performance?" *New England Economic Review* (September 1, 1990): 11.

23. In economic terms, Nadiri estimated cost functions for various industry sectors where Aschauer and a number of others estimated a production function for the nation or production functions for the states.

24. Basically, the two-digit level of the Standard Industrial Classification.

25. Nadiri and Mamuneas, *Contribution of Highway Capital to Industry and National Productivity Growth,* Table 16, p. 97.

26. Nadiri and Mamuneas, *Contribution of Highway Capital to Industry and National Productivity Growth,* p. 96.

27. Ishaq Nadiri and Theofanis Mamuneas, "The Effects of Public Infrastructure and R&D Capital on the Cost Structure and Performance of U.S. Manufacturing Industries," C. V. Starr Center Research Report 91-57, New York University, 1993.

28. M. Ishaq Nadiri and Theofanis P. Mamuneas, a summary of "Contributions of Highway Capital to Output and Productivity Growth in the U.S. Economy and Industries," Office of Policy Development, Federal Highway Administration, U.S. Department of Transportation, Washington, D.C., August, 1998, first page of Chapter IX.

29. Information on the Caltrans 1998 TIP was provided to me in an electronic transmission from Mahmoud Mahdavi on April 27, 1999. I should note that, along with Michael Grant (a colleague at Hagler Bailly), I have recently been assisting Caltrans with development of improvements on their benefit-cost model.

30. Mark A. Delucchi, "The Annualized Social Cost of Motor-Vehicle Use in the U.S., 1990–1991: Summary of Theory, Data, Methods, and Results," p. 45.

31. Both emissions factors and health costs of air pollution were drawn from an unpublished report prepared by Booz-Allen and Hamilton, Hagler Bailly, and Parsons Brinckerhof. Booz-Allen and Hagler Bailly were responsible for the air pollution work. The emissions factors are based on the EMFAC 7 emissions model of the California Air Resources Board. The health-cost values were chosen from the ranges offered by Delucchi in Mark A. Delucchi, "Air-Pollution Costs of Motor-Vehicle Use in the U.S.," report 11 in Delucchi and others, *The Annualized Social Cost of Motor-Vehicle Use in the United States,* p. 236.

32. Apogee Research, unpublished draft report to Federal Highway Administration, 1994.

CHAPTER 5

1. "Americans View the Social Security Debate" (Washington, D.C.: Peter D. Hart Research Associates, 1998).

2. National Commission on Social Security, *Report of 1983,* no. 0396-938 (Washington, D.C.: U.S. Government Printing Office, 1983), statement (7), p. 5.

3. Robert Ball, *Social Security Plus: Straight Talk on Social Security* (New York: The Century Foundation Press, 1998).

4. E. J. Dionne, "Why Social Insurance?" National Academy of Social Insurance, Social Security Brief no. 6 (March 1999), p. 1.

5. The Century Foundation (formerly Twentieth Century Fund), New York, http://www.socsec.org/facts/Basics/basics_index.htm.

6. Martha Derthick, *Policy Making for Social Security* (Washington, D.C.: Brookings Institution Press, 1979).

7. Paul Samuelson, "An Exact Consumption-Loan Model of Interest with or without the Social Contrivance of Money," *Journal of Political Economy* 66, no. 6 (1958): 467–82.

8. World Bank, *Averting the Old Age Crises* (Oxford: Oxford University Press, 1994); Yung-Ping Chen and Stephen Goss, "Are Returns on Payroll Taxes Fair?" in Eric Kingson and James H. Schultz, eds., *Scoial Security in the 21st Century* (New York: Oxford University Press, 1997), pp. 76–90.

9. See also Teresa Ghilarducci, "Do the Old Eat the Young? Intergenerational Equity and Public Pensions," paper presented at the Second International Research Conference on Social Security, "Summing Up the Evidence: The Impact of Incentives and Targeting in Social Security," sponsored by the International Social Security Association: ILO AISS-ISSA-IVSS Jerusalem, January 25–28, 1998.

10. Cato Institute Web page: www.cato.org/research/ss_prjct.html.

11. P. J. O'Rourke, "The Great Ponzi Scheme Rescue Act of 1999," *Rolling Stone,* April 15, 1999, pp. 15–17.

12. Dean Baker, "Saving Social Security in Three Steps," Economic Policy Institute Briefing Paper, Washington, D.C., December 1998.

13. Derthick, *Policy Making for Social Security.*

14. "Trends in Pensions" (Washington, D.C.: U.S. Department of Labor, Pension and Welfare Benefits Administration, 1992); Virginia P. Reno, "The Role of Pensions in Retirement Income," in *Pensions in a Changing Economy* (Washington, D.C.: Employee Benefits Research Institute, 1993).

15. Joseph Quinn, "Microeconomic Determinants of Early Retirement: A Cross-Sectional View of White Married Males," *Journal of Human Resources* 12, no. 3 (1977): 329–46.

16. Eugene Steurele and Jon Bakija, *Retooling Social Security for the Twentieth Century* (Washington, D.C.: The Urban Institute, 1994).

17. Barry Bluestone and Teresa Ghilarducci, *Making Work Pay: Wage Insurance for the Working Poor* (Annandale-on-Hudson, N.Y.: Jerome Levy Institute at Bard College, 1996).

18. Richard Freeman, "Unions and Fringe Benefits," *Industrial and Labor Relations Review* 34 (July 1981): 499–509.

19. Edward Lazear, "Agency, Earnings Profiles, Productivity and Hours Restrictions," *American Economics Review* 71, no. 4 (1980): 606–19.

20. Teresa Ghilarducci, *Labor's Capital: The Economics and Politics of Private Pensions* (Cambridge, Mass.: MIT Press, 1992).

21. World Bank, *Averting the Old Age Crises.*

22. Martin Feldstein, *The Missing Piece in Policy Analysis: Social Security Reform* (Cambridge, Mass.: National Bureau of Economic Research, 1996).

23. Stephen Farkas, "Promises to Keep: How Leaders and the Public Respond to Saving and Retirement," report from the Public Agenda in collaboration

with Employee Benefit Research Institute, Public Agenda, Washington, D.C., 1994.

24. Michelle Singletary and Albert B. Crenshaw, "Credit Card Flood Leaves Sea of Debt," *Washington Post,* November 24, 1996, p. A1.

25. Bureau of Labor Statistics, "Employer Costs for Employee Compensation," various years, http://stats.bls.gov/news.release/ecec.nws.htm.

26. Sylvester J. Schieber and John B. Shoven, "The Consequences of Population Aging on Private Pension Funds, Saving, and Asset Markets" (paper prepared for the NBER-JCER joint conference *The Economics of Aging,* Hakone, Japan, September 14–16, 1994), *NBER Working Paper* no. 4665; Miriam Bensman, "The Baby Boomer Boomerang," *Institutional Investor* (September 1994): 53–56.

27. Bensman, "The Baby Boomer Boomerang."

28. J. Robert Kerrey and John C. Danforth, *Final Report to the President* (Washington, D.C.: Bipartisan Commission on Entitlement and Tax Reform, January 1995).

29. The Century Foundation, http://www.socsec.org/facts/Basics/basics_index.htm.

30. Barbara Bovbjerg, "Social Security Reform: Raising Retirement Ages Improves Program Solvency but May Cause Hardship for Some," statement prepared for the Senate Special Committee on Aging, July 16, 1998.

31. Gary Burtless, "Increasing the Retirement Age for Social Security Pensions," statement prepared for the Senate Special Committee on Aging, July 16, 1998.

32. Bovbjerg, "Social Security Reform: Raising Retirement Ages Improves Program Solvency but May Cause Hardship for Some."

33. Dean Baker, "Saving Social Security with the Stock Market," Twentieth Century Fund/Economic Policy Institute report, Economic Policy Institute, Washington, D.C., 1997.

34. Steurele and Bakija, *Retooling Social Security for the Twentieth Century,* p. 50.

CHAPTER 6

1. P. D. Sorlie, E. Backlund, and J. B. Keller, "U.S. Mortality by Economic, Demographic, and Social Characteristics: The National Longitudinal Mortality Study," *American Journal of Public Health* 85, no. 7 (1995): 949–56.

2. J. E. Williams, M. Massing, W. D. Rosamond, P. D. Sorlie, and H. A. Tyroler, "Racial Disparities in CHD Mortality from 1968–1992 in the State Economic Areas Surrounding the ARIC Communities," *Annals of Epidemiology* 9, no. 8 (1999): 472–80; G. Pappas and others, "The Increasing Disparity in

Mortality between Socioeconomic Groups in the U.S., 1960–1986" *New England Journal of Medicine* 329, no. 2 (July 8, 1993): 103–09.

3. National Center for Health Statistics, *Health, United States, 1999*, with Health and Aging Chartbook (Hyattsville, Md.: National Center for Health Statistics, 1999).

4. J. A. Martin and others, "Births and Deaths: Preliminary Data for 1998," *Vital Statistics Reports* 47, no. 25 (October 5, 1999): 1–45.

5. J. Daric, "Mortality, Occupation, and Socio-Economic Status," *Vital Statistics, Special Reports* 33, no. 10 (1951): 175–87; M. G. Marmot and others, "Health Inequalities among British Civil Servants: The Whitehall II Study," *Lancet* 337, no. 8754 (1991): 1387–93; M. Wolfson and others, "Career Earnings and Death: A Longitudinal Analysis of Older Canadian Men," *Journal of Gerontology* 48, no. 4 (1991): S167–79; Lars Spencer Osberg, "Economic Policy Variables and Population Health," in *Canadian Health Action: Building on the Legacy*, vol. 3 (Sainte Foy: Editions Multimondes, 1998), pp. 579–610; U.S. Department of Health and Human Services, *Healthy People 2000: National Health Promotion and Disease Prevention Objectives Summary* (Washington, D.C.: U.S. Government Printing Office, 1990); R. G. Wilkinson, *Unhealthy Societies: The Afflictions of Inequality* (London: Routledge, 1996); B. C. Amick and others, eds., *Society and Health* (New York: Oxford University Press, 1995); D. R. Williams and C. Collins, "U.S. Socioeconomic and Racial Differences in Health: Patterns and Explanations," *Annual Review of Sociology* 21 (1995): 349–86; Sorlie, Backlund, and Keller, "U.S. Mortality by Economic, Demographic, and Social Characteristics," 949–56; G. Davey Smith and others, "Socio-economic Differentials in Mortality Risk among Men Screened for the Multiple Risk Factor Intervention Trial: I. Results for 300,685 White Men," *American Journal of Public Health* 86, no. 4 (April 1996): 486–96; G. Davey Smith and others, "Socio-economic Differentials in Mortality Risk among Men Screened for the Multiple Risk Factor Intervention Trial: II. Results for 20,224 Black Men," *American Journal Public Health* 86, no. 4 (April 1996): 497–504; Nancy Adler and others, "Socioeconomic Inequalities in Health: No Easy Solution," *Journal of the American Medical Association* 269, no. 24 (June 23–30, 1993): 3140–45; J. S. Feinstein, "The Relationship between Socioeconomic Status and Health: A Review of the Literature," *Milbank Quarterly* 71, no. 2 (1993): 279–322; J. P. Bunker, D. S. Gomby, and B. H. Kehrer, eds., *Pathways to Health: The Role of Social Factors* (Menlo Park, Calif.: Henry J. Kaiser Family Foundation, 1989); E. G. Stockwell, "Socioeconomic Status and Mortality in the United States, *Public Health Reports* 76, no. 12 (1961): 1081–86; A. Antonovsky, "Social Class, Life Expectancy, and Overall Mortality," *Milbank Memorial Fund Quarterly* 45, no. 2 (1967): 31–73; S. L. Syme and L. F. Berkman, "Social Class, Susceptibility, and Sickness," *American Journal of Epidemiology* 104, no. 1 (1976): 1–8; S. H. Preston and P. Taubman, "Socioeconomic Differences in Adult Mortality and

Health Status," in Linda G. Martin and Samuel H. Preston, eds., *Demography of Aging* (Washington, D.C.: National Academy Press, 1994).

6. E. Rogot and others, eds., *A Mortality Study of 1.3 Million Persons by Demographic, Social, and Economic Factors: 1979–1985 Follow-Up* (Bethesda, Md.: National Institutes of Health, 1992).

7. Adler and others, "Socioeconomic Inequalities in Health," 3140–45; Sorlie, Backlund, and Keller, "U.S. Mortality by Economic, Demographic, and Social Characteristics," 949–56; S. Macintyre, "The Black Report and Beyond: What Are the Issues?" *Social Science and Medicine* 44, no. 6 (1997): 723–45.

8. S. A. Robert and J. S. House, "Socioeconomic Inequalities in Health: Integrating Individual, Community and Societal-Level Theory and Research," in Gary L. Albrecht, Ray Fitzpatrick, and Susan Scrimshaw, eds., *Handbook of Social Studies in Health and Medicine* (Thousand Oaks, Calif.: Sage Publications, 2000).

9. K. D. Kochanek, J. D. Maurer, and H. M. Rosenberg, "Why Did Black Life Expectancy Decline from 1984 through 1989 in the United States?" *American Journal of Public Health* 84, no. 6 (1994): 938–44.

10. U.S. Department of Health and Human Services, *Report of the Secretary's Task Force on Black and Minority Health* (Washington, D.C.: U.S. Government Printing Office, 1985).

11. A. T. Geronimus and others, "Excess Mortality among Blacks and Whites in the United States," *New England Journal of Medicine* 335, no. 21 (November 21, 1996): 1552–58.

12. C. McCord and H. P. Freeman, "Excess Mortality in Harlem," *New England Journal of Medicine* 322, no. 3 (January 18, 1990): 173–77.

13. P. McDonough and others, "Income Dynamics and Adult Mortality in the U.S., 1972 through 1989," *American Journal of Public Health* 87, no. 9 (1997): 1476–83; G. King and D. R. Williams, "Race and Health: A Multidimensional Approach to African-American Health," in Amick and others, *Society and Health*, pp. 93–130.

14. Williams and Collins, "U.S. Socioeconomic and Racial Differences in Health," 349–86; D. R. Williams and others, "Racial Differences in Physical and Mental Health: Socioeconomic Status, Stress, and Discrimination," *Journal of Health Psychology* 2, no. 3 (1997): 335–51; N. Krieger and S. Sidney, "Racial Discrimination and Blood Pressure: The CARDIA Study of Young Black and White Adults," *American Journal of Public Health* 86, no. 10 (1996): 1370–78.

15. Williams and others, "Racial Differences in Physical and Mental Health," 335–51.

16. J. Smith, "Healthy Bodies and Thick Wallets: The Dual Relation between Health and Economic Status," *Journal of Economic Perspectives* 13, no. 2 (1999): 145–66.

17. D. Blane, G. Davey Smith, and M. Bartley, "Social Selection: What Does It Contribute to Social Class Differences in Health?" *Sociology of Health and Illness* 15, no. 1 (1993): 1–15; Wolfson and others, "Career Earnings and Death," S167–79; McDonough, "Income Dynamics and Adult Mortality in the U.S.," 1476–83; J. W. Lynch, G. A. Kaplan, and S. J. Shema, "Cumulative Impact of Sustained Economic Hardship on Physical, Cognitive, Psychological, and Social Functioning," *New England Journal of Medicine* 337, no. 26 (December 25, 1997): 1889–95; R. G. Wilkinson, "The Epidemiological Transition: From Material Scarcity to Social Disadvantage?" *Daedalus* 123, no. 4 (Fall 1994): 61–77; J. S. Feinstein, "The Relationship between Socioeconomic Status and Health," 279–322; J. P. Hirdes and W. F. Forbes, "Estimates of the Relative Risk of Mortality Based on the Ontario Longitudinal Study of Aging," *Canadian Journal on Aging* 8, no. 3 (1989): 222–37; A. J. Fox, P. O. Goldblatt, and D. R. Jones, "Social Class Mortality Differentials: Artifact, Selection, or Life Circumstances?" *Journal of Epidemiology and Community Health* 39, no. 1 (1985): 1–8; P. L. Menchik, "Economic Status as a Determinant of Mortality among Black and White Older Men: Does Poverty Kill?" *Population Studies* 47, no. 3 (November 1993): 427–36.

18. G. J. Duncan, "Income National Center for Health Statistics Dynamics and Health," *International Journal of Health Services* 26, no. 3 (1996): 419–44.

19. R. G. Evans and G. L. Stoddart "Producing Health, Consuming Health Care," in R. G. Evans, M. L. Barer, and T. R. Marmor, eds., *The Determinants of Health of Populations* (New York: Aldine De Gruyter, 1994), pp. 27–64.

20. Adler and others, "Socioeconomic Inequalities in Health," 3140–45; N. P. Roos and C. A. Mustard, "Variation in Health and Health Care Use by Socioeconomic Status in Winnipeg, Canada: Does the System Work Well? Yes and No," *Milbank Quarterly* 75, no. 1 (1997): 89–111.

21. M. G. Marmot, M. Kogevinas, and M. A. Elston, "Social Economic Status and Disease," *Annual Review of Public Health* 8, no. 8 (1987): 111–35.

22. J. P. Machenbach, M. H. Bouvier-Colle, and E. Jougla, "'Avoidable' Mortality and Health Services: A Review of Aggregate Data Studies," *International Journal of Health Services* 44, no. 2 (1990): 106–11; C. J. Marini, G. H. Allan, and J. Davidson, "Health Indexes Sensitive to Medical Care Variation," *International Journal of Health Services* 7, no. 2 (1977): 293–309.

23. S. Macintyre, S. Maciver, and A. Sooman, "Area, Class, and Health: Should We Be Focusing on Places or People?" *Journal of Social Policy* 22, no. 2 (1993): 213–34.

24. J. Barry Figueroa and N. Breen, "Significance of Underclass Residence on the Stage of Breast or Cervical Cancer Diagnosis," *American Economic Review* (May 1995): 112–16.

25. M. F. MacDorman and H. M. Rosenberg, "Trends in Infant Mortality by Causes of Death and Other Statistics," *Vital Health Statistics*, DHHS publication PHS 93–1857 (1993), p. 1; This is based on data compiled by the Organization for Economic and Cooperative Development (OECD) and can be found at http://www.oecd.org.

26. J. Horowitz, "Toward a Social Policy for Health," *New England Journal of Medicine* 329, no. 2 (1993): 110–16.

27. P. M. Lantz and others, "Socioeconomic Factors, Health Behaviors, and Mortality," *Journal of the American Medical Association* 279, no. 21 (June 3, 1998): 1703–8; Adler and others, "Socioeconomic Inequalities in Health," 3140–45.

28. B. G. Link and J. Phelan, "Social Conditions as Fundamental Causes of Disease," *Journal of Health and Social Behavior* extra issue (1995): 80–94.

29. M. Marmot and J. F. Mustard, "Coronary Heart Disease from a Population Perspective," in Evans, Barer, and Marmor, *The Determinants of Health of Populations*, pp. 189–214.

30. I. Kawachi, B. P. Kennedy, and R. C. Wilkinson, eds., *The Society and Population Health Reader: Income Inequality and Health* (New York: New Press, 1999).

31. G. B. Rodgers, "Income and Inequality as Determinants of Mortality: An International Cross-Section Analysis," *Population Studies* 33, no. 2 (1979): 343–51; A. T. Flegg, "Inequality of Income, Illiteracy, and Medical Care as Determinants of Infant Mortality in Underdeveloped Countries," *Population Studies* 36, no. 3 (1982): 441–58; J. LeGrand, "Inequalities in Health: Some International Comparisons," *European Economic Review* 31 (February 1987): 182–91; R. J. Waldman, "Income Distribution and Infant Mortality," *Quarterly Journal of Economics* 107, no. 4 (1992): 1283–1302; I. Wennemo, "Infant Mortality, Public Policy, and Inequality: A Comparison of Eighteen Industrialized Countries, 1950–1985," *Sociology of Health and Illness* 15, no. 4 (1993): 429–46; R. G. Wilkinson, "Income and Mortality," in R. G. Wilkinson, ed., *Class and Health: Research and Longitudinal Data* (London: Tavistock, 1986), pp. 88–114; R. G. Wilkinson, "Income Distribution and Life Expectancy," *British Medical Journal* 304, no. 6820 (January 18, 1992): 165–68; R. G. Wilkinson, "Health, Redistribution, and Growth," in A. Glyn and D. Miliband, eds., *Paying for Inequality: The Economic Cost of Social Injustice* (London: Rivers Oram Press, 1994), pp. 24–43; M. C. Daly and others, "Macro-to-Micro Links in the Relation between Income Inequality and Mortality," *Milbank Quarterly* 76, no. 3 (1998): 315; B. P. Kennedy and others, "Income Distribution, Socioeconomic Status, and Self-Rated Health in the United States: Multi-Level Analysis," *British Medical Journal* 317, no. 7163 (October 3, 1998): 917–21; G. A. Kaplan and others, "Inequality in Income and Mortality in the United States: Analysis of Mortality and Potential Pathways," *British Medical Journal* 312, no. 7037 (April 20, 1996): 999–1003; B. P.

Kennedy, I. Kawachi, and D. Prothrow-Stith, "Income Distribution and Mortality: Cross-Sectional Ecological Study of the Robin-Hood Index in the United States," *British Medical Journal* 312, no. 7037 (April 20, 1996): 1004–7.

32. United Nations, *Human Development Report 1996* (New York: Oxford University Press, 1996).

33. D. H. Weinberg, *A Brief Look at Postwar U.S. Income Inequality*, Current Population Reports No. P60–191 (Washington, D.C.: U.S. Census Bureau, June 1996). Data in this report has been updated by the Census Bureau and is available at http://www.census.gov.

34. *Employment Outlook* (Paris: Organization for Economic Cooperation and Development, July 1996); A. Atkinson, L. Rainwater, and T. Smeeding, *Income Distribution in Advanced Economies: Evidence from the Luxembourg Income Study*, Maxwell School of Citizenship and Public Affairs, Syracuse University, Working Paper No. 120, October 1995.

35. U.S. Bureau of the Census, *Measuring Fifty Years of Economic Change Using the March Current Population Survey*, Current Population Reports, P60–203 (Washington, D.C.: U.S. Government Printing Office, 1998).

36. L. A. Karoly, "Growing Economic Disparity in the U.S.: Assessing the Problem and the Policy Options," in J. A. Auerbach and R. S. Belous, eds., *The Inequality Paradox: Growth of Income Disparity* (Washington, D.C.: National Policy Association, 1998).

37. Edward N. Wolff, *Top Heavy: A Study of the Increasing Inequality of Wealth in America* (New York: Twentieth Century Fund Press, 1995); Edward N. Wolff, "Recent Trends in Wealth Ownership," paper presented at a conference, Benefits and Mechanisms for Spreading Asset Ownership in the United States, held at New York University, December 10-12, 1998.

38. K. Fiscella and P. Franks, "Poverty or Income Inequality as Predictor of Mortality: Longitudinal Cohort Study," *British Medical Journal* 314, no. 7096 (June 14, 1997): 1724–28; A. Deaton and C. Paxson, "Mortality, Education, Income, and Inequality among American Cohorts," NBER Working Paper no. 7140 (Cambridge, Mass.: National Bureau of Economic Research, 1999).

39. Kennedy and others, "Income Distribution, Socioeconomic Status, and Self-Rated Health in the United States," 917–21; Daly and others, "Macro-to-Micro Links in the Relation between Income Inequality and Mortality."

40. H. Gravelle, "How Much of the Relation between Population Mortality and Unequal Distribution of Income Is a Statistical Artefact?" *British Medical Journal* 316, no. 7128 (January 31, 1998): 382–85.

41. R. G. Wilkinson, "The Epidemiological Transition: From Material Scarcity to Social Disadvantage?"

42. I. Kawachi and others, "Social Capital, Income Inequality, and Mortality," *American Journal of Public Health* 87, no. 9 (1997): 1491–98.

43. J. W. Lynch and G. A. Kaplan, "Understanding How Inequality in the Distribution of Income Affects Health," *Journal of Health Psychology* 2, no. 3 (1997): 297–314.

44. G. M. Little-Hales, "Public Health in the 1990s: Time for a Change of Approach," *Journal of the Royal Society of Health* 116, no. 3 (1996): 149–52.

45. D. Black and others, *Inequalities in Health: The Black Report—The Health Divide* (London: Penguin, 1988); S. MacIntyre, "The Black Report and Beyond: What Are the Issues?" *Social Science and Medicine* 44, no. 6 (1997): 723–45; M. Marmot, "Acting on the Evidence to Reduce Inequalities in Health," *Health Affairs* 18, no. 3 (1999): 42–44.

46. "Strategies for Population Health: Investing in the Health of Canadians," Federal/Provincial/Territorial Advisory Committee on Population Health, Minister of Supply and Services, Ottawa, Canada, 1994.

47. T. McKeown, *The Role of Medicine: Dream, Mirage, or Nemesis?* 2nd ed. (Oxford, England: Basil Blackwell, 1979).

48. U.S. Department of Health and Human Services, *Healthy People 2010 Objectives: Draft for Public Comment* (Washington, D.C.: U.S. Government Printing Office, 1998).

49. J. DiNardo, N. M. Fortin, and T. Lemieux, "Labor Market Institutions and the Distribution of Wages, 1973–1992: A Semiparametric Approach," University of California at Irvine, March 1994; L. Mishel and J. Bernstein, *The State of Working America 1994–95* (Armonk, N.Y.: Sharpe, 1994).

CHAPTER 7

1. Full technical details on data sources and methods can be found in the following works of mine: "Trends in Household Wealth in the United States, 1962–1983 and 1983–1989," *Review of Income and Wealth* 40, no. 2 (June 1994): 143–74; *Top Heavy: A Study of Increasing Inequality of Wealth in America* (New York: New Press, 1996); "Recent Trends in the Size Distribution of Household Wealth," *Journal of Economic Perspectives* 12, no. 3 (Summer 1998): 131–50; "Recent Trends in Wealth Ownership," in Thomas M. Shapiro and Edward N. Wolff, eds., *Benefits and Mechanisms for Spreading Asset Ownership in the United States* (New York: Russell Sage Press, forthcoming).

2. The time trend is similar when the value of vehicles is also included in net worth, as some researchers are wont to do. Instead of rising by 3.8 percent between 1989 and 1998, median net worth increases by 7.5 percent, and the mean rises by 11.3 percent instead of by 11.0 percent.

3. A proper analysis of this issue requires the use of panel data, tracking individual families over time, in order to test the hypothesis that the increase in mortgage debt is positively related to the rise in stock equity.

4. It should be noted that these figures do not include stocks held in pension funds run by corporations, banks, other financial institutions, and labor unions. Technically, these securities are owned by the institutions that administer them and therefore are not in the direct control of individuals.

CHAPTER 8

1. Academic research on the causes of these changes in inequality has tended to follow with a lag. Given the lack of policy relevance of income changes from 1940 to 1965, the author of a 1971 text on the subject remarked with surprise about the stability of relative incomes throughout the twentieth century, and there were very few studies on the topic (Jan Pen, *Income Distribution: Facts, Theories, Policies* [New York: Praeger, 1971]).

A few isolated papers found inequality among male earners to be rising from the mid-1960s onward, but interest in the inequality problem did not begin in earnest until the mid-1980s. Robert Kuttner used the phrase "shrinking middle class" in "The Declining Middle," an article in the July 1983 issue of *Atlantic Monthly* (pp. 60–72), but reported no data to support this claim. Later that year, Bruce Steinberg and Stephen Rose, working separately, used Census data to show that incomes were breaking apart (see Bruce Steinberg "The Mass Market Is Splitting Apart," *Fortune*, November 28, 1993, pp. 76–82; Stephen Rose, *Social Stratification in U.S.*, 2d ed. [Baltimore, Md.: Social Graphics Co. 1983]). Finally, Barry Bluestone and Bennett Harrison in two major books, *The Deindustrialization of America* (New York: Basic Books, 1982) and *The Great U-Turn: Corporate Restructuring and the Polarizing of America* (New York: Basic Books, 1988), developed fuller, more theoretical approaches to growing inequality.

2. Two papers in 1992 began to formalize the theory of skill-biased technological change: John Bound and George Johnson, "Changes in the Structure of Wages in the 1980s: An Evaluation of Alternative Explanations," *American Economic Review* 823, no. 3 (1992): 71–92; and Lawrence Katz and Kevin Murphy, "Changes in Relative Wages, 1963–87: Supply and Demand Factors," *Quarterly Journal of Economics* 107, no. 1 (1992): 35–78. A good summary of the current argument can be found in Lawrence Katz, "Technological Change, Computerization, and the Wage Structure," paper presented at the Conference on Understanding the Digital Economy, Washington, D.C., 1999. Finally, the following are reviews of the overall literature on wage inequality: Frank Levy and Richard Murnane, "U.S. Earnings Levels and Earnings Inequality: A Review of Recent Trends and Proposed Explanations," *Journal of Economic Literature* 30 (September 1992): 1333–81; and Peter Gottschalk and Timothy Smeeding, "Cross-National Comparisons of Earnings and Income Inequality," *Journal of Economic Literature* 35, no. 2 (June 1997): 633–87.

3. Many economists use hourly wage rates rather than annual earnings on the grounds that this measure comes closer to being a "price" and that workers can supply as many hours as they wish at the going wage. We reject this notion because most jobs come with fixed hours. In particular, for many of the highest-paying jobs, fifty-hour workweeks and beyond are the norm. Because higher-wage workers work more hours as well, the differences among workers based on annual earnings are greater than they are if based on hourly wage. It should also be noted that these compensation measures do not include benefits and amenities of work. Since the higher-paid job tends to have more of these as well, the exclusion of this factor tends to understate total compensation inequality.

4. In making multiyear earnings comparisons, an inflation adjustment must be used. The standard government inflation indicator is the consumer price index. The methodology to construct it has changed over time. The most widely used adjustment is the CPI-U-X1 and this is what we use in this paper. A number of researchers, however, argue that inflation has been overestimated by as much as 1.1 percent a year. Another important issue is what year to use for historical comparison. Average men's earnings reached a peak in 1973 that was not reached again until 1995. For this reason, many people use 1973 as a starting point. From 1973 to 1979, many baby boomers graduated from college and entered the labor force. This unusually large cohort drove down the average earnings of college graduates and led to a fall in their earnings premium versus high school graduates. Since we are interested in tracking inequality (which began to rise sharply after 1979) and also in the increasing earnings premium enjoyed by college graduates, we make our historical comparison with 1979 rather than 1973.

5. Proponents of the political explanation for growing earnings differences argue that the increase in college-educated workers is a red herring because many employers simply are hiring candidates with college degrees for jobs that don't require college-level skills. But this view does not explain why employers are willing to pay more for college-educated workers even as their supply increases.

6. Jeremy Greenwood, *The Third Industrial Revolution: Technology, Productivity, and Income Equality* (Washington, D.C.: American Enterprise Institute, 1997).

7. Steven Davis and Robert Topel, "International Trade and American Wages in the 1980s: Giant Sucking Sound or Small Hiccup?" in *Brookings Papers on Economic Activities,* vol. 2, pp. 214–21.

8. Gottschalk and Smeeding, "Cross-National Comparisons of Earnings and Income Inequality," p. 649.

9. Alan Krueger, "How Computers Changed the Wage Structure: Evidence from Micro Data," *Quarterly Journal of Economics* 108, no. 1 (1993): 33–60.

10. John Dinardo and Jorn-Steffen Pischke, "The Returns to Computer Use Revisited: Have Pencils Changed the Wage Structure Too?" *Quarterly Journal of Economics* 112, no. 1 (1997): 291–303.

11. Eli Berman, John Bound, and Zvi Griliches, "Changes in the Demand for Skilled Labor within U.S. Manufacturing Industries: Evidence from the Annual Survey of Manufactures," *Quarterly Journal of Economics* 109 (1994): 367–97.

12. Eli Berman, John Bound, and Stephen Machin, "Implications of Skill-Biased Technological Change: International Evidence," *NBER Working Paper* no. 6166 (Cambridge, Mass.: National Bureau of Economic Research, 1998).

13. David Autor, Lawrence Katz, and Alan Krueger, "Computer Inequality: Have Computers Changed the Labor Market," *NBER Working Paper* no. 5956 (Cambridge, Mass.: National Bureau of Economic Research, 1997); David Autor, Lawrence Katz, and Alan Krueger, "Computer Inequality: Have Computers Changed the Labor Market," *Quarterly Journal of Economics* 113, no. 4 (1998).

14. Mark Doms, Timothy Dunn, and Kenneth Troske, "Workers, Wages, and Technology," *Quarterly Journal of Economics* 112, no. 1 (1997): 253–90.

15. James K. Galbraith, *Created Unequal: The Crisis in American Pay* (New York: Free Press, 1998).

16. Timothy Bresnahan, "Computerization and Wage Dispersion: An Analytical Reinterpretation," unpublished paper, Stanford University, Stanford, California, 1997.

17. Council of Economic Advisers, "Job Creation and Employment Opportunities: The United States Labor Market, 1993–1996," April 23, 1996; David Howell and Maury Gittleman, "Job Quality and Labor Market Segmentation in the U.S.: A New Perspective on Employment Restructuring by Race and Gender since 1973," unpublished manuscript, New School for Social Research, New York, 1993; Anthony Carnevale and Stephen Rose, *Education for What? The New Office Economy* (Princeton, N.J.: Educational Testing Service, 1998); Steven Hertzenberg, John Alic, and Howard Wial, *New Rules for a New Economy: Employment and Opportunity in Postindustrial America* (Ithaca, N.Y.: Cornell University Press, 1999).

18. William Baumol, "Macroeconomics of Unbalanced Growth: The Anatomy of Urban Crisis," *American Economic Review* 57 (June 1967): 415–26.

19. Office of Technological Assessment, *Technology and the American Economic Transition: Choices for the Future* (Washington, D.C.: U.S. Government Printing Office, 1986).

20. Robert Frank and Philip Cook, *The Winner-Take-All Society* (New York: Free Press, 1995).

21. For many other examples of this phenomenon see Michael Wolf, *The Entertainment Economy: How Mega-media Forces Are Transforming Our Lives* (New York: Times Books, 1999).

22. National Adult Literacy Survey (NALS), U.S. Department of Education, National Center for Education Statistics, 1992.

23. Katherine McFate, Roger Lawson, and William J. Wilson, eds., *Poverty, Inequality, and the Future of Social Policy: Western States in the New World Order* (New York: Russell Sage Foundation, 1995); Harry J. Holzer and Keith R. Ihlanfeldt, "Customer Discrimination and Employment Outcomes for Minority Workers," *Quarterly Journal of Economics* 113, no. 3 (1998): 835–67.

24. Anthony Carnevale and Donna Desrochers, *Getting Down to Business: Matching Welfare Recipients' Skills to Jobs That Train* (Princeton, N.J.: Educational Testing Service, 1999).

CHAPTER 9

1. K. Arrow, "Some Mathematical Models of Race Discrimination in the Labor Market," in A. Pascal, ed., *Racial Discrimination in Economic Life* (Lexington, Mass.: Lexington Books, 1972), p. 91.

2. M. Friedman, *Capitalism and Freedom* (Chicago: University of Chicago Press, 1962).

3. Strictly speaking, one would also have to assume that race is not a consumption good.

4. W. Darity, Jr. and Patrick L. Mason, "Evidence on Discrimination in Employment: Codes of Color, Codes of Gender," *Journal of Economic Perspectives* 12, no. 2 (Spring 1998): 63–90.

5. Douglass S. Massey and Nancy A. Denton, *American Apartheid: Segregation and the Making of the Underclass* (Cambridge, Mass.: Harvard University Press, 1993).

6. Cedric Herring and Charles Amissah, "Advance and Retreat: Racially Based Attitudes and Public Policy," in Steven A. Tuch and Jack K. Martin, eds., *Racial Attitudes in the 1990s: Continuity and Change* (Westport, Conn.: Praeger, 1997), pp. 121–43. Herring and Amissah's results are net of individual differences in education, income, age, sex, middle class status, Protestant or Catholic identity, nativity, location, region, or political ideology.

7. John Donohue and James Heckman, "Continuous versus Episodic Change: The Impact of Civil Rights Policy on the Economic Status of Blacks," *Journal of Economic Literature* 29, no. 4 (December 1992): 1606.

8. All data are taken from the Current Population Survey, Annual Demographic File, 1962–1997. Each individual is a non-institutionalized civilian adult, sixteen to sixty-four years of age, with at least one year of education (Panel Study on Income Dynamics, 1968–93). Wage data are from the year preceding the survey. So the 1968 survey contains information on 1967 wages. All monetary figures are in 1999 dollars.

9. Gary S. Becker, *The Economics of Discrimination* (Chicago: University of Chicago Press, 1957).

10. Arrow, "Some Mathematical Models of Race Discrimination in the Labor Market."

11. Ibid., p. 97.

12. Glen Cain, "The Economic Analysis of Labor Market Discrimination: A Survey," in O. Ashenfelter and R. Layard, eds., *Handbook of Labor Economics* (Amsterdam: North Holland Press, 1986), pp. 693–785.

13. Darity and Mason, "Evidence on Discrimination in Employment."

14. One of the earliest treatments on racial inequality and educational quality is Finis Welch, "Education and Racial Discrimination," in Orley Ashenfelter and Albert Rees, eds., *Discrimination in Labor Markets* (Princeton, N.J.: Princeton University Press, 1974). Thomas Sowell discusses the role of culture and racial inequality; see T. Sowell, *Race and Economics* (New York: McKay, 1975). Richard Herrnstein and Charles Murray provide one of the more recent presentations of biological racism; see Richard J. Herrnstein and Charles Murray, *The Bell Curve: Intelligence and Class Structure in American Life* (New York: Free Press, 1994). James Heckman as well as Derek Neal and William Johnson cite the importance of racial differences in household and community environment for labor market outcomes; see James Heckman, "Detecting Discrimination," *Journal of Economic Perspectives* 12, no. 2 (Spring 1998): 101–16; D. Neal and W. Johnson, "The Role of Pre-Market Factors in Black-White Wage Differences," *The Journal of Political Economy* 104 (1996): 869–95.

15. Brent Bratsberg and Dek Terrell, "Experience, Tenure, and Wage Growth of Young Black and White Men," *Journal of Human Resources* 23, no. 3 (Summer 1998): 658–77; Francine D. Blau, Marianne A. Ferber, and Anne E. Winkler, *The Economics of Women, Men, and Work* (Upper Saddle River, N.J.: Prentice Hall, 1998).

16. Glenn C. Loury, "Discrimination in the Post-Civil Rights Era: Beyond Market Interactions," *Journal of Economic Perspectives* 12, no. 2 (Spring 1998): 117–26.

17. Sowell, *Race and Economics*.

18. J. Cotton, "Color or Culture? Wage Differences among Non-Hispanic Black Males and Hispanic White Males," *Review of Black Political Economy* 21, no. 4 (Spring 1993): 53–67.

19. Edward Telles and Edward Murguia, "Phenotypic Discrimination and Income Differences among Mexican Americans," *Social Science Quarterly* 71, no. 4 (December 1990): 682–94.

20. Patrick L. Mason, "Male Interracial Wage Differentials: Competing Explanations," *Cambridge Journal of Economics* 23 (May 1999): 261–99. In my study, the term *Latinos* excludes persons from Spain. Brown Latinos are

those individuals who gave their race as Chicano, Boricua, moreno, black, brown, or some similar Spanish-language descriptor.

21. W. Darity, Jr., D. Guilkey, and W. Winfrey, "Ethnicity, Race, and Earnings," *Economic Letters* 47, no. 3/4 (1995): 401–8.

22. Welch, "Education and Racial Discrimination."

23. James Smith, "Race and Human Capital," *American Economic Review* 74, no. 3 (June 1984): 685–98; J. Bernstein, "Where's the Payoff? The Gap between Black Academic Progress and Economic Gains," Economic Policy Institute, Washington, D.C., 1995.

24. C. Jencks, *Rethinking Social Policy: Race, Poverty, and the Underclass* (New York: HarperPerennial, 1993), pp. 177–79; Bernstein, "Where's the Payoff?"

25. G. Jaynes and R. Williams, Jr., eds., *A Common Destiny: Blacks and American Society* (Washington, D.C.: National Academy Press, 1989), pp. 351–52.

26. Although the racial gap in educational quality declined throughout the 1970s and 1980s, the residual wage difference might still have increased if the rate of return to skill grew faster than the rate of decrease of the racial gap in educational quality. However, Ferguson fails to find any evidence to support this particular speculation; see Ronald Ferguson, "Shifting Challenges: Fifty Years of Economic Change Toward Black-White Earnings Equality," *Daedalus* 124 (Winter 1994): 37–76.

27. The data in this table are for individuals who were of school age (six through seventeen) in 1972, but who were young adults between 1983 and 1992. I analyzed the wages, hours, and educational attainment of these individuals as they moved from seventeen to twenty-eight years of age in 1983 to twenty-six to thirty-seven years of age in 1992. The family values and class levels are established by the individual's residence in 1972. All data are taken from the Panel Study on Income Dynamics.

I define *values* to include the following elements: desire to help parents and other family members if individual had more money, efficacy and planning skills, emotional attachment to society, aspirations and ambitions, engagement in self-help activities, engagement in economizing activities, engagement in safe behavior, future-orientation, connection to potential sources of information and help or community institutions, engagement in activities to raise income, and achievement orientation.

28. C. Juhn, K. Murphy, and B. Pierce, "Accounting for the Slowdown in Black-White Wage Convergence," in M. Kosters, ed., *Workers and Their Wages* (Washington, D.C.: The AEI Press, 1991), pp. 107–43.

29. Neal and Johnson use Armed Forces Qualification Test Scores from the National Longitudinal Survey of Youth to measure cognitive ability; see Neal and Johnson, "The Role of Pre-Market Factors in Black-White Wage Differences." They did claim that the racial gap in test scores can explain all

(or nearly all) of the racial wage inequality. Using the same data, Rodgers and Spriggs find that once AFQT scores are corrected for measurement bias the gap in test scores has only a nominal impact on racial wage inequality; see William Rodgers III and William E. Spriggs, "What Does AFQT Really Measure: Race, Wages, Schooling, and the AFQT Score," *Review of Black Political Economy* 2, no. 4 (Spring 1996): 13–46. Mason uses intelligence test scores from the Panel Study on Income Dynamics and also finds that test scores do not explain a sizable portion of the racial wage gap; see Mason, "Male Interracial Wage Differentials"; P. Mason, "Persistent Discrimination: Racial Disparity in the U.S., 1967–1988," *American Economic Association Papers and Proceedings*, forthcoming. See also Darity and Mason, "Evidence on Discrimination in Employment," for a greater discussion of the relationship between test scores and racial wage inequality.

30. Mason, "Persistent Discrimination."

31. Mary Corcoran, "The Economic Progress of African American Women," in Irene Brown, ed., *Latinas and African American Women in the U.S. Labor Market* (New York: Russell Sage Foundation, 1999), pp. 35–60; John Bound and Laura Dresser, "Losing Ground: The Erosion of the Relative Earnings of African American Women During the 1980s," in Brown, *Latinas and African American Women in the U.S. Labor Market,* pp. 61–104. Both studies use a sample restricted to women above the age of eighteen with no more than ten years of potential labor market experience, drawn on the 1973–1991 waves of the Outgoing Rotation Group of the Current Population Survey. Young rather than older women are examined because their labor market outcomes are more likely to reflect current changes in the market.

32. Thurow provides a highly accessible but all too brief discussion of some of the theoretical and empirical inconsistencies of the literature on skill-biased technical progress; see Lester Thurow, "Wage Dispersion: Who Done It?" *Journal of Post Keynesian Economics* 21, no. 1 (Fall 1998): 25–37. Unlike the criticisms discussed in the text, Thurow does not focus his criticism of this hypothesis on institutional changes. Rather, he argues quite persuasively that empirical research has not adequately explained the role of factor price equalization (the equalizing effect on international wage differences associated with increased globalization of trade) on wage inequality. Thurow also points out that the distribution of acquired skills is nowhere near as unequal as the distribution of earnings. Indeed, there has been a much greater increase in wage inequality among workers of similar skill classes (for example, same education and experience) than between skilled and unskilled workers. Finally, Thurow points out that an increase in the demand for educated workers is not the same thing as an increase in the demand for skill. Wages are attached to the job and not to potential individual productivity. As employment slackens or tightens in the labor market, firms raise or lower, respectively, the educational credentials required of new employees.

33. David R. Howell, Margaret Duncan, and Bennett Harrison, "Low Wages in the U.S. and High Unemployment in Europe: A Critical Assessment of the Conventional Wisdom," working paper, New School University, 1998.

34. Dennis Snower, "Causes of Changing Earnings Inequality," in *Income Inequality: Issues and Policy Options* (Kansas City: Federal Reserve Bank of Kansas City, 1998), pp. 69–133.

35. See J. Leonard, "The Federal Anti-Bias Effort," in Emily Hoffman, ed., *Essays on the Economics of Discrimination* (Kalamazoo, Mich.: W. E. Upjohn Institute for Employment Research, 1991), pp. 85–113; J. Leonard, "The Impact of Affirmative Action Regulation and Equal Employment Opportunity Law on Black Employment," *Journal of Economic Perspectives* 4, no. 4 (Fall 1991): 47–63.

36. W. Darity, Jr. and Samuel L. Myers, Jr., *Persistent Disparity: Race and Economic Inequality in the United States since 1945* (Northampton, Mass.: Edward Elgar Publishing Company, 1999); Mason, "Male Interracial Wage Differentials"; Patrick L. Mason, "Race, Competition, and Differential Wages," *Cambridge Journal of Economics* 19, no. 4 (August 1995): 545–68.

37. See the NBER Web page at http://www.nber.org/cycles.html.

38. Rudiger Dornbusch, Stanley Fischer, and Richard Startz, *Macroeconomics,* 7th ed. (New York: Irwin McGraw-Hill, 1998), Appendix.

39. Dornbusch, Fischer, and Startz, *Macroeconomics,* Appendix.

40. Mason, "Race, Competition, and Differential Wages"; W. Darity, Jr. and Rhonda Williams, "Peddlers Forever? Culture, Competition, and Discrimination," papers and proceedings, *American Economic Review* 75, no. 2 (May 1985): 256–61; William A. Darity, Jr., "What's Left of the Theory of Discrimination," in S. Shulman and W. Darity, eds., *The Question of Discrimination: Racial Inequality in the U.S. Labor Market* (Middletown, Conn.: Wesleyan University Press, 1989); Rhonda Williams, "Racial Inequality and Racial Conflict: Recent Developments in Radical Theory," in W. Darity, Jr., ed., *Labor Economics: Problems in Analyzing Labor Markets* (Norwell, Mass.: Kluwer, 1993), pp. 209–36.

41. The job is defined by its industry, occupation, and firm location.

42. J. Braddock II and J. McPartland, "How Minorities Continue to Be Excluded from Equal Employment Opportunities: Research on Labor Market and Institutional Barriers," *Journal of Social Issues* 43, no. 1 (1987): 5–39.

43. Although Herrnstein and Murray tend to think of race in biological terms (Herrnstein and Murray, *The Bell Curve*), neither is an economist. Some of the most conservative economists have sought to distance themselves from the work of these authors. (See, for example, Neal and Johnson, "The Role of Pre-Market Factors in Black-White Wage Differences.") Herrnstein, now deceased, was a social psychologist; Murray is a sociologist.

44. Racial identities may carry with them distinct cultural practices, but a person may refrain from engaging in those practices and still be identified with the group that shares them because of other ascriptive characteristics.

45. Cheryl Harris, "Whiteness as Property," *Harvard Law Review* 106, no. 8 (June 1993): 1709–91.

46. *Passing* is when an African American with European features adopts a white identity. To preserve that white identity, the individual does not allow anyone in the new environment to know of the black past. The individual then has passed from black to white.

47. Mason, "Male Interracial Wage Differentials."

48. W. Darity, Jr., Patrick L. Mason, and James Stewart, "Race, Class, and the Economics of Identity: A Theory of Racism," working paper, Florida State University, 2000.

49. See Mason, "Male Interracial Wage Differentials" and "Race, Competition, and Differential Wages," for an extended discussion on this issue.

CHAPTER 10

1. See Phyllis B. Eveleth and James M. Tanner, *Worldwide Variation in Human Growth* (New York: Cambridge University Press, 1976 and 1990).

2. L. A. Malcolm, "Ecological Factors Relating to Child Growth and Nutritional Status," in Alexander F. Roche and Frank Falkner, eds., *Nutrition and Malnutrition: Identification and Measurement* (New York: Plenum Press, 1974), pp. 329–52.

3. Reynaldo Martorell and Jean-Pierre Habicht, "Growth in Early Childhood in Developing Countries," in Frank Falkner and J. M. Tanner, eds., *Human Growth: A Comprehensive Treatise*, vol. 3 (New York: Plenum Press, 1986), pp. 241–62.

4. An alternative view of stature is the "small but healthy" paradigm emphasized by P. V. Sukhatme, *Newer Concepts in Nutrition and Their Implications for Policy* (Pune, India: Maharashtra Association for the Cultivation of Science Research Institute, 1982), in which it is claimed that many individuals adapt with low costs to nutritional deprivation. For a critique of this view see Partha Dasgupta, *An Inquiry into Well-Being and Destitution* (New York: Oxford University Press, 1993).

5. Of course, it is possible that higher incomes could purchase products such as alcohol, tobacco, or drugs that impair health.

6. The countries are Czechoslovakia, West Germany, the Netherlands, New Zealand, United States, Japan, South Korea, Egypt, India, Belgium, Denmark, Hungary, Italy, Argentina, and Australia. Three countries have two height studies conducted at different dates.

7. Richard H. Steckel, "Stature and the Standard of Living," *Journal of Economic Literature* 33 (December 1995): 1903–40.

8. These countries have about the same per capita GDP as the United States.

9. For additional discussion of nutrition and health see U.S. Department of Health and Human Services, *The Surgeon General's Report on Nutrition and Health*, DHHS Publication PHS 88-50210 (Washington, D.C.: U.S. Government Printing Office, 1988); and Charlette R. Gallagher and John B. Allred, *Taking the Fear Out of Eating: A Nutritionists' Guide to Sensible Food Choices* (New York: Cambridge University Press, 1992).

10. Adding to the confusion, some recommendations that have been "overturned" were never based on solid evidence, and for various reasons the media have perpetuated some nutritional myths.

11. See "Health: Eating Smart for Your Heart," *Time*, July 19, 1999, pp. 40–54.

12. Data presented in this section are taken from various reports of U.S. government agencies, and are compiled in Richard H. Steckel, ed., "Health, Nutrition, and Well-being," in *Historical Statistics of the United States, Millennial Edition* (New York: Cambridge University Press, forthcoming).

CHAPTER 11

1. L. Mishel, J. Bernstein, and J. Schmitt, "Tight Labor Markets Continue to Generate Strong, Broad-Based Wage Growth, without Inflation," Washington, D.C.: Economic Policy Institute, 1999.

2. Council of Economic Advisers, *Economic Report of the President, 1999* (Washington, D.C.: U.S. Government Printing Office, 1999), p. 94.

3. The Congressional Budget Office made similar estimates in its most recent Economic and Budget Outlook. See Congressional Budget Office, *The Economic and Budget Outlook: Fiscal Years 2000–2009* (Washington, D.C.: U.S. Government Printing Office, 1999), p. 30.

4. For example, Robert Gordon, one of the nation's leading macroeconomists, who has also done extensive work measuring quality improvements in durable goods, has argued that the BEA's measurement of computer quality improvement is substantially overstated. See Robert Gordon, "Some Experts Say Inflation Is Understated," *New York Times*, November 6, 1997, p. D1.

5. For example, see W. M. Cox and R. Alm, *Myths of Rich and Poor: Why We're Better Off Than We Think* (New York: Basic Books, 1999).

CHAPTER 12

1. See, for example, Lawrence Mishel, Jared Bernstein, and John Schmitt, *The State of Working America, 1998–99* (Ithaca, N.Y.: Cornell University Press, 1999), chapter 3.

CHAPTER 13

1. World Bank, *Global Development Finance, Country Tables* (Washington, D.C.: World Bank, 1998), p. 390.

2. International Monetary Fund, *World Economic Outlook: Financial Turbulence and the World Economy* (Washington, D.C.: International Monetary Fund, October 1998), p. 72.

3. Mark Weisbrot, testimony to the General Oversight and Investigations Subcommittee, House Committee on Banking and Financial Services, September 10, 1998. See http://www.house.gov/banking/91098ppp.htm.

4. Boris Kagarlitsky, testimony to the General Oversight and Investigations Subcommittee, House of Representatives Committee on Banking and Financial Services, September 10, 1998. See http://www.house.gov/banking/91098kag.htm.

5. International Monetary Fund, *Direction of Trade Statistics, March 1999* (Washington, D.C.: International Monetary Fund, 1999), pp. 4–5.

6. William Pfaff, "Redefining World Power," *Foreign Affairs* 70, no. 1 (1991): 34–48.

7. And elaborated in an interview with the author for BBC Radio 4 *Analysis* documentary "Russian Roulette," transmitted March 23, 1996.

8. See George Breslauer, "Aid to Russia: What Difference Can Western Policy Make?" in Gail W. Lapidus, ed., *The New Russia: Troubled Transformation* (Boulder, Colo.: Westview Press, 1995), pp. 223–44.

9. See Stephan Haggard and Steven B. Webb, eds., *Voting for Reform: Democracy, Political Liberalization and Economic Adjustment* (Washington, D.C.: World Bank, 1994).

10. Prepared statement of Lawrence H. Summers, *Impact of IMF/World Bank Policies toward Russia and the Russian Economy*, Hearing before the Committee on Banking, Housing, and Urban Affairs, S. Hrg 103–508, February 8, 1994, p. 52.

11. See Anders Aslund, "Possible Future Directions for Economies in Transition," in Joan Nelson, Charles Tilly, and Lee Walker, eds., *Transforming Post-Communist Political Economies* (Washington, D.C.: National Academy Press, 1998).

12. See Simon Johnson and Marzena Kowalska, "Poland: The Political Economy of Shock Therapy," in Stephan Haggard and Steven B. Webb, eds., *Voting for Reform: Democracy, Political Liberalization and Economic Adjustment* (Washington, D.C.: World Bank, 1994), pp. 185–241.

13. Aslund, "Possible Future Directions for Economies in Transition."

14. See Anders Aslund on the necessity of such institutions: "Are Radical Reforms Unpopular," Carnegie Endowment for International Peace, Washington, D.C., 1994, p. 4.

15. In the words of Secretary of State James Baker, cited in *Financial Times*, December 13, 1991, p. 18.

16. See Jeffrey Sachs, "The Grand Bargain," in Anders Aslund, ed., *The Post-Soviet Economy: Soviet and Western Perspectives* (London: Pinter, 1992).

17. These figures are from *Ekonomika i zhizn'*, no. 4 (February 1993): 13–15 and no. 6 (February 1994): 7–9, as analyzed by Richard E. Ericson, "The Russian Economy since Independence," in Lapidus, *The New Russia*, p. 45.

18. *Izvestiya* 4 (April 1992) as cited in *Current Digest of the Post-Soviet Press* 44, no. 14 (1992): 12.

19. Lilia Shevtsova, "Russia's Post-Communist Politics: Revolution or Continuity," in Lapidus, *The New Russia*, pp. 23–24.

20. See discussion in Aslund, "Possible Future Directions for Economies in Transition."

21. There was shock and uproar when in early 1996 a U.S. diplomat outlined the new elite of "clans" that was ruling Russia: Thomas Graham, "Who Rules Russia," reprinted in *Prospect* (January 1996): 15–16.

22. As calculated by Anders Aslund, *How Russia Became a Market Economy* (Washington, D.C.: The Brookings Institution, 1995).

23. Aslund, "Possible Future Directions for Economies in Transition," p. 6. The figures used in the rest of this and the following paragraph are also taken from this article.

24. World Bank, *World Development Report 1998* (Washington, D.C.: World Bank, 1998), Box 7.1.

25. John Vickers and Vincent Wright, *The Politics of Privatization in Western Europe* (London: Cass, 1988).

26. See International Monetary Fund, *World Economic Outlook* (Washington, D.C.: International Monetary Fund, 1998 and 1999).

27. European Bank for Reconstruction and Development, *Transition Report 1998* (London: European Bank for Reconstruction and Development, 1998).

28. International Monetary Fund, "Crisis in Emerging Market Economies: The Road to Recovery," Address by Michel Camdessus, New York, *Press Release 98/17*, September 15, 1998.

29. International Monetary Fund, *Press Release 97/5*, April 2, 1997.

30. International Monetary Fund, *World Economic Outlook* (May 1998), p. 100; International Monetary Fund, *World Economic Outlook* (October 1998), p. 70.

31. This argument draws upon Nigel Gould-Davies and Ngaire Woods, "Russia and the IMF," *International Affairs* 75, no. 1 (January 1999): 1–22.

32. *Nezavisimaya Gazeta*, December 18, 1997, *Current Digest of the Post-Soviet Press* 49, no. 51 (1997): 8.

33. Radio Free Europe/Radio Liberty Newsline, December 30, 1997.

34. See comments by John Odling-Smee as cited in Richard W. Stevenson, "Did Yeltsin Get a Sweetheart Deal on I.M.F. Loans?" *New York Times*, March 11, 1996.

35. See Gould-Davies and Woods, "Russia and the IMF."

36. See "A Few Favoured Cliques," in Janine R. Wedel, *Collision and Collusion: The Strange Case of Western Aid to Eastern Europe 1989–1998* (London: Macmillan, 1998), chapter 3.

37. Karl Thalheim, "Russia's Economic Development," in George Katkov and others, *Russia Enters the Twentieth Century 1894–1917* (London: Temple Smith, 1971).

38. Thalheim, "Russia's Economic Development."

39. Joseph E. Stiglitz, "Whither Reform? Ten Years of Transition," Annual Bank Conference on Development Economics, April 28–30, 1999 (Washington, D.C.: World Bank, 1999), citing the quip of a colleague, n. 12, p. 9.

40. See summary in Michael D. Intriligator, "Round Table on Russia: A New Economic Policy for Russia," *Economics of Transition 5*, no. 1 (1997): 225–27.

CHAPTER 14

1. John Maynard Keynes, *The Collected Writings of John Maynard Keynes*, Volume 25: *Activities 1940–1944: Shaping the Postwar World* (London: Macmillan, 1980), p. 52.

2. Dani Rodrik, *The New Global Economy and Developing Countries: Making Openness Work* (Washington, D.C.: Johns Hopkins University Press, 1999), p. 68.

3. For contrasting explanations of the breakdown of Golden Age and the rise of Neoliberalism, see Samuel Bowles, David Gordon, and Thomas Weisskopf, *After the Wasteland* (Armonk, N.Y.: Sharpe, 1990); and Robert Brenner, "The Economics of Global Turbulence," *New Left Review* 229 (May/June 1998): 1–264.

4. John Eatwell, *International Financial Liberalization: The Impact on World Development* (New York: United Nations Development Programme, Office of Development Studies, 1996), p. 38.

5. Reported in David Felix, "Asia and the Crisis of Financial Globalization," in Dean Baker, Gerald Epstein, and Robert Pollin, eds., *Globalization and Progressive Economic Policy* (Cambridge: Cambridge University Press, 1998), p. 184.

6. Angus Maddison, *Monitoring the World Economy 1820–1992* (Paris: Organization for Economic Cooperation and Development, 1995), p. 60.

7. Data is from United Nations Conference on Trade and Development, *Trade and Development Report, 1999* (New York: United Nations, 1999), p. 4; World Bank, *World Development Indicators*, November 1999, p. 190.

8. Data is taken from the Council of Economic Advisers, *Economic Report of the President* (Washington, D.C.: U.S. Government Printing Office, 2000).

9. Data in this paragraph is from Lawrence Mishel, Jared Bernstein, and John Schmitt, *The State of Working America 1998–99* (Ithaca, N.Y.: Cornell University Press, 1998), pp. 51, 131, 132, and 157.

10. United Nations Conference on Trade and Development, *Trade and Development Report 1997* (New York: United Nations, 1997), pp. 65–66.

11. Some of the arguments in this section are taken from James Crotty and Gerald Epstein, "In Defense of Capital Controls," in *The Socialist Register 1996* (London: Merlin Press), pp. 118–49.

12. The argument in this section focuses on financial capital mobility. The benefits and costs of foreign direct investment to developing countries are analyzed in James Crotty, Gerald Epstein, and Patricia Kelly, "Multinational Corporations in the Neoliberal Regime," in Baker, Epstein, and Pollin, *Globalization and Progressive Economic Policy,* pp. 117–43.

13. The economic functions exercised by the state in Korea and Taiwan are clearly explained in Alice Amsden, *Asia's Next Giant* (New York: Oxford University Press, 1989); and in Robert Wade, *Governing the Market* (Princeton, N.J.: Princeton University Press, 1990).

14. "The Price of Uncertainty," *Economist,* June 12, 1999, p. 65.

15. United Nations Conference on Trade and Development, *Trade and Development Report 1998* (New York: United Nations, 1998), p. 55.

16. For an extensive analysis of the Asian crisis, see James Crotty and Gary Dymski, "Can the Neoliberal Regime Survive Victory in Asia? The Political Economy of the Asian Crisis," *International Papers in Political Economy,* no. 2 (1999): 1–47.

17. Joseph Stiglitz, "Sound Finance and Sustainable Development in Asia," keynote address to the Asia Development Forum, March 12, 1998, emphasis in original, http://www.worldbank.org/html/extdr/extme/jssp031298/htm.

18. United Nations Conference on Trade and Development, *Trade and Development Report 1998,* p. 61.

19. An excellent discussion of the Korean crisis can be found in Ha-Joon Chang, Hong-Jae Park, and Chul-Gyne Yoo, "Interpreting the Korean Crisis: Financial Liberalization, Industrial Policy, and Corporate Governance," *Cambridge Journal of Economics* 22, no. 6 (November 1998): 735–46.

20. Jason Furman and Joseph Stiglitz, "Economic Crises: Evidence and Insights from East Asia," *Brookings Papers on Economic Activity,* no. 2 (1998): 1–114.

21. *Financial Times,* September 30, 1998.

22. "Germany's Schroeder Backs Controls," *Wall Street Journal,* October 9, 1998.

23. "How to Reshape the World Financial System," *Business Week,* November 12, 1998, pp. 113–14.

24. "As Free-Flowing Capital Sinks Nations, Experts Prepare to 'Rethink System,'" *New York Times,* September 20, 1998.

25. Quoted in Robert Wade, "The Asian Debt-and-Development Crisis of 1997–?: Causes and Consequences," *World Development* 26, no. 8 (1998): 1550.

26. Steven Radelet and Jeffrey Sachs, "The East Asian Financial Crisis: Diagnosis, Remedies, Prospects," *Brookings Papers on Economic Activity*, no. 1 (1998): 71.

27. The Tobin Tax is explained and defended in David Felix, "Financial Globalization vs. Free Trade: The Case for the Tobin Tax," *UNCTAD Review* (New York: United Nations, 1996).

28. Manfred Bienefeld, "Capitalism and the Nation State in the Dog Days of the Twentieth Century," in *The Socialist Register 1996*, p. 122.

29. Crotty and Epstein, "In Defense of Capital Controls."

30. John Maynard Keynes, *The Collected Writings of John Maynard Keynes*, Volume 7: *The General Theory of Employment, Interest, and Money*, p. 160.

31. United Nations Conference on Trade and Development, *Trade and Development Report 1998*, pp. 103, 105.

32. *Economist*, October 7, 1995, p. 16.

33. Rodrik, *The New Global Economy and Developing Countries*, p. 15.

CHAPTER 15

1. See also my earlier paper, "Technology, Growth, and Policy: Theory, Evidence, and Interpretation," *Nordic Journal of Political Economy* 25, no. 1 (1999): 5–14.

2. For an overview see Luigi Pasinetti, *Growth and Income Distribution* (Cambridge: Cambridge University Press, 1974).

3. See Moses Abramovitz, "Resources and Output Trends in the United States since 1870," *American Economic Review* 46, no. 2 (May 1956): 5–23; and Edward F. Denison, *Why Growth Rates Differ: Post-War Experience in Nine Western Countries* (Washington, D.C.: Brookings Institution Press, 1967). A good overview of the research in this area is to be found in Angus Maddison, "Growth and Slowdown in Advanced Capitalist Economies: Techniques of Quantitative Assessment," *Journal of Economic Literature* 25, no. 2 (June 1987): 649–98.

4. Richard R. Nelson, "Aggregate Production Functions and Medium-Range Growth Projections," *American Economic Review* 54, no. 5 (September 1964): 575–606.

5. Alwyn Young, "The Tyranny of Numbers: Confronting the Statistical Realities of the East Asian Growth Experience," *Quarterly Journal of Economics* 110, no. 3 (August 1995): 641–80.

6. Robert E. Lucas, "Making a Miracle," *Econometrica* 61, no. 2 (March 1993): 251–72.

7. Hence, I use the notion *evolutionary* in a broad sense. In a more narrow sense the notion is also used to characterize a specific class of formal economic models inspired by the use of evolutionary models in biology. As in biology, these economic models operate with a set of competing "species," which in economics might be firms or technologies or both, and a selection environment that sets the rules for their survival and growth. The central reference here is Richard R. Nelson and Sidney G. Winter, *An Evolutionary Theory of Economic Change* (Cambridge, Mass.: Harvard University Press, 1982). For an overview and discussion of work in this area see Esben Sloth Andersen, *Evolutionary Economics: Post-Schumpeterian Contributions* (London: Pinter, 1994).

8. It is worth mentioning that the emphasis on historical analysis and technological change was quite widespread among German economists around the beginning of the twentieth century, particularly among the adherents of the so-called historical school, and that Schumpeter—although he never regarded himself as belonging to any school—was probably influenced by this. For his own view on the "historical school" in Germany and the controversies that followed in its wake, see Joseph Schumpeter, *History of Economic Analysis* (New York: Oxford University Press, 1954), Part IV, Chapter 4, Section 2.

9. Joseph Schumpeter, *The Theory of Economic Development* (Cambridge, Mass.: Harvard University Press, 1934; first German edition, 1911).

10. Nicholas Kaldor, "A Model of Economic Growth," *Economic Journal* 67 (December 1957): 591–624; Nicholas Kaldor, *Strategic Factors in Economic Development* (Ithaca, N.Y.: State School of Industrial and Labor Relations, Cornell University, 1967). Similar ideas, though in a more neoclassical framework, were proposed by Kenneth Arrow, "The Economic Implications of Learning by Doing," *Review of Economic Studies* 29, no. 3 (June 1962): 155–73.

11. Bengt Åke Lundvall, "Innovation as an Interactive Process: From User-Producer Interaction to the National System of Innovation," in Giovanni Dosi and others, *Technical Change and Economic Theory* (London: Pinter, 1988), pp. 349–69.

12. Nathan Rosenberg, "Learning by Using," in Nathan Rosenberg, *Inside the Black Box: Technology and Economics* (Cambridge: Cambridge University Press, 1982), pp. 120–40.

13. See Bengt Åke Lundvall, ed., *National Systems of Innovation: Towards a Theory of Innovation and Interactive Learning* (London: Pinter, 1992); Richard R. Nelson, ed., *National Innovation Systems: A Comparative Analysis* (Oxford, England: Oxford University Press, 1993); Charles Edquist, ed., *Systems of Innovation: Technologies, Institutions, and Organizations* (London: Pinter, 1997); Christopher Freeman, "The National System of Innovation in Historical Perspective," *Cambridge Journal of Economics* 19, no. 1 (1995): 5–24.

14. Alexander Gerschenkron, *Economic Backwardness in Historical Perspective* (Cambridge, Mass.: Belknap Press, 1962), p. 7.

15. Moses Abramovitz, "The Origins of the Post-War Catch-Up and Convergence Boom," in Jan Fagerberg, Bart Verspagen, and Nick von Tunzelman, eds., *The Dynamics of Technology, Trade, and Growth* (Aldershot, England: Elgar, 1994), pp. 21–52.

16. The pioneer in much of this was John Cornwall, who regressed variables assumed to reflect the scope for catch-up, investment, and endogenous technological progress (the so-called Verdoorn law) on GDP growth for a sample of OECD countries. See John Cornwall, "Diffusion, Convergence, and Kaldor's Law," *Economic Journal* 86 (June 1976): 307–14. Since then many studies of this type, including the scope for catch-up and some other conditioning variables as determinants of GDP and productivity growth, have been published. For overviews of this literature see Jan Fagerberg, "Technology and International Differences in Growth Rates," *Journal of Economic Literature* 32, no. 3 (September 1994): 1147–75; Jonathan Temple, "The New Growth Evidence," *Journal of Economic Literature* 37, no. 2 (March 1999): 112–56. In the more recent literature, such regression models have for some reason been dubbed "Barro-regressions" after Robert Barro, an economist who did not pioneer this type of research but picked it up at a rather late stage.

17. Although relevant, many applied studies did not include R&D or innovation performance, often with reference to lack of data (although this was not always entirely justified). For an exception to this trend see Jan Fagerberg, "A Technology Gap Approach to Why Growth Rates Differ," *Research Policy* 16, nos. 2–4 (August 1987): 87–99.

18. Bradford De Long, "Productivity Growth, Convergence, and Welfare," *American Economic Review* 78, no. 5 (December 1988): 1138–54.

19. Robert Summers and Alan Heston, "The Penn World Table (Mark 5): An Expanded Set of International Comparisons, 1950–1988," *Quarterly Journal of Economics* 106, no. 2 (May 1991): 327–68.

20. William J. Baumol, Sue Anne Batey Blackman, and Edward N. Wolff, *Productivity and American Leadership: The Long View* (Cambridge, Mass.: MIT Press, 1989).

21. Baumol, Blackman, and Wolff, *Productivity and American Leadership*.

22. Another reason might be that growth models assuming economies of scale may fail to produce a stable equilibrium. In fact, such models may easily, depending on the parameterization, predict explosive growth or, alternatively, no growth at all in the long run.

23. See Paul M. Romer, "Increasing Returns and Long-Run Growth," *Journal of Political Economy* 94, no. 5 (October 1986): 1002–37.

24. See the survey by Zvi Griliches, "The Search for R&D Spillovers," *Scandinavian Journal of Economics* 94, supplement (1992): S29–47.

25. Paul M. Romer, "Endogenous Technological Change," *Journal of Political Economy* 98, no. 5 (October 1990): S71–102. Models along similar lines were also suggested by a number of other authors. See for instance Pierre Aghion and Peter Howitt, "A Model of Growth through Creative Destruction," *Econometrica* 60, no. 2 (March 1992): 323–51; and Gene M. Grossman and Elhanan Helpman, *Innovation and Growth in the Global Economy* (Cambridge, Mass.: MIT Press, 1991).

26. Robert E. Lucas, "On the Mechanisms of Economic Development," *Journal of Monetary Economics* 22, no. 1 (July 1988): 3–42.

27. See Grossman and Helpman, *Innovation and Growth in the Global Economy.*

28. Charles I. Jones, "Time Series Tests of Endogenous Growth Models," *Quarterly Journal of Economics* 110, no. 4 (1995): 495–525; Charles I. Jones, "R&D-Based Models of Economic Growth," *Journal of Political Economy* 103, no. 2 (1995): 759–84. See also the overview and discussion of this issue in Temple, "The New Growth Evidence."

29. The method consists of selecting a set of basic variables, which are always included in the regression. Other possible variables are included one by one and the sensitivity of the result is then tested by including up to three other variables drawn from a large pool of possible explanatory factors. If the variable is always significant, the relationship is termed "robust." If it is insignificant in at least one case it is considered "fragile." See Ross Levine and David Renelt, "A Sensitivity Analysis of Cross-Country Growth Regressions," *American Economic Review* 82, no. 4 (September 1992): 942–63.

30. In a later study by Robert King and Ross Levine, the level of financial development of the country was added to the list of robust variables. See Robert King and Ross Levine, "Finance and Growth: Schumpeter Might Be Right?" *Quarterly Journal of Economics* 108, no. 3 (August 1993): 717–37.

31. Christopher D. Carrol and David N. Weil, "Saving and Growth: A Reinterpretation," *NBER Working Paper* no. 4470 (Cambridge, Mass.: National Bureau of Economic Research, 1993).

32. World Bank, *The East Asian Miracle: Economic Growth and Public Policy* (New York: Oxford University Press, 1993). In this report the bank argues that 60–90 percent of productivity growth of the so-called high-performing Asian economies can be explained by accumulation and thus that other "unconventional" factors were of relatively little importance. However, I have shown elsewhere (Aadne Cappelen and Jan Fagerberg, "East Asian Growth: A Critical Assessment," *Forum for Development Studies* no. 2 [1995]: 175–95) that this conclusion is not warranted. In fact, the models applied by the World Bank predict very poorly for the fast-growing countries of Asia! For a critical assessment of the World Bank's view see also Dani Rodrik, "King Kong Meets Godzilla: The World Bank and the East Asian Miracle," in Albert Fishlow and others, eds., *Miracle or Design? Lessons*

from the East Asian Experience, policy essay no. 11 (Washington, D.C.: Overseas Development Council, 1994), pp. 13–53.

33. See, for instance, Robert Wade, *Governing the Market: Economic Theory and the Role of Government in East Asian Industrialization* (Princeton, N.J.: Princeton University Press, 1990).

34. See the survey by Griliches, "The Search for R&D Spillovers."

35. See Adam B. Jaffe, "Real Effects of Academic Research," *American Economic Review* 79, no. 5 (December 1989): 957–70; Adam B. Jaffe, Manuel Trajtenberg, and Rebecca Henderson, "Geographic Localization of Knowledge Spillovers as Evidenced by Patent Citations," *Quarterly Journal of Economics* 108, no. 3 (August 1993): 557–98; Per B. Maurseth and Bart Verspagen, "Europe: One or Several Systems of Innovation," in Jan Fagerberg, Paolo Guerrieri, and Bart Verspagen, eds., *The Economic Challenge for Europe: Adapting to Innovation-Based Growth* (Aldershot, England: Elgar, 1999), pp. 149–74.

36. See David T. Coe and Elhanan Helpman, "International R&D Spillovers," *European Economic Review* 39, no. 5 (May 1995): 859–87.

37. The conclusion, then, would be that foreign R&D embodied in imports is the primary source of growth in most countries, particularly the developing ones, and that openness to trade is what is required if a country is going to benefit from the global process of innovation and diffusion. See Coe and Helpman, "International R&D Spillovers," and David T. Coe, Elhanan Helpman, and Alexander Hoffmaister, "North-South R&D Spillovers," *Economic Journal* 107 (January 1997): 134–49.

38. Maury Gittleman and Edward N. Wolff, "R&D Activity and Cross-Country Growth Comparisons," *Cambridge Journal of Economics* 19, no. 2 (March 1995): 189–207.

39. See Gittleman and Wolff, "R&D Activity and Cross-Country Growth Comparisons"; Jonathon Eaton and Samuel Kortum, "Trade in Ideas—Patenting and Productivity in the OECD," *Journal of International Economics* 40, nos. 1–2 (1996): 251–78; Jonathon Eaton, Eva Gutierrez, and Samuel Kortum, "European Technology Policy," *Economic Policy* no. 27 (October 1998): 405–38. Bart Verspagen argues that failure to take into account such differences in absorptive capacity across countries may in fact explain some of the conflicting evidence reported in the literature on the importance of other carriers of technology diffusion. See Bart Verspagen, "Estimating International Technology Spillovers Using Technology Flow Matrices," *Weltwirtschaftliches Archiv* 133, no. 2 (1997): 226–48.

40. See Christopher Freeman, *The Economics of Industrial Innovation,* (Harmondsworth, England: Penguin Books, 1974).

41. This does not, of course, invalidate the use of other methods that are currently in more use in economics. Arguably, empirical work will need to proceed at several levels, not in isolation, but in interaction.

INDEX

Page references followed by t, f, and n refer to tables, figures, and notes, respectively.

ABOUT THE CONTRIBUTORS

PETER S. ARNO is an economist and professor in the department of epidemiology and social medicine at Albert Einstein College of Medicine and Montefiore Medical Center in New York City. His research has focused on the economic, financial, and public policy dimensions of the AIDS and tuberculosis epidemics. Arno has been a Pew Postdoctoral Research Fellow at the Institute for Health Policy Studies and the Institute for Health and Aging at the University of California, San Francisco, and a scholar of the American Foundation for AIDS Research, and he currently holds an Investigator Award in Health Policy from the Robert Wood Johnson Foundation. He is coauthor (with Karyn L. Feiden) of *Against the Odds: The Story of AIDS Drug Development, Politics & Profits* (Harper Collins, 1993), which was nominated for a Pulitzer Prize.

DEAN BAKER is the codirector of the Center for Economic and Policy Research. He previously worked as a senior economist at the Economic Policy Institute. He has written extensively on Social Security and macroeconomic issues. He is the coauthor (with Mark Weisbrot) of *Social Security: The Phony Crisis* (University of Chicago Press, 1999) and the coeditor (with Robert Pollin and Jerry Epstein) of *Globalization and Progressive Economic Policy* (Cambridge University Press, 1998). He also is the author of the weekly online commentary on economic reporting, the *Economic Reporting Review* (www.fair.org).

JANIS BARRY FIGUEROA is an economist and associate professor in the department of economics at Fordham University in New York City. Her research interests involve the fields of labor, health economics, and industrial organization. Recent investigations have considered the impact of family-provided elder care on the labor supply and the significance of place of residence in determining the likelihood of a late-stage cervical or breast cancer diagnosis. Her publications are

371

found in *The American Journal of Preventive Medicine* (1996), *The New England Policy Journal* (1996), *The American Economic Review* (1995), and the book *Hispanics in the Labor Force*, which she coedited (with Edwin Melendez and Clara Rodriguez; Plenum, 1991).

ERIC BESHERS is an economist who has specialized in transportation issues throughout his career. He currently works as senior transportation economist with ICF Consulting, Inc. He has provided analysis and advice for the U.S. government, foreign governments, the World Bank, and other bodies. He served for some years in the policy office in the Office of the Secretary of Transportation (U.S. Department of Transportation). He is an acknowledged authority on transportation economic and policy issues. He has worked on all aspects of transportation but is best known for work relating to highway and railroad questions.

ANTHONY P. CARNEVALE is vice president for public leadership at the Educational Testing Service. He is an internationally recognized authority on education, training, and employment. He chaired the National Commission for Employment Policy during President Clinton's first term while serving as vice president and director of human resource studies at the Committee for Economic Development. Earlier, he had been president of the Institute for Workbased Learning, an applied research center affiliated with the American Society for Training and Development. Carnevale has held senior staff positions in the U.S. Senate and House of Representatives and the U.S. Department of Health, Education, and Welfare.

JAMES CROTTY is professor of economics, research fellow in the Political Economy Research Institute, and a member of the Center for Popular Economics at the University of Massachusetts, Amherst. Recent publications include: "Multinational Corporations in the Neoliberal Regime" (with Gerald Epstein and Patricia Kelly), in Dean Baker, Gerald A. Epstein, and Robert Pollin, editors, *Globalization and Progressive Economic Policy* (Cambridge University Press, 1998); "Was Keynes a Corporatist? Keynes's Radical Views on Industrial Policy and Macro Policy in the 1920s," *Journal of Economic Issues* (September 1999); and "Structural Contradictions of the Global Neoliberal Regime," *Review of Radical Political Economy* (forthcoming). He is grateful to the Ford Foundation for research support.

PAULA ENGLAND is professor of sociology at the University of Pennsylvania, where she is also director of women's studies. Her research focuses on gender inequality in labor markets and on changing roles of men and women in the family. She is the author (with George Farkas) of *Households, Employment, and Gender* (Aldine de Gruyter, 1986) and *Comparable Worth: Theories and Evidence* (Aldine de Gruyter, 1992). From 1994 to 1996 she served as the editor of the American Sociological Review. She has testified as an expert witness in a number of Title VII discrimination cases.

JAN FAGERBERG is professor of economics at the University of Oslo, where he is affiliated with the Centre for Technology, Innovation and Culture. Previous affiliations include the Norwegian Institute for Foreign Affairs and the University of Aalborg. Fagerberg specializes in research on the impact of technology on trade, competitiveness, and growth and has published extensively on these and related topics in books and major journals. He also has been active in comparative studies of economic policy and has served as a consultant to the OECD and the EU. His latest book is *The Economic Challenge for Europe: Adapting to Innovation-Based Growth* (with Paolo Guerrieri and Bart Verspagen; Edward Elgar, 1999)

NANCY FOLBRE, professor of economics at the University of Massachusetts, Amherst, is the author of *Who Pays for the Kids? Gender and the Structures of Constraint* (Routledge, 1994) and an associate editor of the journal *Feminist Economics*. She is a staff economist at the Center for Popular Economics and coauthor, with James Heintz, of *The Ultimate Field Guide to the U.S. Economy* (New Press, 2000). Her forthcoming book, *The Invisible Heart: Economics and Family Values* (New Press, 2001), explores the economics of care in more detail.

ROBERT H. FRANK currently holds a joint appointment as professor of economics in Cornell University's Johnson Graduate School of Management and as Goldwin Smith Professor of Economics, Ethics, and Public Policy in Cornell's College of Arts and Sciences, where he has taught since 1972. For the past several years, his research has focused on rivalry and cooperation in economic and social behavior. His books include *Choosing the Right Pond: Human Behavior and the Quest for Status* (Oxford University Press, 1985), *Passions within*

Reason: The Strategic Role of the Emotions (W. W. Norton, 1988), *Microeconomics and Behavior* (McGraw-Hill, 1991), *The Winner-Take-All Society* (coauthored with Philip Cook; Free Press, 1995), and *Luxury Fever* (Free Press, 1999).

TERESA GHILARDUCCI is associate professor of economics at the University of Notre Dame. Her work focuses on the evolutionary development of American capitalism—of how Social Security and private pensions distribute both income and power. She works within the field of institutional labor economics and is concerned with the relationship between economic development, equality of income distribution, and the quality of life in retirement for workers. While on leave from Notre Dame, she served as the assistant director for employee benefits at the AFL-CIO. Ghilarducci is the author of *Labor's Capital: The Economics and Politics of Private Pensions* (MIT Press, 1992).

JEFF MADRICK is the editor of *Challenge*, the economic affairs magazine, and most recently the author of *The End of Affluence* (Random House, 1997). He is also a columnist for the *New York Times*, a regular contributor to the *New York Review of Books*, and adjunct professor of social sciences at Cooper Union. A former NBC News correspondent and columnist for *Business Week*, he is the recipient of several major awards, including the Emmy and the Page One Award. He is a senior fellow of the World Policy Institute. Madrick is currently working on a book about America's productivity.

PATRICK L. MASON is associate professor of economics at Florida State University. His recent research has concentrated on examining the causes of rising wage inequality, changes in the nature and extent of racial discrimination in the labor market, and the economics of identity. His recent edited books include *Race, Markets, and Social Outcomes* (with Rhonda Williams; Kluwer Academic Publishers, 1997) and *African Americans, Labor, and Society: Organizing for a New Agenda* (Wayne State University Press, 2000).

LAWRENCE MISHEL is the vice president of the Economic Policy Institute and specializes in the fields of productivity, competitiveness, income distribution, labor markets, education, and industrial relations. He is the coauthor (with John Schmitt and Jared Bernstein) of *The State of Working America*, a comprehensive review of incomes, wages, employment, and other dimensions of living standards, published biennially by the Economic Policy Institute. He holds a Ph.D. in economics from the University of Wisconsin, an M.A. in economics from American University, and a B.S. from Pennsylvania State University. He has published in a variety of academic and non-academic journals.

STEPHEN J. ROSE is senior economist at the Educational Testing Service. He has conducted innovative research on labor market trends, using cross-sectional and longitudinal data to track individuals' career pattern and thus distinguish "permanent" income from yearly fluctuations, measure changes in earnings over time, and measure workers' stability within companies and industries. Previously, he held policy positions at the U.S. Department of Labor, the National Commission for Employment Policy, and the Joint Economic Committee of the Congress. His *Social Stratification in the U.S.* was originally published in 1978, and the fifth edition came out in January 2000 (New Press).

JOHN SCHMITT is an economist with the Economic Policy Institute in Washington. He has written for popular and academic publications on wage inequality, unemployment, the minimum wage, education, comparative economic performance, and other topics. He is a coauthor, with Lawrence Mishel and Jared Bernstein, of three editions of *The State of Working America*. He has a Ph.D. in economics from the London School of Economics.

RICHARD H. STECKEL joined the economics department at the Ohio State University in 1974. His approach to research is interdisciplinary, bringing medical knowledge into the social sciences. Widely recognized as a pioneer in the field of anthropometric history, he has published numerous articles that integrate ideas from economics, history, and human biology. His latest book is *Health and Welfare during Industrialization* (coedited with Roderick Floud; University of Chicago Press, 1997). In 1982 he was elected to the National Bureau of Economic Research. Active in several professional organizations, he has served on the editorial boards of various journals in economic history, history, and human biology.

EDWARD N. WOLFF received his Ph.D. from Yale University in 1974 and is currently a professor of economics at New York University.

He is managing editor of *The Review of Income and Wealth*, a senior scholar of the Jerome Levy Economics Institute, and a council member of the International Input-Output Association. In addition, Wolff is an associate editor of *Structural Change and Economic Dynamics* and an editorial board member of *Economic Systems Research*. Wolff has published widely, including *Top Heavy: A Study of the Increasing Inequality of Wealth in America* (Twentieth Century Fund Press, 1995).

NGAIRE WOODS is a fellow in politics and international relations at University College, Oxford University. Her recent publications include *The Political Economy of Globalization* (Macmillan 2000), *Inequality, Globalization and World Politics* (with Andrew Hurrell; Oxford University Press, 1999), *Explaining International Relations since 1945* (Oxford University Press, 1996), and several articles on the international financial institutions, global governance, trade, and globalization. She is at present completing a book on the politics of the IMF and the World Bank.